Theory and Design in the First Machine Age

*This book is dedicated to those who made it possible and
necessary to write it:*

to Nikolaus Pevsner for the original impulse, and for guidance constantly
and ungrudgingly given

to Giovanni Bernasconi and H. L. C. Jaffé, for publications on Sant'Elia
and *de Stijl* that materially altered the direction of these studies

to André Lurçat, Ernö Goldfinger, Pierre Vago, Rob van t'Hoff, Mart
Stam, Walter Segal, Marcel Duchamp and Artur Korn, for the use of their
memories or their libraries

to Alison and Peter Smithson, James Stirling, C. A. St. John Wilson, Peter
Carter, Colin Rowe, and Alan Colquhoun, my own contemporaries, for a
constant view of the mainstream of modern architecture flowing on, and to
the last named in particular for a proposition that, true or false, has been
the lodestone of these studies:

'What distinguishes modern architecture is surely a new
sense of space and the machine aesthetic.'

REYNER BANHAM

Theory and Design in the First Machine Age

Second Edition

FREDERICK A. PRAEGER, Publishers

New York · Washington

BOOKS THAT MATTER

Published in the United States of America in 1960
by Frederick A. Praeger, Inc., Publishers
111 Fourth Avenue, New York, N.Y. 10003
Second edition, 1967

Contents

5

SECTION 5: GERMANY: BERLIN, THE BAUHAUS, THE VICTORY OF THE
NEW STYLE

ACKNOWLEDGEMENTS

Acknowledgement is made to the following for the use of illustrations.
The numbers refer to the figure numbers.
Arphot 86–88, 96; Photo Chevojon, Paris 13; Mario Chiattone 50, 51;
Doeser Fotos, Holland 56, 77; E. M. van Ojen 123; Buckminster Fuller 13, 137;
Gemeente Musea van Amsterdam 54, 65, 67, 69; Lucien Hervé 131, 132;
Lucia Moholy-Nagy 121, 122; Museo Civico, Como 42–49; Museum of Modern Art,
New York 79; Mart Stam 71; Stedlijk Museum, Amsterdam 58, 59.

6

Illustrations

7

8

Introduction—the machine age

THIS BOOK WAS conceived and written in the late years of the Nineteen-fifties, an epoch that has variously been called the Jet Age, the Detergent Decade, the Second Industrial Revolution. Almost any label that identifies anything worth identifying in the period will draw attention to some aspect of the transformation of science and technology, for these transformations have powerfully affected human life, and opened up new paths of choice in the ordering of our collective destiny. Our accession to almost unlimited supplies of energy is balanced against the possibility of making our planet uninhabitable, but this again is balanced, as we stand at the threshold of space, by the growing possibility of quitting our island earth and letting down roots elsewhere. Again, our explorations into the nature of information have made it possible, on the one hand, to set electronics to work to take the drudgery out of routine thought, and on the other hand to tailor human thinking to suit the needs of some narrow-minded power-*élite*.

These, of course, are the grand prospects that affect economics, morality and sociology, in the same remote and statistical way as did the perfection of cavalry, the growth of feudal organisations, the rise of money economy. But, unlike those developments of the past, which left the objects of daily life, the hierarchy of the family and the structure of sociable intercourse almost untouched, the technical revolutions of our own time strike us with infinitely greater force because the small things of life have been visibly and audibly revolutionised as well.

Even a man who does not possess an electric razor is likely—in the Westernised world at least—to dispense some previously inconceivable product, such as an aerosol shaving cream, from an equally unprecedented pressurised container, and accept with equanimity the fact that he can afford to throw away, regularly, cutting-edges that previous generations would have nursed for years. Even a housewife who does not possess a washing machine dispenses synthetic detergent from synthetic plastic packs on to synthetic fabrics whose quality and performance makes the jealously-guarded secrets of silk seem trivial. A teen-ager, curled up with a

9

transistorised, printed-circuit radio, or boudoir gramophone, may hear a music that literally did not exist before it was committed to tape, reproduced at a level of quality that riches could not have bought a decade or so ago. The average automobile of today, running on such roads as have been especially contrived for it, provides transport more sumptuous in vehicles more gorgeous than palanquin-borne emperors knew how to desire.

Many technologies have contributed to this domestic revolution, but most of them make their point of impact on us in the form of small machines —shavers, clippers and hair-dryers; radio, telephone, gramophone, tape recorder and television; mixers, grinders, automatic cookers, washing machines, refrigerators, vacuum cleaners, polishers. . . . A housewife alone, often disposes of more horse-power today than an industrial worker did at the beginning of the century. This is the sense in which we live in a Machine Age. We have lived in an Industrial Age for nearly a century and a half now, and may well be entering a Second Industrial Age with the current revolution in control mechanisms. But we have already entered the Second Machine Age, the age of domestic electronics and synthetic chemistry, and can look back on the First, the age of power from the mains and the reduction of machines to human scale, as a period of the past.

Although the earliest stirrings of that First Machine Age must have appeared with the availability of coal-gas for lighting and heating, the mechanism of light and heat remained a flame, as it had been from the Stone Age onwards. Mains electricity made a decisive alteration here, one of the most decisive in the history of domestic technology. In addition, it brought small, woman-controlled machinery into the home, notably the vacuum cleaner. Electrical techniques brought the telephone as well, and for the first time domestic and sociable communication did not depend on the sending of written or remembered messages. The portable typewriter put a machine under the hands of poets, the first gramophones made music a domestic service rather than a social ceremony.

All these machines are still with us in the Second Machine Age, supplemented and improved by more recent technological advances, but there is a more than quantitative difference between the two ages. In the Second, highly developed mass production methods have distributed electronic devices and synthetic chemicals broadcast over a large part of society— television, the symbolic machine of the Second Machine Age, has become a means of mass-communication dispensing popular entertainment. In the First, however, only cinema was available to a broad public, whose home life was otherwise barely touched and it was in upper middle-class homes that the First Machine Age made its greatest impact, the homes that could afford these new, convenient and expensive aids to gracious living, the homes that tend to breed architects, painters, poets, journalists, the creators of the myths and symbols by which a culture recognises itself.

Thus, it was into the hands of an *élite*, rather than the masses, that the symbolic machine of that First Machine Age was delivered, the automobile. It was more than a symbol of power, it was also, for most of that *élite*, a heady taste of a new kind of power.[1] One of the uncommented curiosities of the early part of the Industrial Age is that, in spite of its massive dependence on mechanical power, few of its *élite*, if any, had any personal experience of controlling that power. They could buy the use of it with money, and ride in its great ships and famous expresses, but they did not dirty their hands with the controls. That was left to a separate, working-class *élite* of ships' engineers, engine-drivers and so forth, who retired into the middle-classes when their service was complete.

But, with the coming of purchasable motor-cars, it became possible, and fashionable, for the opinion-forming classes to own and personally control units of motive power of up to sixty, or even a hundred horse-power. Although they brought over into this new situation certain horse-and-groom social usages, the psychological effect was a revolution that struck deep. Many of them were clearly aware that the men who made and serviced their cars were of an utterly different breed and mind to those who had bred and cared for their horses. Over and above this, the jump in speed from a spanking twenty-five miles an hour to the roaring sixties, with the magic century an ever approaching goal for the really rich and determined, brought in changes of experience that were qualitative, not merely quantitative—the dynamics of a fast-moving car are different in kind to the dynamics of even a race-horse. The Man Multiplied by the Motor, to use Marinetti's phrase, was a different kind of man to the horse-and-buggy men who had ruled the world since the time of Alexander the Great.

Under these changed circumstances, that barrier of incomprehension that had stood between thinking men and their mechanised environment all through the nineteenth century, in the mind of Marx as much as in the mind of Morris, began to crumble. Men whose means of moving ideas from place to place had been revolutionised at their writing desks by the type-

[1] John Davidson, Scots chemist and journalist, who died in 1909, expressed the *élite* aspect of motoring more explicitly than any other writer of the time, and contrasted it with the mass experience of railway travel in a late poem entitled *The Testament of Sir Simon Simplex concerning Automobilism*, of which the following lines are typical:

> Class, mass and mob for fifty years and more
> Had all to travel in the jangling roar
> Of railways, the nomadic caravan
> That stifled individual mind in man,
> Till automobilism arose at last!
> . . .
> And things that socialism supposed extinct,
> Degree, nobility and noble strife,
> A form, a style, a privacy in life
> Will re-appear; and, crowning nature's plan
> The individual and the gentleman
> In England reassume his lawful place. . . .

writer and the telephone, could no longer treat the world of technology with hostility or indifference, and if there is a test that divides the men from the boys in say, 1912, it is their attitude to Ruskin. Men whose view of the aims of art and the function of design were as diverse as could be, nevertheless united in their hatred of *ce déplorable Ruskin*.

The human chain of Pioneers of the Modern Movement that extends back from Gropius to William Morris, and beyond him to Ruskin, Pugin and William Blake, does not extend forward from Gropius. The precious vessel of handicraft aesthetics that had been passed from hand to hand, was dropped and broken, and no one has bothered to pick up the pieces. When Gropius, in the Bauhaus Proclamation of 1919, talked of handicrafts he was, effectively, talking to himself. His re-establishment as one of the leaders of Modern design after about 1923 was as the head of a school devoted to Machine Age architecture and the design of machine products, employing a Machine Age aesthetic that had been worked out by other men in other places.

Naturally that Machine Age aesthetic was not an entirely new creation —the men who wrought it came to the First Machine Age bowed down with two-thousand years' culture on their backs, but the very minimum of the new mental equipment needed to handle their new environment. At one extreme, the Futurists proposed to dump their cultural load, and rush forward equipped only with a new sensibility; at the other extreme, men like Perret and Garnier in France felt that the new should be, in Paul Valéry's phrase, subject to the old, or at least the outlines of the old. Between Futurist dynamism and this Academic caution the theory and design of the architecture of the First Machine Age were evolved. Whether those theories, and that architecture were what we, looking back from the Second Machine Age, would regard as proper, or even adequate, to their situation, is a question which will be held over until the last chapter, after the events and theories of the period have been described. Nevertheless, while we yet lack a body of theory proper to our own Machine Age, we are still free-wheeling along with the ideas and aesthetics left over from the first. The reader may therefore, at any turn, find among these relics of a past as economically, socially, and technologically dead as the city-states of Greece, ideas that he is using every day of his life. Should he do so, may he ask himself two things; firstly, are any of his ideas as up-to-date as he thinks them to be, this is the Second Machine Age not the First; and secondly, how out-moded in truth are the ideas he dismisses as mere fashions of the Jazz Decades, for one Machine Age is more like another Machine Age than any other epoch the world has ever known. The cultural revolution that took place around 1912 has been superseded, but it has not been reversed.

Section one

This printing differs from earlier versions in the addition to the bibliographies of a few substantial works of scholarship that have come to my notice since the original text was completed. So far, their content does not seem to require any major revisions of the text, but the reader is enjoined to refer to any books listed in the bibliographies with dates later than 1957—most of them should be available in specialised architectural libraries—in order to bring himself up to date.

Footnotes are given only for quotations from publications of subsidiary importance, and the main works are listed in a bibliography at the beginning of the section in which they are discussed.

PREDISPOSING CAUSES: ACADEMIC AND RATIONALIST WRITERS, 1900–1914

Guadet, J: *Éléments et Théories de l'Architecture*, Paris, 1902.
Blanc, C: *Grammaire des Arts de Dessin*, Paris, 1867.
Ferran, A: *Philosophie de la Composition Architecturale*, Paris, 1955.
Choisy, A: *Histoire de l'Architecture*, Paris, 1899.
Morancé and Badovici: *L'Œuvre de Tony Garnier*, Paris, 1938.
Garnier, T: *Une Cité Industrielle*, Paris, 1918.
Jamot, B: *Auguste Perret et l'Architecture du Beton Armé*, Brussels, 1927.
Collins, P: *Concrete—The Vision of a New Architecture*, London, 1959.
Lethaby, W. R: *Form in Civilization*, London, 1922.
     Architecture, London, 1911.
Goodhart-Rendel, H: *English Architecture since the Regency*, London, 1953.
Scott, G: *The Architecture of Humanism*, London, 1914.
Lindner and Steinmetz: *Die Ingenieurbauten und ihre Entwicklung*, Leipzig, 1923.
Muthesius, H: *Stilarchitektur und Baukunst*, Berlin, 1902.
Pevsner, N: *Pioneers of the Modern Movement*, London, (1st edn.) 1936 (for a brief account of the Deutscher Werkbund).
Loos, A: *Trotzdem*, Innsbruck, 1930 (for *Ornament und Verbrechen*, *Architektur* and excerpts from *Das Andere*).
Periodicals
 Die Form, VII, 1932 (for a fuller account of the beginnings of the Deutscher Werkbund, by Peter Bruckmann).
 Jahrbuch des Deutschen Werkbundes, 1912 and 1913 (for Muthesius's *Wo stehen wir*, Grosz's *Probleme der Ornamente*, essays by Muthesius, Gropius and others on factory design, etc.).

13

1: The academic tradition and the concept of elementary composition

WHILE A SERIES OF revolutionary gestures around 1910, largely connected with the Cubist and Futurist movements, were the main point of departure for the development of Modern architecture, there were also a number of particular predisposing causes that helped to guide the mainstream of development into the channels through which it flowed in the Twenties. These predisposing causes were all of nineteenth-century origin, and may be loosely grouped under three heads: firstly, the sense of an architect's responsibility to the society in which he finds himself, an idea of largely English extraction, from Pugin, Ruskin, and Morris, which was summed up in an organisation founded in 1907, the Deutscher Werkbund: secondly, the Rationalist, or structural approach to architecture, again of English extraction, from Willis, but elaborated in France by Viollet-le-Duc, and codified in Auguste Choisy's magisterial *Histoire* at the very end of the century, though the parallel tradition in Germany has no major exponent after Gottfried Semper; and, thirdly, the tradition of academic instruction, world wide in distribution, but owing most of its energy and authority to the *École des Beaux-Arts* in Paris, from which there emerged, just after the turn of the century, Julien Guadet's compendious summary of his course of professorial lectures—though again no equivalent work appeared in Germany at that time.

The attitude of those who were to become the masters of Modern architecture to these traditions from the past was apt to be equivocal. The Werkbund and its members were the object of suspicion in some quarters, though most of the younger architects accepted the moral imperatives bound up in it. The Rationalist attitude was held in high regard, yet effectively repudiated by most of them, and the academic tradition was generally vilified, yet many of the ideas it embodied were taken over by them.

The last circumstance makes the evaluation of Guadet's contribution to modern theory difficult to assess. Those who rejected the academic discipline did so because they felt it to be hostile to their conception of architecture, which they held to be functional, scientific and divorced from

14

stylistic considerations. Yet, on the evidence of his five volumes of *Éléments et Théories de l'Architecture*, Guadet—the very embodiment of the academy —was as functional, scientific and un-stylistic as they. Conversely, they in their turn, while repudiating the 'false standards of the academies', accepted many academic ideas without knowing where they had come from. Thus Gropius in 1923, having criticised the academies for not nurturing aesthetic science, goes on in the succeeding paragraphs to make use of a number of aesthetic concepts that resemble those of French academic origin.[1]

This state of affairs was, to some extent, the product of specialisation and compartmentation inside the academies themselves, and also of certain silences that were observed in academic teaching on subjects held to be too obvious or too sacred for discussion. On the first count, one must note that many of the academic ideas accepted by architects came not from the architectural side of *Beaux-Arts* instruction, but from the painterly. The *Grammaire des Arts de Dessin*, written by Charles Blanc, the librarian of the *École des Beaux-Arts*, and published in 1867, had become part of the racial sub-conscious, so to speak, of many tribes of creative artists in the Western world and its ideas can be paralleled (e.g. in Germany) even where they had no direct influence. Its emphasis on technical methods of expression (brushwork, colour, composition, etc.) as against subject-matter, in painting—128 pages of the former, only 19 of the latter—helped to pave the way for the rise of Abstract art. It may well have helped to pave the way for Guadet as well: Blanc's insistence on the *ordonnance* of a painting as its prime means of expression, was echoed over and over again by Guadet's insistence on the importance of *composition* in architecture.

Again, Blanc's relative lack of interest in subject-matter, is matched in Guadet by a complete absence of interest in style. This is one of the conspicuous silences in the *Éléments et Théories*; the other concerns axial planning. Guadet's attitude to both subjects, both so crucial to academic teaching, seems to be a product of his own intimate and lifelong entanglement with that teaching system. He became Professor in 1886, after fifty-two years of blameless academic respectability, suitably adorned with numerous firsts, medals and the Prix de Rome. His own master had been Henri Labrouste, the 'rogue' academician of the middle of the century, and through him Guadet was a link in an unbroken academic chain that went right back to the early days of the nineteenth century, and to the heyday of neo-Classical architecture in France. So truly did the tradition run through him, that his own insistence on composition, the assembly of a building from its component volumes, is only an echo of J. N. L. Durand saying, in 1821[2]

[1] See chapter 20.
[2] On page 6 of his *Partie Graphique* (Paris, 1821), a supplementary volume to his well-known *Précis* (Paris, 1809) which had a wide distribution in Europe,

15

> Any complete building whatever is not, and cannot be, anything but the result of the assembly and putting together (composition) of a greater or lesser number of parts.

But the specific mode of putting the parts together is something that Guadet barely discusses—it occupies one chapter out of eight in the second book of the first of the five volumes of *Éléments et Théories*, is not very informative and is completely swamped by the mass of practical information contained in the other four volumes. The fact was, simply, that the symmetrical disposition of the parts of a building about one or more axes was so unquestionably the master-discipline of academic architecture that there was no need for him to discuss it, any more than he would need to discuss the clothing of the building's forms in one or another of a number of recognised 'catalogued styles' (as Lethaby was to call them). The details of those styles could be had from a good crib-book, such as Normand's *Parallèle*, the axial discipline would be part of the air a student breathed, and Guadet's business as Professor was to handle the information that could not be acquired from these two sources. It was not until the idea of axial composition had ceased to be unquestionable, that any justification or explanation of it appeared in print—Albert Ferran's *Philosophie de la Composition Architecturale*, published as late as 1955, but cast entirely in the frame of mind of the first decade of the century, when Ferran was among Guadet's last pupils, and largely illustrated with Rome Prize projects of that epoch.

The resultant state is a curious one: here was the man who was the master of Auguste Perret and Tony Garnier, the twin progenitors of the Modern Movement in France, whose book formed the mental climate in which perhaps half the architects of the twentieth century grew up, and provides valuable clues to the atmosphere in which the other, German, half matured, and yet contained neither of the main themes—axial planning and historical styling—of the mental discipline that produced it. The direct influence of the book has, in fact, always been slight. Bulky, sumptuous, expensive and largely unreadable, its place has been the shelves of reference libraries, rather than in the students' lodgings. But it has been much consulted for information, if rarely read for instruction. Guadet himself saw his position thus

> I do not aspire to role of a guide for the whole journey; to those who leave after me I indicate the luggage wanted on the voyage

and the bulk of its five thick volumes is taken up with luggage wanted on the voyage, by a student at the *École*—instruments and techniques of draughtsmanship, systems of proportion, walls and their openings; porticoes, bays

including a German translation, and made Durand's ideas one of the international neo-Classical bases on which modern architectural theory was (often unwittingly) built.

and orders; roofs, vaults, ceilings and stairs: type plans and schedules of accommodation for all conceivable sorts of public and semi-public buildings, down to such matters as the provision of toilet facilities for infant schools. In sum, five volumes of pre-digested wisdom on functional matters, all second-hand, much of it out of date, all of it vital to success wherever the *Beaux-Arts* system flourished—hence its continuing influence deep into the century, and hence, too, the various attempts to write 'a new Guadet', culminating in Talbot Hamlin's *Forms and Functions of Twentieth-Century Architecture.*

Nevertheless, between the lines of this mass of information, and in annexed texts, such as the introduction, and the reprint of his inaugural lecture of 1894, a certain amount of Guadet's theory emerges, and some of it deserves comment, either for its intrinsic interest or for the echoes of it that can be heard later in the century. For a start, his attitude to the past is not altogether what one might expect from an academician. It is from the masters and monuments of former periods that he prefers to draw his examples, but he recognises the emergence of new building types and functions in the lifetime of his own contemporaries, and concedes that

> Là, il faudra bien que je fasse des emprunts aux vivants.

This may be only prudent, but one notes elsewhere a tendency to be scornful of pure archaeology in the choice of style.

> In Munich they imagine utilitarian Parthenons; in London, in response to the entirely modern needs of clubs, you meet such old friends as the Palazzo Farnese, the Procuratie . . . down to the very mouldings for greater servility of imitation.

Against this, he sets the example of the innovators of the generation of his master, Labrouste.

> Fortunately, certain proud artists—our masters—saw, and made us see, that freedom is not simply the right to change one's uniform, and our art has gradually freed itself from such archaeology. Not everything was a success, but all efforts in this direction bore fruit, and today we know and proclaim that our art has a right to liberty, that only liberty guarantees its life and fecundity; in a word, its health. . . .
> If I insist on these considerations it is not, indeed, to wipe the slate clean of all that went before; on the contrary our art, like our language, like our whole civilisation, is—and must be—the rich inheritor of an estate that has accumulated over the centuries. But I hate artistic proscriptions, like all proscriptions, and artistic exclusiveness like all exclusiveness, and I aim to make you understand the sense, broad and severe, in which I understand that word 'Classic' that I set at the head of these studies.

Leaving aside the libertarian sentiment of the last sentence for the moment, we see here an abstract and ambivalent attitude to history—to be understood, not imitated, its lessons embodied less in the actual monuments of former time than in the principles that can be abstracted from them. This last idea will be seen to be of peculiar importance in evaluating Guadet's understanding of *ce mot de classique.*

This attitude to history was regarded by Guadet as 'scientific'

> The architect today is, or should be, a most manifold man: a man of science in all matters touching construction and its applications, a man of science also in his profound knowledge of the whole heritage of architecture

and this clearly implies a different meaning of the word *science* to that which was current even among the generation of his own pupils. He means science in the generalised sense in which Leonardo de Vinci understood science, as erudition plus logical method (Paul Valéry's *Introduction à la Méthode de Leonardo da Vinci* came out only five years before Guadet's book was published, and it is probably no coincidence that Leonardo is Ferran's most quoted authority) not as most twentieth-century writers understand it, as a mental discipline based on experimental research. If anything, Guadet was hostile to exact physical studies as a basis of design

> He must be shown what can be built; later he will see by what means he can secure its construction, that is, the realisation of a thing he must already have conceived

yet he certainly regarded his own teaching methods as scientific, and at one point draws an energetic parallel between the *ateliers* of the *École* and the laboratories of a scientific institute.

The confusion that he introduced here was widespread in later years, though the blame is not always to be laid upon his influence. Much of the academic aesthetics of Blanc and his followers, which was scientific in the older and more generalised sense, acquired the prestige accruing to science in the newer and more specialised sense, in spite of the inconclusive result of Charles Henry's attempts in the Nineties to render them scientific in the experimental sense as well.[3] The statement of Ozenfant and Jeanneret that

> l'art et la science dépendent du nombre[4]

suggests that they too, while claiming for their theories the prestige of the advanced science of the twentieth-century, are still thinking of science in terms of its condition before it became 'the experimental philosophy'. This confusion over the meaning of 'scientific' has been paralleled by an equal confusion between the two possible meanings of 'objective', and the aesthetics of Abstract art, largely derived from Charles Blanc, which are capable of being rendered objective in the sense of logically impeccable, have been regarded as also objective in the sense of substantiated by experiment, which they have not been so far.

The connection with Abstract art needs to be made at this point,

[3] For the most recent assessment of Charles Henry, see Christopher Gray, *Cubist Aesthetic Theories* (Baltimore, 1953). Henry was the director of a Laboratory of the Psychology of Perception, annexed to the *École des Beaux-Arts*, and his ideas were still sufficiently in vogue in the Twenties to be reprinted at some length in *L'Esprit Nouveau*, on which, see chapter 17.
[4] See chapter 15.

because Guadet has occasionally been represented as favouring an Abstract architecture. Colin Rowe, for instance, has proposed that he 'envisaged an architecture of pure form',[5] but the illustrations in *Éléments et Théories*, the work done at the *École* under his professorship, and the few buildings to emerge from his office do not substantiate this idea. It would be truer to say that he facilitated the emergence of an architecture of pure form in much the same way that Blanc facilitated the emergence of Abstract art. Blanc pays little attention to subject-matter, Guadet even less to stylistic details, but this does not imply that either envisaged doing without them. Guadet regards style as something outside the competence of his course, open to the choice and temperament of the individual designer and the examples in his book are drawn from all styles and periods; he is a sort of negative eclectic, and—as was pointed out above—his attitude is libertarian, he hated proscriptions and exclusivism.

The key point in his avoidance of the stylistic problem is the *large et sévère* sense in which he understands the word *classique*. It is something like the 'unhistorical Classicism' later proposed by Oud,[6] or the diagrammatic Classicism of Labrouste and, even more, the masters like Ledoux and Durand in whose work the roots of the *Beaux-Arts* tradition were struck. It is like the sense of *Greek* intended by Alois Hirt, also in the early years of the nineteenth century when he said

Whoever constructs correctly, builds even as the Greeks

—that is, rational and straightforward, a sense that comes back many times in Le Corbusier's comparisons of machinery with Greek architecture.[7]

Thus, on at least three topics current in the Twenties, the meaning of history, the status of science, and the status of the Classical tradition, we find Guadet anticipating widely held opinions, though it would be risky to propose any influence or historical connection. On one topic, however, and that of the greatest importance, an historical connection can certainly be proposed: his conception of the actual process of designing buildings. If his views on style were too negative to reach the printed page, his views on symmetrical composition were too positive to do so. It was under his professorship that the *Beaux-Arts* training became almost completely focused on the elaboration of multi-axially symmetrical plan patterns of abstract, but unfunctional elegance. Elevational design became so secondary that Ferran, for instance, feels no need to illustrate anything but the plans and leaves the reader to infer the elevations from the columniation, etc. shown on them; and where Ferran expresses a preference between one plan and another—preferences which seem always to follow those of the

[5] In the *Art Bulletin* (New York, June 1953, p. 170).
[6] See chapter 12.   [7] See chapter 17.

19

Rome Prize jury—it is always for schemes that are symmetrical about more axes.

But this hammering of axiality is not found in *Éléments et Théories* indeed, Guadet mocks absolute axial symmetry as '*du non-sens*'; what he does emphasise is the manner of fitting the parts of the building into the axial plan

> This course has for object the study of the composition of buildings in their elements and their totality, from the double viewpoint of adapting them to defined programmes and to material necessities

and he expands this viewpoint on more than one occasion

> To compose is to make use of what is known (*ce qu'on sait*). Composition has materials, just as construction has, and these materials are, precisely, the Elements of Architecture.

and again

> Nothing, to be sure, is more engaging than composition, nothing more seductive. It is the true realm of the artist with no limits or frontiers but the impossible. What is it, to compose? It is to put together, weld, unite, the parts of a whole. These parts, in their turn, are the Elements of Composition, and just as you will realise your conceptions with walls, openings, vaults, roofs—all elements of architecture—you will establish your composition with rooms, vestibules, exits and staircases. These are the Elements of Composition.

These elements are *ce qu'on sait*, the utilitarian information that makes up the contents of the last three volumes of *Éléments et Théories*; composition is the manner of putting them together, and the two concepts make up a design philosophy that was common to Academics and Moderns alike. The approach is particulate; small structural and functional members (elements of architecture) are assembled to make functional volumes, and these (elements of composition) are assembled to make whole buildings. To do this is to compose in the literal and derivational sense of the word, to put together.

But it is not the only way of designing buildings, or the only way of creating great architecture. To take an example that will be discussed in a later chapter, Mies van der Rohe's flats at Weissenhof were designed by subdividing a bulk volume to create functional spaces out of it. Although there have been a number of later buildings conceived in this mode, by Mies himself, by office-block designers like Skidmore, Owings and Merrill, and by engineers like Buckminster Fuller, examples of this approach were rare in the period covered by the present study, and it may be taken as a general characteristic of the progressive architecture of the early twentieth century that it was conceived in terms of a separate and defined volume for each separate and defined function, and composed in such a way that this separation and definition was made plain.

In view of the dependence of Guadet's theory of elementary composition on neo-Classical writers like Durand, it should come as no surprise to find that this clear separation of the parts of buildings has been identified as a characteristic of neo-Classical architecture in general—by Kaufmann, who also drew attention to its reappearance in twentieth-century architecture[8] —and even of its earliest phase—by Wittkower, who drew attention to the distinction of the parts in Lord Burlington's designs.[9] The theory seems to have survived throughout the nineteenth century, the practice was somewhat submerged except where unstylistic aesthetic practices, such as those of the Picturesque flourished, and the re-emergence of this piece-by-piece mode of design may well have been due to the impact of the picturesque 'English Free Architecture' on an established neo-Classical tradition, as in Germany, where it cannot be due to the impact of Guadet direct.

Thus, while it comes as little surprise to find Le Corbusier, a pupil of Perret, persistently using elementary composition, and even paying direct tribute to Guadet by captioning an alternative version of his League of Nations design:[10]

Here . . . an alternative proposal, employing the same elements of composition.

the presence of Gropius among the architects of this persuasion must be due, presumably and in part, to the impact of Muthesius's enthusiasm for English free planning on the *Schinkelschuler* tradition of neo-Classicism. Yet it is worth noting that while two of Gropius's most famous and most original designs, the Fagus factory of 1911–13 and the Bauhaus at Dessau, of 1925–6, both compose their elements in a free manner, the equally famous Werkbund Pavilion at the Cologne exhibition of 1914 composes its disparately conceived elements according to purely *Beaux-Arts* rules of symmetrical composition, complete even with secondary and tertiary axes, such as were discussed later, and quite independently in Ferran's book.

However, mention of the Bauhaus raises the question of another theory of elementary composition, which may have influenced Gropius in its design. This was propagated by the Elementarist Movement, and took the form of supposing pictures, sculptures, etc. to be composed of certain fundamental geometrical elements.[11] This movement drew its inspiration from Dutch and Russian Abstract art, and thus owes something to the theories of Charles Blanc. It chimed in well with ideas that came from the architectural side of academic thought and were current at the time, but its

[8] Kaufmann made this point in both *Von Ledoux bis Le Corbusier* (Vienna, 1935) and in *Architecture in the Age of Reason* (London, 1955) but in neither case does he give close documentation, though the latter work contains some suggestive quotations from Gropius and others.
[9] See 'Lord Burlington and William Kent' (*Archaeological Journal*, London, 1945) where Professor Wittkower points out that in the elevation of Lord Burlington's designs for Tottenham Park, each part of the house forms a distinct unit of its own.
[10] *Une Maison, Un Palais* (Paris, 1928, p. 97).
[11] See chapter 14.

tendency was to focus attention on what Guadet would have called elements of architecture, not of composition; that is, on structural components, and it is in this sense that the word 'element' has passed into the common vocabulary of the mainstream of development.

2: Choisy: rationalism and technique

IF GUADET'S MAIN thesis is almost lost beneath a flood of miscellaneous information, Choisy's, to which information is everywhere subservient, is always in view, even if it continually opens side issues or casts light on other matters. His book[1] is history, but it is history with a single theme—Form as the logical consequence of Technique—that makes the art of architecture always and everywhere the same

> With every people, the art will undergo the same choices, obey the same laws; prehistoric art seems to contain all the others in embryo.

For Guadet, composition was the perennial theme, for Choisy it was construction. The difference is one of background and work, not of generation, for they were men of almost the same age, Guadet, born 1834 died in 1908, Choisy, just seven years younger, died in 1909. There was a difference of temperament also; Guadet was, apparently, very much the *Grand Professeur*, and in his later years almost as diffuse in personality as in his writings, but

> Though short in stature, M. Choisy, was a man of very fine presence, with something military about his personality[2]

and photographs taken of him at the time he received the RIBA Gold Medal, 1904, show a rather hard-faced, business-like man in the sort of square-rigged jacket affected by sea captains and constructional engineers.

An engineer by training, he took a down-to-earth, practical-minded view of architecture which remained for him, as for Henri Labrouste, *L'Art de Bâtir*. For him, the essence of good architecture, was always construction, the business of the good architect was always this: to make a correct appraisal of the problem before him, after which the form of the building

---

[1] This discussion of Choisy and his ideas is based on the *Histoire* exclusively, since this was the work of his that was most widely read and exercised the most general influence among the next two generations of architects. His other books, such as the exhaustive *Art de Bâtir* series, each dealing with some major phase of architectural history, such as the Roman or the Byzantine, were more specialised and more bulky, and therefore hardly known to general architectural readers, though their effective conclusions are summarised in the relevant parts of the *Histoire*.

[2] Obituary in *The Builder* (London, 25 September 1909).

23

would follow logically from the technical means at his disposal

> Style does not change according to the caprice of more or less arbitrary fashion, its variations are nothing but those of processes . . . and the logic of methods implies the chronology of styles.

in which, of course he was not alone, Semperian Rationalists having taken a similar view in Germany, and Gothicising Rationalists in England as well. Thomas Graham Jackson, for instance, saw the matter in a less absolute light, but in very similar terms.[3]

> To clamour with some people for a new style as if it could be had for the asking, to parade your Art Nouveau . . . is to ignore the whole teaching of history.
> Not so did the great styles of the past come into being. . . . It was in the suggestions of construction that the architect of the great artistic ages found his truest inspiration.

But, in terms of influence, Choisy had certain advantages over other Rationalist theorists—historical, technical and literary advantages. The historical advantage lay in his book appearing, in 1899, just as Art Nouveau was about to go into its decline. T. G. Jackson's objections came when it was already past its peak, but those who read Choisy early would see his view of the origins of style being proven before their eyes over the next decade. Art Nouveau, widely regarded by then as a *caprice de mode* was visibly proving deciduous, a distaste for the arbitrary among the younger generation was hardening into an admiration for the logical, and Choisy's obituary on late Gothic must have sounded to them like a *rappel à l'ordre* applicable to their own situation.

> Complexity had reached its peak, a return to simple forms was the only way to rejuvenate the art.

Choisy's technical advantages lay in the appearance of his book and its illustrations. The *Histoire de l'Architecture* is packed into two substantial, but not bulky volumes; it is not too big to take home. The text is set out in shortish paragraphs, each of which makes—normally—only one particular point, so that reference is easily made, and on almost every page there is at least one of his remarkable illustrations. Nothing could so well reinforce the idea of the continuity of architectural practice than the complete homogeneity of style of these 1,700 illustrations, all drawn by his own hand according to an almost invariable formula. The deviations from that formula are not numerous—an occasional perspective, pure elevation or plan—but, more important, they are not memorable. The formula is: isometric in its setting out, it presents plan, section and elevation in a

---

[3] Thomas Graham Jackson, *Reason in Architecture* (London, 1906, pp. 156–7). This book was the reprint of Graham's lectures given at the Royal Academy Schools in that year, a late outcropping of nineteenth-century Rationalist Gothicism and part of the background to the ideas of Walter Richard Lethaby, discussed in chapter 4.

single image, detailing is suppressed and one is left with an elegant and immediately comprehensible diagram.

There is no attempt at artistic effect in them, they are the careful and learnedly drawn representations of fact.

So convincing were they at the time that even the obituarist of *The Builder*, who is elsewhere critical of Choisy's methods, failed to observe that they are pure abstractions, and don't deal with such facts as what the building looks like to an observer inside it or in front of it. Nevertheless, it was almost certainly this quality of abstraction, of a logical construct rather than the accidents of appearance, the elegant pattern of black and white on the page, that endeared these illustrations to the generation born in the Eighteen-eighties, the generation which, outside architecture though never out of touch with it, also perfected Abstract art. Le Corbusier, at least, took these illustrations for his own, and used many of them in *L'Esprit Nouveau*, through which agency they gained a fresh and wider circulation.

His literary advantage lies in the style of writing that goes with the short paragraphs that have been discussed already. His overall argument is often too diffuse to be read consecutively, but individual paragraphs, crisp and aphoristic in manner, stick in the mind by virtue of their balanced concision and eminent reasonableness. Thus, of Doric pediments he says

The pitch of the gable is that of the roof, which is governed by this double condition, that the rain should run off, and the tiles should not.

a tidy and reasonable explanation, even if it lacks any documentary or factual evidence to support it, and rendered convincing by its very reasonableness. As the obituarist in *The Builder* observed

. . . if he was too prone to treat as proved that which he had only succeeded in representing as probable, many of his probabilities as to ancient construction impress themselves on the reader, in his brilliant demonstrations, as at all events more likely to be the true solution than any others that could be offered.

These pithy propositions, which so often appeared to his readers to have tidied up some problem, explained some mystery in a definitive manner, are without doubt, largely responsible for the durability of his reputation. Memorable and quotable, they gave a clear and logical orientation to minds seeking guidance on detail points, as well as guiding principles, and in some cases even furnished the phraseology and form of words for later discussions.

At times this too takes on a tinge of seeming-prophecy, and one wonders if Le Corbusier's willingness to be included among the founders of the review *L'Esprit Nouveau* may not have been conditioned by a mental echo of

We have perceived as a sign of the new spirit (l'esprit nouveau) the search for truth, the independence, of a rejuvenated art that breaks with conventional types.

Choisy was, in fact, discussing the new spirit of emergent Gothic architecture, but nothing could better describe the aims (if not the performance) of *L'Esprit Nouveau* during the five and a half years of its existence than this association of a search for truth with a rejuvenated art that broke with conventional types of architecture.

Underlying the memorability of his writing—or perhaps partly caused by it—was Choisy's success in imposing his mental processes on his readers. When they were stuck with some problem, they went back to his favoured method of correct appraisal from which the answer logically derives.

> La question posée, la solution était indiquée.

They tended, more often than not, to phrase the question in his terms, and thus—almost inevitably—were practically incapable of coming out with any answers but his. He put in circulation a whole coinage of questions and answers that remained current until devalued, much later, not by the experience of his followers, but by a different kind of architectural history, that of scholars like Worringer and Sedlmayr, or—in France itself—Focillon.

That devaluation did not even begin to affect the theoretical approach of architects themselves until well after the period covered by the present study, and Choisy's coinage, embodying major architectural values as well as the small change of discussion, needs to be examined in some detail.

Bearing in mind the basic concept of architectural form as the logical consequence of technique, it should be noted that for Choisy *technique*, *méthode*, *procédé* and *outillage*, are aspects of society as a whole, the complete range of mechanisms and relationships that are put in motion in the erection of a building.

> Buildings classify themselves as witnesses fixing the way of life and the moral condition of humanity, age by age.

This applies, equally, in his eyes to smaller units within the larger social frame. On Gothic cathedral planning he notes that these civic churches had to serve a dual purpose

> . . . to serve both for meetings of the people and for sacred ritual. Hence their mixed character as buildings at once municipal and religious. Sometimes the civic influence prevailed, sometimes the ecclesiastical, and their alternations explain and sum up the history of successive types of plan

and even smaller units within the church had their traceable influence in his eyes, for on conventual planning he observes

> . . . from one group to another the character differs according to the very spirit of the Rule.

'According to the very spirit of the Rule' is a very vague and generalised sort of causation, but there are times when Choisy seems to envisage nothing more definite than a kind of abstract necessity as a determining factor.

L'arc-boutant (the flying buttress) . . . ne fut point inventé, il s'imposa.

and he backs this up later with

It is in the nature of Gothic, as with all discoveries, that we can rarely manage to name the true inventor without dispute; the seeds incubate in obscurity, and suddenly we witness various hatchings that imply only the logic of facts.

Such a position, of constructional fatalism, is probably inevitable in one who adopts a strictly determinist view of architectural history, and it brings out the difference between a Rationalist like Choisy, under the older historiographic dispensation, and a merely reasonable man, under a different historical discipline, who would tend to suppose that an inability to name names derives from an absence of the necessary documentation. At all events, it is an approach that depreciates personal effort, and tended to leave his followers standing about waiting for a new structural principle like the flying buttress, to impose itself. However, such an attitude was understandably welcome in a period of revulsion against Art Nouveau and its supposed excesses of personal wilfulness.

However, since Choisy was not specifically arguing against Art Nouveau, but speaking in more general terms, the drift of his remarks sometimes appears to favour some aspects of Art Nouveau practice. Thus the concept of the all-round designer receives implied support when he speaks admiringly of Renaissance architects who

. . . possessed an universality of talent; all matters touching form were their domain . . . the superiority of the Renaissance lies in not having arts independent of one another, but a single art in which all expressions of the beautiful were fused.

Ideas like these helped to prepare French architects, who did not have the backing of Germany's kind of Arts and Crafts Movement, for post-War forays into the neighbouring arts of painting and product design, circulated the concept of a single overriding art of design embracing all others, and began to give currency to the word *form* as part of the terminology of design theory—a word closely associated with later developments in the field of industrial design.

In that context, form is generally regarded as having laws of its own; laws of harmony, proportion and so forth. But on these laws Choisy is ambiguous. He notes the use of systematic proportion, for instance, wherever he finds evidence of it, but rarely accords it great importance

The Egyptians did not accept that the effect of a monument resides entirely in the abstract harmony of its lines

and although he records the use of *tracés regulateurs* in the Middle Ages and Renaissance, to advance him as a justification for their use, as Le

Corbusier seems to wish to do on occasion, is to misrepresent him. In fact, his best-known remarks on geometrical *tracés* appear in a gloss on Serlio that seems to be intended only as an ironic comment on regulating lines as an intellectual exercise

> We take from Serlio . . . the proportional setting out of a door in a panel of width m', n' . . . (construction C).
> In reality, construction C, results in giving the door a width equal to one third of $m'n'$ and a height equal to twice the width, but the graphical method that leads to this result is interesting in itself and contains a whole method.

but one does not feel that Choisy really considers this method worth the trouble, if the same result could have been attained by simple measurement.

However, as a Rationalist, he naturally inclined toward the orderly and the logical, and some sort of system in dimensioning and proportion receives his implied approval from his use of faintly derogatory language

> ce vague sentiment de l'harmonie qu'on nomme le goût

to describe the alternative; personal taste. In any case it seems likely that what interests him is not the pure harmony of proportions, but the use of dimensional modules implying a sense of scale, deriving from the multiplication of a standard structural component.

> Modular proportions: we have observed that they result, as an inevitable consequence, from the use of brick.
> Classical art had only an abstract harmony based on proportion alone; but, as Lassus observed, it is to the Middle Ages that the art of emphasising the dimensions belongs, and the principle of scale.

This principle of scale seems to subsist, in Choisy's view of the Middle Ages, in two things. Firstly, dimensioning by the size of a man, rather than increasing door-heights, etc. as the building became larger

> Man does not change dimensions according to the importance of the monument.

and secondly, as a consequence of Romanesque and Gothic stone-laying methods, course by course, which, he claims, led to the necessity of making all vertical dimensions into multiples of the course-heights, so that capitals and friezes, door-jambs and column shafts, all answered to the same module. Arguable as this last observation may be, the importance of the idea of building to a human scale, advanced in this influential context, is not to be overlooked.

The Gothic masons who practised this technique were the heroes of his second volume, the heroes of the first had been the builders of the Doric temples. In the words of de Dartien's *Compte Rendu*

> Greek art and Gothic . . . these were the subjects to which we may say M. Choisy has dedicated himself for preference. It is always Greek architecture and Gothic architecture that stand out, the one for nearly half the first volume, the other for half the second.

and he continues to justify Choisy in this distribution of emphasis.

And it is just that it be so, for these two architectures, so absolutely different in spirit, stand in the front rank of all the styles by the high value of the qualities they hold in common—clarity of methods, sincerity of expression, spontaneity, delicacy and intensity of artistic feeling.[4]

Choisy's views on these two preferred styles are of the greatest interest, and were of great seminal power, but before passing on to them there is an oddity of his *History* (an oddity that he shared with other Rationalists) that affects his view of the place of Doric in Greek technical culture, and is best dealt with first.

This oddity, which was a certain fascination with the use of the forms and methods of one material in connection with another, has an interest of its own, in any case, as will be seen later. Such a procedure ought, presumably, to be anathema to a Rationalist, but Choisy seems to have no overriding objections to it. Inevitably, almost, he compares Doric to wooden structure, as generations of neo-Classicists had done, but in a way that seems to invert the normal implications of this comparison. Doric for him owes nothing to carpentry, which he believes to be a borrowing from shipbuilding technique, and

. . . the difference from our system of carpentry is radical; Greek woodwork . . . is a piling up pure and simple, a veritable masonry of wood.
The Doric order was to be the application of this mode of building to stone.

so that, if anything, pre-Doric was a wooden architecture imitating the, as yet, undiscovered modes of stone construction. However, Choisy finds the Classic type of reversal in Indian architecture.

The stone is put to work in the manner of wood, with all the jointing techniques that suit wood . . . a carpentry of stone.

This was for the past, of course, but for the materials of his own time, notably iron, Choisy believed that appropriate forms and methods had already been evolved.

At the *Halles de Paris* we can see realised a whole body of forms that arise naturally from the material employed.

But not all Rationalists were quite so sure as this, and Thomas Graham Jackson in his Royal Academy lectures of 1906, after demanding that iron should not be used after the manner of brick and stone, nevertheless continues

It has often struck me that the half-timber work of the fifteenth and sixteenth centuries contains many suggestions for this new way of construction. In the

[4] This *Compte Rendu* adopts throughout an extremely eulogistic tone, and appeared immediately upon the publication of the *Histoire*. It has the air of being either a piece of 'inspired' puffing (which a work by Choisy could hardly have needed by that date) or of interested flattery. It may yet, however, be read with profit as an 'official' Rationalist evaluation of the master's work.

first place it is a trabeated style in the literal sense of the word, a style of posts and beams. . . . And iron construction is very like carpentry. It too is a system of trabeation, of posts and beams, ties and braces; it has the tensile strength and rigidity of timber to a superior degree, and hangs together by its joints, cleats and bolts, much as carpentry by its tenons and mortices.[5]

This transposition of forms and methods must appear a muddle to later readers, but the greatest muddle—a very productive and influential muddle—was Auguste Perret's transposition of wood-framing techniques on to reinforced construction,[6] a procedure which he, apparently, held to be warranted by Choisy. Right or wrong, however, this act of transposition served an important purpose in bringing a new material within the accepted body of formal procedures in building design, and by endowing it with a rectangular aesthetic of posts and lintels, made it accessible to integration with the rectangular aesthetics of Abstract art that appeared after 1918, and thus, in a very real sense, determined the appearance of the new architecture.

But Perret's structural methods owe a further debt than this to Choisy, and to his views on Gothic structure in particular. Gothic, as has been said above, was one of Choisy's two preferred styles, because it constitutes in his eyes, the culmination of logical method in structure.

> Comes the Gothic period . . . the new structure is the triumph of logic in art; the building becomes an organised being whose every part constitutes a living member, its form governed not by traditional models, but by its function, and only its function.

This is Choisy's view of Gothic, but, as so often happens with him, it sounds in retrospect like a directive to his successors. Logic, analysis, function, economy, performance—

> Everywhere, in the detailing of the forms, we have recognised the spirit of analysis that governs the economy of the whole work . . . in effect, a construction where stone works to the limit of its resistance.

and the consequence of this was, as in later Modern-Movement theory, that the appearance of the building was supposed to some extent to be fixed thereby

> By the very fact that the stone works to its maximum effort, the absolute size is in no way arbitrary; and the eye, most sure of mathematical instruments, at once establishes the scale, which calculations may figure out in due course.

This paragraph brings forward a number of important ideas that were to enjoy further currency. The idea of an unavoidable mathematical relationship of the parts of a building, on an absolute, not a relative scale, which clearly ties in with the idea of modular dimensioning discussed above, and the idea of the eye as an accurate judge of measurement, an idea that played a vital part in the so-called objective aesthetics of post-War Abstract art.

[5] *Reason in Architecture*, p. 167.   [6] See chapter 3.

Choisy's whole view of Gothic structure is clearly coloured by his early readings in Willis and Viollet-le-Duc, and it was a view of Gothic that one of his own supposed followers, Pol Abraham, was to call seriously in question by demonstrating the considerable redundancies and large margins of safety of all those Gothic structures that have managed to survive.[7] Abraham also did much to discredit Viollet-le-Duc's theory that Gothic vaulting was a light panelled structure carried on a framework of ribs, an idea that was also used by Choisy, and extended by him to wall-structures of the period as well.

> The Gothic vault is nothing but a ridged vault where the panels are independent and supported by the rib-work . . . and the wall is nothing but an infill.

Frame and fill, the posts that bear the load, and the screen panels that do not—these concepts seem to have been current wherever the Willis/le-Duc view of Gothic had encountered nineteenth-century iron construction —for what was dubiously true of the *Sainte Chapelle*, was abundantly so for the *Galérie des Machines*, where the arches were grounded on rollers, and the glass infill of the roof was carried by a system of riblets that span the spaces between the main trusses—a contemporary reworking in iron and glass of Viollet-le-Duc's vision of Gothic as a form of elastic, self-compensating structure. But most important from our point of view is the fact that Auguste Perret took over from Choisy the idea of a load-bearing frame with lightweight infilling, and from there forward, the concept of the separation of support and cladding became one of the most discussed, if least practised ideas of the Modern Movement.

The mood of Gothic, as Choisy saw it, was progressive, forward looking and enabled its practitioners to tackle

> . . . the most daunting problems with the zest of that spirit of progress and reform that animated society as a whole.

and again the use of the historic present (*anime*) must have struck his younger readers as a call to themselves. It would also be a call to model themselves on the Greeks for

> Ancient Greece and our Middle Ages meet in this faith in progress.

The Greece he has in mind is the Greece of the Periclean Empire, Doric not Hellenistic, and in writing of Doric architecture he is at his very best —better even than on Gothic, on which he has, in fact, one slight reservation; the buttresses cannot be seen from within the main vessel of the

---

[7] Pol Abraham, *Viollet-le-Duc et le Rationalisme Médiévale* (Paris, 1933). Though there can be little doubt that this 'demolition' of Viollet-le-Duc is overdone, and has been too enthusiastically quoted out of context, and that mediaeval builders may indeed have believed that the ribs carried the panels and so forth, Abraham's demonstration of structural redundancies is entirely convincing, and makes it very clear that in surviving Gothic buildings the stone very rarely works to its limit.

building and this causes him *inquietude*

> . . . at first sight one does not understand its stability

but he has no such qualms about Doric. But in his discussion of this other preferred style of his, he brings into juxtaposition two ideas very rarely found together in works of theory—pure form and picturesque composition—though of course they had existed together in neo-Classical practice, in Nash and Schinkel particularly. The way in which he arrives at this position is as interesting as the juxtaposition was to be productive.

Doric, for him, is a reformist style, a revolution against the applied decoration of previous ages

> . . . the Mycenaean age only thought of decoration as an applied and outward show

but this was not good enough for Choisy's Greeks

> They would need a more masculine accent,[8] a firmer expression; they placed their ideal in an architecture that scorned the easy seductions of ornament, an architecture that aimed, above all, at a severe beauty of line . . . new types, more abstract and more simple

and it was the revival of these qualities that Choisy found admirable in Renaissance architecture.

> What architecture had just regained was the sense of classic beauty in its highest and most abstract purity.

But this style, praiseworthy for its abstract purity of undecorated form (triglyph and metope were not decoration to him) is set firmly by Choisy in the context of picturesque grouping. And picturesque is to be understood in its strict sense, not the eroded picture-postcard sense. It is to be understood from a succession of pictures (*tableaux*) seen by the visitor approaching the Parthenon, and as a deliberate, not an accidental, mode of procedure. He compares the plans of the Acropolis before and after the fire had razed most of its buildings and comments that though the earlier plan was the result of an accumulation of accidents

> . . . the other is methodically conceived according to an overall view and adapted to a site that had been cleared by the fire, and in this new Acropolis the apparent asymmetries are only a means of giving a picturesque aspect to the most cunningly balanced group of architecture there ever was.

This is putting a very high value on picturesque composition, and makes a striking contrast to *Beaux-Arts* practice with its routines of major and

---

[8] The idea of a male or masculine architecture was transmitted primarily through academic channels. Thus, Charles Blanc had written in his *Grammaire*, 'In the Doric order the proportions are male . . . the architecture of the Dorians was to be solid, massive, powerful, and it was to demonstrate its strength as an athlete flexes his muscles'—a grotesque, though reassuringly down-to-earth, foreshadowing of Geoffrey Scott's somewhat otherworldly theory of humanist values in architecture, discussed in chapter 4.

minor axes. He identifies the components of the picturesque method with complete accuracy: the respect for site.

> The Greeks never visualised a building without the site that framed it and the other buildings that surrounded it . . . siting it as nature would have done

profiting by given factors

> Architecture bent itself to these subjections, and turned them to account

balancing of masses

> Each architectural motif, on its own, is symmetrical, but every group is treated like a landscape where the masses alone balance out

as seen by the eye of a walking viewer at ground level

> The method of balancing will emerge from a study of the successive pictures that the Acropolis of the fifth century presented to the visitor.

And not only is the picturesque good enough for the Greeks, it is also nature's way.

> So proceeds Nature . . . symmetry reigns in each part, but the whole is subject only to those laws of equilibrium for which the word 'balance' is at once the physical expression and the mental image.

To Choisy as a practical man, this *ad hoc* and natural mode of composition would obviously appeal, but nevertheless the association of Greek Doric, an ultimate term in architectural discipline and regularity, with asymmetrical composition remains a remarkable achievement in the context of French late nineteenth-century design. The message did not go by default, and though the asymmetries of post-War building were to have a more complicated aesthetic basis than this, Choisy's illustrations turn up, and his arguments too, in support of Le Corbusier's anti-axial views on planning. All the same it may be doubted if Choisy realised that he was putting a mine under accepted planning methods for a younger generation to explode. His last words on Greece are conventional.

> Greek art . . . seems to be a disinterested cult offered to the idea of harmony and abstract beauty.

Choisy, indeed, has his soft passages, when he falls short of his best form. His logical and teleological view of architectural development makes little allowance for such random factors as the exercise of the human will, with the result that his attitude to the Renaissance is muddled and self-contradictory, largely because he failed to take into account the full range of social determinants. Similarly his study of the nineteenth century is unsatisfactory because he failed to take into account the full range of technical determinants. He seems not to have observed that, at the time that the book was writing, both equipment and materials were in revolution, and that—by his own standards even—architecture ought to be in revolution as well. But he stops with Labrouste's *Bibliothèque Nationale* observing that it was a *début* that contained *plus que des promesses*, and remains silent about the last third of the century. In the meantime *outillage* was being revolutionised by electricity and the internal combustion engine, *construction* by steel and reinforced concrete. Yet he could say of Gothic building tackle

> We recognise there our present engines, near enough, the crane, the capstan, all our machinery, which itself is nothing but the machinery of antiquity.

However great his contributions to the mental equipment of the Modern Movement, his failure to appreciate the emergence of its mechanical equipment meant that he could contribute nothing final to it. But something like final contributions were to come from his own direct successors, Auguste Perret and Tony Garnier.

3: The academic succession: Garnier and Perret

OUTSIDE THE contribution of engineers like Freyssinet, France gave to the developing practice of a new architecture before 1914, only the work of two members of the academic succession to Guadet: both Auguste Perret (1874–1954) and Tony Garnier (1869–1948) had been his pupils and imbibed both the progressive and the negative aspects of his teaching. Both also owe something to Choisy, but the debt is slighter in the case of Garnier, whose career was academically respectable, much greater in the case of Perret, who did not stay the course.

But whatever the debt to Choisy, the prime one in their mode of designing buildings—composing, that is—is to Guadet, whose course they heard, whose influence they underwent in the Nineties, when he was in his prime as a professor. Garnier bore off the Rome Prize in 1899 (two years after Perret had left) with a design that is still cited (by Ferran)[1] as a model of composition and, indeed, represents the *Beaux-Arts* ideal at its most abstract and most elegant. It is a design for the central office of a State Banking House, with its main work-spaces distributed peripherally around an enormous covered court in the centre of which, but occupying barely a tenth of its area, is the main banking room. The scale is grandiose, the space given to monumental circulation, entrance facilities, etc. is utterly disproportionate—yet this scheme was preferred by the Prize jury to others with far more efficient circulations, far greater functional sense. One can understand how a generation rendered suspicious of the arbitrary by Choisy's teaching would be in revolt against such design principles as these, and against the juries that enforced them.

But to suppose that Garnier made his design with his tongue in his cheek, as was apparently supposed by students in Paris after 1918,[2] jealous of his reputation as a father of Modern architecture, seems not to be borne out by the evidence. Had he done so, it is unlikely that so astute an academic critic as Ferran would be taken in by his design fifty years later, and the

---

[1] In his *Philosophie*, mentioned in chapter 1.
[2] André Lurçat told the author that it was a great source of embarrassment to young progressive architects of the early Twenties, to have to explain away such a design.

evidence rather points to the probability that he turned to his *Cité Industrielle* project in revulsion against ideas he had previously held with some sincerity.

To occupy one's time with such a scheme while a *pensionnaire* at the Villa Medici was an unprecedented and, indeed, revolutionary course of action, but there is evidence that he also occupied some part of his time with more conventional academic exercises.[3] However, he seems to have been in an unacademic and troubled frame of mind while he was there, for one of his few recorded statements on architecture,[4] written in 1900, reads

> Since all architecture rests on false principles, the architecture of antiquity was an error. TRUTH ALONE IS BEAUTIFUL. In architecture truth is product of the calculations made to satisfy known needs with known means.

There is an echo here of Guadet's '*Composer, c'est faire l'emploi de ce qu'on sait*', but the use of *calculs* sounds more like Choisy, whose book was new in men's minds, though the sentiment goes far beyond anything in it. But this seems to signal fairly accurately the frame of mind in which an architect might turn from the unreality of a Rome Prize programme, to the *verité* of an industrial town.

That *verité*, however, was by no means utterly removed from *Beaux-Arts* connotations. Unlike Sant'Elia's *Città Nuova* fragments of 1913–14,[5] Garnier's project is not concerned with the problems of any actual town or city.[6] *La Cité Industrielle* stands upon an imaginary site—an ideal site, in fact, for a more-than-convenient flat-topped ridge lifts the residential area clear above the industrial zone. The zones, too, though they are of the sort generally envisaged by early twentieth-century town-planning thought, are treated almost as Guadetesque elements. Residence, industry, transportation, sport and health are allotted separate and compact areas of land, all industry in one unit, all residential in another, with—as between industry and residence—quite inadequate communications, the single axial road that runs the length of the residential ridge bottle-necking all traffic to and from the industrial zone into a single artery without relief roads.

But the academic survivals go deeper than this. The residential zone, though irregular in outline, has its streets laid out on a regular rectangular grid with *axe d'équilibre* and *axe secondaire*, with its *salles d'assemblées* at its intersection, in the centre. The houses, though freely sited—more or less —are squared up to the road grid. The pattern, indeed, is like Camillo

---

[3] In 1912 Tony Garnier published plans of a reconstruction of Tusculum.
[4] Quoted in the introduction to *L'Œuvre de Tony Garnier* (Paris, 1938) edited by Badovici and Morancé.
[5] See chapter 10.
[6] Though most of the work on the *Cité Industrielle* was supposedly sufficiently finished for exhibition in 1904, it should be noted that it was not definitely published (as a large and complex portfolio) until 1918, by which time it was possible for Garnier to incorporate into it some of the buildings he had actually constructed at Lyons, as mentioned below.

Sitte with the serpentinings taken out. In smaller detail the house plans—though asymmetrical, in some cases—seem derived from those precepts upon *la salle et ses dépendances* that Guadet derived from Blondel, while individual public and institutional places seem drawn directly from Guadet's ideas, notably the *salle des collections* of his art school. In elevational treatment the various buildings tend to follow Guadetesque precedent when they are largely fenestrated and, indeed, establish already a number of norms to which Garnier returned in his later work. But it should be emphasised that it is not the Guadet of the *Cours de Théorie*, nor the Guadet of the *Hôtel des Postes* that he follows here, but the Guadet revealed in his son's small house in the Boulevard Murat, which will be discussed later. The small houses of the *Cité Industrielle*, however, are even simpler than this, solidly-walled with plain rendered surfaces, flat roofs and no cornices. It is in these smaller buildings that Garnier is most truly a forerunner of later developments in architecture, and Morancé and Badovici, when they published their book on Garnier in 1931, drew special attention by means of footnotes to the table of plates, to such features as *toît-terrasse jardin*, and *suppression totale de la corniche*.

It was in this that he was a forerunner of detail developments in architectural form, but as a forerunner of developments in architectural thought he must be remembered and valued simply for having considered an industrial town (indeed, any town) as a subject worthy of the architect's drawing board. By this gesture he extended architecture's terms of reference, and he brought the art closer to the reality—*la verité*—of an industrialised epoch. However, the impact of this gesture was somewhat softened, as far as his own contemporaries were concerned, by the fact that—though substantially completed by 1904—it had to wait until the end of the War for publication, and it was upon the men of a generation younger that it made its greatest effect. This was a generation that had been prepared for ideas about industrial cities by the Futurists, and had, by then, some completed works by Garnier to look at.

Although Garnier's unconventional attitude to architecture would not recommend him to the regularly constituted elements of the French administrative hierarchy that handed out big commissions, it did bring him the attention of one of France's most enlightened politicians of the time, Edouard Herriot, then Mayor of Lyons, Garnier's native town. *Les Grands Travaux de la Ville de Lyon*, put in hand under Herriot's leadership, occupied Garnier for fourteen years, from 1906 to 1920. The work is partly a realisation and extension of ideas that already existed in the *Cité Industrielle*, such as the stadium, and the great hospital centre at Grange Blanche; and partly a making good of the most conspicuous deficiency of the *Cité*.

In spite of the name, this project had been weak on the industrial side. Out of one hundred and sixty-five pages and several large sheets of plans in the 1918 edition of *La Cité Industrielle*, only five pages are given to industry alone. And of these, two are borrowings from his actual work on industrial construction at Lyons. For a large part of his work for Herriot was in laying out marketing and abbatoir facilities on the very largest scale. This work included a large hall with its roof carried on lattice trusses in the manner of Contamin's *Galerie des Machines*, and a remarkable group of auxiliary buildings housing power-plants, cold-storage, etc. in which he combines his Classicist learnings (cornices and a form of Doric column-fluting on the chimneys) with the satisfaction of industrial requirements to produce an architecture which can stand comparison on the one hand with early nineteenth-century industrial buildings, and with the projects of contemporaries like Behrens, Poelzig or Sant'Elia on the other.

A similar interaction between Classicist leanings and technical necessities underlies the work of Auguste Perret, but similarities between him and Garnier go little further than this. As has been said above, he left the *École des Beaux-Arts* in 1895 before completing his course, but after showing considerable aptitude for his studies, in order to join his father's contracting business. He had been designing independently from about 1890, the year he entered the *École*, so that he had possessed, almost from the start, that combination of the architect and the practical man of affairs that makes him comparable with Peter Behrens in status, as well as influence on the rising generation—for it seems clear that these two transitional Classicists were among the most influential figures in the formation of the generation that produced, rather than pioneered, Modern architecture.

With Perret, that influence depends chiefly on three complete buildings and the frame of another, all but one of them completed before 1914, and on a brief period as teacher and elder statesman in the Nineteen-twenties. An examination of these buildings will show that his achievement was to have imposed on reinforced concrete structure an eclectic aesthetic—derived from Guadet as much as Choisy—that his contemporaries, and the following generation too, believed to be the natural form of reinforced-concrete construction. In fact, he left concrete structure no more advanced than he found it and some, more recent, criticism has even suggested that he retarded its development. On the other hand he left concrete an aesthetically acceptable material (in the eyes of the younger generation at least) which is what it certainly was not before him, in spite of the efforts of Hennebique. And this acceptability was achieved by finding concrete a place within the possibilities of time-honoured structural and architectural concepts, not by extending those concepts to include the possibilities of concrete construction.

The three pre-1914 buildings depend, as Perret himself admitted, on a Choisyesque transposition of reinforced concrete into the forms and usages of wooden construction—a rectangular trabeated grid of posts and beams. This procedure which makes little use of the monolithic qualities, and less of the plastic ones, of the material, the assertions of Perret's followers notwithstanding, appears to have a complicated derivation. Perret himself is reported as claiming its descent from the half-timbering of northern France (much as Thomas Graham Jackson wished to have iron construction based upon English half-timbering) but there is more to the matter than this. The house in the Boulevard Murat, executed by Perret for Paul Guadet in 1912, has a short-span grid of beams and posts clearly exposed on its street-front, the voids being filled in with glazing, and stone spandrels—the uppermost run of spandrels, directly under the projecting cornice, being treated somewhat as a Doric frieze—the whole design has the quality of a rationalised, geometricised pilastered elevation, somewhat on the model of a Chicago school office building, but perfectly conceivable as a direct derivation from the elder Guadet's approach to 'les elements de l'architecture'. If, on the other hand, Perret derived this type of structure from woodwork practice independently of Guadet, he had here again good visible precedent in Paris. The piecemeal replacement of timber beams by concrete ones can be seen at a vernacular level in the long factory sheds of the Rue des Cordeliers area. Bay-widths and beam depths are often identical for wood and concrete, even in the case of complete concrete structures, some of which even retain the corner brackets used in wooden work, and theoretically unnecessary in concrete. The dates of these structures are difficult to determine, but details of door-furniture, etc. suggest that some of the complete concrete sheds, even, may go back to the Eighteen-nineties.

Certainly, Perret's early use of concrete is no more adventurous than is to be found in the Rue des Cordeliers, and in his first important concrete manifesto-building, 25bis Rue Franklin, only one beam—the fascia at first floor level—spans a distance that would be quite inconceivable in wood. Nevertheless, this is a most original building, if only for the way it avoids the inhuman results of the light-well requirements of the Paris town-planning code. The solution devised by Perret—that of putting the requisite courtyard area on the front of the building, instead of behind it—has already in 1903, the Gordian quality of some of Le Corbusier's ways of avoiding difficulties, and results in a floor-plan arranged in a hollow U facing the street—something completely unprecedented in Paris at the time. But this has nothing to do with reinforced concrete; even the cantilevers that bring the arms of the U forward over the street are of such a form that they could probably have been achieved in wood or corbelled brickwork.

What is equally important is the way in which Perret uses his façade to express both his material and his Choisyesque attitude to structure. The main supporting members, both horizontally and vertically, are exhibited on the face of the wall, but without putting any concrete on show, since the beams are tile-faced. At the top of the building the areas between the

39

frame members are unfilled, thus creating open loggie, but on any typical floor, these spaces are filled with fenestration, or with pot-tiles faced with brownish ceramic mosaic, making a raised pattern of giant daisies—a pattern which effectively emphasises the unstructural nature of these panels of fill. But there is no attempt to separate the load-bearing and sheltering functions of the wall, the fill is effectively co-planar with the face of the structural grid, and, internally, though the plan is free (but no freer than some of the fragments of Blondel's planning to which Guadet referred) wall surfaces tend to run simply from one structural upright to the next, and there are no free-standing columns.

The importance of this building lies, indeed, more in the originality of its plan, the use of concrete, and its bold display of framing as an exterior effect, than in its structural aspects. His next important pre-War building, the Garage Ponthieu of 1905, marks a recession from this advanced position towards one which is more nearly Guadetesque though the structural concrete is now exposed. This building has been discussed as if it were a simple, unassuming structure whose forms were the simple outcome of purpose and materials 'barren of all refinements . . . exhibiting all the clumsiness of a new architecture in the making' and 'the reinforced-concrete skeleton is given full opportunity to determine the character of the façade'.[7] The latter statement is questionable, the former false.

Rebuttal comes from Perret himself, claiming the Garage Ponthieu to be the *première tentative* (*au monde*) *de béton armé esthétique*,[8] and it seems clear that the aesthetic he had in mind was that of the *Beaux-Arts*. The façade is composed as a rhythmic *travée* of pseudo-pilasters disposed 3 : 5 : 3, the rhythm being counted off by the windows that occupy what would (in a Chicago school building) be termed an 'attic frieze', and the vertical composition is closed by a projecting cornice. The elements of the façade are, indeed, those of the later house in the Boulevard Murat, and though they lack the particular decorative devices used by Paul Guadet, the square edged *modenature* employed throughout is far from unrefined, while the great rose-window over the doors and the stained glass of the doors themselves, not to mention the bronze window-surrounds at ground floor level seem to suggest aesthetic pretension rather strongly.

As to the general form of this façade, and its relationship to the material employed, it is to be observed that only one span on the façade is as long as the beams inside, and that is the one that crosses the top of the rose-window, the equivalent beam beneath it being supported, visually, at its outer quarter-spans by two colonettes, as it were *in antis*. The effect of these columns is to muddle, not reinforce the expression of the garage's

[7] An opinion expressed by Peter Collins in 'The Doctrine of Auguste Perret', *Architectural Review* (London, August 1953) and an opinion expressed by Sigfried Giedion in *Space, Time and Architecture* (London, 3rd edition, 1954 p. 329).

[8] The opinion of Auguste Perret, cited (remarkably enough) on the same page by Sigfried Giedion.

interior economy on the outside, the central gangway between the parking bays being the same width as the major central span, not of the door opening. It cannot truthfully be said that this exterior elevation has been determined either by the material employed, or the function of the building, but rather, one senses a compromise between the positions of Choisy and Guadet, that is between the expression of the technique of the period (including automobiles and reinforced concrete) and the *Beaux-Arts* concept of 'design first, structure afterwards'.

In his next major design task of the pre-War period, Perret found himself driven explicitly into the latter position, serving initially on the design staff of the *Théâtre des Champs Élysées* as structural consultant to Henry van de Velde. This was an unhappy collaboration that ended in quarrels, public polemics and considerable bad blood,[9] but whoever, in fact designed the exterior and detailed the interior, the main structure is undoubtedly Perret's own, and stands as a witness to his mode of thought at the time of its design (1912) and is one of his most prized works in the eyes of his followers. Since this structure was entirely hidden, there was no need for him—as in the Garage Ponthieu—to put an aesthetic face on it while concealing his more daring employment of the material for the interior, the whole frame is consistent in feeling, and incorporates curved and bracketed members that could not be accommodated in his trabeated exteriors.

It is imbued throughout with the feeling of a wooden framing built of standard timber sections; thus, none of the vertical members is diminished toward the top but becomes increasingly redundant in section and farther away from the Choisyesque ideal of materials working to their limits. Bracketed corners under constant-section beams are used instead of arches to take up heavy distributed loads, and although there are undoubted good reasons concerned with simplification of shuttering for these practices, the general appearance of the frame is of a complicated piece of joiner's work, with beams threaded through upright stiles, and glued fillets in some of the corners. The monolithic qualities of the frame are used only to attain those torsional resistances that derive, in joinery, from dove-tailed or mortised joints. However, viewed out of context—the only way it can be viewed as a visual image—this frame is an exciting artefact in its own right, and one that differently clad might have looked very like the framed architecture of the Twenties. There can be no doubt that it must have appeared to be very close to their own hearts' desires to the succeeding generation— the generation that flocked to admire his church at le Raincy.

Notre Dame du Raincy is a confusing monument, but of considerable importance. Almost all its visible surfaces were concrete faced—the facing

[9] The authority on these graceless bickerings is Paul Jamot in *Auguste Perret et l'Architecture du Béton Armé*. Such squabbles, which are basically disputes over priority and self-esteem, have been unusually frequent in the present century, but the trend is not necessarily to be blamed on the interest shown by art historians in the architecture of their contemporaries.

41

being no less than the carefully shuttered surface of the structure—and its completion in 1922 confirmed Perret's standing as the master of reinforced concrete in the eyes of a generation that was convinced that new materials would revolutionise architecture. But their acceptance of the church aesthetically must have been considerably eased by the fact that there was little new here structurally. In its widths of span it lags well behind what had already been achieved by Freyssinet, though the very tall slim columns —almost thirty-five feet high but barely fourteen inches thick—represent a bold stroke for the period.

However, the general form of the construction is well covered by Choisyesque precedents that had had, by then, more than two decades of acceptance. At first sight the form is Gothic, even though it lacks the pointed arches of Anatole de Baudot's earlier concrete church,[10] for it has a nave slightly higher than its aisles, from which it is separated by a row of tall 'aspiring' columns and its vast windows are filled by a tracery—that is literally a *remplissage*—of precast geometrical units. But this *Sainte Chapelle du béton armé*[11] avoids Choisy's difficulties with Gothic's external buttressing that was invisible from within by adopting a general procedure that lies close to his analysis of the Basilica of Maxentius, and similar structures. There are no external *organes de butée*, and the lateral thrusts of the nave vault are absorbed—visually at least—in the structure of the aisles, whose vaults lie at right angles to the main axis, as do the side vaults of the Basilica of Maxentius, while the thrusts of the aisle vaults are visibly taken up by an upstand edge-beam interposed between them and the main vault.[12] Such a procedure had Choisy's approval

> The eye takes in at one glance the vault that covers the building and the buttressing that supports it. Nothing that is not self-explained, the clarity of Greek art itself

and in the eyes of his followers Notre Dame du Raincy would have the double prestige of being Gothic and Greek at the same time.

The younger of those followers were being directed to Perret and to his works at this time both by his direct successors like Le Corbusier, and by independent Rationalists like Adolf Loos. He was in the process of being elevated to the rank of a patron of the new architecture, the formal canonisation coming in 1923, when a body of dissatisfied students from the *École des Beaux-Arts* persuaded him to set up as their *maître d'atélier*[13]—the actual atélier being established in one wing of an interesting building of his, the Palais de Bois, a temporary wooden structure whose spans, in

---

[10] i.e. Saint-Jean de Montmartre, a gothicising design of 1894.

[11] This neat and misleading description appears to be a coinage of Jamot's.

[12] The main departures from the Classical prototype are the use of a continuous barrel vault over the main vessel of the building, and the use of posts and lintels, instead of diaphragm walls under the troughs of the lateral vaults.

[13] For an eye-witness account of this phase in Perret's career, see the memoir by Ernö Goldfinger in the *Architectural Review* (London, May 1954).

timber, were slightly greater than those of the Garage Ponthieu, though admittedly less heavily loaded.

In the same year he was invited to contribute a preface to the first volume of Morancé's periodical *L'Architecture Vivante*, which was one of the most important recording organs of the Modern Movement. This *page liminaire* took the form (and the layout) of a Classical inscription, though the phraseology was hardly lapidary

LIVING ARCHITECTURE IS THAT WHICH FAITHFULLY EXPRESSES ITS TIME WE SHALL SEEK IT IN ALL DOMAINS OF CONSTRUCTION WE SHALL CHOOSE WORKS THAT STRICTLY SUBORDINATED TO THEIR USE AND REALISED BY THE JUDICIOUS USE OF MATERIAL ATTAIN BEAUTY BY THE DISPOSITION AND HARMONIOUS PROPORTIONS OF THE NECESSARY ELEMENTS OF WHICH THEY ARE COMPOSED

MCMXXIII   AUGUSTE PERRET

and contained nothing, beyond the offer to go to 'all domains of construction', that Choisy and Guadet might not have approved.

Perret's later development towards full Classicism, lies beyond the scope of the present study psychologically, since it had no appreciable influence on the development of the Modern Movement, while his work on the rationalisation and standardisation of building elements lies beyond its scope in time, not taking notable form until 1930 in his *Garde-Meuble Nationale*. His importance in the present context is as a teacher and example to the next generation, and as the man who, more than any other, made reinforced concrete acceptable as a visible building material in the eyes of those who practised architecture as an art, and did so by endowing it with an easily recognised, and easily digested, rectangular aesthetic.

4: England: Lethaby and Scott

SPEAKING TO THE Architectural Association, London, in 1915, W. R. Lethaby proposed that one of the things that might be learned from Germany was

> . . . how to appreciate English originality. Up to about twenty years ago there had been a very remarkable development of English art of all kinds. For five or six years round about the year 1900, the German Government had attached to its Embassy in London an expert architect, Herr Muthesius, who became the historian (in German) of the English Free Architecture. All the architects who at that time did any building were investigated, sorted, tabulated and, I must say, understood. Then, just as our English free building arrived, or at least 'very nearly did', there came a timid reaction and the re-emergence of the catalogued styles. It is equally true or even more true that the advances in German industrial design have been founded on the English Arts and Crafts.

This characteristic piece of Lethaby's prose, loosely organised but by no means artless, entangles two issues that are really independent of one another, though one can well see how a feeling that some virtue had gone out of English architecture, might become coupled with the feeling that it had gone with Muthesius to the adoptive Fatherland of the Arts and Crafts. Indeed, the synchronisation of the stages of decline in England and of advance in Germany is so close that it is all too easy to suppose a connection.

Thus the foundation of the Deutscher Werkbund in 1907 had been preceded by Thomas Graham Jackson's denunciation of Art Nouveau in 1906 and was followed in 1908 by an attack on the Glasgow School in the *Architectural Review*. One must suspect that one of the reasons for the English decline was a failure to see that Glasgow Art Nouveau was a part of the 'English Free Architecture', and not an opposition movement. Sensitivity about this decline is apparent in the *Review* as early as 1909.

> Our reputation in domestic architecture, on which we are wont to pride ourselves, is being taken away. . . . A writer in the *Architectural Record*, New York, criticising our special issue—which, it will be remembered, was devoted to domestic architecture, pines for variety and complains of a lack of rational development.

In 1911, the year of the completion of Gropius's *Fagus* factory, the *Review* first gave prominence to a 'catalogued style' in an article by A. E. Richardson entitled '*Le Style Neo-Grec*'. An eulogistic study of Schinkel followed in the next year, and the trend, exemplified in both these articles towards (*a*), a revival of neo-Classicism and (*b*), a dependence on foreign, not native, models, is fully confirmed by another article later in the same year 'Architecture from the Classic Standpoint', unsigned, but Richardsonian in tone and Guadetesque in attitude, e.g.

> The great fault in modern art is the lack of studied composition.

However, the drift of the argument is anti-Parisian

> France, for centuries the Academy of Europe, is allowing the Classical spirit to be usurped by base modern tendencies . . . the fooleries of the Grand Palais, the ornamental excrescences of the Gare d'Orléans, have captured the imagination of the present generation.

and salvation is believed to lie in 'the reticence of the Anglo-Saxon' and in an appeal to Rome

> Now, with the establishment of the British School at Rome, we can look to the future with hope, because the importance of the Classic spirit to modern architectural development is at length receiving attention.

The appearance of such wooden sentiments in a magazine that had once been more or less the mouthpiece of the Lethaby connection, illustrates a change not only in editorial policy (it had been changing ever since 1905, when Mervyn Macartney took over editorship) but also a general change in the intellectual climate of English architecture. That change also dates from 1904–5, and involves the almost simultaneous completion of the Ritz Hotel, by Mewés and Davis, the new wing of the British Museum, by John Burnet, and the Central Hall, Westminster, by Lanchester and Rickards. The conception of all three was Classicising, academic and French, and to the rising generation of English architects, of whom H. S. Goodhart-Rendel seems typical, they exhibited 'Expertise Restored'. The changed direction continued to 1914 and beyond; the *Architectural Review* sustained it in 1914 with articles by A. E. Richardson on Jean-Charles Krafft and Jacques Hittorf, and confirmed the tendency away from Paris in an enthusiastic review of by far the most interesting product of this period and trend, Geoffrey Scott's *Architecture of Humanism*.

Scott's book marks the culmination of the Classicising tendency, the apex of his generation's revolt against Victorian earnestness, insularity and empiricism. It is both implicitly and explicitly hostile to Lethaby, marks the late intrusion into architectural criticism of the tradition of donnish aestheticism that stems from Walter Pater, and probably suffered a condign fate in becoming the aesthetic hand-book of the neo-Georgian and Playboy phases of English architecture. But it is of more than provincial interest, for though it lies outside the mainstream of architectural thought, it illustrates explicitly certain processes that took place below the surface of the mainstream, and it illumines both the strengths and weaknesses of the free style of the Lethaby connection.

Lethaby's own position was never as explicit as Scott's. He and his connection were not systematic thinkers, but men of feeling, who carried the moralistic attitude of Ruskin and Morris forward into the new century, and made a present of it to the German movement. But Lethaby himself, at least, marries this morality to a Rationalist interest in construction and engineering. His work contains echoes of Viollet-le-Duc

> These ribs and bars and shafts are all at bowstring tension; a mason will tap a pillar to make its stress audible; we may think of a cathedral as so 'high-strung' that if struck it would give a musical note.

and of Choisy

> A fine fishing-rod, a well-tuned fiddle, have their just proportions; and Gothic architecture was developed not by any aesthetic view of the proportions, but by getting the nerved vault, the ramping buttress and the stone-barred window to do the utmost possible.

The comparison with non-architectural design in this last quotation is typical of him. He desired an architecture without affectation, created in the satisfaction of understood needs, and so he frequently turns to objects like railway viaducts and bicycles whose value, for him, lay 'in their nearness to need'. Such design he termed scientific, and it must be observed that the use of the term is far less improper in his case than in Guadet's.

> What I do urge, in the simplest and plainest words, is concentration on practical, experimental and scientific education.
> The method of design to a modern mind can only be understood in the scientific, or engineer's sense, as a definite analysis of possibilities—not as a vague poetic dealing with poetic matters.

These passages, with their emphasis on experiment and analysis, come from a lecture given by him in 1910 at the RIBA *The Architecture of Adventure*, an apotheosis of the activities of engineers and scientists—notably Sir Christopher Wren, a native, not foreign Classicist—in architecture. But it would appear from other writings and lectures of his that his admiration went—as did that of many other architects—only to the mental disciplines of engineering. He is contemptuous of the practical disciplines that complement and make possible the intellectual ones.

> Human work, I say, not machine-grinding. Machining is no more real work than hand-organ noises are real music.

In view of this hostility, one cannot but wonder who was the author of a remarkable anonymous note contributed to the *Architectural Review* for July 1905. The tone of the opening paragraph suggests a source close to Lethaby, and the use of his contemptuous tag 'Architects' Architecture' confirms it. But the forceful tone and directness of statement outbid him

> Why should we architects live in perpetual rebellion with the present? We talk

46

about picking up the thread of architectural tradition where it was broken. Is it not really an excuse to go back a couple of hundred years or so, that we may get away from the needs and conditions and stern realities of modern life? We cannot so quietly leave out centuries of history, nor is the thread of national tradition so easily broke, history will see to that.

The scientists have been truer to their generation. The impressive dignity, the beauty, the perfect fitness and the style of a modern express locomotive is incomparably finer than the best work of the best architect of today.

If only we could build with the same fitness, the same science, the same *unchallenged acceptance of modern material and modern conditions*, and the same sincerity; if we could only think of our building as an entirely modern problem without precedent (and it is an entirely modern problem without precedent) just as the railway engine is, then, without doubt the same beauty, the same serene dignity would inevitably accompany our efforts, and the ruins of the past might crumble to dust but the architectural tradition would remain with us still. We must begin at the foundation and not at the cornice. We must put aboriginal constructive force into our work, and leave it to speak for itself: tricky combinations of style and smart inventions are fools' play.

The grave yawns for Architects' Architecture.

The demands of our tasteless clients for plate glass fronts and the like are rational enough; but we, schooled from our apprenticeship in traditions and unreality, rebel against any problem that cannot be solved by traditional methods.

We are ashamed of our nakedness—and yet it is in the confession of our nakedness that our regeneration lies.

In conclusion, let it be said that only the aboriginal force in any building can be called architecture, and to introduce any form that is not contemporary is to hinder progress and the true expression of the modern in architecture.

This uncompromising and radical statement of faith, which pre-echoes nearly all the significant moral and intellectual attitudes of the ensuing quarter-century of architectural thought, shows how close to the mainstream of development the English Free architecture could have been. The dramatic reduction of that Free architecture to a mere provincial vernacular, in competition with a provincial version of *Beaux-Arts* Classicism, is a singular example of failure of nerve and collapse of creative energy. To some extent this may be due to muddled thinking and squeamishness— the failure to identify the Glasgow School as an ally, or to accept machine production, are examples of the squeamishness. The muddled thinking is exemplified by the case of C. F. A. Voysey.[1] His domestic architecture is the ultimate proof of the importance and value of the Free Style, and through Muthesius and others it had a critical influence on the develop-

[1] In Voysey's defence it should be said that other members and supporters of the English Free architecture were capable of being quite as muddle-headed as he. Lethaby, for instance, went on record with his contempt for 'mouldy Picturesque' and Muthesius was equally scathing about it, in spite of the fact that the Free architecture they so much admired was more the product of the Picturesque than of anything else, and was in many ways no more advanced than early Picturesque architecture had been. A late tenant of John Nash's pioneer and highly Picturesque free-plan dower-house at Cronkhill (1804) expressed his admiration of it to the author in terms that would have gratified any Free Architect of 1900—'It is very convenient.' Choisy's admiration for the Picturesque is something that other Rationalists might profitably have emulated (and in the case of Le Corbusier, profitably did).

ment of the Modern Movement. Yet it is common hearsay knowledge that Voysey's own intention was only to improve and continue the native cottage vernacular of southern England. He had no conception of the importance of what he was doing (he seems to have had that almost pathological modesty of some English provincial intellectuals) and angrily deprecated any attempt to link his name with the Modern Movement. Under these circumstances it should not surprise us that his practices and aims should be aesthetically at variance with one another. His work excels by the sharp definition of one smooth plain surface from another, the fine precision of his arrises and the bold geometry of his forms, and yet he was quoted in 1908 as saying that he preferred

> The soft effect of the outline of an old building where the angles were put up by eye, compared with the mechanical effect of the modern drafted angle.

Even without such muddled thinking, the pure empiricism of the free style would have been difficult to pass on. An endless perspective of *ad hoc* decisions, based on first principles and personal responsibility, for the whole of one's career is much less attractive than a neat package of cut-and-dried answers such as a *Beaux-Arts* training could offer, and only a rigorous moral and intellectual discipline—such as the free style acquired in Germany—could have made it convincing enough to be transmissible. But its masters were mostly coasting along on the accumulated moral momentum of the previous epoch. Worse still, the masters of the previous generation, like Norman Shaw, were turning full Classicist in their old age (Regent Street, Gaiety Theatre) and lending their authority to the restoration of French *expertise*. The buildings that possessed this *expertise* offered suave new aesthetic pleasures of a superficial kind, plus a certain snob appeal, and the generality of the smart young London architects were soon full of contempt for the masters of the Art Nouveau and the free style—Goodhart Rendel's satirical wit is at its best on Mackintosh and Voysey, but of Lethaby he cannot even bring himself to be funny.

But, as has been said, a desire to return to Italian fundamentals is mixed with this admiration for France. The foundation of the British School in Rome gave this desire an institutional body, Geoffrey Scott gave it an intellectual head. *The Architecture of Humanism*, was written in Florence, the traditional home of Anglo-Saxon *far niente*, but if its tendency is to preach a kind of architectural irresponsibility, it is neither a trivial book nor a superficial one. It is the by-product, so to speak, of a serious and respectable academic programme of work

> My intention had been to formulate the chief principles of Classical design in architecture

and one whole chapter out of the nine that compose the book is devoted to a devious defence of the academic tradition. It must be said that by the time Scott has finished defending it, the academic tradition has become almost

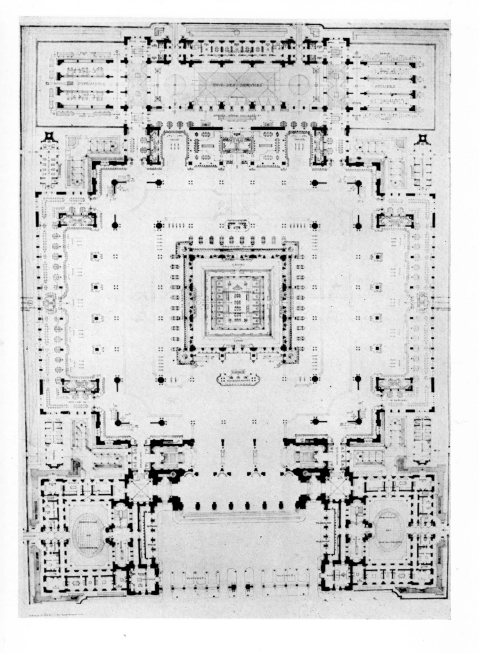

1. Tony Garnier. Project for a national bank, Prix de Rome-winning design of 1899. French academic planning at its most skilful and systematic, the plan 'composed' of 'elements' according to Guadet's precepts by his most brilliant pupil.

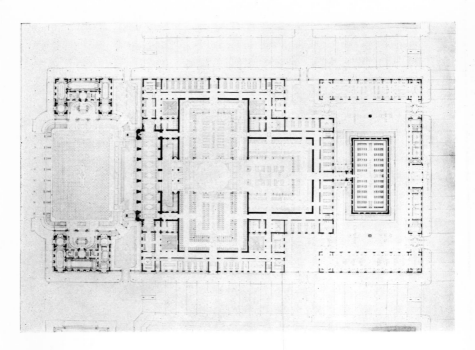

2. Sirot. Project for a national bank, unsuccessful Prix de Rome entry of 1899. Elementary composition even more clearly displayed in plan.

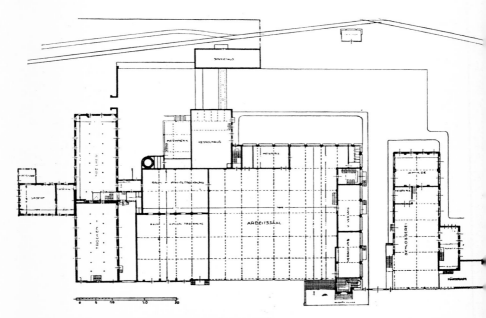

3. Walter Gropius and Adolf Meyer. Plan of the Fagus factory, Alfeld, 1911–1913. Elementary composition according to a purely functional discipline.

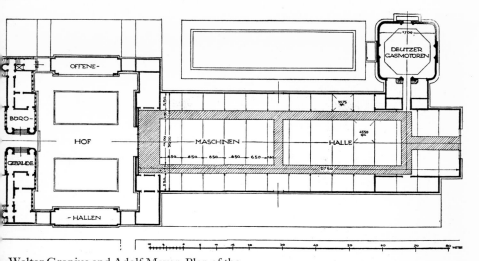

5. Walter Gropius and Adolf Meyer. Plan of the
Werkbund Pavilion, Cologne, 1914. Elementary
composition according to academic precepts.
6. Walter Gropius. Plan of the Bauhaus buildings,
Dessau, 1926. Elementary composition according to
elementarist precepts.

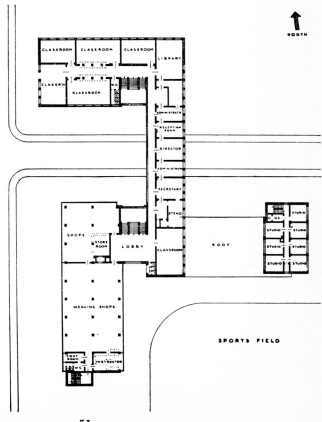

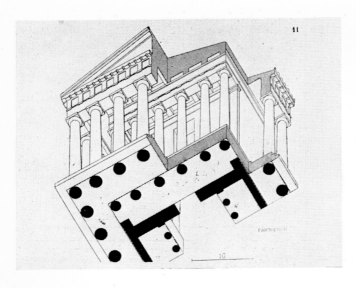

6. Auguste Choisy. The Parthenon, a plate from his *Histoire de l'Architecture* (1898), showing his characteristic mode of projecting a simplified version of the building in section, elevation and plan.

arrive à réduire l'édifice à ses parties agissantes. Privé des moyens puissants, il y supplée à force de combinaisons.

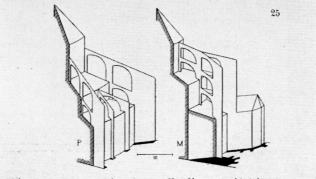

L'architecture gothique est celle d'une société à ressources

7. Auguste Choisy. Flying buttresses, from the *Histoire*, the facts of structure reduced to diagrammatic and insubstantial form.

des évangiles, l'autre à la lecture des épîtres et à la prédication.

L'ensemble. — La fig. 23 montre, d'après les dispositions actuellement existantes de Saint-Clément de Rome, l'aspect

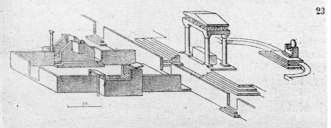

l'un chœur latin; l'édifice a été remanié au 9ᵉ siècle, mais tous

8. Auguste Choisy. The choir of San Clemente from the *Histoire*: a simplified rendering of liturgical furniture that appears to have done a good deal to suggest a simplified architecture.

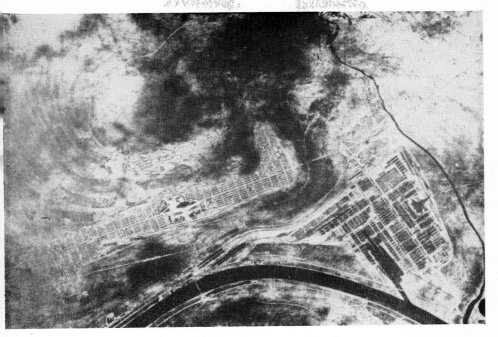

9. Tony Garnier. La Cité Industrielle, imaginary town-planning project, 1904–1918. A city laid out according to the concept of elementary composition, with the residential 'element' in the centre, industrial 'element' lower right.
10. Tony Garnier. Refrigerator Tower of the abattoir, *Grands Travaux de la Ville de Lyon*, ca. 1913. The stripped classicism of an advanced academic architect.
11. Paul Guadet. House in the Boulevard Murat, 1910: stripped classicism in the academic tradition.

12. Auguste Perret. Apartment block in the Rue Franklin, Paris, 1903; a pioneer use of reinforced concrete in domestic work, notable for the ingenuity of its hollow U-fronted plan and the clear exhibition of its frame construction, although both structural and infill materials are clad in ceramic tiling.

13. Auguste Perret. Garage in the Rue Ponthieu, Paris, 1906; exposed concrete construction, within the discipline of the stripped Classicism of the academies.

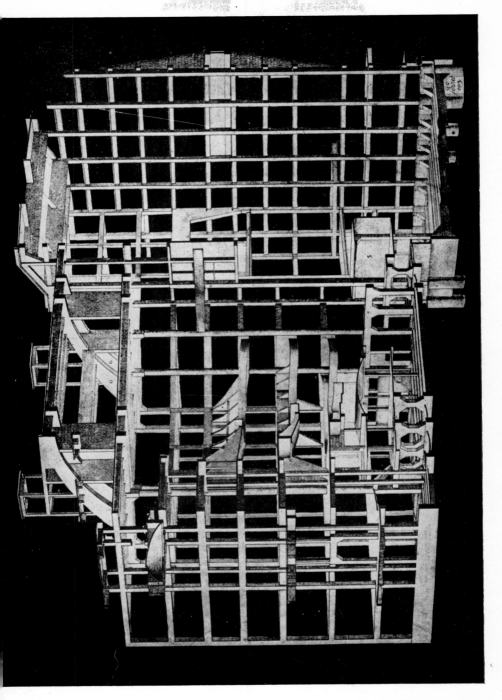

14. Auguste Perret. Part-sectional drawing of the frame of the *Théâtre des Champs Elysées*, dated 1913. Although the credit of the design of the whole building goes, in part, to Henry van de Velde, the frame is undoubtedly Perret's, and exemplifies his manner of handling concrete as if its nature resembled that of wood.

55

15. Auguste Perret. Church of
Notre Dame, Le Raincy, 1923: a
elaborate (and influential)
realisation of Choisy's
Rationalism in terms of
reinforced concrete.
16. Walter Gropius and Adolf
Meyer. Fagus factory, Alfeld,
1911–1913: south-western corne
of the workshop block, showing
the famous glazed corner.

17. Walter Gropius and Adolf
Meyer. Fagus factory, Alfeld,
1911–1913: the very advanced
treatment of the workshop block
is in contrast to the design of the
other elements of the composition.
18, 19. Bruno Taut. Steel Industry
Pavilion, Leipzig, 1913, and Glass
Pavilion, Cologne, 1914: two
structures intended to display the
nature of the material they
advertised. The Glass Pavilion is
one of the most advanced concepts
of its time.

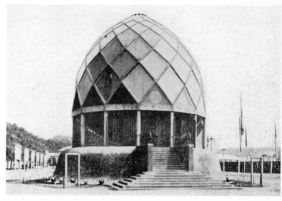

20. Max Berg. Jahrhunderthalle, Breslau, 1913. The
least inhibited employment of reinforced concrete in a
non-industrial building in the first 30 years of the
century, ranking with Taut's Glass Pavilion in
originality.

21, 22. Hans Poelzig. Water tower, Posen, 1910; and Chemical factory, Luban, 1911. Poelzig may be taken as the leader of the Werkbund Expressionists, and both these works deviate notably from the Classicism of the other wing of the Werkbund. 23. Albert Marx. Boiler House, Bad Nauheim, 1912: Werkbund Expressionism betraying some of its Art Nouveau origins.

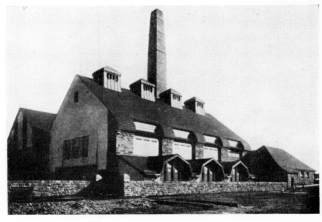

24. Heinrich Stoffregen. Anker linoleum factory, Delmenhorst, 1912: a tough-minded version of Werkbund Expressionism almost comparable to: 25. Peter Behrens. AEG Heavy erection hall, Berlin, 1912, but not to: 26. Peter Behrens. AEG Turbine erection hall, Berlin, 1908, his first, and most classical, factory building for AEG.

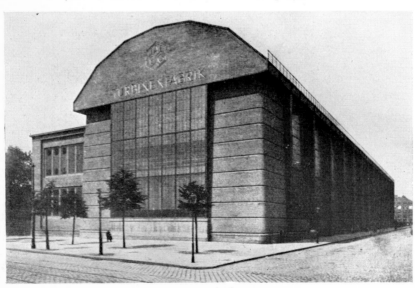

27. Peter Behrens. Buildings for the gasworks, Frankfurt am
Main, 1911: a rare departure from classical models in Behrens'
industrial work before 1914.
28. Walter Gropius. Farm-workers' housing, Jankow, 1906.

29, 30. Walter Gropius and Adolf Meyer. Werkbund Pavilion, Cologne, 1914. In the elevations, the Classicism of the plan (cf. fig. 4) is barely apparent because of the differing styles of the parts, and critical comment has concentrated on the employment of glass, which is, however, less advanced than that of Bruno Taut at the same exhibition (cf. fig. 19).

31. Frank Lloyd Wright. Hotel, Mason City, 1909. The European influence of Wright, which first becomes visible in Gropius and Meyer's work at Cologne, depended chiefly on the two picture-books published by Wasmuth—even the brickwork of the front of the Werkbund Pavilion can be traced back to Wright by way of these books.

32. Adolf Loos. Steiner House, Vienna, 1910: view from the garden, contrasting the square, almost Classical handling of the garden front with the rounded roofline of the street side.

33. Adolf Loos. Tzara House, Paris, 1926 (photograph reworked to show intended final state). One of Loos' most sophisticated designs, yet taking a tinge of local Montmartre character—cf. fig. 88.

non-existent. The main product of that tradition as it stood at the time that Scott was writing (1911–14) was the body of theory epitomized in Guadet, but

> An academic *tradition*, allied, as it was in the Renaissance, to a living sense of art, is fruitful, but academic *theory* is at all times barren.

Indeed, all that seems to remain, with him, of that tradition is the right to ignore the precepts of the only academic writer he discusses—Vitruvius. Nevertheless this tenuous body of academic tradition could achieve great things.

> The academic influence rescued the architecture of England and France. It provided a canon of forms by which even the uninspired architect could secure at least a measure of distinction; and genius, where it existed, could be trusted to use this scholastic learning as a means, not as an end. . . .

This is clearly something very like Goodhart Rendel's restored *expertise* which guaranteed, on the security of the accumulated experience of the *École des Beaux-Arts*, that

> if the pupil chose to experiment, he experimented with his feet on firm ground

though 'experiment' manifestly does not mean here what it meant for Lethaby, but something purely formalistic.

However, as has been said above, the *Architecture of Humanism* was a deviation from the original aim of writing an academic handbook. The reason for this deviation was Scott's feeling that Classical architecture could not be appreciated, much less understood, by his countrymen because their judgement had been clouded by a number of erroneous architectural criteria, or fallacies, which he lists, before setting out to demolishing them, as the Romantic, the Picturesque, the Naturalistic, Mechanical, Ethical and Biological Fallacies. His attempted demolitions do not appear very convincing now, partly because they were—more or less in the order listed—the frames of mind that had saved Victorian architecture from stagnation and sterility, and partly because he normally attacks hearsay versions of these theories without going back to original sources. Thus, unacquainted with Choisy at first hand, and ignorant of Choisy's extension of *technique* to cover the whole fabric of society, he can only confess himself amazed that Professor Moore who 'bases his whole treatment quite consistently upon a mechanical ideal of architecture' can yet preface his work 'by a rapid and liturgical recitation of all the ethical formulae', since he regards these two approaches as *utterly opposed* (Scott's italics).

He himself is quite consistent, however, and does not defend Renaissance architecture by an appeal to sources (though he appears to have consulted, e.g. Alberti, Serlio and Palladio) but in terms of academic theory as it existed in his own time, stripped of moral and social overtones. Going only a little way beyond Guadet's indifference to particular styles, and thus to particular symbolic and narrative contents, he shrugs off all symbolic and narrative qualities and offers instead an architecture of pure form. He defines his position thus

> Architecture, simply and immediately perceived, is a combination, revealed through light and shade, of spaces, masses and lines.

and this puts him very close to certain post-War theorists of Abstract art who also took the view that simple and immediate perception took in only the formal or geometrical aspects of the object seen. As with later Abstract theorists he also took this simple and immediate perception to be absolute and fundamental.

> These few elements make the core of our architectural experience; an experience which the literary fancy, the historical imagination, the casuistry of conscience, the calculations of science, cannot constitute or determine, though they may encircle or enrich.

The 'few' elements mentioned above are later rendered as 'four' by Scott

> By the direct agency of Mass, Space, Line and Coherence upon our physical consciousness, architecture communicates its value as an art.
> Such are the four great elements of building from whose laws the finest masters of the Renaissance, however various their impulse and achievement, did not deviate. Theirs is an architecture which by Mass, Space and Line responds to human physical delight, and by coherence answers to our thought.

The formation of this concept has a complex background. It is clear that French academic theory has been laid under tribute both on the architectural side and the painterly. If *elements* comes from Guadet so does *coherence*, which Scott uses to mean either an acceptance of mathematical order, or simply *composition*. The connection between this *coherence* and *thought* sounds like Charles Blanc's

> The painter's prime means of expressing his thought is 'ordonnance'

and the insistence on *line*, one of the factors that responds to *human physical delight* recalls Blanc's

> Straight or curved, horizontal or vertical, parallel or divergent—all lines have a secret relationship with our feelings

It is not necessary to refer these ideas back to direct French academic sources; not only were *Beaux-Arts* ideas on architecture current in England in the decade before the War, but ideas on painting, from a similar source, had been put in circulation by Roger Fry and his circle.

But there is a new 'element' among Scott's four—Space. This was not being discussed in architectural circles in France at the time, neither within the *Beaux-Arts* curriculum as recorded by Guadet, nor by Choisy and his followers. Choisy uses the word *espace* to mean an area to be spanned by an arch or covered by a roof, and where we might nowadays use the word 'space' to indicate an unbuilt volume within a building he is more inclined to use *la vide*. By Space, Scott means, effectively, *Raum*, with most of the overtones that the word had acquired in German aesthetics, and he himself had avowedly taken it over from the writings of Theodor Lipps, along with the theory of *Einfühlung*.

Lippsian theory seems to have been common currency in the Anglo-Florentine circle in which he moved (Berenson, Vernon Lee *et al.*)[2] and it is used by Scott to give a show of objectivity to the extremely solipsistic attitude he is taking up, viz., that architecture affects us by its mimic correspondence with human attitudes and actions. His position depends, on examination, on a kind of pun on the word 'Humanist', which he uses indiscriminately to refer either to the world of humane learning, or to the projection of human sentiments into the forms of architecture. This *double-entendre* appears to be quite unconscious, but it is upon it, and nothing else, that his theory of Renaissance architecture as an art of pure form, pure taste and pure pleasure is founded. Presumably the material, from which Professor Wittkower later developed his entirely different view of Renaissance architecture as an art of symbolic form, was also available to Scott had he wanted to use it, but, under the academic dispensation which set symbolic and narrative values aside, he could explain his liking for Renaissance architecture only by assuming it to be meaningless at any but the empathetic level.

But in his borrowing of the idea of *Raumempfindung* from Lipps, and his introduction of it into the context of academic theory, he achieved an innovation. The introduction was not seminal, but it retains its interest as an illustration of a process which must have happened elsewhere, though not explicitly. The change-over from the Lippsian idea of space, as felt volume, which is the sense it has in the writings of, e.g. Muthesius, to the later concept of space as a three-dimensional continuum, capable of metrical subdivision, without sacrifice of its continuity, appears to depend largely from its assimilation to the Blanc/Guadet idea of composition, and the extension of that idea to operate in three dimensions instead of the two dimensions of the building-plan or the picture surface, both of which are two-dimensional fields metrically subdivided without sacrifice of their continuity. Such ideas are manifest—if not verbally explicit—in the work of both Mies van der Rohe and Le Corbusier after about 1923. The routes by which they acquired such ideas are devious, but it seems fairly certain that somewhere along the route, a fusion of Lippsian and academic ideas, on the Scott pattern, must have taken place.

[2] Scott came in contact with this circle as Berenson's librarian, and the currency of Lippsian ideas among this connection will be found discussed in an appendix to Arnold Whittick's book *Eric Mendelsohn* (London, 2nd edition, 1956).

5: Germany: industry and the Werkbund

THE YEAR 1907 must appear, in retrospect, a decisive one for German (and, by that token, international) architecture. If no new themes are introduced into architectural thought, attitudes toward certain contemporary problems were as resolutely taken up as they were, a little later, by the Futurists, and —what is more—were shortly translated into practice. That is to say, discussion and exposition among architects and those connected with design were primarily devoted to evolving programmes and organisations for immediate action, and not to the formulation of bodies of encyclopaedic theory in the manner of Choisy or Guadet. There was indeed a parallel current of pure intellectual speculation about the aesthetics of architecture, descending from Lipps and producing one of its classics in Worringer's *Abstraktion und Einfühlung* of 1908, but there seems to have been no important mingling of the two streams of thought—the men of action tapped the Lippsian stream at source, not at Worringer.

The heart-theme of the practical body of thought was the problem of mechanism—or rather, the relationship of architecture, as an art of design, to mechanical production at all its phases, from the factory work-hall to the advertising of the finished product. This relationship was scrutinised most closely at two critical points: the aesthetics of engineering construction, and the aesthetics of product design. To take the first point first, leaders of German architectural thought, like the Italian Futurists, deplored the application of art-work to engineering structures, but whereas the Futurists intended to conjure an aesthetic out of machinery and engineering, the Germans hoped to conjure some aesthetics into them.

> Already, therefore, in 1907, the *Verband Deutscher Architekten- und Ingenieurvereine* was challenging expert opinion on this point: How shall we force up the importance of aesthetic considerations in engineering construction to a higher level than at present.

Phrased thus, as a sort of collision between two separate entities, aesthetics and engineering, the problem tended to indicate two equally separate answers, as Lindner and Steinmetz go on to record

> We soon arrived at the conclusion that any solution for our new situation

68

involved the discovery of a new, appropriate and heartfelt mode of expression. The architecture of the styles having broken down, everybody changed their aim and began to shoot in different directions. Some preached Pure Functional Art (Reine Zweckkunst) while others saw the ideal in untramelled artistic creation 'each according to his own powers' finding new forms for new problems.

This latter paragraph identifies, perhaps unwittingly, a basic division in the work of the years immediately after 1907. Lindner and Steinmetz associate 'new forms for new problems' with 'untramelled artistic creation' and not with 'Pure Functional Art' and it is to be noted that those most closely associated with the pure service of function—Behrens, Muthesius, Mies van der Rohe and Gropius (with one notable exception[1])—were not formally inventive, while the Individualists, later termed Expressionists, of that generation in Germany—Poelzig, Berg, Marx, Stoffregen—were among the most fertile creative minds in their profession at that time, and the most vigorous continuers of the spirit of the English Free architecture. It should be emphasised here that this division of practical method does not imply, at that time, any notable division of theoretical approach—that did not appear until after 1922, when *Zweckkunst* finally acquired a formal language of its own—nor any difference of organisational loyalty. All these architects were connected with the Werkbund, and the two whom it is most customary to contrast; Hans Poelzig and Peter Behrens, both enjoyed the support of Hermann Muthesius, the Werkbund's founder.

But, in any case, it was events connected with the Werkbund and with Peter Behrens that made 1907 a decisive year, rather than the beginnings of a stylistic division among the progressive German architects. For it was in 1907 that Behrens joined AEG (*Allgemeine Electricitätsgesellschaft*) and Muthesius founded the Deutscher Werkbund. The two events are related, if not connected, and are the two faces of the same coin—a *rapprochement* between creative designers and productive industry, in which industry was a more willing participant than the designers.

The foundation of the Werkbund took place in the teeth of some fairly spirited opposition from the 'establishment' of the German Arts and Crafts Movement, and Muthesius's success is a tribute to his diplomacy, as well as his determination and his influential supporters. He was held in suspicion for a variety of reasons. As a Prussian civil servant who regarded himself as an instrument in the furtherance of German economic policy, he naturally stood for order and discipline, and not for the Bohemian individualism and aestheticism of the loosely organised German *Kunstgewerbe* craftsmen and designers. Furthermore, he seems to have been regarded as the importer of a foreign style to be imposed on German Arts and Crafts. This arose naturally from his having been in England from 1896 to 1903 as a supplementary trade attaché to the German Embassy,

[1] The exception being Behrens's remarkable gas-works buildings at Frankfurt am Main, which stand well away from the line of development towards a chastened neo-Classicism that characterises his other work of the period.

with a brief to study and report back on the high prestige of English architecture and design. His reports covered not only domestic and church architecture, but teaching methods as well—even amateur work done in evening classes. His masterpiece as *rapporteur* was undoubtedly *Das Englische Haus*, which covered, in three volumes of which the last appeared in 1905, every aspect of the English free style from Stokesey Castle to Sanitary Ware. The impact of this book can be seen as early as Peter Behrens's Obenauer House of 1906, and persisted until it was overtaken by the Wasmuth publications of the work of Frank Lloyd Wright. Thus these attempts to weld industry and the unattached artists and designers into a single, effective organisation that could make a useful contribution to the national economy were regarded in some quarters as an attack on German art.

The polemical situation came to a head in the early part of 1907. Muthesius opened with a speech at the new Commercial College in Berlin (of which he was then head) in the course of which he complained of the superficiality of the 'so-called style' then in use in German Kunstgewerbe, but his complaint has an economic basis. As Peter Bruckmann (a progressive industrialist who employed designers like Lauwericks) reports

> He prophesied a sharp economic recession if the motifs used in the shaping of their products continued to be thoughtlessly and shamelessly borrowed from the form-treasury of the previous century.
> What Muthesius put forth publicly in this lecture was vigorously rebutted both by the Crafts and Industry, and the *Verband für die wirtschaftlichen Interessen des Kunstgewerbes* in Berlin battled fiercely against him, putting on the order-paper for their meeting of June 1907 an item headed 'Der Fall Muthesius'.

Bruckmann himself took part in this meeting as an interested party. Not that he was in any personal way connected with Muthesius, but

> I felt in Düsseldorf that a change was imminent, and that there should be representatives from Industry for Muthesius and his ideas. . . . On the Muthesius case, the Chairman made play with the complaints of Industry and the Crafts, calling him their traducer and enemy of German art . . . Dohrn, Lux, and myself confronted the whole assembly, which we left in complete uproar. This Congress took place in June, yet as early as the sixth of October the Deutscher Werkbund was founded. How was it possible to achieve this object so quickly?

Bruckmann's question must be rhetorical, rather than naïve, since he must have known as well as anybody, as a representative from progressive industry, why things had moved so quickly between June and October. Major German industrial enterprises were becoming interested in quality products and better design, as witness the appointment in the same month of October of Peter Behrens as design consultant for everything that AEG built, manufactured or printed. Nor were AEG alone in this; wherever German industries had set up selling organisations they soon turned to designers—as in the case of the *Stahlwerksverband* and their employment of Bruno Taut—for their publicity material if nothing else. From the other

70

side, the more responsible section of the German Kunstgewerbe movement, the Deutsche Werkstätten, had already in 1906 begun to develop furniture for mass production, and was associated with the Werkbund from its inception. Bruno Paul,[2] the designer of this furniture was appointed in 1907 as head of the Berlin *Gewerbeschule*—an appointment in which Muthesius must have been as much interested as that of Behrens to AEG, though there seems to be no record of his having directly influenced either appointment.

In any case, the whole tendency to a union of crafts and industry was given urgency by the economic situation and national interest. Muthesius had issued his warning in 1907, but Karl Schmidt, the director of the Deutsche Werkstätten at Hellerau, had warned before him, in 1903, that German industrial products were so inferior that

> Within a year we might be hard put to buy sufficient raw material from abroad to keep running, and the social problem would then become sharper and sharper until it (*scil.* design) was no longer just a cultural problem.

and it was this same economic situation that gave force to Muthesius's insistence that the problem

> was not the business of a single government office, but a concern worthy of the German people as a whole.

Now, Karl Schmidt's condemnation of German industrial production had been phrased in general terms; he merely says that it is *minderwertig*, without specifying in what aspects it is deficient in quality. This was to be expected; as head of the Hellerau Werkstätten he spoke from within the Arts and Crafts tradition of not distinguishing between visual and material quality in products, of believing them to be automatically related. Muthesius, in complaining of the 'so-called style' used in German *Kunstgewerbe* is clearly on a different tack. But for the first few years of the Werkbund's existence, it followed Schmidt's more generalised approach and made *Qualität*[3] its watchword. In this condition the most that can be said was that it was a triumph of organisation—an influential part of German production by machine and hand had been brought within the scope of a single body, and within that body, the attention of industry had been drawn to the availability of a body of independent designers, the attention of designers and craftsmen had been drawn to the opportunities that existed for them in industry, while the problem of design, at large, had been brought to the attention of the German nation. But it lacked, as yet, any specific aesthetic direction.

That came in 1911, and from Muthesius. At the Werkbund's Congress in that year he delivered what, in a later terminology, would be called the Key-

---

[2] On Bruno Paul, see Nikolaus Pevsner, *Pioneers of the Modern Movement* (London, 1st edition, 1936, pp. 38, 198).
[3] The idea of *Qualitätsarbeit* is also discussed in *Pioneers of the Modern Movement*.

note speech, entitled *Wo stehen wir?* It was a contribution to the general theme of the Congress 'The Spiritualisation of German Production', and so closely involved is this general theme with the detailed argument in Muthesius's speech that it seems possible that he had a large share in deciding the general theme himself. The speech is a long and complex one, its structure is rhetorical rather than logical, but its interest to the present study is that it introduced to the Werkbund the idea that aesthetics could be independent of material quality, it introduced the idea of standardisation as a virtue, and of abstract form as the basis of the aesthetics of product design, and it introduced these ideas to an audience that included not only the young men who were going to shape the architecture of post-War Germany—Mies van der Rohe, Walter Gropius, Bruno Taut—but of France as well, for Charles Edouard Jeanneret, later Le Corbusier, had been sent to Germany in 1910 by the Art School of Chaux de Fonds (Switzerland) to make a study of German progress in design, and of the Werkbund in particular. At the time of the Congress he had ceased working with Behrens, but had only transferred himself to the Werkstätte colony at Hellerau where he was working with Heinrich Tessenow, and was still within the Werkbund orbit. A good deal of what Muthesius said reappears, suitably modified, in Le Corbusier's publications of the early Twenties.

Like the later, but apparently unrelated, *Manifesto of Futurist Architecture*, and like that earlier work of Muthesius himself, *Stilarchitektur und Baukunst*,[4] it opens with an historical survey whose aim is to demonstrate the decay of architecture in the nineteenth century, but here it is linked to a more general theme of the special aptitudes and tasks of different races of men and periods of time—a theme which reappears at the end of the speech, made specific as the destiny of the German people to revivify the arts of design in the twentieth century. Unlike most historical perspectives of this kind, it ends on a note of rising optimism. A recovery had already begun as early as 1890 for

> The first clear and representative literary indication of the beginning of a new spiritual orientation was that forceful book *Rembrandt als Erzieher*, which recalled to the mind of Germany the importance of artistic as against scientific culture.

It may be only a coincidence that Julius Langbehn[5] in this book also invited the German people to look for leadership in this spiritual regeneration to Low Germany (a Holsteiner himself, he took Rembrandt as a Low German) and that Peter Behrens, who so often appears as the personification of Muthesius's ideal designer, was a Low German too, from Hamburg.

---

[4] An orthodox Lethabitic diatribe against the 'catalogue styles' (except for an un-Lethabitic show of interest in Schinkel and neo-Classicism) published in 1902.

[5] On Langbehn, see, for instance, Jethro Bithell, *Modern German Literature* London, 1946, p. 497).

The foundation of the Werkbund, Muthesius proposes, had been another step forward in this spiritual regeneration, but

> The Deutscher Werkbund was founded at a time when a close association of all men of good will was needed against hostile forces. Its campaigning days in that direction are over now, the ideas that were then in question are nowhere denied today, and enjoy general approval. Has its existence thereby become superfluous? One could only think so by taking a narrow view of the Arts and Crafts. . . . In truth . . . the specific task of the Werkbund is only just beginning. Up till now, considerations of quality stood in the forefront of our activities, and and we can now be sure that in Germany a sense of good materials and methods has gained a swift ascendancy; but by that very token it follows that the work of the Werkbund is not completed. Far higher than the material is the spiritual; far higher than function, material and technique, stands Form. These three material aspects might be impeccably handled but—if Form were not—we would still be living in a merely brutish world. So there remains before us as an aim a much greater and more important task—to awaken once more an understanding for Form, and the revival of architectonic sensibilities.

Form, as it appears here—and not for the first time in the speech—is a thing of the spirit, but before Muthesius has finished it becomes many other things as well; he covers, in fact, pretty well all the shades of meaning that the word was to carry in later writings—except that of mathematically proportioned shapes

> Form that is not the result of mathematical calculation, that is not fulfilled by mere function, that has nothing to do with systematic thought

but if he is vague about its origins, he is precise about its manifestations

> It is, above all, architectonic, its creation a secret of the human spirit, like poetry and religion. Form, that is for us an unique and shining achievement of human art—the Greek Temple, the Roman *Thermae*, the Gothic Cathedral, and the princely salon of the eighteenth century

and it will be observed that his canon of good form, while it subsumes the Rationalist triumphs of Doric and Gothic structure, adds to them a triumph of the shaping of interior volumes, the Roman *Thermae*, and a triumph—as he saw it—of the fruitful collaboration of the various arts, the eighteenth-century interior. But eighteenth-century architecture had, for him, an interest beyond that of collaboration, it was also the last time that Form had received its due, and then with Schinkel disappeared. Schinkel's output therefore appeared as

> something higher, more exalted, than what came after it, something that we have subsequently lost

and lost so completely that Gottried Semper could observe, as early as the Great Exhibition of 1851 that

> taken all round, the barbaric and semi-civilised peoples have taken the lead over the cultured ones in the arts.

Given this admiration for the eighteenth century, and particularly his admiration for Schinkel, often expressed, it is not surprising to find that

Form, as he felt it, was a kind of geometrical essence distilled from neo-Classical design. This is confirmed in part by the architecture of the designer who stood closest to him, Peter Behrens, in whom the echoes of neo-Classicism are as clear as they are simplified, and in part by a suggestive literary parallel drawn by Muthesius himself. Towards the end of the speech he refers contemptuously to the instability and changeability of taste in his own lifetime, and to the fallibility of '-isms', and contrasts with them the stability of the 'inmost essence' (*innerste Wesen*) of architecture, which has

> . . . its own constancy, calm and endurance. Throughout the millenia of its continually enriched tradition, it represents, as it were, the permanent in human history.

This, of course, is yet another appeal to the power of tradition over the head of the styles and Art Nouveau, but Muthesius follows it with a side-look at other arts that gives it a new twist.

> In its constancy of mind it is unfavourable to the prevailing Impressionist approach in the other arts. In painting, in literature, to some extent in sculpture, Impressionism is conceivable and has conquered these realms of art. But the thought of an Impressionist architecture is altogether terrible—*Denken wir ihn nicht aus*! There have already been individualistic essays in architecture that fill us with alarm—as will the first signs of Impressionism.

The point need not be laboured here that reactions against Impressionism in painting were called a *renaissance du sentiment classique*, and that the reaction of Maillol and other sculptors against Rodin has been termed neo-Classical.[6] The chief German representative of this sentiment was Adolf Hildebrand, though his book *Problem der Form* was not directed at any named artists, but only at what he termed *Positivism*, that is, the concept of truth to nature implicit in Impressionism, and the artistic anarchy, as he saw it, that followed from it. Hildebrand makes, in short form, a linkage between a scientific culture and a failure of architectonic sensibility, that Muthesius makes only diffusely and at great length

> It is significant of our scientific times that a work of art today seldom rises above the level of imitation. The architectonic feeling is either lacking entirely, or replaced by a purely external . . . arrangement of forms

and it is not inconceivable that the insistence in Muthesius on such themes as Form, Architectonic Discipline, and the importance of Space, may be due directly to the influence of Hildebrand's book, which had already achieved five editions,[7] two outside Germany, by 1907.

[6] Robert Rey used this phrase as the title of a book (Paris, 1931) on the anti-Impressionist painters of the Eighteen-eighties and Nineties. The term neo-Classical is used for Maillol and his connection in Gischia and Vedrés, *La Sculpture en France depuis Rodin* (Paris, 1945).

[7] The first edition appeared in Strassburg in 1893; this quotation is taken from the introduction to the New York edition of 1907.

In German literature the situation was analogous, except that the movements were simultaneous, not sequential, the pioneers of both Impressionist novel-writing, and neo-Classic theatre, being men of Muthesius's own generation (e.g. Emil Strauss, born 1861 as was Muthesius, and Paul Ernst only five years later). The aims, and indeed the terminology, of the neo-Classicists are often remarkably close to those of Muthesius. Paul Ernst's book, in which their aims were set forth, was called *Der Weg zur Form*,[8] and had appeared in 1906. It demanded the restoration, in drama, of a logical inevitability in the action, the preservation of the Classical unities, and the use of blank verse. These tenets hardly need paraphrasing to be made applicable to Werkbund architecture with its attempts to develop buildings logically from their functions, its tendencies toward simple, axial compositions, and its use of simplified neo-Classical detailing for which 'blank verse' is an apt metaphor. Ernst prefigures Muthesius also in his demand for the exclusion of the inessential—*Nebensachen auszuschliessen*—while his couplet

> Wer ist weise, wer ist gut?
> Wer nach seinem Wesen tut.

might stand as a motto not only for Muthesius himself, but for the factories designed by young Werkbund architects like Walter Gropius, who tried to design according to the *innerste Wesen* not only of architecture, itself, but of the functional programme with which they were confronted.

One further point about Muthesius's rejection of Impressionism needs to be noted here: the Individualistic essays that alarmed him so much are, presumably, to be equated with Lindner and Steinmetz's class of designers who opted for untrammelled artistic creation, and were therefore, Expressionists, not Impressionists. Muthesius shows himself less perceptive here than Worringer who, also in 1911, actually coined the word Expressionist to describe, roughly, what Roger Fry had termed post-Impressionism—but only in painting; the word was only later applied to German painting even, and not till very much later to German architecture, in spite of the fact that the tendency to which it was applied had been noticed as early as 1907.

What alarmed Muthesius about these Individualistic essays was that they deviated from his concept of the typical, for he goes on immediately to say

More than any other art, architecture strives toward the typical. Only in this can it find fulfilment. Only in the all-embracing and continuous pursuit of this aim can it regain that effectiveness and undoubted assurance that we admire in the works of past times that marched along the road of homogeneity. And only that way might it meet painting and sculpture of equal quality . . . in those times the feeling for the rhythmic and the architectonic was universally alive and governed all the works of man, whereas in more recent times, architecture

[8] Ernst and his opinions are also extensively discussed in Bithell's book, pp. 282–9.

—called by Semper 'the lawgiver and support that no art dare lack'—has been dragged along in the wake of its sister arts.

and in saying this he formulated a group of related ideas that became a kind of unspoken prejudice that underlies a great part of subsequent architectural thought: that under the leadership of architecture, all the arts of design ought to evolve towards the establishment of standards (types, norms) of a homogeneous style—a prejudice that was translated into visible fact for a few years at the Bauhaus in the Twenties.

But homogeneity and the typical have more than aesthetic connotations for Muthesius. For him the overtones of these words extend as deep into sociology and history as do those of *technique* in the hands of Auguste Choisy.

> Thus, the re-establishment of an architectonic culture is a basic condition of all the arts. . . . It is a question of bringing back into our way of life that order and discipline of which good Form is the outward manifestation.
> In modern social and economic organisation there is a sharp tendency to conformity under dominant viewpoints, a strict uniformity of individual elements, a depreciation of the inessential in favour of immediate essentials. And these social and economic tendencies have a spiritual affinity with the formal tendencies of our aesthetic movement.

And here he has laid the foundation of another prejudice: that certain formal usages are proper to certain conditions of society. This is implicit still in his next paragraph, but his main theme is now a return to the idea of a German destiny in design.

> Germany enjoys a reputation for the most strict and exact organisation in her businesses, heavy industry and state institutions of any country in the world— our military discipline may be cited as the ground of this. Such being the case, perhaps this is an expression of Germany's vocation—to resolve the great problem of architectonic form. Well as our great economic trusts may appreciate the architectonic tendencies of our time, circumstances make us ask whether we can still rely directly on firms and unions of this kind alone to support the progress of architecture. For it to succeed, the whole class of educated Germans, and above all our wealthier private individuals, must be convinced of the need for pure Form, in order that it may progress farther in our land.

If this sounds uncomfortably like a nineteenth-century politician trying to enlist liberal support for some military enterprise, rallying the intellectuals behind the professional soldiers, then it is because that is broadly how Muthesius did regard the situation. The new insistence on spiritualisation and good Form was, in part at least, only another tactic in a continuing trade war in which aesthetics were still a competitive margin. Le Corbusier later accused Behrens of having designed buildings to further Prussian propaganda, citing, e.g. the AEG factories, and there is certainly a nationalist tone about the closing lines of the speech that reminds us that the Werkbund was seen by Muthesius as an adjunct of state policy.

> Only when every member of our nation instinctively clothes his needs in the best Form, shall we achieve as a race a level of taste worthy of the former pro-

76

gressive efforts of Germany. This development of taste, the enjoyment of the handling of Form, hold a decisive meaning for the future status of Germany in the world. First we must set our own house in order, and when all is clarity and light within, we can begin to have some effect outside. Only then shall we appear in the world as a nation worthy to be entrusted, among other things, with the handling of this task—to restore to the world and our age the lost benefits of an architectonic culture.

Just as those who owed most to the Futurists started off, as it were, by discounting Marinetti's patriotic intentions, so those who owed most to Muthesius soon put the Prussianism to one side, but—French and German alike—they did tend to retain the authoritarian tone that accompanied his theory of types and uniformity. Their intention is to legislate for, rather than serve, their public. But as far as the Werkbund Congress of 1911 was concerned, the patriotic issue was not the one they wanted to discuss. It was Form, and Type, that dominated the early part of the debate on his paper.

Cornelius Gurlitt, in the first speech from the floor, made it clear that the intention to change policy was understood

> The question of quality alone can no longer be decisive, but the word Form deserves to be set alongside it in the spearhead of our effort

and the Muthesian consequence as well

> So, then, another important question arises; the question: Type or Individuality?

but in spite of his standing as a serious historian of art and architecture he was not prepared to treat this question with quite the earnestness that Muthesius intended.

> That question—when you come to Hellerau—you will find, not solved, but under examination, and that in many witty and interesting ways. There you can see, in the houses and in the house planning, individual creations cheek-by-jowl with types—the former after the taste of the designers, the latter after that of the people who live in them. . . .

The question of the typical was not completely new—not in Werkstätte circles anyhow, since Bruno Paul's designs for mass-production furniture of the previous year had been termed *Typenmöbel*—and the second contribution from the floor has the smooth look of a prepared response. K. E. Osthaus of the Folkwang Museum in Hagen,[9] used an argument that was to be repeated *ad nauseam* for the next forty years as he brought the eighteenth century forward as an historical justification for standardisation and the typical

> I have come straight here from France, where I found to my surprise a whole series of towns all developed on the same aesthetic pattern. I might take Rennes

[9] Osthaus was one of the 'culture heroes' of the period (to misuse a useful phrase) and was active in commissioning work from progressive designers such as Behrens, van de Velde, Gropius and Bruno Taut.

as an example, where the town was completely gutted in the eighteenth century, and subsequently rebuilt according to an unified architectural scheme. Essentially it is a question there of a Typical plan-form that makes it almost impossible to tell one house from another. Yet though the town expresses a more uniform appearance than perhaps any other in the world, men derive a most vigorous artistic life from it, in spite of outward uniformity. The Typical, as one sees it fully developed there, has formed itself by the equalisation and refinement of personal needs. So it need not necessarily function as a stumbling block to artistic creation.

This exposition of the virtues of eighteenth-century typicality more or less closes the ring of the argument begun by Muthesius when he referred his audience back to the eighteenth century for the last visible examples of good Form. The attitudes adopted in 1911 remained good, for the most part until 1914 and far beyond—Henry van de Velde's polemic against Muthesius at the 1914 Congress still left the question in the form 'Type or Individuality' and should be regarded, like his elegant theatre at the Werkbund exhibition in Cologne that year, as a spirited rearguard action by an outgoing type of designer. Beyond this it should be noted that Muthesius's preoccupations with problems like national standing, aesthetics, standardisation and mechanisation were to find partial fulfilment—like those of the Futurists—in the ensuing World War. Under the pressure of military necessity and a tight economic situation, *DIN-Format* began to be applied to an increasing range of industrial products. It was essentially the freezing, *ad hoc*, of a number of widely-used dimensionings as standard measures for that particular class of product (*Deutsche Industrie-Normen*), and so 'our military discipline' became indeed the ground of standardisation and the Typical. *DIN-Format* was never fully abandoned after the war, and was revived and revised in the Second World War. It is commonly taken to be the inspiration of Bauhaus studies in dimensional standardisation of building components, and thus lies at the root of the whole trend toward modular co-ordination that runs right through the Modern Movement.

6: The factory aesthetic

THE FAGUSWERKE AT Alfeld, designed from 1911 onwards by Gropius and Meyer, and in construction until 1913, is frequently taken to be the first building of the Modern Movement properly so-called, the end of the pioneer phase in Modern architecture. There can be little doubt that it owes this high esteem in part to Gropius's personal relationship to the historians of the Modern Movement, and also, in part, to the accidents of photography—it is possible, by a hostile selection of photographs,[1] to make it appear no more 'Modern' than, say, Behrens's Eppenhausen development of 1907. The modernity of this group of buildings is visible, indeed, only on parts of two sides, where the machine-shop and power-house present glazed walls to the south. These two blocks are in such strong contrast to the unadventurous neo-Classical regularity of the rest of the buildings that one may suspect that—like the informal planning, and the strong sculptural forms of the dust-extractor plant—they must have been an unsought consequence of the *innerste Wesen* of the functional programme. The rest of the factory lies well within the scope and intentions of the current body of Werkbund practice and ideas, but these glazed blocks, with their windows rising continuously through three stories, and wrapped round the corners of the block without corner piers, stand out as major innovations but may not have been designed until as late as the beginning of 1913 when Gropius and Meyer were already working on the Werkbund Pavilion for the 1914 Exhibition in Cologne.

But they still lacked the support of any accumulated experience in Werkbund circles of the aesthetics of glazed envelopes, and serious visual research on this subject seems not to have been attempted until the beginning of the Twenties. Nevertheless, if practice lagged, in theoretical writings Muthesius ran well ahead. At an early date he had begun to assemble that canon of nineteenth-century glass and iron masterpieces that was to be

---

[1] Such a hostile selection, made for polemical reasons, may be found in Bruno Zevi's book *Poetica dell'Architettura Neo-Plastica* (Milan, 1953).

extended by Meyer, by J. A. Lux,[2] by Lindner and Steinmetz, and receive its definitive form in Giedion's *Bauen in Frankreich* of 1928. Already in his *Stilarchitektur und Baukunst* of 1902, Muthesius lists the Crystal Palace, the two *Bibliothèques* of Labrouste, the Galerie des Machines and the Eiffel Tower, and he comments on the 'failure' of the Chicago Centennial to maintain the standard set by earlier exhibitions. To this canon of accepted masterpieces is appended a general encomium of station halls, covered markets, glazed museum-courts and department stores. Though he did not labour this list when he came to contribute to a symposium on factory design in the Werkbund *Jahrbuch* for 1913, he did revise it

> A good deal of engineering structure, bridges, station halls, lighthouses and grain silos, are good aesthetically.

and though this list includes structures of a solidly plastic type (lighthouses, silos) it was prefaced by Lethabitic excursion into machine design that throws the emphasis very heavily the other way.

> The contrary sense appears in the invention of the bicycle wheel with its wire spokes and pneumatic tyre. No one nowadays any longer finds anything abnormal in this, and the light structure of the wire spoking strikes us as fine and elegant.

One might expect to find such sentiments echoed by the designer of the transparencies of the Faguswerke and the Cologne pavilion, but in so far as Gropius's humane and intelligent reflections on factory design show any aesthetic preferences, they go against the grain of Muthesius's ideas

> Compared to other European countries, Germany has a clear lead in the aesthetics of factory-building. But in the motherland of industry, in America, there exist great factory buildings whose majesty outdoes even the best German work of this order. The grain silos of Canada and South America, the coal bunkers of the leading railroads and the newest work halls of the North American industrial trusts, can bear comparison, in their overwhelming monumental power, with the buildings of ancient Egypt.

and he continues the monumental theme when he praises Behrens's buildings for AEG as *Denkmäler von Adel und Kraft*. This clearly is not the quality that Muthesius found admirable when he singled out the Eiffel Tower, or station halls, or bicycle wheels for praise, and Muthesius's theoretical position stood far ahead of any support from the practical men.

Such support as he did receive came, not from the *Zweck-Kunst* Classicists who otherwise stood nearest to him, but from the 'Expressionists' of the Breslau group, and from a survivor of Art Nouveau. The latter was

---

[2] Meyer's book *Eisenbauten* (Berlin, 1908) was to exercise considerable influence in an underground way; it was little read by architects, as far as one can make out, but much used by historians. The effect of Lux's *Ingenieuraesthetik* (Berlin, 1913) seems to have been much less.

August Endell, whose grandstand for the Mariendorf race-track, Berlin, a work of 1910 may be regarded as a late, self-conscious, but perfectly controlled survival of nineteenth-century lattice-structure sensibility, enriched by the experiments in three-dimensional arabesque which had characterised some sections of continental Art Nouveau (e.g., Horta, house in Rue Paul-Emile Janson). It is a rare and early approximation to a true space-frame structure.[3]

The Breslau group had the advantage of an exhibition to create an opportunity to exercise their talents, and two small exhibition buildings by Bruno Taut should be discussed first, before turning to the buildings for the Breslau *Jahrhundertfeier*. These two buildings were both pavilions for industrial marketing combines: one for the *Stahlwerksverband* (Leipzig, 1913) the other for the Glass Industry, at the Cologne Exhibition of 1914. The former is the less interesting, consisting of a glazed stepped-back pyramid of steel post-and-lintel construction on an octagonal base, but surmounted by a large sphere, whose diameter fills the highest octagon, and is seen through the structure immediately below. The glass pavilion is of much greater originality, the greater part of its volume being enclosed by a tall dome of approximately geodesic structure, with steel ribs and glazed panels. This stands on a regular, sixteen-sided lower storey, in which stairs with glass treads and risers ascend in curves between walls of glazed bricks. Both structurally and visually this is the most brilliant combination of glass and steel achieved by any architect in the years immediately preceding 1914. Quite apart from the possibility of its having been influenced by Paul Scheerbart's book *Glasarchitektur*[4] which came out in the same year, its rare qualities suggest that it was produced in a moment of genius that Taut was unable to repeat. The same must be said of Max Berg's *Jahrhunderthalle* at Breslau (1913). No other work of Berg's long career, both as city architect of Breslau, or as an independent designer, is to be compared to this giant dome, and like Taut's glass dome, this structure in reinforced concrete must rank as the most brilliant use of its materials achieved by anybody in its period (with the possible exception of some of Freyssinet's early vaults). By comparison with the sense of plasticity and three-dimensional form, the understanding of concrete as a material to be poured and moulded, that performs most efficiently in arcuate and vaulted forms, such as Berg exhibits here, the contemporary work of Perret cannot but appear wooden and intellectually circumscribed. Here, alone, in Germany or elsewhere, was a building that could face comparison with Muthesius's canon of nineteenth-century exhibition buildings in terms of scale, originality and exploitation of the material. The way in which it was forgotten and its lessons ignored (much as the lessons of Freyssinet's hangars were

[3] Endell, like Muthesius, was an admirer of such structures as glazed station halls.
[4] See chapter 19.

ignored, even while lip-service was paid to their designer) in the Twenties, is a mark of the success with which an aesthetic could be applied in defiance of the best use of the material, even by architects who accepted truth to materials as a fundamental tenet in their philosophy of design, and is a tribute also to the power of conviction carried by the Abstract aesthetics of immediately post-War art movements.

The other main buildings for the *Jahrhundertfeier* were the work of Hans Poelzig. They do not show him at his best or his most inventive, their detailing is in a kind of smudged Greek Doric and the planning is academic. But outside such 'representational' contexts Poelzig was one of the most consistently and persuasively inventive designers of his generation in Germany. His buildings for industry really did produce new forms for new needs, were the chief ornament of the Expressionist, or Individualist wing in the Werkbund, and were the prime inspiration of the short-lived Expressionist phase in German architecture after 1918.

The chemical plant at Luban, near Berlin, is the best-known of the buildings of this phase of his work; its mannered distribution of Roman windows over otherwise unmodulated façades has attracted criticism, but it was effected with conviction, and appears to bear a functional relation to the *innerste Wesen* of the building's use. It is a work of the same year as the *Faguswerke*, but completed more quickly, and it has none of that building's inconsistencies or uncertainties. The effect of the whole is homogeneous and deliberate, even if it bears little superficial resemblance to later Modern buildings. As an exercise in unadorned, but carefully modulated, brick structure, this work of Poelzig's does not stand entirely alone, for a similar aesthetic, though more austerely handled, can be seen in Stoffregen's factory for the Anker Linoleum Company, a work of 1912 whose reputation survived the War but subsequently fell from regard. In the same way, the sculptural treatment of the exterior of Poelzig's water-tower at Posen, designed in 1910, finds an echo in the boldly formed roof of Albert Marx's boiler-house at Bad Nauheim, which like the Anker Company, was also a work of 1912. In fact, one can see building up around Poelzig and Berg in the last four years before the war an incipient school of factory designers,[5] independently descended from the English Free architecture, almost unaffected by the Classicising preferences of the Behrens wing in the Werkbund, eschewing decoration and handling sculptural forms with great boldness—a boldness to be matched only in Futurist projects at that time. Immediately after the War it looked as if this school could resume where it had broken off, and in a generally expressionist atmosphere that affected even Gropius and Mies van der Rohe, the early works of Erich Mendelsohn and Hugo Häring promised a real

[5] Designers of this persuasion in the Werkbund were well-represented in the *Jahrbuch* for 1913.

continuance.[6] But the movement was quickly inhibited by the Dutch and Russian Abstract aesthetics mentioned above, and came to nothing.

The comparison with the Futurists may be taken a little further than outward formal similarities, though, as some of Poelzig's immediately pre-War projects show, these were remarkably close—there is one sketch for a factory store that could serve equally well as a prototype of the drying shed of Mendelsohn's Luckenwalde factory, or of some of Sant' Elia's *Dinamismo Architettonico* sketches. But it is clear beyond this, that Poelzig had something of the Futurists' mechanical sensibility, even as early as 1910, at which time it is doubtful if he could have read any of the manifestoes. The interior of the water-tower at Posen, with its emphasis on mechanical equipment and metallic structure, reveals, beyond the mere fulfilment of operating needs, a sense of the dramatic possibilities inherent in these factors, and the creation of forms and spaces that emphasise them.

Compared with the work done on this wing of the Werkbund's creative programme, that achieved on the other side, by Behrens, Gropius and Muthesius himself must appear less adventurous and imaginative. The development of Behrens's great work-halls for AEG does show a consistent growth, away from the massive pseudo-Classicism of the *Turbinenfabrik* of 1908–9, where the management of the massively rusticated and battered corners seems to make nonsense of the frame-and-fill and glass-and-steel structure of the sides, to the *Grossmaschinenfabrik* of 1911–12, where he seems at last to sense that glazed or solid, the walls and roof are only a light envelope drawn over a vast bulk of industrially usable space. Even the brick panels between the windows of the sides seem to have a light and tenuous quality that is quite unlike the solid walling of any of his earlier industrial work. On the other hand, this block also has a rather cheap and unfinished air, as if restrictions on budget had played a larger part in its design than in, say, the *Turbinenfabrik*, which was clearly intended as a piece of prestige building. But whatever alternative influences may have been at work, he remains faithful to a standard envelope for all these factory halls—the envelope of a Classical temple, qualified only by an industrial necessity (viz. the need to give head-clearance to gantry runs) that militated against plain single-ridged roofs, and accounts for his polygonal gable-forms. The only important exception to this type of gable occurs on the *Hochspannungsfabrik*, 1910, where paired Classical pediments appear low down on the main façade to express the presence of a pair of

[6] Mendelsohn's factory at Luckenwalde, and Häring's farm buildings at Gut Garkau, promised, in the very first years of the Twenties, an architecture extraordinarily open-minded in its attitude to materials and planning—the use of wood on exteriors of boldly sculptural form and the employment of exposed concrete portal frames in the interiors of these two schemes, coupled with the most remarkable horseshoe plan of Gut Garkau, all suggest a mode of design that could have greatly enriched the architecture of the Twenties.

parallel work-halls within the building, though these halls do not appear functionally to penetrate to the outer wall at this point.

Curiously, these more enterprising designs of Behrens left less mark on subsequent architectural thought and feeling than did the *Turbinenfabrik*, which seems to have served as a model even for post-War Expressionist architecture. But it is clear, anyhow, that the long-term significance of Behrens's pre-War industrial architecture does not lie altogether in the buildings themselves—except in so far as they demonstrated his ability to clothe industrial needs in forms that would be recognised by his contemporaries as 'architectural' in almost the normal sense of the word. Here Behrens is most closely to be compared with Auguste Perret, the latter having brought a new material—concrete—within the accepted canons of architectural thought,[7] just as Behrens brought a new set of functional programmes within the accepted formal disciplines, and of this last the *Turbinenfabrik* was the most exemplary demonstration. It is also another demonstration of the exemplary way in which Behrens embodied Muthesius's ideal of the good designer. Coming from painting, by way of graphic design and *Gewerbekunst*, to domestic architecture and thence to industrial design in the very broadest sense, he liberated himself from the influence of Art Nouveau and achieved, in the *Turbinenfabrik*, that kind of Schinkelesque form that Muthesius was to demand in so many words of the Werkbund designers two years later.

Yet his Schinkelism was by no means consistent. In 1911, at the same time as the extremely neo-Classical Wiegand house in Dahlem, his office also produced the gasworks buildings in Frankfurt, perhaps the most formally inventive industrial buildings of his pre-War career. It may be because of some such indecision in his own mind, or within his office hierarchy, that he did not exercise an equal, or equally beneficial, neo-Classical influence on his pupil-assistants. Mies van der Rohe clearly accepted it, and—to judge from his project for the Kröller House—could practise it with even greater facility than his master. Le Corbusier rejected it, in practice, and in written word, Gropius, it seems, accepted it, but without benefit to his architecture.

There may have been some fundamental disposition of Gropius's mind that accounts for the seeming division of intentions here. His training, at the Charlottenburg *Hochschule* and in Munich was one that, on other personalities (Poelzig, Berg, Mendelsohn) produced designers of an Expressionist turn of mind, and the blank, plain, glyptic shapes of his early houses at Jankow in Prussia (1906) suggest, within a neo-Classical envelope, a sculptural attitude to design that might be compared to Poelzig's. The solidly walled storehouse block of the *Faguswerke* seems to continue this tendency, while the tight functional programme prevented any neo-Classical idea, acquired from Behrens in the intervening years, from appearing

[7] See chapter 3.

in the plan. But in the offices and '*Fabrik*' for the Werkbund at their Exhibition in Cologne in 1914, the enforced discipline of an industrial pro-gramme did not exist, Gropius and Meyer were at liberty to arrange the elements of the building as they thought fit. A comparison of the finished building with the block plan shown in the *Jahrbuch* for 1913 reveals an extensive rearrangement of the parts, probably connected with a change in the function of half the building—that part which was labelled *Werk-stätte* on the 1913 plan becoming a hall for the display of machine tools, etc. with an additional pavilion for the Deutz motor-company.

The plan finally used is fully as academic as that employed by Poelzig in his buildings for the Breslau *Jahrhundertfeier* but with the addition of certain usages that seem uncommonly French. The office block is disposed axially about the main entrance, and the axis runs back through an open courtyard and down the centre of the Machine Hall. The courtyard is traversed by an *axe secondaire*, and—on paper, though not as seen by the eye in fact—has bi-axial symmetry, the linking passages between the open sheds that flanked the court and the office on the one hand, the Machine Hall on the other, being disposed in such a way as to create identical patterns of set-backs on both sides, even though the two con-fronted elevations were utterly different. As can sometimes be seen on more 'experimental' types of *Beaux-Arts* plans, there is an asymmetrical element, the Deutz Pavilion, aligned on a tertiary axis at the other end of the machine hall.

Stylistically, the various elements of this group of buildings are a fairly complete florilegium of the modern eclectic sources from which an up-to-date Werkbund designer could draw at the time. That which seems most homogeneous with the aims of the Werkbund and its expressed attitudes is the Machine Hall, clearly based on gable-ended train-sheds such as Muthesius had admired, simple in form and entirely convincing in its shape, as are the open sheds that flank the court, though these have every appearance of being at least the prototypes of standard units drawn from industrial production. An equal certainty of design, though a far less adven-turous form, is exhibited by the Deutz Pavilion. Clearly related in its de-tails, plan-form and constructional methods to Taut's *Stahlwerksverband* Pavilion of the previous year, it makes a strong contrast with Taut's Glass Industry exhibit of 1914. Where this latter steps forward to further struc-tural and formal adventure with its geodesic dome and so forth, the Gropius version is a step back towards an accepted Classicising form, that of the *Tholos* or polygonal temple—a point which is emphasised by the copy of the Parthenon Hermes that was placed at its base at the end of the long pool which ran down the side of the Machine Hall.

But the office block is the most complex part of the whole assembly, stylistically speaking, and also architecturally the weakest. Its overall silhouette can only be described as Palladian, in the manner of Wilton

House, with a long two-storey central body, a weakly-marked central entrance, and terminal towers—or nearly so; the position of these towers is architecturally the most debatable part of the design. The source of the silhouette is Wrightian as are some of the details (e.g. the framing of the entrance) and this is the first clear demonstration of Wright's influence in Werkbund circles. Wright's work was fairly well known by 1913–14, not only through the Wasmuth publications but also through the activities of H. P. Berlage. There is a striking similarity between the block form of Gropius's building and Wright's bank in Mason City, Iowa, completed a year earlier, particularly as to the flanking towers and their deeply overhung cornices. Drawings for this building, published in the first Wasmuth volume, are also the source for the use of a close-spaced rhythm of brick piers with narrow slit-like windows between them, and for much of the detailing of the brickwork throughout the whole block.

Had Gropius and Meyer been content to follow out this Wrightian exercise to its natural formal conclusion, the result would have been, it seems, a distinguished pioneering work in an idiom new to Europe, though clearly sympathetic to neo-Classic modes of thought. However, their neo-Classical disposition of mind seems to have been insufficiently strong to resist the temptation to make the building a manifesto of Muthesian transparency and fine-structure at the same time. On the courtyard face, the Wrightian basement storey and the Wrightian roof-structures, are separated by a storey of total glazing, carried some three feet clear of the rear structural wall of the block, making a covered passage that links the various first-floor offices with the staircases at the end of the block. These staircases are not as might be imagined, within the towers, but stood proud in front of them on the other façade, in semicircular projections in the manner of the end pavilion of Hoffmann's Villa Ast (Vienna, 1909). But whereas Hoffmann had used a solidly-walled form with two cornices to emphasise its shape, Gropius and Meyer continue their total glazing round the ends of the building at first-floor level and wrap it around the staircases, at which point it is brought down to ground-level, to produce glazed half-drums rising the full height of the main façade. The staircases are thus visible from outside, as is the corner stair of the *Faguswerke*, and this technical innovation has enjoyed a considerable *succès d'éstime* ever since, as well as providing the inspiration for some of Mendelsohn's most characteristic designs. But it is difficult to rate it a visual success. The two turns of staircase that are revealed rise at different rates, due to the presence of a half-landing in the upper one, an uncomfortable sight that would have been better hidden, while the glazing of the whole end of the building at first-floor level, reveals the fact that the towers, instead of being firmly based on a continuous structure down to ground level—as they are in the Wrightian prototype—are half-heartedly cantilevered from the internal structure at the level of the main roof.

The cantilevers are slight, but in this context most unhappy. The whole building seems to lack any experienced awareness (such as Paul Scheerbart already possessed) of the difficulties of glass walling from the visual angle. The simple strongly-marked rhythm of the vertical ordering of the *Faguswerke* windows is replaced by an uncontrolled horizontal spread without, however, the appearance of being intended for what would later have been called an 'endless' façade, and the effect of transparency seems not to have been studied. Compared to van de Velde's Theatre at the same exhibition, this must appear a more clumsy piece of design. But van de Velde's building, though immensely sophisticated, is without innovations, architecturally speaking. The future lay with Gropius and those who felt as he did. All they lacked was an aesthetic discipline that would make sense of transparencies, cantilevers, glass-walling and other technical innovations.

That aesthetic discipline was not, however, one that any school of architecture seems to have been capable of finding for itself, and the resolution of the architectural difficulties was to come from the realm of painting and sculpture, from that development towards purely Abstract art that had already been launched by the Cubists and Futurists, but did not become available as a usable discipline until after the War.

7: Adolf Loos and the problem of ornament

AMONG THE EFFECTIVE contributors to the body of ideas that supported the Modern Movement, one must certainly number Adolf Loos. Yet his contribution was sporadic, personal and not always very serious in tone. As an architect he appears as one of the first to build in a manner that really valued simplicity of form as a virtue in itself, yet usually spoiled that simplicity by usages that wilfully departed from it, or materials that concealed it. As a writer he was prolific and usually well-informed, yet much of his influence depends upon one, or possibly two, of his most opinionated essays. As a person he was turbulent, combative, contradictory and capable of turning personal quarrels into public crusades, yet he was admired and courted, and people are still proud to claim his acquaintance,[1] twenty or more years after his death.

His active career divides itself into three main parts. The first, down to his return from the U.S.A. in 1897 does not concern us immediately at this point. The second, of active building, teaching and journalism in Vienna, reaching a peak of productivity around 1910, produced his most influential writings, his most characteristic buildings. The third, which begins with his arrival in Paris in 1923 as an acknowledged celebrity, is the phase of his greatest personal influence, but one that is hardest to deal with historically —one has to accept the testimony of those who knew him then that they were pleased when they pleased him,[2] and were flattered to be accepted into his circle of friends and admirers.

But this third phase was the product of the second. His celebrity on arrival depended only in part on his personal reputation, and hardly at all

[1] Many architects came, or claim to have come, under his influence either in Vienna or Paris—most notably André Lurçat, Richard Neutra, Raymond Schindler and Eric Mendelsohn.

[2] Lurçat, in conversation with the author, volunteered the information that one of his early designs *faisait grand plaisir à Adolf Loos*. Somewhere in this connection, by way of Loos's notorious Anglomania, may lie the explanation of what appear to be quotations from the work of Charles Rennie Mackintosh that appear in Parisian architecture in the early Twenties—the tall 'oriel' window of Lurçat's Maison Guggenbuhl is a case obviously in point.

on his buildings, which seem to have been known only by hearsay. He was famous primarily for certain of his writings which had just been reprinted for the second time in French, writings from the peak years of the second phase, writings which he himself regarded as the most essential expressions of his credo. Like practically everything else he wrote, these had appeared first in Viennese newspapers and periodicals, and were mostly occasional works—as a witty and spritely controversialist he was in demand for *feuilletons* and exhibition notices, and he wrote on a wide variety of subjects, such as clothing, manners, furnishing, music, etc. besides architecture. These writings all exhibit a similar tendency, anti-Romantic, fastidious, puritanical (though never inhumane) and authoritarian (though opposed to established authorities). The possible appeal of these qualities to later Modern Movement theorists is clear, but they might well have been forgotten and lost in post-War Vienna, but for the activities of one man whose connection with Modern architecture is important, though oblique.

This was Herwarth Walden, proprietor of a gallery and magazine, both called *Der Sturm*, who was one of the chief representatives of revolutionary art, and primarily Expressionism, in Berlin. A conscientious *avant-gardiste*, and despiser of conventions, on the model of Marinetti, he made his magazine, founded in 1910, and gallery, which ran until 1924, a clearing-house of ideas on an international scale, somewhat like Léonce Rosenberg in Paris after 1919. He was one of those who introduced Futurism to the German public, in 1912; and also in 1912 he published in his magazine five of Loos's essays.[3] These may have been brought to his attention by Arnold Schoenberg, who was a friend of Loos, and also in touch with German Expressionist painters (he was a member of the Munich *Blaue Reiter* group) at all events, the tone of voice of the essays that appeared in *Der Sturm* was of a kind to appeal to despisers of convention, even if the logical outcome of their arguments was not. In particular the tone of *Ornament und Verbrechen*, which Loos had written in 1908, was likely to appeal by its use of sexual and anthropological arguments, and that of *Architektur*, by its apotheosis of peasant design.

Access to the pages of *Der Sturm* was access to a limited, but international audience, and bore fruit in an almost immediate reprinting in Paris, in the pages of *Les Cahiers d'Aujourd'hui* in 1913, in what became the standard French translation, by Georges Besson. The Besson version is lively, but somewhat bowdlerised, and fairly heavily cut, as far as *Ornament und Verbrechen* is concerned, drastically cut and shortened in the case of *Architektur*. Nevertheless, the main substance of the argument is present in both cases, and these two essays (all that ever were translated) would appeal to similar persons and frames of mind in Paris as in Berlin—in this case, those who later became members of Dada. For when *Ornament*

[3] A bibliography of these reprintings is given in Schreyer and Walden, *Der Sturm* (Baden-Baden, 1954).

und Verbrechen was reprinted again in French, in 1920 in *L'Esprit Nouveau* —perhaps its most influential reprinting, and the one that prepared the way for Loos's arrival in Paris—it was during the period when Paul Dermée, an active fringe Dadaist who did much to break up the attempt to revive *La Section d'Or*, was still one of *L'Esprit Nouveau*'s editors. It thus carried a double sense; it supported the demand of Le Corbusier for a reform in architecture and an abandonment of the catalogue styles, and it also supported the Dadaists' campaign of mockery against the fine arts, thus gaining Loos the entrée to the circle of Tristan Tzara and other Dadaists.

L'Esprit Nouveau also promised the forthcoming publication of *Architektur* (under the title of *L'Architecture Moderne*) but this never took place and the essay finally appeared again in French in Morancé's *L'Architecture Vivante*, in 1923. Between these two second reprints of his essays in France, Loos had gathered together his papers of the 1897–1900 period and published them in 1921 as *Ins Leere gesprochen*, a publication that bears strong witness to his international reputation at that time—a German language text appearing over a French imprint (that of Crès et Cie, Le Corbusier's publishers). *Ornament und Verbrechen*, and *Architektur* achieved their second German reprintings in a further book of collected essays, *Trotzdem*, which appeared in Innsbruck in 1930.

Also in Austria appeared a *Festschrift* for his sixtieth birthday (1930) and Kulka's study of his work as an architect (1931). This return to a purely Austrian status should be noted, for it is clear that at the beginning of the Thirties Loos was not the commanding figure that he had been at the beginning of the Twenties, and *Trotzdem* does not appear to be so widely known and cited as *Ins Leere gesprochen*—in fact, architects who have read the latter are sometimes unaware of the existence of *Trotzdem*, even though they know *Ornament und Verbrechen*.[4] The reasons for this fall from grace are probably to be sought in the difference of generation between Loos and the practising masters of the New architecture, and for a drastic change in sensibility during the Twenties (occasioned largely by the diffusion of Abstract and Futurist ideas, that made Loos look old-fashioned) and in the probability of personal quarrels with (e.g.) Le Corbusier. At all events, Loos's main impact on his younger contemporaries was made via Paris in the early Twenties, and—beyond his personal influence—appears to depend primarily upon *Ins Leere gesprochen* and *Ornament und Verbrechen*. The former acted as a support to Corbusian ideas of architecture as equipment but *Ornament und Verbrechen*, because it exercised influence of some sort from the time of its first writing, and because it was very clearly a product of a particular time and place, will be dealt with here.

The subject of this essay—the status of architectural decoration—was

---

[4] In spite of his personal acquaintance with Loos in the Twenties, Lurçat, for instance, seemed to know *Ornament und Verbrechen* only from the reprint of it in *L'Esprit Nouveau*.

not a new one, and in the early years of the century was a very live issue. But Loos's attitude towards the subject goes far beyond that of any of his contemporaries, and directly contradicts that of some of the most influential bodies of opinion, notably the Werkbund. It will be helpful, therefore, to survey the state of opinion briefly around 1910. The attitude of the Rationalists, and of the Academics, was effectively one of indifference. T. G. Jackson makes a familiar gibe when he observed

> The man who cannot design flies naturally to ornament

but he seems not to have actually envisaged an entirely undecorated architecture, any more than Guadet did, in spite of his indifference to style. Similarly Geoffrey Scott regards ornament as unimportant if the basic control of form is sufficiently sure

> These means sufficed them (i.e. Renaissance architects). Given these they could dispense at will with sculpture and colour

a view which is flatly contradicted by Choisy's

> The Renaissance in Italy involved only a reform in the system of ornament

and although Choisy does once express a preference for a building because it is free from ornament;[5] he is not, in general, hostile to it. Among the English Free architects one finds contempt for the catalogued styles, but no hesitation in using ornament of their own invention, and an exploitation (though less vigorous than in the case of Loos) of the inherent decorative qualities of natural materials. Voysey is on record as objecting to ornamental plaster-work on ceilings, but only because he cricked his neck in looking at it, and one cannot but notice how Voysey turns minor functional necessities (such as the owl-ports in some of his gables) to decorative profit.

But what is most remarkable, in view of later developments, is to find within the line of descent from the English Free architecture and the Deutscher Werkbund, no sense of impropriety in the ornamentation of machinery, engineering structures and machine products. The development of such a sense is a tribute to the revolution in taste effected by Loos himself and the Abstract aesthetics of the war years. Before this revolution it is possible to find an anonymous Lethabist in the *Architectural Review* observing that there is

> . . . a firestation just outside of Vauxhall where the lookout stage is a simple piece of iron lattice work wonderfully agreeable in its lines. Add to a skeleton like this a little bit of daintily designed and disposed modelling and the result would be charming.

More remarkable than this is the Werkbund's only official pronunciation on the subject in the period, an article by Karl Gross in the *Jahrbuch* for

---

[5] 'Saint Front in Perigueux, more imposing in its severe nakedness than San Marco . . . with all its mosaics and marbles.' Choisy's observations on Doric quoted in chapter 2, go some way in this direction as well.

1912. It is easy to suppose that Muthesius's demands for the elimination of the *nebensächlich* refers to ornament specifically, but an examination of Werkbund products suggests that it only refers to 'superfluous' ornament, which is not the same thing. It is unlikely that Muthesius would have been able to hold together his heterogeneous organisation if he had deprived one whole wing of it—the artist-designers—of the only element they were trained in or capable of contributing, and he nowhere inveighs against ornament as such. Behrens likewise shows a divided attitude on the subject—his products for industrial users (e.g. arc lamps) are undecorated, but those for domestic use (e.g. electric ovens) are ornate, and Gropius shows himself a capable ornamentalist in his fabric designs, etc. of 1913–14.

But Karl Gross's article also reveals a qualifying factor in Werkbund discussions that may be no more than a verbal quibble, or may be the touchstone that distinguishes justifiable ornament from superfluous ornament. It first appears as a question that can hardly be rendered into English

Muss Schmuck denn ohne weiteres Ornament sein?

because no two English words (e.g. Decoration/Ornament) carry the distinction that Gross makes between *Schmuck* and *Ornament*. The general sense of *Schmuck* appears clearly enough in a later sentence

Der erste Schmuck eines Gebäudes ist eine gute Massenverteilung
(The prime ornament of a building is a good arrangement of the masses)

which seems to be comparable to the implication of a passage from Lamprecht cited by Worringer

. . . architecture, apart from its more or less ornamental accessories, such as the comprehension of space. . . .

But, in any case, this is only the *erste Schmuck*, and he nowhere renders precise the point at which the degrees of *Schmuck* begin to shade off towards *Ornament*. And beyond this, though he is clearly dissatisfied with some contemporary ornament (in his second sense), he does not turn his back on it in general. In fact he looks forward to an *Ornamentik* of the twentieth century. His views about this suggest that, though that ornament may be in a new style, his main interest in it is one that had been declared outmoded at the Werkbund Congress of 1911. Thus, while he admits that

Beauty of form is pleasing, even without ornament

and complains that industrial style consists of

seeking to mislead, by means of worthless ornamental rubbish covering poorly-conceived form

his solution does not envisage those formal and intellectual disciplines proposed by Muthesius, nor the absolute anathema proposed already by Loos, but simply a call for *Qualität*

Decoration, even ornament in the technical sense, must remain quality work when we set out on the road to twentieth-century ornament.
If ornament is to be again what it once was and must remain, a particular distinction that lifts an object out of the general mass, it must be quality work. The power of survival of the artistic handicrafts rests directly on this premise.

Here we have a writer belonging to the most progressive body in the field of design at the time, taking a line that was to be specifically rejected by the next generation of designers belonging to that body, who turned against ornament of any kind, and accepted Loos's views on the subject so wholeheartedly that he had to complain of plagiarism. For him, the idea of a nineteenth-century *Ornamentik*, was insupportable, let alone an *Ornamentik* of the twentieth century, and for him ornament was irretrievably connected with poor-quality goods.

The reason why Loos's ideas prevailed over a more cautious attitude lies largely in three factors. Firstly, his absolute anathema on ornament solved Gross's problem (and everyone else's) by a swift and surgical means. Secondly, he was timely and specific. At a time when Art Nouveau was falling into discredit, his attack on ornament was launched against named Art Nouveau designers, as well as more generally. And thirdly, his mode of expression gave his argument unwonted force. Both argument and style are effectively summed up in the opening paragraphs of *Ornament and Crime*.

The human embryo goes through the whole history of animal evolution in its mother's womb, and a newborn child has the sensory impressions of a puppy. His childhood takes him through the stages of human progress; at the age of two he is a Papuan savage, at four he has caught up with the Teutonic tribesman. At six he is level with Socrates, and at eight with Voltaire. For at this age he learns to distinguish violet, the colour that the eighteenth century first discovered—before that violets were blue and tyrian was red. Physicists can already point to colours they have named, but that only later generations will be able to distinguish.
Children are amoral, and so—by our standards—are Papuans. If a Papuan slaughters an enemy and eats him, that doesn't make him a criminal. But if a modern man kills someone and eats him, he must be either a criminal or a degenerate. The Papuans tattoo themselves, decorate their boats, their oars, everything they can get their hands on. But a modern man who tattooes himself is either a criminal or a degenerate. Why, there are prisons where eighty per cent of the convicts are tattooed, and tattooed men who are not in prison are either latent criminals or degenerate aristocrats. When a tattooed man dies at liberty, it simply means that he hasn't had time to commit his crime.
The urge to ornament oneself and everything within reach is the ancestor of pictorial art. It is the baby talk of painting. All art is erotic.
The first ornament born, the cross, is of erotic origin; the earliest art-work, the first creative act of the original artist was smudged on the cave wall to let off emotional steam—a horizontal stroke, the reclining woman; a vertical one, the man who transfixes her. The man who did this felt the same impulse as Beethoven, was in the same heaven of delight as Beethoven composing the Ninth. But the man of our own times who smudges erotic symbols on walls is either a criminal or a degenerate. It is clear that this violent impulse might seize one or two unbalanced individuals in even the most advanced cultures, but as a general rule one can rank the cultures of different peoples by the extent to which

their lavatory walls have been drawn upon. With children this is a natural con
dition, their first artistic expressions are erotic scribblings on the nursery walls.
But what is natural to children and Papuan savages is a symptom of degenera-
tion in modern man.
I have therefore evolved the following maxim, and pronounce it to the world:
the evolution of culture marches with the elimination of ornament from useful
objects.

Rarely—outside the Futurist Manifestoes—has a new doctrine been
enunciated in so drastic and dynamic a manner, or in a way which persuades
by chiming in with so many bodies of received opinion—albeit combined in
new patterns. Loos never made any significant extensions to the argument
set out here except the idea (not original) of ornament as wasted effort, but
almost unlimited embroideries were possible because of the great number
of levels of reference. Many of the ideas were fairly common property. The
evolutionary fallacy may be found in Worringer for instance

Springer justly compares these productions (cave paintings) to the 'artistic
achievements' of African natives; another comparison not far to seek would
have been the scribblings of a child

but whereas Worringer believed these primitive scribblings to be 'linear
abstract' Loos, profiting from Freud (in which he is a pioneer) rates them
all symbolically representational. On the other hand, the comparison between tattooing and some kinds of architectural decoration can be found
in Lethaby as early as 1911,[6] presumably in complete isolation from
Loosian ideas.

Above all, there was his specific attack on named masters of Art Nouveau,
which undoubtedly helped to galvanise a hitherto vague and unorganised
distrust into a definite feeling that—at least—Art Nouveau was a past mis-
take that should not be made again.

Now that ornament is no longer organically integrated into our culture, it has
ceased to be a valid expression of that culture. The ornament that is designed
today has no relevance to ourselves, to mankind at large, nor the ordering of
the Cosmos. It is unprogressive and uncreative.
What has happened to the ornamental work of Otto Eckmann? What has happened to van de Velde? The artist used to stand for health and strength at the
pinnacle of humanity, but the modern ornamentalist is either a cultural laggard
or a pathological case. He himself is forced to disown his work after three
years. His productions are already unbearable to cultured persons now, and will
become so to others in a little while. Where are now the works of Eckmann,
and where will those of Olbrich be ten years from now. Modern ornament has
neither forbears nor descendants, no past and no future. It may be received with
joy by uncultivated folk, to whom the true greatness of our time is a book with
seven seals, but even by them it will shortly be forgotten.

The specificity and personal nature of this attack have subsequently been
somewhat obscured, but they need to be re-emphasised here for reasons
that will appear later. *Ornament and Crime*, whatever else it may have become, was originally an attack on the *Wiener Sezession*, and the *Wiener*

[6] *Architecture*, p. 188.

Werkstätte, with whom Loos had a quarrel going back into the Nineties, occasioned, it would appear, by Josef Hoffmann's failure to entrust him with the decoration and furnishing of the *Sezession* council chamber. The fact that he is only attacking contemporary ornament and contemporary ornamentalists is brought out by the last paragraph of the essay which ends

> . . . and modern man may use the ornament of historic and exotic cultures at his discretion, but his own inventive talents are reserved and concentrated on other things.

Loos, in fact, is quite permissive to the ornamental activities of those whom he regards as culturally lagging—earlier civilisations, primitive persons, even the labouring poor of Vienna. It is only sophisticated decoration by trained artists of his own time that he attacks, and he himself is fully prepared to use, e.g. the Doric order, when he feels that the situation requires it.

Also, like many reformers, he was a Traditionalist and tended to look backward, not forward. One does not find him attacking Ruskin, as Marinetti was to do. In spite of his inevitable distrust for the Deutscher Werkbund (which he seems to regard as a plot of artists to batten on classes of production that ought to be unornamented, the imposition of a false style) he thanked Muthesius in print for *Das Englische Haus*, and was attached to the English cottage tradition as epitomised in the English Free architecture. He took tradition-bound English tailoring as a model of reticent good taste. Though he admired some consequences of American industry and the whole of American plumbing, he had none of the Futurists' sense of machinery as an aid to personal expression, and he mocks the ideas of a high-obsolescence, scrapping economy, such as was already appearing in the U.S., and was accepted enthusiastically by the Futurists in the next five years. He tends to see furniture and utensils as a class of possessions whose market value must be maintained, not as a class of equipment to be discarded when outmoded.

A Traditionalist, he was also a Classicist, as the frequent use of Classical details—the coffered ceiling of the American Bar in Vienna, for instance— in his buildings shows, but one can be more specific than this; he was also a Schinkelist. Just as the last paragraph of *Ornament and Crime* reveals, unexpectedly, a permissive attitude to the ornament of the past, the concluding paragraph of *Architektur* reveals, somewhat unexpectedly in view of the rest of the essay, a touching faith in the value of the *Schinkelschüler* tradition

> Fischer von Erlach in the south, Schlüter in the north, were justly accounted the greatest masters of the eighteenth century. Then on the threshold of the nineteenth century stood Schinkel—but we have forgotten him. May the radiance of his towering achievement shine forth on the coming generations of our builders.

95

One cannot help finding this parting apotheosis of Schinkel somewhat surprising, because the preceding paragraphs of *Architektur* had been rather anti-Greek in tendency. The ancient Greeks are abused for excessive attention to original detailing and, by inference from the fact that Romans were praised for not doing so, inventing new orders after Doric. The Parthenon is despised for being painted—a point that later Modern-Movement Classicists were happy to overlook. It is Rome and Roman architecture (as he understood them) that receive Loos's approbation.

From the Romans we derive our social sense and our spiritual discipline

> It was no accident that the Romans were not in a position to discover new orders of columns, new decorative styles. . . . The Greeks squandered their inventiveness on the Orders, the Romans spent theirs on the plan. And he who can resolve the larger problems of the ground plan does not concern himself with new mouldings.

Taking a stand on the authority of the plan, Loos brings himself close—closer than anywhere else—to the body of academic discipline. But it is strange that he should praise Roman architecture here and not mention what other German-speaking theorists found praiseworthy in it, *Raumgestaltung*, nor mention what French theorists found praiseworthy, *construction*. This highly abstract view of Roman building is balanced against a curiously primitive view of the nature of architecture in general. Continuing to work backwards through the essay, we find him preceding his praise of Rome with a demonstration of his idea that architecture must affect the emotions, and using as an illustrative image the following

> When we find a mound of earth in the woods, six feet long and three feet wide, shovelled up into the shape of a pyramid, then we turn serious, and a voice inside us says 'Here lies . . .' *That is Architecture.*

Now this is not Abstract; as with the cross, the first art work smudged on the cave wall; it is symbolic, it communicates information as well as emotion, unlike Geoffrey Scott's empathetic responses to architectural form. In spite of the apparent contradiction of his insistence on the plan in Roman architecture, it seems doubtful if, for Loos, the seeming Abstract was ever completely so, whether the purity of Pure Form ever really interested him as anything other than a symbol of purity of mind.

This view of Loos is reinforced by the opening paragraphs of *Architektur*, which bring together several of his pet aversions and admirations. He sets a scene on the shores of a mountain lake, and commends the homogeneity of character of the scene; everything in it, mountains, water, peasant houses, trees and clouds, all seem shaped by the hand of God. But

> Here—what is this? A false note, a scream out of place. Among the houses of the peasants, which were made not by them but by God, stands a villa. Is it the work of a good architect or a bad one? I don't know. I only know that the peace and beauty of the scene have been ruined.
> . . . how is it that every architect, good or bad, causes harm to the lake?

The peasant doesn't do this, nor the engineer who builds a railway on the shore or sends ships to plough their deep furrows in the waters of the lake.

It is clear, though hardly explicit, in the following paragraphs that the peasant builds well, in harmony with the universe, because he builds without thinking about architecture, and without interference from architects. So, presumably, does the engineer in Loos's view, though he does not refer to engineers again in the essay. Now, to build without interference from architects, and their preoccupations with style and the Styles, has for Loos at this juncture an important consequence. Without direction from an architect

der Baumeister könnte nur Häuser bauen: im Stile seiner Zeit.

In the style of his own time, can only mean, in Loos's view of the evolution of ornament and culture, in an undecorated style. Freedom from ornament is the symbol of an uncorrupted mind, a mind which he only attributes to peasants and engineers. In this view succeeding generations were to follow him, thus laying further foundations to the idea of engineers as noble savages (to which Marinetti also contributed) and also—and this is vital in the creation of the International Style—laying further foundations to the idea that to build without decoration is to build like an engineer, and thus in a manner proper to a Machine Age.

Section two

ITALY: FUTURIST MANIFESTOS AND PROJECTS,
1909–1914

Boccioni, U: *Pittura, Scultura Futurista*, Milan, 1914
(for a general account of the movement's attitudes and the texts of the earlier manifestos).

Marinetti, F. T: *Le Futurisme*, Paris, 1912.
La Splendeur Géometrique et Mécanique (manifesto), Milan, 1914.

Caramel and Longatti: *Antonio Sant'Elia* (catalogue of the permanent exhibition at Villa Olmo), Como, 1962.

Sartoris, A: *L'Architetto Antonio Sant'Elia*, Milan, 1930.
(for the best text of the *Manifesto dell'architettura futurista*).

Gambillo and Fiori: *Archivi del Futurismo*, Rome, 1958.

Periodicals
Rivista Tecnica, 7, 1956.
(for the text of the *Messaggio sull'architettura moderna*).

8: Futurism: the Foundation Manifesto

THE QUALITIES WHICH made Futurism a turning-point in the development of Modern theories of design were primarily ideological, and concerned with attitudes of mind, rather than formal or technical methods—though these attitudes of mind were often influential as vehicles in the transmission of formal and technical methods which were not, in the first place, of Futurist invention.

The new ideological orientation of the Futurists can be seen as early as the Foundation Manifesto, published in *Le Figaro*, 20 February 1909. This Manifesto was entirely the work of Fillipo Tomaso Marinetti, the founder and continuous animator of the Futurist Movement. Though originally written in French (Marinetti was a graduate of the Sorbonne, in Letters) and only subsequently translated into Italian, it was apparently written *in* Milan, and is, certainly, substantially autobiographical.[1] It consists of three parts, not separately titled but different in structure and style. The first (or Prologue) is narrative, the second sets out a programme of action and beliefs in tabulated form, and the third is a reflective Epilogue.

The first and second sections are of the greatest interest in the present context, the Prologue in identifying Marinetti's state of mind and the social setting that enframed it, the second in formulating the Futurist attitude to various aesthetic and cultural problems.

The Prologue opens with a piece of *fin-de-siècle* stage-setting

> We had been awake all night my friends and I, under the mosque-lamps whose filigree copper bowls were constellated like our very souls . . . we had trampled out our ancestral *ennui* on opulent turkey carpets, arguing to the limits of reasoning, and blackening innumerable sheets of paper with our frantic scribblings. . . .

In the middle of the next paragraph, the tone of voice begins to change

> We were alone before the hostile stars . . . alone with the stokers who sweat

[1] The two best sources on early Futurism are the contributions of Paolo Buzzi and Benedetta Marinetti to the special issue of *Cahiers d'Art* devoted to Italian painting (Paris, 1950), and Libero di Libera's '*Antologia Futurista*' in *Civiltà delle Macchine* (Rome, March 1954).

before the satanic furnaces of great ships, alone with the black phantoms who ferret in the red-hot bellies of locomotives as they hurtle forward at insensate speeds. . . .

and then the change of tone is gathered up into two powerfully contrasted poetic images

> We all started up, at the sound of a double-deck tram rumbling past, ablaze with multi-coloured lights, like a village in festival dress that the flooded Po tears from its banks and sweeps through gorges and rapids, down to the sea. But afterwards, the silence grew deeper, and we heard only the muttered devotions of the old canal and the creaking of the arthritic, ivy-bearded old palaces until —suddenly—we heard the roar of famished motor-cars beneath the windows.

These passages have a precise topographical location, which adds point to their superficial poetic meaning. The opening lines are not a pastiche of a decadent novel, but are a factual description of the interior of the Casa Marinetti, furnished with oriental bric-à-brac acquired by his parents during their stay in Alexandria (where Marinetti himself was born). The *Casa* stood in the via del Senato (it has since been pulled down) and backed on to the ancient *Naviglio* canal (an alleged work of Leonardo da Vinci, now abandoned) whose noise of waters was still a feature of the district, although it had ceased to be used for navigational purposes. The old palaces stood on its further bank. The tram would have passed down the via del Senato itself, and the contrast between an outmoded technology at the back of the house, and a new and visually stimulating one at the front must have made a very forcible impression on a person like Marinetti, already sensitive about the backward looking *borghese* culture of northern Italy and its contrast to the experimental and adventurous atmosphere of Paris, his other home.

The sense of the overriding of an old, tradition-bound technology, unchanged since the Renaissance, by a newer one without traditions was something which poets and philosophers of other European countries had already felt, and it had left its mark on their writings. The experience had in some cases been so gradual that, as in England, it had produced no cultural crisis (outside the 'Arts and Crafts' reaction) or had been preceded by other disturbances so radical—as in the case of France where the Encyclopedists had built much of the new technology into their work, and the Revolution had dominated other cultural changes—so radical that technology did not rank, of itself, as a major psychological impact.

But the scale of nineteenth-century technological developments had been both large, and remote. Apart from the introduction of gas-lighting, the appearance of the streets of most capital cities hardly altered between 1800 and 1880, after which the increasing use of buses and trams, and their subsequent mechanisation began to alter the urban pattern more rapidly. But the early growth of industry in the Black Country, for instance, made little difference to the daily, horse-drawn, flame-lit life of the English opinion-forming classes.

To a north-Italian, the impact was neither gradual nor remote, however. Though railways began to be built in Italy soon after 1850, they were in the centre or the south (Florence, Posilippo) and the large scale industrialisation of the north did not begin until after the *Risorgimento*.[2] Towns like Milan and Turin suddenly found themselves changed from princely or ducal capitals into subsidiaries of a revived Rome, but they also found themselves transformed into industrial centres. The existing aristocracy and intelligentsia of the north found its social foundations drastically altered (in contradistinction to the gradual shift of authority in, e.g. England) and the appearance of their towns dramatically altered at the same time—new tram replacing old canal. Furthermore these changes took place not in some remote province, but literally on the doorsteps of their ancestral palaces.

It was this manifest and radical change-over to a technological society which animated the whole of Futurist thought, and it was the sense of sudden change which, in all probability, enabled them to exploit more quickly than other European intellectuals the new experiences which they had in common with the poets and painters of Paris, London, New York, Brussels and Berlin. For the Prologue to the Manifesto continues

> We drew near to the snorting beasts and laid our hands on their burning breasts. Then I flung myself like a corpse on a bier across the seat of my machine, but sat up at once under the steering-wheel, poised like a guillotine blade against my stomach

and there follows a lengthy and highly-coloured description of an early-morning impromptu motor-race through the outer suburbs of Milan. The tone of this passage is very pro-automobile, and this is one of the earliest appreciations of the pleasures of motoring to appear in European literature. However, the pages that describe the car-race have a deeper significance than this. If the events described in the Prologue to the Manifesto took place in 1908, then they are events of a kind that could hardly have taken place ten years earlier—it is extremely doubtful if any group of young men in their twenties could have commanded, in 1898, a number of reliable automobiles at 5 a.m., and driven them themselves. The cultural importance of this situation is this: not only had the new technology invaded the street (trams, electric-lighting, lithographed posters) and the home (tele-

---

[2] At the time of the unification of Italy, the country's economy was primarily agrarian—and in 1910 it was still so. But the process of industrialisation in the north, which had begun with the introduction of steam power into textile factories in the 1860's was violently accelerated in the period of Futurism. Production of textiles trebled in the period between 1900 and 1912, the output of iron and steel rose from 300,000 metric tons to almost 1,000,000 metric tons in the same period, and other industries experienced comparable increases. At the same time, the creation of an automobile industry capable of producing machines that could hold their own in international competition gave industry a glow of psychological prestige that mere increase in quantity of established products could not have done.

phone, sewing machine, electric-lighting, fans, vacuum cleaners, etc.) but with the advent of the motor-car the poet, painter, intellectual, was no longer a passive recipient of technological experience, but could create it for himself. The command of vehicles of the order of 60 h.p. and upwards had hitherto been in the hands of professional specialists—engine drivers, ships' engineers and so forth. But the advent of the automobile brought such experiences and responsibilities within the scope of the rich amateur in the years immediately after 1900, and although experience of motoring was to leave its mark on much of the literature of the twentieth century no one was to treat it in so high and lyrical a strain as the Futurists, and none with so strong a sense of its being a new cultural factor, without poetic precedent. As Boccioni later phrased it[3]

> The era of the great mechanised individuals has begun, and all the rest is Palaeontology . . . therefore we claim to be the primitives of a sensibility that has been completely overhauled.

No such precise form of words appears in the Foundation Manifesto, but it is implied in at least one place where Marinetti interrupts the wild flow of automotive rhetoric to say

> Ours was no ideal love, lost in the soaring clouds, nor a cruel queen to whom we must offer our bodies contorted like Byzantine jewellery

and this, on the evidence of his later writings, is to be interpreted as a gibe at d'Annunzio, whose sensibility, the Futurists always claimed, had never been properly overhauled (though he too turned to automobilism in the next year). Any survival of nineteenth-century sensibility, whether symbolist or decadent, they regarded as improper to the changed situation of the new century, even though Marinetti himself was deeply indebted to such characteristic nineteenth-century figures as Whitman and Mallarmé for the growth of his own sensibility. Yet Whitman, whose work he knew in translation, could offer—as no European poet could at that time—a vision of a world of grandiose individuality, a world where machinery was an accepted part of life. Such a world was still, for a cultured European, an alien one, that could only be entered through a violent psychological change, such as Marinetti pantomimes at the end of the Prologue.

> . . . I swung the car round in its own length, like a mad dog trying to bite its own tail, and there, wobbling towards me were two cyclists, as confusing as two equally convincing arguments, right in my line of travel. I pulled up so short that the car, to my disgust, looped into the ditch and came to rest with its wheels in the air.
> O maternal ditch, brimming with muddy water—O factory drain! I gulped down your nourishing mud and remembered the black breasts of my Sudanese nurse. And yet, when I emerged, ragged and dripping from under the capsized car, I felt the hot iron of a delicious joy in my heart.

[3] In his preface to the catalogue of the first exhibition of Futurist painting in Paris, 1912.

This is clearly to be taken as a mimic baptism in Jordan, an initiation—from the ground up—into the experiences and mental categories of the alien world of mechanical sensibility, for immediately after it comes

> And so, face covered in good factory mud—plastered in swarf and slag, sweat and soot—bruised and in splints, but undaunted yet, we pronounce our fundamental will to all the live spirits of the world.

and then follow the tabulated propositions of the second section.

There are eleven of these propositions, declamatory in style, and not all of sufficient relevance to the present context to justify quotation at length. The first and second praise danger, energy, audacity, etc. the third contrasts the Futurist passion for movement and activity against 'Literature' (probably meaning d'Annunzio) which exalts repose, ecstasy and dreams. The fourth is the best known of all pieces of Futurist writing.

> 4. We declare that the splendour of the world has been enriched by a new beauty—the beauty of speed. A racing car with its bonnet draped with exhaust-pipes like fire-breathing serpents—a roaring racing car, rattling along like a machine gun, is more beautiful than the winged victory of Samothrace.

And this exaltation of the spectacle of turbulent, noisy motion above the contemplation of silent Classical repose, is followed by an exaltation of the dynamic experience of automobilism.

> 5. We will hymn the man at the steering wheel, whose ideal axis passes through the centre of the earth, whirling round on its orbit.

Succeeding propositions praise speed, announce the annihilation of space and time, and praise war as the cleanser of society (something for which later critics have never forgiven the Futurists, but which remains understandable when it is remembered that with Italian populations around the northern Adriatic still *Irredenti*, the *Risorgimento* remained a war that was still in progress for many Italian patriots)[4] as the cleanser of society from the adiposities of an unadventurous *borghese* peace, attacked also in the tenth proposition.

> 10. We will destroy all museums and libraries, and academies of all sorts; we will battle against moralism, feminism, and all vile opportunism and utilitarianism

This was a proposition on which he later had second thoughts, for while the hostility to academies and the past remained, feminism (of a sort) was later built into the Futurist programme as (*a*), the epitome of a new kind of unromantic woman, in opposition to d'Annunzio's heroines, and (*b*), as something which would break up liberal parliamentarism (and thus 'vile

---

[4] Many Futurist manifestations had political intentions—or at least acquired them—particularly in Trieste and Venice, where the sense of *Italia Irredenta* was, understandably, still highly inflamed. This strain in Futurist thought led, logically, to demands for intervention in the War, and less logically, though understandably given the dynamics of politics, to Futurist participation in Fascist uprisings after 1918.

opportunism and utilitarianism') as soon as women had the right to vote. The eleventh proposition concludes this sequence with an apotheosis of the urban and mechanised setting of Futurist life.

> 11. We will sing of the stirring of great crowds—workers, pleasure-seekers, rioters—and the confused sea of colour and sound as revolution sweeps through a modern metropolis. We will sing the midnight fervour of arsenals and ship-yards blazing with electric moons; insatiable stations swallowing the smoking serpents of their trains; factories hung from the clouds by the twisted threads of their smoke; bridges flashing like knives in the sun, giant gymnasts that leap over rivers; adventurous steamers that scent the horizon; deep-chested loco-motives that paw the ground with their wheels, like stallions harnessed with steel tubing; the easy flight of aeroplanes, their propellers beating the wind like banners, with a sound like the applause of a mighty crowd.

Though many of these images are derived from nineteenth-century sources (the locomotive, for instance, from Whitman and Huysmans,[5]) many could be nothing but new, particularly the aeroplane, since practic-able aircraft had existed in Europe only since 1906. But, in any case, such a concatenation of mechanistic images seems to be without precedent in European literature at the time, and the emphasis on motion and disorder is in strong contrast to the static and monumental aspects of engineering which seem to have been admired by German writers of the same period.[6] The third section of the Manifesto, which is in the nature of a personal apologia has little to add to the position already taken up—except to add a rather pathetic note on the youth of the Marinetti circle

> The oldest among us is only thirty, and we have therefore at least ten years in which to do our work

and to couple with it the first intimation of that sense of transience which was to become a regular motif in Futurist thought. A sense of transience in which the ageing of human beings is linked to the obsolescence of their technical equipment. Marinetti envisages a younger generation, more truly Futurist than his own that would find him, and his friends

> squatting fearfully by our aeroplanes . . . and all, exasperated by our daring, will rush to kill us, driven by hatred made more implacable by the extent to which their hearts are filled with love and admiration.

This is something more than the routine Romantic contempt for old men, just as the whole Manifesto is more than the provincial juvenilia which it is

---

[5] Huysman's enthusiasm for locomotives became a by-word and was still a subject for comment in the Twenties—Le Corbusier used it as a point of reference in a potted history of locomotives in *Urbanisme* (see chapter 18). For aircraft there was not, and could not be, any comparable tradition of enthusiasm. The first demonstrably successful European machine was the Voisin *Canard* flown by Santos Dumont in 1906 near Paris. However, any widespread eye-witness ex-perience of aircraft, such as Marinetti must have enjoyed in order to write a passage so conspicuously different from H. G. Wells's imaginative projections of aviation, must have waited on the Wright Brothers' European tour of 1908.

[6] See the opinions of Muthesius, Gropius and others quoted in chapter 5.

commonly made out to be. As will be seen, simply by being a young man, by being both a cosmopolitan intellectual by training and a provincial patriot by disposition, Marinetti was able to give a widespread feeling of disgust with the old and craving for the new, a positive orientation and a point of attachment in the world of fact; Marinetti ordered his generation into the street with his Manifestoes, in order to revolutionise their culture, just as the political Manifestoes from which he took over the literary form had ordered men into the street to revolutionise their politics.

9: Futurism: theory and development

THE ATTITUDE ADOPTED by Marinetti in the Foundation Manifesto was a poet's attitude, adopted for the benefit of other poets. Their response was direct and before three years had elapsed a characteristic type of Futurist lyric had appeared, written in short-lined *vers libre* revealing an overall debt to late nineteenth-century French poetry, and taking as its subject-matter *l'Elettricità* (Luciano Fulgore) *A un Aviatore* (Libero Altomare), *Il Canto della Città di Mannheim* (Paolo Buzzi), etc. The magazine *Poesia*, and Marinetti's associated publishing activities, became the main instruments of Futurist literary activity.

As early as 1909, however, there is a poem of Buzzi's dedicated to Umberto Boccioni, beginning

Érige les constructions massives pour la ville future
Qu'elle s'élève dans le ciel libre des aviateurs

which indicates that the *Poesia* circle were already in contact with practitioners of the plastic arts, and that at least one of the great Futurist themes, the City of Tomorrow,[1] was already in circulation. The memoirs of Signora Benedetta Marinetti state that in the same month as the publication of the Foundation Manifesto, Marinetti met Umberto Boccioni, Carlo Carrà, and Luigi Russolo, and later in the year Giacomo Balla. These four, with the addition of Gino Severini, constitute the main body of Futurist painters, and together they signed the *Manifesto of the Futurist Painters* (11 February 1910) and the *Technical Manifesto of Futurist Painting*, published in April of the same year, on the 'canonical' eleventh day (no fewer than eight of the Manifestoes were published on the eleventh of the month).

These two Manifestoes concerned with painting, and the later one on sculpture, are basic points of departure for all Futurist activity in the plastic arts. But they need to be taken in a complicated context which must include the continuing literary activity of Marinetti (some of which was not published in permanent form until after the two painting Manifestoes) and must also include developments in the painting of the School of Paris.

[1] As exemplified by Antonio Sant'Elia's projects *La Città Nuova* and *Milano 2000*; which are discussed in the next chapter.

However, there is a gap before this second context becomes fully effective, for in 1910 only Severini had actually been to Paris, and seen Fauve and Cubist painting at first hand. The February Manifesto is, in fact, almost purely literary, not to say political. The young artists of Italy are called upon to rebel against the senseless and snobbish cult of the past. Other nations treat Italy as a whited Pompeii of sepulchres, whereas, in fact Italy has been reborn; the political *Risorgimento* has been followed by an intellectual one, etc. etc. This is for the most part Marinettian, but the Manifesto does contain some new material, some of a primarily professional nature, some of more general aesthetic consequence. Thus

> Just as our ancestors found their inspiration in the world of religion which weighed upon their souls, so we must draw ours from the tangible miracles of contemporary life. . . .

indicating a rather subtle approach to the problem of the painters' inspiration, transferring it to the world of ideas, rather than visual facts.

The attack which follows on academic officialdom for not recognising the talents of Segantini, Previati and Medardo Rosso is more than the 'trade union' affair that it might appear. These men were the representatives of a Milanese tradition of Modernism of which the Futurists were the culmination, and Medardo Rosso was particularly important to them as an innovator in both iconography and method.

The one reference to architecture (which appears among the denunciations): *An end to Big Business architecture and reinforced concrete contractors*, is in direct contradiction to the later architectural policy of the Futurists and probably opposed to Marinetti's own views at that time. It suggests that Futurist painting did not yet exist in visible or material form, and that their theories existed only on paper, for, once they had found themselves as painters, materials like concrete, cardboard, etc. were soon in favour with them.

The Technical Manifesto of April was written in this same vacuum, but it is less rhetorical (the February Manifesto had been 'launched' at a quasi-political Futurist demonstration in Turin)[2] and penetrates far deeper into the basic mental orientations of its authors. It emphasises the dynamic against the static, the deformation and multiplication of visual images caused by retinal persistence. It emphasises that art is based upon conventions and that 'truths' are expendable, that space is (visually) merely one of these conventions, that X-rays have introduced new analogues of normal vision.

For practical confirmation of the destruction of traditional and static modes of vision, the Manifesto instances

---

[2] The celebrated meeting at the Politeama Chiarella, 9 February 1910, which later became a legend in Futurist circles since its more violent passages made excellent newspaper copy and thus established the movement in the public mind.

The sixteen people around you in a tram are successively one, ten, four, three. They hold still momentarily, but then they shift again, coming and going with the swaying and bouncing of the tram . . . persistent symbols of universal motion.

a passage which draws heavily upon Medardo Rosso, who had not only insisted on the transience of appearances

↗ We are all of us merely lighting effects[3]

but had, in physical fact, created precisely the visual image under discussion in his sculpture-group *Impressione d'Omnibus* (1884) where the figures seem to be undergoing precisely the same kind of dissolution in movement and flickering light as the Futurists had in mind.

Futurist paintings from this period are now extremely rare, having been destroyed or painted over, but a number of Boccionis from before 1911 have survived, and often show an attempt to translate back into painting the atmospheric style of sculpture which Medardo himself had derived from the paintings of the Impressionists. Medardo was passionately admired by Boccioni and provided a link back to a live Milanese Impressionist tradition, skipping the generation of Synthetists and Nabis in Paris, whose work he could only know about through Severini. This link with the Impressionist tradition is important because it is part of the anti-academic heritage which the Futurists were to pass on to later Modern-Movement theory, even though it was contradicted in so much of their practice.

For the Technical Manifesto still gives no directives as to what a Futurist painting should look like in material fact. Its tabulated propositions formulate a frame of mind only

WE PROCLAIM

1. That an inherent complementarity is as necessary to painting as *vers libre* to poetry or polyphony to music
2. That the universal dynamism must be rendered as dynamic sensation
3. That in the interpretation of nature there must be sincerity and chastity
4. That light and motion destroy the solidity of bodies

WE COMBAT

1. Patina and the obscurity of false antiques
2. Superficial archaism . . .
3. False Futurists, secessionists and independents, the new academics of every country.
4. The nude in painting, just as tiresome and depressing as adultery in literature.

It is interesting to observe that the positive propositions are their own (or Medardo's) while the negative ones, except no. 3, are essentially Marinetti's, the attack on the nude being an extension of the attack on the Dannunzian preoccupation with adultery ('d'Annunzio, toujours penché sur le corps nu d'une femme'). Negative proposition no. 3, however, is

[3] The most informative short study of Medardo Rosso in English is that by P. M. Fitzgerald in *World Review* (London, June 1951

rather remarkable for its date, for the general tendency of European *avant-garde* aesthetics at the time was to continue the academicising tendencies of the Nineties, as can be seen from the writings of Roger Fry,[4] or the Cubist circle in Paris. Even so truculent an anti-Secessionist as Adolf Loos remained a Classicist at heart,[5] and the Futurists seem to have been almost alone in seeing that Platonic and Classicising aesthetics were out of tune with their mechanolatry, or, indeed, any positive and fruitful accommodation to the new technology.

Before the next major Manifesto on the plastic arts appeared, however (that on Sculpture, over Boccioni's unsupported signature, 11 April 1912) the scope of Futurism had been broadened by further writings and lectures from Marinetti, and the painters had visited Paris. The whole aspect of the movement was altered. The visit to Paris was organised, and largely paid for, by Marinetti, but his own contacts in Paris (e.g. Gustave Kahn) were not of much direct value to the painters. Severini, however, could claim acquaintance with Braque, and through him the Futurists met Picasso and the rest of the Cubist circle. The situation of Cubism at this moment was extremely interesting. 1911, in retrospect, appears to be the year of culmination, in which the promise of Picasso's 'Girl with the Mandolin' (1910) was fully realised in the 'Portrait of Kahnweiler', the year of Braque's *'Le Portugais'*, in both of which formalised fragments of representational painting are splintered down into a shallow layer of space, whose depth is indicated without recourse to academic perspective. The contact with such painters and such paintings had a galvanic effect on the Futurists and uncertainty as to the appearance of their painting disappeared, they took over from the Cubists a repertoire, a *linguaggio*, of formal devices and surface treatments and turned them to their own ends.

That those ends were not those of Cubism needs to be emphasised at this point. Cubism stood at the end of a long reformist tradition that runs back through Cezanne towards Courbet; and Boccioni, at least, recognised this. Its aesthetics when they came to be written were traditionalist and academic, and in no way as revolutionary as those of Futurism—chiefly because Cubism was a revolution within painting itself, and not part of a profound reorientation towards a changed world.[6] Nevertheless, the for-

[4] For these tendencies in Roger Fry see his *'Essay on Aesthetics'* in *Vision and Design* (London, 1923) and for the Cubists see the works discussed in chapter 15.

[5] The Classical streak appears not only in his writings, which are discussed in chapter 7, but also in the persistent use he made of such motifs as the Doric column; the Goldmann and Salatsch store in Vienna (1910) which, like Peter Behrens's Mannesmann office block, uses Doric to mark the entrance, and his entry for the Chicago *Tribune* Tower competition employing a Greek Doric column, magnified to a giant scale, to give the form of the whole upper part of the block, with the windows let into the flutings!

[6] In Boccioni's preface to the catalogue of the first Paris exhibition he asserts, 'If our pictures are Futurist, it is because they represent the result of conceptions of ethics, aesthetics, politics and sociology that are absolutely Futurist!'

mal and superficial resemblances in the paintings, coupled with certain literary resemblances between Apollinaire's writings and those of the Futurists, have led to a belief that Futurism was derived from Cubism. In fact, Apollinaire's book *Les Peintres Cubistes* did not appear until 1913 and had been anticipated by Futurist Manifestoes on painting, sculpture, literature and music, as well as in prefaces to the catalogues of Futurist exhibitions in Paris (1912, 1913) while, as will appear from what has been said above, Futurist interest in the dissolution of bodies antedates their encounter with Cubism by over a year. Their interest in the dismemberment of forms was their own; it was a method for doing it which they picked up in Paris. Their interest in bodies in motion was their own, it was a convention for representing motion which they learned from the Cubists.

The Cubists from whom they acquired this device were the *Groupe de Puteaux*, a group centring round the Duchamp family, on the fringe of the Picasso/Braque circle. The Puteaux group[7] were to make more than one contribution to the development of modern design, and what they could offer to the Futurists at this point was an intellectual and diagrammatic approach to painting, rather than the intuitive and quasi-representational approach of Braque or Picasso. In Marcel Duchamp's 'Coffee Mill' (an occasional work undertaken as a wedding present for his brother) of early 1911 they would be able to see[8] not only a machine 'dismantled' in order to show its functions, but also a convention for showing the different successive positions of the crank as turned. This work was probably done under the influence of the early Futurist Manifestoes, but that does not alter the fact that the Futurists themselves had not yet arrived at any such set of conventions for either motion or the dissolution of forms.

The influence of the Paris visit was apparent in their work immediately on their return to Milan, successive-state representation of motion soon appears in the work of Balla (e.g. the celebrated 'Dog on a Leash' of 1912) but it was upon Boccioni that the impact was greatest.

He had put in hand, shortly before the departure for Paris, a series of three paintings entitled *Stato d'Animo*: 'The Farewells', 'Those who Go', 'Those who Stay'. The earliest sketches for these are almost completely abstract fields of waving, hurrying, or loitering forms. All were drastically reworked on his return, and the abstract fields were filled with broken, superimposed, and transparent elements of engines and rolling stock, carriages and faces, hats, macintoshes and buildings. The pictorial conventions employed in creating these elements are an intelligent and original blend of the methods of Duchamp and those of Braque—systematically geometrical in construction but richly dappled and textured as to the actual paint

[7] On the subject of the *Groupe de Puteaux* see chapter 15.
[8] Duchamp, himself, does not believe there can have been any influence from this painting, and modestly proposes photographic motion studies as a common source.

surface. The first of these paintings ('The Farewells') also contains elements of typography, used as part of the planimetric composition of the picture. Such a usage, which lies at the root of much typographical reform later in the century, and also paved the way for the reintegration of typography into architectural composition, is generally regarded as a Cubist invention of 1911 (Braque: '*Le Portugais*'), but if so Boccioni may have arrived at it in the same months, for one late drawing for 'The Farewells' in which typographical elements occur, seems datable to 1911, not 1912. Though this could still be a borrowing from Braque, of course, it should be further noted that the person close to Boccioni who was most interested in typography was Marinetti, who had acquired from his contacts with Mallarmé an interest in free, varied and open page-composition,[9] in which words and even letters were treated as elements in an abstract design. Although Marinetti's *Les Mots en Liberté* was not published until 1919, the word *Motlibriste* was in Futurist circulation before 1914, and Boccioni refers to *parole in libertà* early in 1912.

It is in connection with Boccioni's sculptural activities of 1912 that the growing fusion between Parisian practice and Milanese theory is most clearly manifested. One of his best-known works in sculpture, '*Sviluppo d'una Bottiglia nello Spazio*' dates from that year. It is a still-life subject, something which he had not attempted before Paris, but a drawing connected with this work shows more radical changes than merely a new subject-matter.

The fundamental method of this sketch, both in terms of composition and study of the object depends upon a rotation of the bottle about in its own axis, while observing it from different heights. In a remote sense, such a method had been accidently employed by Cézanne, intuitively by Picasso. But here it is systematically employed and fully exploited. The bottle is resolved into a series of sweeping convex-concave forms which interpenetrate those of a glass standing beside it. There is a powerful plastic sense of them being bodies of rotation, which is quite contrary to the flattening tendencies of Cubism at that date, even though both the drawing technique and the method of geometrical sectioning probably go back to *École de Puteaux* sources. But even more remarkable is the treatment of the table-top. Where, in Cézanne or Picasso the multiplication of table-tops due to the changing viewpoint is disguised or ignored, it is here given full value as part of the image. Three main table-top planes are defined, almost parallel to one another, and their boundaries cross and

[9] On the subject of the origins of Futurist typography see Carlo Martini, '*Mallarmé-Marinetti-Gide*' in *Idea* (Rome, 17 May 1953) and Renato Mucci, '*Mallarmé Pubblicista*' in *Civiltà delle Macchine* (Rome, November 1954). In this connection it is interesting to note that Michel Seuphor has suggested that it may have been Marinetti who introduced the idea of the calligram, or figurate poem, into the circle of Apollinaire, and this could have triggered the Cubists' interest in typography.

override one another at the corners. Since these effects are created within a more or less conventional perspective we are presented with a spatial experience analogous to the Prairie House architecture of Wright, or the work of architects under *de Stijl* influence in the early Twenties.[10]

Boccioni's *Technical Manifesto of Futurist Sculpture* appeared in April 1912; it was entirely his own responsibility, and since the actual turn of phrase is not particularly Marinettian, probably entirely his own work. The first section is a routine rhetorical denunciation of the past and un-originality. In the second section however it justifies the word technical far more fully than does the painting Manifesto, since after Paris he now knew what the result should look like.

> We must begin from the central nucleus of an object as it strives for realisation, in order to discover the new laws, that is, the new forms, that relate it invisibly but mathematically to the plastic infinity within, and visible plastic infinity with-out. The new plasticity will thus be the translation into plaster, bronze, glass, wood, or any plother material, of the atmospheric planes that unite and intersect visible objects. . . . Thus sculpture must bring objects to life by rendering apprehensible, plastic and systematic their prolongations into space, since it cannot be doubted any longer that one object finishes where another begins, and that there is not an object around us—bottle, automobile, tree, house or street—that does not cut and section us with some arabesque of curved or straight lines.

The drawing discussed above is, of course, a more or less programmatic demonstration of this field theory of aesthetic space, a space which exists as a field of force or influence radiating from the geometrical centre of the objects which give rise to it, and is a remarkable poetic achievement born, presumably, of Bergson and Einstein.[11]

The third section compares Rodin, Bourdelle, and Meunier unfavourably to Medardo Rosso, who is apotheosised (correctly) as the father of 'atmos-

---

[10] Most obviously, the overlapping planes of the Robie House of 1909. Possible influence from Wright on Boccioni can be discounted, in spite of his wide reading and interests. In the case of Sant'Elia, discussed in the next chapter, the possibility cannot be so easily dismissed.

[11] Bergson was widely discussed at the time: in the circle of the magazine *Poesia*, in the Apollinaire circle (on this see Christopher Gray's *Cubist Aesthetic Theories* once more) and by the Vorticists in England. The situation with Einstein is less clear: ideas marginal to the theories of relativity were certainly current in Cubist circles, and Gleizes refers confusedly to Reimannian geometry in *du Cubisme*, and Apollinaire, in a much-quoted and over-rated passage of his *Peintres Cubistes* refers to *la quatrième dimension* as a piece of established studio jargon by 1912. Although doubt has been cast on the ability of the Cubists to know about such matters, it is clear that the Braque-Picasso circle picked up a certain amount of mathematical gossip from the actuary Maurice Princet (see chapter 15) while the interests of the Puteaux group were notoriously mathematical and philosophical. Boccioni appears to have picked up some of his interests in these quarters but seems to have an independent source as well, since he later became very critical of Apollinaire's views on the fourth dimension. Lumping Cubists and Futurists together for the purpose of argument, however, it would appear that Giedion's proposition that resemblances between the painting of the period and Einsteinian ideas are simply 'a temporal coincidence' should be treated with some reserve—the possibility of consciously 'Relativistic' art cannot be ruled out.

34. Medardo Rosso. *Impressione d'Omnibus*, 1884: a pioneer work in the observation of mechanised life by the father of Milanese Modernism.
35. Georges Braque. *Le Portugais*, 1911: one of the works by which Cubism may be defined, with its highly fragmented simultaneous vision of scattered aspects of the visual scene.

36. Pablo Picasso. Portrait of
D-H. Kahnweiler, 1911:
another canonical Cubist
work of the kind that assisted
the Futurists in the creation of
their characteristic mode of
vision.

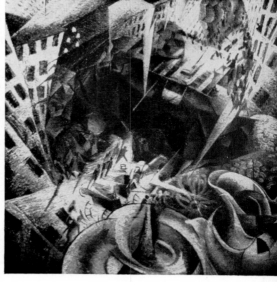

37 (left). Marcel Duchamp. The Coffee
Mill, 1911: much closer to Futurist ideas
than any comparable Parisian work of the
period, it analyses the workings of the
machine, the rotation of its parts.
38. Umberto Boccioni. *La Strada entra
nella casa*, 1911: an early realisation of the
Futurist concept of the city as a field of
interacting powers and influences.

39. Umberto Boccioni. *Stati
d'Animo II, Quelli chi vanno,
1912*: the second panel of a
triptych expressing the
emotions felt in a railway
terminal; here, departure.
40. Umberto Boccioni.
Composition sketch for *Stati
d'Animo I, Gli Adii*: once in
the Walden collection, this
version of 'The Farewells'
played a part in making
Futurist interests in
typography known outside
Italy.

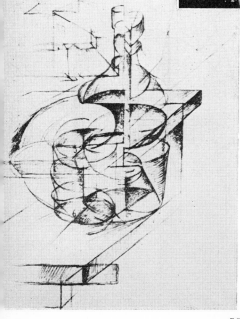

41. Umberto Boccioni.
*Bottiglia + Tavola
+ Caseggiata*, 1912: a sketch
connected with the sculpture
Bottle evolving in Space,
combining the concepts of
moving viewpoint and field
theory of space.

42. Antonio Sant'Elia.
Stazione Aeroplani, 1912: one
of the sequence of sketches
deriving from the problem of
rebuilding Milan Central
Station: multi-level planning
and an aircraft landing strip
are already present.

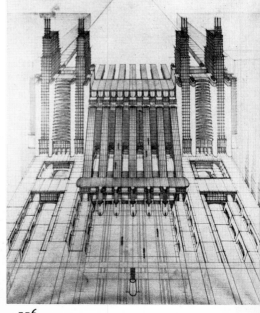

43. Antonio Sant'Elia.
Central Station of the *Città
Nuova*, 1913–1914: derived in
its turn from the above, but
with far greater formal and
mechanical definition, this was
one of the carefully rendered
drawings of a new city (*Milano
2000*) exhibited in 1914.

116

44, 45. Antonio Sant'Elia.
Projects for an airship hangar
and electric generating station,
both 1913. In sketches such
as these Sant'Elia gave almost
'Werkbund Expressionist'
form to the Futurists'
admiration for certain types of
industrial buildings.

46. Antonio Sant'Elia. *Casa a Gradinate*, 1914: one of the *Città Nuova* projects, this drawing of a stepped-back block of flats with illuminated skyline advertising became one of the best known of Sant'Elia's designs outside Italy. 47, 48. Antonio Sant'Elia. Projects for a lighthouse and an electric generating station, 1913. Some of Sant'Elia's drawings reveal an undecorated and geometrically pure mode of design that seems to anticipate the architecture of the 1930's.

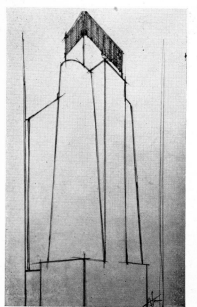

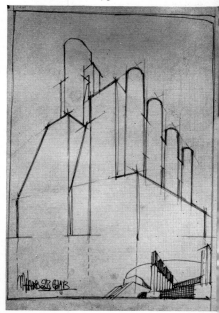

49. Antonio Sant'Elia. *La Città Nuova*, 1914: the most
fully worked out of all the perspectives of Sant'Elia's
new city, bringing together skyscraper towers and
multi-level circulation in an image that has dominated
modern ideas of town-planning right down to the
present time.

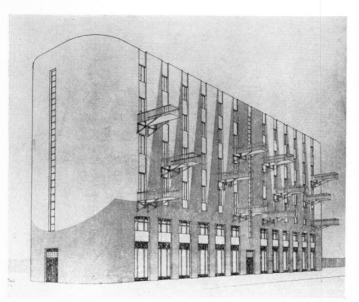

50. Mario Chiattone.
Project for a block of
flats, 1914. Chiattone
Sant'Elia's associate
1914–1915, produced
number of projects fo
apartment-blocks tha
were known and—in
case of this one—som
what influential in
northern Europe.
51. Mario Chiattone
Project for a block of
flats, 1914: one of the
most prophetic of
Futurist drawings—
detail at least, though
the remarkable use o
colour-wash has not
been imitated.

pheric' sculpture, and of 'unheroic' sculptural subjects. However, Medardo is criticised for remaining pictorial in inspiration, and for not developing in the direction of '*lo stile del movimento*'. This style, by systematising the vibrations of light and the interpenetration of planes

> . . . will produce Futurist sculpture, whose basis is architectonic, not only as a construction of masses, but also because the sculptural block will contain within itself architectonic elements from the sculptural environment in which the object exists.

This idea is clearly a development from the previous quotation, and it was to lead in Sant'Elia's work to a remarkable redefinition of the man/building relationship, but for Boccioni it was to have only the crudest consequences.

> Thus, from the armpit of a mechanic there could protrude a gearwheel, the line of a table could slice through the head of a man reading, and the fanned pages of the book could section his stomach.

Though at a more theoretical and metaphysical level this idea clearly anticipates, again, developments of the Twenties

> . . . we proclaim the absolute and complete abolition of determined lines and closed statues. We split open the figure and include the environment within it

anticipating the breakdown of the barriers between inside and out which is to be seen in the architecture of 1927–33, and there follows (from a discussion of the concept *lines-of-force*) a further, and rather subtle, prevision of the aesthetics of the Twenties

> For us, the straight line will be alive and palpitating; will lend itself to all the expressive necessities of our material, and its basic bare severity will be a symbol of the metallic severity of the lines of modern machinery

in which the subtlety lies in seeing that the straight line would be symbolic of, and not inherent in, mechanical design.

Two other points from this Manifesto deserve to be noted here. The adumbration of kinetic sculpture, hardly surprising in this context

> a source of power capable of giving a rhythmic movement properly related to its planes and lines

and a call for the extension of the range of the sculptor's materials, which appears among the tabulated propositions at the end of the Manifesto. One sees Boccioni here in one of his most influential roles, as a codifier and systematiser of *ad hoc* Cubist practices, and their inclusion within the body of Futurist theory, even before they had been systematised and included within Cubist theory.

> 4. Destroy the purely literary and traditional nobility of bronze and marble. Deny that any one material should be used exclusively for the whole of a sculptural construction. Affirm that even twenty different materials can join in one work to increase the scope of its plastic emotion. We enumerate some: glass, wood, iron, cement, hair, leather, cloth, electric light, etc.

This list, in which it will be observed that concrete makes its return, is an intelligent extension of the principles of Cubist *papiers collés*, composed of various different materials, invented by Braque in 1911. It is also positive and mandatory in its tone, whereas Apollinaire's reference to collage in *Les Peintres Cubistes*, which did not appear until more than a year later, is merely permissive (if that)

> I have not one prejudice with regard to the painter's materials

In the same year as the sculpture Manifesto, the general theory of Futurism was carried forward and broadened by Marinetti, who published a book composed of stray pieces, lectures, etc. which he welded into a roughly continuous rhetorical exposition of his position under the title of *Le Futurisme*, which seems to exist only in the French version, and was thus clearly intended for international rather than Italian circulation.

A great deal of what is in this book contradicts widely-held beliefs about Futurism, and brings it nearer to the accepted canons of Puritanism, Humanitarianism, etc. on which mainstream Modern design is supposed to rest. Marinetti proclaims that the Futurists are against Anarchism (this is another aspect of dissociation from the immediate Symbolist past) and against Nietzsche, whose Supermen are dismissed as an antiquarian Grecian dream. Against eternal permanent values (also anti-Symbolist)

> We who insist that a masterpiece must be burned with the corpse of its author ... against the conception of the immortal and imperishable we set up the art of the becoming, the perishable, the transitory and the expendable

a theme which was to be passed on to the architectural theories of the Twenties.[12]

Equally contrary to what is commonly supposed to be the Futurist frame of mind is the curious streak of puritanism which runs through this work. Marinetti declares himself opposed to 'clair de lune', 'Femme-Beauté idéal et fatale', Luxury, adultery, incest, the sense of sin as subjects for literature. Though this occurs in a passage specifically aimed at d'Annunzio 'frère cadet des grands Symbolistes Français', the theme of an anti-romantic attitude to woman appears elsewhere in this book, equality of the sexes is urged, the Suffragettes are encouraged (though for the reason cited *supra*), and poets are denounced in almost Platonic terms for keeping alive the enervating myth of romantic love.

The alternative is to be the beauty of the machine, and the love of a machine that may be seen reddening the cheeks of mechanics

> You may have noticed in the last great railway strike in France that the Sabotage Committees could not persuade a single mechanic to put his locomotive out of action.
> I find this natural enough. How could a man kill so faithful and devoted a friend?

---

[12] In his books of the early Twenties Le Corbusier was much concerned with the problem of scrapping and the impermanence (aesthetic and otherwise) of engineering structures (see chapters 17 and 18).

and a note of mechanistic irrationality is allowed to creep in

> You have doubtless heard the observations currently made by motorists and factory directors—Motors are truly mysterious, they say. It is as if they had personalities, minds, souls. You have to humour them . . . and then, suddenly, this machine of cast steel, made after the most precise calculations, will unexpectedly produce not merely its designed output but twice, three times as much.

but this, in fact, paves the way for an observation that mechanics are not as other men are, and seem equipped with alternative sets of sensibilities and values.

> . . . One finds today, with increasing ease, men of the people without culture or education, who are nevertheless endowed already with what I call the gift of mechanical prophecy, or the flair for metals. They are workmen who have already undergone the education of the machine, and in some way are affiliated to machinery.

This is one of the first appearances of the idea of the engineer as a form of noble savage, which also appears in Loos and reappears in the writings of Le Corbusier,[13] but does not seem to be, in Marinetti's mind, the same concept as 'l'homme multiplié par le moteur', who also appears in this book and seems rather to be a species of educated dilettante who makes maximum use of the technological and mechanical extensions of his experience which the twentieth century offers, one of Boccioni's 'great mechanised individuals'. Besides this reinforcement of the Futurist orientation towards technology and technologists, *Le Futurisme* also introduces three themes of prime importance to the development of modern design: opposition to handicraft, the un-monumental architecture of democracy, and the power-station as an apotheosis of technology.

Whereas Adolf Loos's opposition to handicraft was an immediate reaction to the excesses of Sezessionist Art Nouveau in Vienna, Marinetti's objections go back to the theoretical sources of the Arts and Crafts Movement, to Ruskin. The reasons for this are, essentially, of an occasional nature—his lecture to the Lyceum Club in March 1912, for which he needed a figure to symbolise English *Passéisme*

> When, then, will you disencumber yourselves of the lymphatic ideology of your deplorable Ruskin, whom I intend to make utterly ridiculous in your eyes. . . .
> With his sick dream of a primitive pastoral life; with his nostalgia for Homeric cheeses and legendary spinning-wheels; with his hatred of the machine, of steam and electricity, this maniac for antique simplicity resembles a man who in full maturity wants to sleep in his cot again and drink at the breasts of a nurse who has now grown old, in order to regain the carefree state of infancy

and this is followed by an attack on English supporters of the brick-for-brick rebuilding of the campanile at Venice, and general abuse for the

---

[13] In *Vers une Architecture* Le Corbusier wrote an extraordinary eulogy of engineers as 'healthy and virile, active and useful, balanced and happy', as if they were the uncorrupted aborigines of an imaginary land dreamed up by an early nineteenth-century Romantic (see chapter 17).

English for giving all their attention to Rome, Venice and Florence—
'which we consider running sores on the face of the Peninsula'—and not
to Genoa, Turin and Milan, the cities of the 'new renascent Italy that we
love'.

The architecture of mechanised democracy, as envisaged by Marinetti,
also makes a strong contrast with Loos's views—at least as far as the democracy is concerned, for, whereas Loos, in *Das Andere*,[14] eulogises a simple
Jeffersonian frontier democracy where top hats and frock-coats need not
be worn, Marinetti is talking about big-city democracy of the mob and the
trade union.

> And besides, I reply to you that a life of cosmopolitan travel, the spirit of de-
> mocracy and the decay of religions have made completely useless the vast
> permanent and ornate buildings that once used to express royal authority, theo-
> cracy and mysticism.
> The contradictory forces of the banks, the leaders of fashion, revolutionary
> syndicates, metallurgists, engineers, electricians and aviators, the right to
> strike, equality before the law, the authority of numbers, the usurping power
> of the mob, the speed of international communications and the habits of hygiene
> and comfort, demand instead large well-ventilated apartment houses, railways
> of absolute reliability, tunnels, iron bridges, vast high-speed liners, hillside
> villas open to the breeze and view, immense meeting halls and bathrooms
> designed for the rapid daily care of the body.
> Aesthetics, responding directly to utility, have nothing to do nowadays with
> royal palaces of imposing line and granite basement . . . we oppose them with
> a fully mastered and definitive Futurist aesthetic of giant locomotives, spiral
> tunnels, Ironclads, torpedo boats, Antoinette monoplanes and racing cars

These three paragraphs contain, in miniature, the arguments and contrasts
of the theories of the Twenties. Classical architecture contrasted against
engineering products, buildings equated with railways and bridges—seen,
that is, as equipment; and three main building types identified, outside of
the field of transport and communications: large, well-ventilated low-
rental blocks, suburban villas sited for view and breeze, halls of assembly.
These were to be the dominating architectural themes of Le Corbusier; the
most striking difference between this passage and similar writing after the
Great War, however, is the absence of social conscience—Marinetti sees
this range of better equipment not as the transcendental social right of
democratic man, but as things that must be given to a politically conscious
and active working class. Here is realism bordering on a cynicism that
could become Fascist.

The theme of the power-station is one that was peculiarly Marinetti's
own. Widely distributed in Modern Movement rhetoric after the War, it
seems to be found in his writings alone, before 1914. It occurs in *Le
Futurisme* at the end of a highly emotive passage in which Marinetti has
envied the men of the Two-thousands, who will live in an Italy

> . . . entirely revivified, shaken and tamed by new electrical energies

[14] A periodical pamphlet on manners and morals published by Loos in the first
years of the century and anthologised in *Trotzdem*.

whose power, derived from the harnessing of the sea, will be controlled by a kind of technocracy of engineers who

> ... live in high tension chambers where a hundred-thousand volts flicker through great bays of glass. They sit at control panels with meters, switches, rheostats and commutators to right and left, and everywhere the rich gleam of polished levers. These men enjoy, in short, a life of power between walls of iron and crystal; they have furniture of steel, twenty times lighter and cheaper than ours. They are free at last from the examples of fragility and softness offered by wood and fabrics with their rural ornaments. ... Heat, humidity and ventilation regulated by a brief pass of the hand, they feel the fullness and solidity of their own will. ...

The tone of voice is that of science-fiction, and fairly clear debts to Jules Verne can be seen, but this is science-fiction of the rare type that comes true in detail. Power-stations are uncommonly like this nowadays and the passage has, anyhow, the singing tones of prophecy. It fixes a vision of a smart, glittering, businesslike technological life, and a corresponding architecture, which was to haunt the imagination of the next generation.

Two years later, Marinetti returned to this theme in his *Manifesto of Geometrical and Mechanical Splendour, and the Sensibility of Numbers* (March 1914), but with a difference

> Nothing is more beautiful than a great humming power-station, holding back the hydraulic pressures of a whole mountain range, and the electric power for a whole landscape, synthesised in control-panels bristling with levers and gleaming commutators

The science-fiction quality is missing; apart from the control-panel, the point of human contact, the qualities of the image are now an abstract immensity, pressures and powers, *bourdonnante* has a low-toned and suppressed quality about it which is rare among Marinetti's epithets of praise.

This more restrained and adult view of technology seems to have been part of a change which was coming over Futurism as a whole. The more abstract vision here proposed can be paralleled by the increasing abstraction of the paintings of Balla through 1912 and 1913. The tone of other parts of the *Manifesto of Geometrical and Mechanical Splendour* is dry and tough, rather than rhetorical. This splendour is compounded of (besides the usual Futurist ingredients like speed and the city)

> ... harnessed power ... order, discipline, method ... the aggressive optimism that comes from physical culture and sport ... the ubiquity, laconic tone and simultaneity that characterise tourism, big business and journalism ... conciseness ... harmonious precision.

These qualities were perceived for the first time, according to Marinetti, and their mechanical splendour, in a thoroughly Futurist place—on the bridge of a dreadnought, but though the source of inspiration was much as it had ever been, the qualities deduced were not those that he would have noted in 1909. If these qualities can be categorised, they are abstract, intellectual—and French (*ordre, discipline, méthode*).

The continuous contact with Paris, never broken after 1911, and reinforced by the temporary absorption of the Florentine Cubist group and their magazine *La Voce*, after 1912, had undoubtedly modified Futurist sensibilities. Their enthusiastic acceptance of machinery and urban life remained untouched, but their view of the proper artistic consequences of their social orientation had undoubtedly altered. Boccioni's preference expressed for straight lines (mentioned *supra*) probably marks the beginning of the change, and his painting, toward the end of 1914 was becoming increasingly Parisian, until in 1915 and 1916 (the year in which he died) he was painting, in all but colour, imitations of Cézanne.

The Cubists had not gone untouched either. The Orphic faction of Delaunay was largely Futurist in inspiration and the qualities attributed to it by Apollinaire were, in fact, slightly altered quotations from Boccioni. The Futurist magazine *Lacerbá*[15] circulated in Cubist circles and appears in two Picasso still lifes. Under pressure from Boccioni. Apollinaire 'turned Futurist' and wrote a Manifesto, *L'Antitradition Futuriste*, which was distributed as a broadside in Paris (June 1913). Futurism, oriented toward the world of machinery and technology, and Cubism, regarded by Apollinaire as a pure geometrical construct of the mind, were drawing very close together, and, by the beginning of 1914 it was time to realise the mechanistic inspiration of Futurism in terms of the pure geometrical forms towards which Parisian art was tending. The achievement was Sant'Elia's, and the product was Futurist architecture.

[15] *Lacerbá* was—effectively—*La Voce* modified to serve the interests of both the Florentine group and Marinetti's circle. This happy consummation was only achieved at the expense of vociferous arguments, a pitched battle with café tables and chairs, and much backstage manoeuvring. Nevertheless, Marinetti's view that Italy was not big enough for two *avant-gardes* was accepted in the end, and the uneasy alliance lasted till just after the beginning of the War, when it quietly fell apart.

10: Sant'Elia and Futurist architecture

THE APPLICATION OF the term 'Futurist' to the opinions and designs of Antonio Sant'Elia has been contested with legalistic enthusiasm by Italian scholars since 1955, but only on biographical grounds, not in terms of the ideas involved. The biographical facts[1] are not in doubt and may be briefly stated. Sant'Elia was born in Como in 1888, and was thus a little younger than the masters of the Twenties. His studies, first in Milan, and later at the University of Bologna, were interrupted by a period of apprenticeship to the Villoresi Canal Company, and of service in the works department of the commune of Milan. On his return from Bologna to Milan in 1912 he set up as an architect, but most of his time seems to have been taken up in work for other offices, and no buildings designed under his own name appear to survive with any certainty.

Sartoris has stated that Sant'Elia was in touch with the Futurists from the time of his return, and this has not been questioned in the recent polemics. In 1912, 1913 and 1914 he made a number (possibly several hundred) of imaginative drawings of buildings and town-planning ideas, and a group of these under the title of the *Città Nuova* were shown at an exhibition of the group *Nuove Tendenze* in May 1914. In the catalogue of this exhibition there appeared, over Sant'Elia's name, a *Messaggio* on the problems of Modern architecture: and a reworked version of this *Messaggio* appeared on the canonical eleventh day of July 1914, as the Manifesto of Futurist architecture, still over the name of Sant'Elia, and without other signatories. After the outbreak of War, Sant'Elia, like Marinetti and Boccioni volunteered for the Army, even before Italy entered the fighting. Eventually he died a hero's death in the battle of Monfalcone in October 1916, two months after Boccioni. His name and reputation were nurtured with unusual care by Marinetti, who, for instance, brought his work to the attention of the Dutch *de Stijl* group in 1917, but it is this Marinettian connection that seems to have provoked the recent attempts to diminish the

[1] See the biographical memoir at the beginning of Alberto Sartoris's book *L'Architetto Antonio Sant'Elia*.

importance, even to deny the existence, of Sant'Elia's Futurist affiliations.[2]

The argument hinges upon the differences between the texts of the *Messaggio* and the Manifesto. Neither now appears to have been actually written by Sant'Elia himself, even the *Messaggio* having been worked up, apparently, by Ugo Nebbia from ideas expounded to him by the architect 'alle quali perfettamente aderivo'.[3] If Nebbia's word is to be trusted—and even the anti-Marinettians appear to trust it—then a scrutiny of the text of the *Messaggio* should not only give a fair view of the ideas that were indisputably Sant'Elia's own, but also make it possible to evaluate their relationship to Futurism, without any suspicion of Marinetti's interference, such as exists with the Manifesto. The text[4] of the *Messaggio* reads in its entirety

> The problem of Modern architecture is not a problem of rearranging its lines; not a question of finding new mouldings, new architraves for doors and windows; nor of replacing columns, pilasters and corbels with caryatides, hornets and frogs; not a question of leaving a façade bare brick or facing it with stone or plaster; in a word, it has nothing to do with defining formalistic differences between the new buildings and old ones. But to raise the new-built structure on a sane plan, gleaning every benefit of science and technology, settling nobly every demand of our habits and our spirits, rejecting all that is heavy, grotesque and unsympathetic to us (tradition, style, aesthetics, proportion), establishing new forms, new lines, new reasons for existence, solely out of the special conditions of Modern living, and its projection as aesthetic value in our sensibilities.
> Such an architecture cannot be subject to any law of historical continuity. It must be as new as our state of mind is new, and the contingencies of our moment in history.
> The art of building has been able to evolve through time and pass from style to style while maintaining the general character of architecture unchanged, because in history there have been numerous changes of taste brought on by shifts of religious conviction or the successions of political regimes, but few occasioned by profound changes in our conditions of life, changes that discard or overhaul the old conditions, as have the discovery of natural laws, the perfection of technical methods, the rational and scientific use of materials.
> In modern life, the process of consequential stylistic development comes to a halt. Architecture, exhausted by tradition, begins again, forcibly, from the beginning.
> [continued on facing page]

[2] The leader in anti-Marinettian polemics has been Giovanni Bernasconi, in the pages of *Rivista Tecnica*, a magazine published in Lugano of which he was editor. He has been able to draw on the eye-witness accounts of Mario Chiattone, up till the time of the latter's death in 1957. The argument depends chiefly on the niceties of interpretation of remembered conversations, and the differences between the texts of the Messaggio and the Manifesto (see below). It does not, however, involve any confrontation of the ideas that were indisputably Sant'Elia's with those current among the Futurists. Such a confrontation gives a different picture, as will be seen later in the present chapter, to that put forward by those who maintain, usually for commendable political reasons, that Sant'Elia never was a Futurist. For the moment, it appears that Bernasconi has carried his point in Italy, and his view is accepted by, for instance, Bruno Zevi and Giulia Veronesi.

[3] Nebbia has given his version of the writing of the *Messaggio* in a letter to *L'Espresso* (Rome, 9 December 1956).

[4] This is the text established by Bernasconi—to whom thanks are due, whatever his opinions—in *Rivista Tecnica* (Lugano, 1956, No. 7) and subsequently issued by him as a separate pamphlet.

Calculations of the resistance of materials, the use of reinforced concrete and iron, exclude 'Architecture' as understood in the Classical and traditional sense. Modern structural materials and our scientific concepts absolutely do not lend themselves to the disciplines of the historical styles, and are the chief cause of the grotesque aspect of modish constructions where we see the lightness and proud slenderness of girders, the slightness of reinforced concrete, bent to the heavy curve of the arch, aping the stolidity of marble.

The formidable antithesis between the modern world and the old is determined by everything that was not there to begin with. Into our lives have entered elements whose very possibility the ancients could not have suspected; material contingencies have crystallised, spiritual attitudes have arisen, with thousand-fold repercussions: first, the formation of a new ideal of beauty, embryonic still and obscure, but already stirring the masses with its fascination. We have lost the sense of the monumental, the massive, the static, and we have enriched our sensibilities with a taste for the light and the practical. We no longer feel ourselves to be the men of the cathedrals and ancient moot halls, but men of the Grand Hotels, railway stations, giant roads, colossal harbours, covered markets, glittering arcades, reconstruction areas and salutary slum clearances.

We must invent and rebuild *ex novo* our Modern city like an immense and tumultuous shipyard, active, mobile and everywhere dynamic, and the modern building like a gigantic machine. Lifts must no longer hide away like solitary worms in the stairwells, but the stairs—now useless—must be abolished, and the lifts must swarm up the façades like serpents of glass and iron. The house of cement, iron, and glass, without carved or painted ornament, rich only in the inherent beauty of its lines and modelling, extraordinarily brutish in its mechanical simplicity, as big as need dictates, and not merely as zoning rules permit, must rise from the brink of a tumultuous abyss; the street which, itself, will no longer lie like a doormat at the level of the thresholds, but plunge storeys deep into the earth, gathering up the traffic of the metropolis connected for necessary transfers to metal cat-walks and high-speed conveyor belts.

For these reasons I insist that we must abolish the monumental and the decorative; that we must resolve the problem of Modern architecture without cribbing photographs of China, Persia or Japan, nor stultifying ourselves with Vitruvian rules, but with strokes of genius, equipped only with a scientific and technological culture; that everything must be revolutionised; that we must exploit our roofs and put our basements to work; depreciate the importance of façades; transfer questions of taste out of the field of petty mouldings, fiddling capitals and insignificant porticos, into the vaster field of the grouping of masses on the grandest scale: that it is time to have done with funereal commemorative architecture; that architecture must be something more vital than that, and we can best attain that something by blowing sky-high, for a start, all those monuments and monumental pavements, arcades and flights of steps, by digging out our streets and piazzas, by raising the level of the city, by reordering the earth's crust and reducing it to be the servant of our every need and our every fancy.

And I conclude in disfavour of

Modish architecture of every style and nation.

Classically solemn architecture, hieratic, theatrical, decorative, monumental, graceful or pleasing.

Preservation, reconstruction, reproduction of ancient monuments.

Perpendicular and horizontal lines, cubic and pyramidal forms, static grave, oppressive and absolutely foreign to our newest sensibilities.

Use of materials that are massive, bulky, durable and expensive, all opposed to the complexity of Modern culture and Modern experience

and I affirm

That the new architecture is the architecture of cold calculation, temerious boldness and simplicity; the architecture of reinforced concrete, iron, glass, textile fibres and all those replacements for wood, stone and brick that make for the attainment in maximum elasticity and lightness.

That real architecture is not, for all that, an arid combination of practicality and utility, but remains art, that is, synthesis and expression.

That decoration, as something superimposed on or attached to architecture is an absurdity, and that only from the use and disposition of raw, naked and violently coloured materials can derive the decorative value of a truly Modern architecture.

And finally I affirm that just as the ancients drew their inspiration in art from the elements of the natural world, so we—materially and spiritually artificial—must find our inspiration in the new mechanical world we have created, of which architecture must be the fairest expression, the fullest synthesis, the most effective artistic integration.

By any standard of historical judgement this would be a remarkable document to have been produced early in 1914, because it puts together the predisposing causes and the newly emergent ideas of the pre-War epoch in a manner which did not become general until the War was over, and—more important—it takes up attitudes to those predisposing causes according to those new ideas. Thus, the second paragraph rejects the architecture of the past, the third takes a view of the past that Choisy could have approved (and probably inspired), the fourth explains why the past must be rejected, and the fifth explains that rejection further in terms of concepts that derive mostly from nineteenth-century Rationalist sources, or from the moralising tradition of England. This kind of revaluation of older bodies of ideas, accepting much of what they had to say as true, but recasting them in new frames of reference that often completely altered their meaning, was to become the common ground of mainstream ideas in the Twenties—for instance, the reworking of Guadet's idea of elementary composition in terms of asymmetrical planning, or the use of Choisy's own insistence on the importance of technique to make nonsense of his proposition that the technical aids available to modern architects were those of the Gothic or even the prehistoric world.

But Sant'Elia does more than this. He anticipates, in the second of his affirmations, the anti-Functionalist mood of Le Corbusier and Gropius in the Twenties, and in taking up Berlage's view on the impropriety of adding decoration to structure, he moves forward to a position abreast of that adopted by Adolf Loos in *Ornament und Verbrechen*. That he knew Loos's work is entirely possible, but the possibility at once raises the problem of the connection with Futurism. There is a distinct streak of Viennese late Art Nouveau about some of Sant'Elia's earliest surviving designs, such as the project for the cemetery at Monza,[5] of 1912, executed in collaboration with Italo Paternostro. But well before the compilation of the *Messaggio* this quality had disappeared, replaced by a bold glyptic starkness, more extreme than that of any of his contemporaries, even Poelzig, and far beyond anything being done in Vienna by anyone except possibly Loos himself. But there are no stylistic resemblances to Loos at all, and the indications

[5] A very full reprinting of Sant'Elia's drawings and projects was undertaken by Tentori and Mariani in *L' Architettura* (Rome, 1955, No. 2 and 1956, No. 5).

are that by the time Sant'Elia evolved this undecorated style of his own, he was out of direct touch with Vienna—if he had ever been in touch at all.

On the other hand, Marinetti and the Futurists provided a direct line of contact with Paris, where Georges Besson's translation of *Ornament und Verbrechen* had appeared in 1913, and with *Der Sturm* which had reprinted the essay in 1912. If it is maintained that Sant'Elia was not a Futurist at the time the *Messaggio* was composed, these two links with Loos are, presumably impossible. However, in spite of the fact that the words *Futurist* and *Futurism* do not appear in the *Messaggio*, it is difficult to construe it as anything but a work Futurist in spirit, form and inspiration. The Futurist spirit is manifest in its rejection of the past, of Monumentality and Classicism, its insistence on the revolutionary changes in cultural life wrought by science and technique. It is Futurist too in the vehemence of its opinions, and in its form, complete with positive and negative propositions at its end. Above all it contains numerous ideas, echoes and partial quotations from existing Futurist publications.

Thus, the 'new ideal of beauty' connects it with the Foundation Manifesto of Futurism, the 'masses' it fascinated connect it with those 'men of the people' to whom Marinetti attributed the gift of mechanical prophecy in *Le Futurisme*. The proposed new materials to replace wood, stone and brick are directly comparable to the new materials (in some cases they are identical) proposed by Boccioni to replace marble and bronze in the Manifesto on sculpture, the insistence on dynamism is endemic in Futurist writing, while in the final affirmation the contrast between the inspiration of the ancients and the inspiration proper to a Modernist is simply a reworking of Boccioni's pronouncements on the same subjects, though with the curious and significant modification of 'world of religion that weighed upon their souls' to 'elements of the natural world'—where Boccioni saw the church as the inspiration of the great art of the past, Sant'Elia presumably saw tree-trunks as the inspiration of Doric, branches as the inspiration of Gothic, and foliage as the inspiration of most of the ornament known to ancient architecture.

Even so, the sentiment remains Futurist, and the document as a whole stands too close to Futurism in every respect to be capable of consideration under any other heading. Furthermore, the most elaborate of Sant'Elia's sketches of 1913 and 1914 underline the Futurist quality of his inspiration at the time. In order of increasing complexity, rather than chronology, these sketches begin with simple and almost abstract exercises in architectonic form, tall structures titled *Dinamismo Architettonico* and occasionally given the functional justification of lighthouses. Their shapes are bare and smooth, rectangular or semicircular in plan, often battered back in section to give a tapering silhouette, their vertical emphasis uninterrupted by string-courses or cornices, but reinforced by boldly marked vertical arrises. Though nothing designed by him in this idiom was ever built, the monument to the War-dead (and to Sant'Elia himself) in Como was worked up from drawings of this type by Enrico Prampolini and Giuseppe Terragni,[6] and—allowing for the fact that Sant'Elia himself could never, presumably, have designed a monument—gives a fair idea of the plastic qualities he intended in these sketches.

The next order of complexity in his designs is represented by single buildings for relatively uncomplicated functions. These include all the types of buildings that Marinetti had indicated in *Le Futurisme*: villas open to the breeze and the horizon (and one of them visibly influenced by Wright) large apartment houses (though the best-known designs for blocks of flats from Sant'Elia's circle were by the Swiss, Mario Chiattone), great meeting halls (sometimes labelled theatres) and others, such as airship hangars, bridges, factories, and power-stations. In most of these projects, all of them presented in perspectives and very few indeed in plan, the emphasis is on the same elements as appear in the simpler sketches— battered walls, canted buttresses, square podia or basements, and strong semicircular projections, either as apses, or in ranks along the side of the building, the buttresses too being used repetitively in this way. The most striking of all these designs are those for power-stations, which embrace the most grandiose vertical rhetoric in some, an unassuming simplicity in others, and in one, the geometrical rigour of the forms and their mode of grouping is such that only the date 1913 under Sant'Elia's signature and a slight Art Nouveau border would give one to suppose that it had not been done in the late Twenties or even the Thirties.

The most complex of all his sketches are the fragments of town-planning schemes which were put into fairly precise draughtsmanship, as against his usual free-hand style, for exhibition in May 1914. The original inspiration of these projects would appear to have been the proposal to rebuild Milan Central Station, first mooted in 1906, which involved moving it back to its present site, thus creating (*a*) the broad avenue of the present Viale Vittor Pisani and (*b*) the need for a traffic underpass beneath the tracks, such as now exists. The earliest of his Central Station projects exhibit both of these features, with the manifestly Futurist addition that the Viale is shown decked over to provide a landing strip for aircraft between its two ranks of skyscrapers—a suicidal project which reappears, along with a good deal more of Sant'Elia, in Le Corbusier.[7]

[6] Terragni, much under Marinettian influence at the time, was awarded the first prize in the competition in 1926, but the monument was not completed until the early Thirties.

[7] See chapter 18: it is just possible that Sant'Elia's ideas for a multi-level city have a Parisian source, since Gustave Kahn, who was a friend of Marinetti's for some time before 1914, had drawn attention to the ideas of the *communard* doctor, Tony Moilin, who proposed streets at various levels, with railways above and below them converging on a central railway station, as a cure for Paris traffic problems in the late Eighteen-sixties. These propositions clearly anticipate the projects of both Sant'Elia and Le Corbusier, and could have influenced both.

But this particular design is conceived in loosely modelled curved masses, unlike the precise forms of the projects of late 1913, and equally unlike the neatly-detailed, sharp-arrised forms of the Central Station as it appeared redrawn in 1914. These carefully rendered presentation drawings, are united both in style of draughtsmanship, and the style of the buildings they represent, with the rest of the *Città Nuova* series that were exhibited with them, and Sant'Elia's version of Milan in the year 2,000,[8] though fragmentary, is held together by a basic unity of style, and—even more important—a basic unity of vision. Sant'Elia sees his city as based in a complex network of transport services, in some drawings as much as seven levels deep, much as he had proposed in his observations on streets in the Manifesto. Out of this three-dimensional grid of communications rise the buildings, usually *a gradinate*, that is, with the floors stepped back one behind the other towards the top. The floors are of equal, or even increasing depth from back to front, however, and the overhangs at the back are taken up by the rising curve of a parabolic arch whose other half supports the back of the building's twin, which is backed up against it, leaving a tunnel for transport and services between them.[9] The lift-shafts are on the façades, and, rising vertically, stand well clear of the upper floors, to which they are connected by bridges of ever-increasing length as one goes up. This device, which fulfils, again, a proposition in the *Messaggio*, was probably suggested to him by the lifts on the shores of Lake Como rising from landing stages, and connected back to points on the mountainside by bridges.

He appears to have envisaged his city as consisting of knots of building of this type, connected by the network of multi-level circulation at their feet. The resemblance to Boccioni's 'field' concept of space, with bodies connected by geometrical fields of force is very striking, as is the reappearance of purely superficial Boccionisms like the illuminated advertising that appears on the roof of some of these projects. Yet in this minor device of designing the advertising as part of the building, he was a pioneer of later developments, as much as he was in his fully three-dimensional view of town-planning problems. On both counts, the comparison with Tony Garnier is instructive. Garnier has skyline advertising over the principal hotel of his *Cité Industrielle* but it looks like an afterthought attached to a broadly Classical design, even though he was probably the first architect to recognise that such advertising had its place. Similarly, in spite of the fact that he was also the first architect to recognise that the planning of industrial towns had its special problems, his conclusions, though published

[8] Some of the drawings are apparently inscribed *Milano 2000*.
[9] This type of structure was actually used, a decade later by Henri Sauvage for his flats in the Rue des Amiraux, Paris; see chapter 16. Although the street façades of these flats were very Sant' Elian, with *gradinate* and vertical towers standing away from them, the arched construction at the back was used only to span a swimming pool and garages, not a service road.

133

later than Sant'Elia's, are less radical, less well integrated, and were to prove less influential, even though lip-service was often paid to them.

After 1918 it was to be the Sant'Elian concept of the multi-level tower city that held sway in men's imaginations, and the wide distribution of his ideas on the subject seems to have been almost entirely due to the energetic promotion of Sant'Elia's memory by Marinetti. It is fair to say that his reputation is largely of Marinetti's making, outside Italy at least, not only because Marinetti circulated his work to groups like *de Stijl* and *Der Sturm*, but also because some of the most widely admired opinions associated with his name are only to be found in the disputed Manifesto, not in the *Messaggio*, which hardly anyone outside Italy ever saw.

It is generally agreed that the Manifesto is largely Marinetti's responsibility, but there is still some confusion about how much he actually wrote. The differences between the two texts are of two kinds.[10] Firstly, alterations, which consist mostly of inserting the words Futurist or Futurism on the slightest pretext, and leaving the *Messaggio* otherwise almost untouched, and secondly, the addition of new paragraphs at the head of the text, and among the propositions at the end. The authorship of the four new paragraphs at the head is obscure; they do not read like Marinetti, and Sant' Elia's reported objections to the text of the Manifesto were to the additions at the end, not those at the beginning. They do not, in fact, add much to the argument, and their flavour can be adequately typified by the first

> Since the eighteenth century there has been no architecture at all. A bewildering mix-up of the most varied elements of style, employed in masking the skeletons of Modern buildings is called Modern architecture. The new beauty of steel and concrete is being profaned by the superimposition of carnival-style decorative incrustations justified neither by antiquity of the constructional methods nor by our own tastes, drawing their sources from ancient Egypt, India and Byzantium . . .

and so forth, mostly a rhetorical expansion of the sentiments of the body of the *Messaggio*, with even stronger echoes of Loos.

However, the additions at the end are more to the point, the first of them now reading, after 'I combat and despise'

> All *avant-garde* pseudo-architecture from Austria, Hungary, Germany and America

which is simply Marinettian politics and makes his hand very clear in this last part. The next three negative propositions are virtually unchanged, the fifth has been dropped. The first two positive propositions are unchanged apart from the insertion of *Futurist* instead of *new*: the third proposition has been dismissed to fourth to make way for a new one reading

> That oblique and elliptical lines are dynamic by their very nature, have an emotive power a thousand times greater than that of horizontals and verticals, and there can be no dynamically integrated architecture without them.

[10] The most reliable text of the Manifesto is in Sartoris's book mentioned above.

It is difficult to see how Sant'Elia could have disagreed with this since it is a logical extension of his own disapproval of cubic forms, etc. He had no need to disapprove of the next two since they were his own unaltered, except for the usual insertion of the word *Futurist* for *new*, but he might conceivably have objected to the last three, all added, though his status as a pioneer and prophet of the Twenties would be slightly diminished thereby, since these, apart from the patent 'advertisement' in the last paragraph, contain the most forward-looking ideas to which his name has ever been attached, viz.

> That architecture as the art of disposing the forms of a building according to pre-established laws is finished.
> That architecture must be understood as the power freely and boldly to harmonise environment and man, that is, to render the world of things a projection of the world of the spirit.
> That from an architecture so conceived no stock answers, plastic or linear, could arise, because the fundamental characteristics of Futurist architecture will be expendability and transience. Our houses will last less time than we do, and every generation will have to make its own. This constant renewal of the architectonic environment will contribute to the victory of Futurism, already asserting itself through *les mots en liberté*, plastic dynamism, music without bars, the art of noise, through all of which we fight without quarter against *passéiste* cowardice.

Since the idea that every generation must make its own house is by far the best known to which Sant'Elia's name attaches, it appears that his international reputation is indeed of Marinetti's making.

Whether or not he was a Futurist, the possibility of a Futurist architecture perished with Sant'Elia in 1916 just as the development of Futurist painting expired, for certain, with the death of Boccioni in the same year. The most interesting sketches made by Mario Chiattone, Sant'Elia's fellow architect in the *Nuove Tendenze* group, all seem to have been made before the middle of the War, in spite of the fact that he lived until 1957. After 1918, Virgilio Marchi, one of the 'Bar Bragaglia' circle of Roman Futurists converted some Roman remains in the Via Avignonesi into the aforementioned Bar, and an experimental theatre[11] a piece of restoration that shows how far Marchi had receded from the position adopted by Sant' Elia, even while paying lip-service to his name. The recession is underscored by the merely modish style of this work, and further underlined by the text and illustrations of a small book on *Architettura Futurista* that Marchi published about this time. The sketches have some affinities with the work of such Berlin Expressionists as Otto Bartning, but without his structural sense, and achieve their nadir in a project for the 'adaptation of an existing structure to Futurism'—a piece of applied decoration that would have appalled Sant'Elia, spread over a raw concrete skeleton that he would have admired.

But Marchi's inanities are only typical of the downfall of the movement

---

[11] Both are illustrated in his book *Architettura Futurista* (Foligno, 1923).

as a whole. Robbed of its most active and substantial members by deaths and resignations, robbed of relevance by a world that had been rendered forcibly Futurist by the War, robbed of independence of manoeuvre by too close an involvement with the Fascist revolution, it had become an object of ridicule. Only Marinetti and Balla survived of the old brigade, the ten years they had given themselves to achieve their aims having expired in 1919. Yet they had, in fact, achieved most of their aims. The bulk of their irredentist claims had been satisfied, barring Trieste; parliamentary government had been ridiculed and overthrown; the comic-opera politics and back-stage barbarities of the Fascist régime were, so to speak, part of the original specification for a virile and bellicose Italy. Though the official eyes of that Italy were fixed too often on the Roman past, rather than the Milanese future, the Futurists' small place in the hierarchy did help to make progressive architecture possible, and even produce some patronage for it, in the Twenties and Thirties—Terragni's work in and around Como being to some extent a conscious assumption of the mantle of Sant' Elia, but couched in the established idiom of the International Style that had been created in other countries.

Yet it was in those other countries that the Futurists had most fully achieved their aims. As Marinetti sank deeper into political buffoonery, the ideas that he and his circle had propagated before 1914 became more and more part of the inalienable common ground of mainstream developments in Modern architecture as subsequent chapters will show. The growing pressure of mechanisation made the world seem more and more Futurist, and as men felt this increasing pressure, they found Futurist ideas at hand to channel their ideas and give shape to their expression. The general availability of such ideas should occasion no surprise in view of the work that Marinetti had put into their distribution across Europe from Madrid to Moscow, from Rome to Berlin. His own travels, and those of Boccioni (though less extensive) were supported and extended by Futurist manifestations in Paris (1912, 1913, 1914), London (1912–13), Rotterdam and Berlin (both in 1913) while all or part of the exhibition held in Paris in 1912 seems to have been seen in Brussels, Berlin, Hamburg, The Hague, Leipzig, Munich, Vienna, Breslau, Wiesbaden, Zurich and Dresden, and in every case was accompanied by Manifestoes, some of which were available in German, Spanish and Russian by 1914, as well as the 'original' French and Italian. Independent local Manifestoes were also issued by Futurist groups in Madrid and London.

In most of these places, as in London, where the group soon fell apart,[12] interest in Futurism as a movement was short-lived, but the influence lived

[12] The group in London seems to have existed chiefly in the minds of Marinetti, Nevinson and, briefly, Wyndham Lewis. Among those who hastened to disclaim membership was Frederick Etchells, who later translated two of Le Corbusier's books into English, and designed the first Modern office block in London, Crawfords in High Holborn.

on, in manifestations as diverse as Dadaist typography, the rise of kinetic sculpture, the poetry of Mayakovsky—and the theoretical writing that supported progressive architecture all over Europe. In most cases this was due to the tapping of a common deposit of ideas, without direct intervention from any of the surviving Futurists themselves, but in the case of *de Stijl*, to which we must turn next, what might be termed 'sub-conscious Futurism' was supplemented and made conscious by the despatch of documents from Marinetti in 1917, among them some reproductions of Sant' Elia's drawings, and the text of the Manifesto of Futurist Architecture.

Section three

HOLLAND: THE LEGACY OF BERLAGE: DE STIJL, 1917–1925

Berlage, H. P: *Grundlagen und Entwicklung der Architektur,* Berlin, 1908.
    Gedanken über Stil, Leipzig, 1905.
de Groot, J. H: *Vormharmonie,* Amsterdam, 1912.
Wright, F. Ll: Introduction to the 'first Wasmuth volume':
    Frank Lloyd Wright, Ausgeführte Bauten und Entwürfe,
    Berlin, 1910.
Ashbee, C. R: Introduction to the 'second Wasmuth volume':
    Frank Lloyd Wright (Chicago), Berlin, 1911.
de Fries, H: *Frank Lloyd Wright,* Berlin, 1926.
Jaffe, H. L. C: *de Stijl 1917–1927,* Amsterdam, 1956.
Brown, Theodore M: *The Work of G. Rietveld, Architect,* Utrecht, 1958.
Seuphor, M: *Piet Mondriaan,* London, 1957.
Oud, J. J. P: *Holländische Architektur (Bauhausbuch 10),* Munich, 1926.
Mendelsohn, E: lectures reprinted in
    Erich Mendelsohn, Das Gesamtschaffen des Architekten,
    Berlin, 1930.
Whittick, A: *Eric Mendelsohn,* London (2nd edn.), 1956.
Conrads and Sperlich: *Fantastic Architecture* (English version with notes
    by G. and C. C. Collins), London, 1962.
Malevitsch, K: *Die gegenstandslose Welt (Bauhausbuch 11),* Munich, 1927.
Lissitsky, E: *Russland,* Vienna, 1930.
Periodicals
    Wendingen, 1919–1925
    (including special issues on Mendelsohn, 1920, and Frank Lloyd
    Wright, 1925.)
    de Stijl, 1917–1931.
    G and *ABC,* 1923–1925.

11: Holland: Berlage and attitudes to Wright

DURING THE WAR of 1914–18 the Dutch alone, of all nations who had contributed to the growth of a new architecture, enjoyed the benefits of neutrality, and in the development of their architecture alone can the break between the first and second phase of the developing twentieth-century style be seen unobstructed by the confusions of the War. Outside Holland, major architects whose careers effectively span the War years are rare— Gropius and Perret are almost alone in having done work of equal interest before 1914 and after 1918—and most of the personalities who characterised the post-War scene, such as Mendelsohn, Mies van der Rohe, Le Corbusier, Lurçat, have insignificant or non-existent pre-War careers. But in Holland the war years were, if anything, a period of increased building activity, forcing on the development of talents that were maturing after 1910, which rapidly brought young men to the top, and drove pre-War currents of ideas to their logical (or illogical) conclusions—all without any serious breaks or interruptions of development except those precipitated by the ideas and personalities involved. The break—and it is a real break with the past—comes in late 1917 with the foundation of the group *de Stijl*, but the ideas of this group, far from being born of the agonising experiences of the War, were the product of discussions, experiments and building work that had been going on since 1911, or thereabouts. That the ideas of *de Stijl* (and similar bodies of thought) were taken up so enthusiastically in countries that had been involved in the War, seems to be less due to their applicability to post-War conditions (which is doubtful) than to the fact that theorists in most of those countries would have arrived at similar conclusions themselves at about the same time, had they not been otherwise engaged.

The rapid evolution of *de Stijl* theory and practice may be largely attributed to the clear-cut polemical situation in which the group's architects found themselves, with their own Rationalist, mechanistic, abstract approach in direct opposition to the fantasticated, handicraft, figurative approach of the *Wendingen* group in Amsterdam. But, as is so often the case in polemics of this kind, the violent opponents had a great deal in

139

common—in this case the example of H. P. Berlage, and his advocacy of F. Lloyd Wright.

Hendrikus Peter Berlage was born as far back as 1856; he studied in Zurich in the late Seventies and did not return to Holland until after 1881. His studies had brought him into contact with late followers of Gottfried Semper[1] while, after his return to Holland, he was associated with P. J. H. Cuijpers, an admirer and—to some extent—follower of Viollet-le-Duc. From these two sources, Berlage seems to have acquired the strain of careful mid-nineteenth Rationalism that runs through his work and his writings. But since his most notable building, the *Beurs* in Amsterdam, was not completed until after 1900, and his most influential writings all date from after 1905, young Dutch architects confused by the collapse of Art Nouveau were able to turn to the works and writings of a man who conceived of architecture in terms that had been current before Art Nouveau appeared on the scene.

This is not to say that Berlage did not take cognisance of technical and social developments of his own time; to him, as to any true Rationalist, these were of prime importance, but the way in which he regards them is unlike the attitude of most of the other architectural theorists of his time. In particular one notes in his writings a moralistic tone of voice about the right employment of materials, etc. that is very hard to parallel, but gave his views particular force wherever they were heard. In general he seems to have been understood, and regarded, in the sense that he himself would have preferred to be understood and regarded, as a man who insisted on certain elementary truths, and despised side issues and decorative irrelevancies.

The truths on which he insisted were three: the primacy of space, the importance of walls as creators of form, and the need for systematic proportion. As he expresses them, the first two are inseparably linked. In his *Grundlagen und Entwicklung der Architektur* of 1908[2] he relates them thus

> The art of the master-builder lies in this: the creation of space, not the sketching of façades. A spatial envelope is established by means of walls, whereby a space, or a series of spaces is manifested, according to the complexity of the walling.

In view of the brilliant plays upon space later created by his indirect follower G. T. Rietveld and his direct pupil Mies van der Rohe,[3] it is worth noting here that the kind of space that Berlage appears to have in mind is interior space within the building envelope, not space as an extensive

---

[1] Notably Manfred Semper, old Gottfried's son, and others of that generation of Sempers.

[2] Like nearly everything else that he wrote at the period, this was a reprint of ectures given in German to German audiences.

[3] In Rietveld's case, the Schröder house at Utrecht, discussed in chapter 14, and in Mies's case, most notably the project for a brick villa described in chapter 19.

continuum, just as the walling he has in mind is load-bearing and solidly built of brick or masonry. These were both reasonably conventional ideas for the period, but walling, in particular, had for him a more than customary value. In his German texts he persistently speaks of *Mauern* and *Mauerflächen*, emphasising the wall's substantial qualities; and he insists, at the end of his *Gedanken über Stil*

> Before all else the wall must be shown naked in all its sleek beauty, and anything fixed on to it must be shunned as an embarrassment

and in the *Grundlagen*

> And thus walling would receive its due value again, in the sense that its nature as a plane would remain, while a more heavily articulated surface would not register as wall.

Like Adolf Loos after him, he takes as an example of good uncluttered structure, the astylar walling of Roman remains, and in the same year as Loos's *Ornament and Crime* he wrote

> And thus in architecture, decoration and ornament are quite inessential while space-creation and the relationships of masses are its true essentials.

It is not surprising that he was largely remembered as an apostle of 'Truth to Materials', but he himself would have seen both this, and space-creation, as subservient to overriding claims of proportional systems, to which the bulk of his work is devoted. Proportional systems were a preoccupation of many of his Amsterdam contemporaries as well, and most of them are agreed that the originator of this preoccupation was Jan Hessel de Groot. Berlage himself is quite explicit on his debt to him.

> The main thing is to work systematically, which may yield remarkable results for the modern theory of proportions; I myself have worked for years in no other way, and I am an ex-pupil of de Groot.[4]

However complex the mathematics and the forms employed may have been, de Groot's view of the nature and function of proportion was remarkably simple. In the introduction to one of his numerous published books and papers, the *Vormharmonie* of 1912, he states

> This is a book of instructions on how to arrive at harmony of form through formal relationships. I call form harmonious when its internal relationships are such that it creates a whole. The aim of my research is this; to be able to make from, say, twenty forms, one form. Take ten letters, you can make a whole of them through placing them next to one another so that they can be read as a whole, without interruption, as a word.

However, he raises the subject to something more like the mystical plane on which it is customarily discussed, by adding a footnote that introduces

[4] Quoted by Slebos as an introduction to his *Grondslagen voor Aesthetischen Stijl* which appeared in Amsterdam in 1939, a last pathetic rearguard of the mathematical aesthetics of the Amsterdam School.

Berlage's favourite phrase (expressing an idea as old as Aristotle) for formal harmony, which, he says,

> . . . is also defined as 'Unity in Plurality' (*Eenheid in veelheid*).

Berlage was not alone in following de Groot, as has been said, nor was he alone in distributing his influence outside Holland. It is clear that the contribution of J. G. Lauwericks is of great importance in this respect, for, although he was an Amsterdam architect to begin with, he taught for some years at the Düsseldorf *Kunstgewerbeschule*, where Adolf Meyer, later a regular collaborator with Gropius, came under his influence, and he may also have provided Le Corbusier with his first sight of a building designed according to systematic proportion.[5] But whatever Lauwerickx's contribution as a teacher on the practical plane, and whatever may have been written by de Groot himself, and later by his follower Slebos, it was Berlage who gave this school of thought its most eloquent expression, and, although most of his ideas went by default in the work of his followers, they did provide the foundations for a Rational attitude to form.

For Berlage, proportion was a guard against mere passing fashions, a guarantee of permanent value, and he quotes at the head of the *Grundlagen* a phrase from Sheraton's *Cabinet Maker*:

> Time alters fashions . . . but that which is founded on geometry and real science will remain unalterable.

He reinforces this opinion with his own experience

> I have been driven to this conclusion; namely, that geometry (and thus mathematical science) is not only of the greatest usefulness in the creation of artistic form, but even of absolute necessity

he makes the customary appeal to the musical analogy

> Why should architecture—of all arts most often compared to music, as Schlegel brought out with his famous expression *gefrorene Musik*—why should architecture be composed without rhythmical, i.e. geometrical laws.

and the equally customary appeal to the authority of Greece, by way of a quotation from Ferguson's *History*

> The system of definite proportions which the Greeks employed in the design of their temples, was a cause of the effect they produce even on uneducated minds.

This, however, is the only reference he makes to the supposed physiological

[5] Drawings signed by Meyer are reproduced in Berlage's *Grundlagen* as examples of the work being done at Düsseldorf, under Lauwerickx's instruction, but along purely Berlagian lines. As regards Le Corbusier the evidence is only circumstantial, but conclusive. In his *Modulor* (London edition, 1954) he relates that 'looking over a modern villa at Bremen, the gardener there had said to him (i.e. Le Corbusier) "This stuff, you see, that's complicated, all these twiddly bits, curves, angles, calculations, it's all very learned". The villa belonged to someone called Thorn Brick (?) a Dutchman, (about 1909).' The inference seems unavoidable that the answer to the parenthetical question mark is the Dutch artist J. Thorn Prikker, and that this was the house built for him in Bremen by Lauwerickx in 1905—and one wonders if it can have been Berlage who directed Le Corbusier's attention to it.

responses to proportional effects, probably because the production of such effects was not with him the aim of proportional systems. The aim of all artistic creation, in his mind, was the achievement of *repose*, and thus of *style*, the ultimate aesthetic quality

> . . . one leading and essential property strikes the eye; it is Repose—a charming repose in small work, a noble calm in great monumental architecture. Against this (i.e. ancient architecture) our current work gives the impression of being very unrestful. I might almost say that the two words 'Style' and 'Repose' are synonymous; that, as Repose equals Style, so Style equals Repose.

and later he equates these two concepts with proportion as well, by bringing in the characteristic *Eenheid in Veelheid* tag

> Nature is not unrestful, since it has Style, and if we direct our attention to the arts of earlier times, we shall not be misled by them either, since they have Style, i.e. Unity in Plurality

The possession of style seems to have been held by most of Berlage's Amsterdam associates as a quality to be cultivated; they must have acquired the idea from readings in Semper, whose *Der Stil in den technischen Künsten*, is familiarly referred to by de Groot simply as *Der Stil*, and passed it on to the group which, consciously or otherwise, took on the phrase *de Stijl* as both name and watchword. Just what style meant to de Groot himself is obscured by his own tendency to overfine discrimination, but he seems, at least, not to intend the 'catalogue styles' of the academies. Berlage, without ever attempting to define what style really is, nevertheless, clearly means something of use and value to his own time. He decries Ruskin and other 'philosophers' for being only students, not teachers, of style and says

> There are, however, great practising artists like Viollet-le-Duc in France, and the well-known Semper in Germany, who are better teachers, and give in their great books a practical aesthetic . . . of a sort that can be used.
> What then is the problem?
> Why, to have (a) style again.

But style is also order, and not necessarily an obvious order such as is given by axial planning. Order prevails wherever settled laws are effective, and for examples of this he turns once more to the Antique, and to Nature. The order of nature raises another problem, which seems never to have been far from his mind, but which he poses here by means of a quotation from Semper; the problem of Norms or Types

> Just as nature is ever thrifty of motifs even in her endless abundance, constantly repeating her basic forms, but modifying them a thousand different ways according to the condition of her creatures and their mode of life, stretching or curtailing some, hiding or revealing others—just as nature has her evolutionary processes, within whose limits old motifs continually reappear in new creations, so art lies within the scope of a few Norms or Types that derive from old tradition, each constantly reappearing in diverse forms, each with its own history, as in Nature. Nothing, therefore is purely arbitrary, but all is governed by circumstance and relationship.

This was published in Berlin three years before Muthesius delivered *Wo stehen wir?* to the Werkbund Congress of 1911, and though one doubts that Muthesius needed Berlage to remind him of Semper's writings, nevertheless the two men knew one another and one another's ideas, which approach fairly closely in content, though with significant differences in bias. As far as the architect's task in the twentieth century is concerned, there are striking resemblances. Berlage writes as early as 1905

> Architecture shall be the creative art of the twentieth century, as it was down to 600 years ago, and painting and sculpture shall advance together as its servants and, in that employment, could reach their highest development.

and thus far he is close to Muthesius's vision of an unified hegemony of the arts under architecture. But he then goes on to prophesy, as a consequence of this and

> . . . on the basis of present social and artistic evolution: One will soon observe an interest in the growing body of useful arts, and a yearly decrease in the number of easel paintings and statues.

This, whatever its debts to William Morris, goes beyond anything Muthesius had prophesied, but for all that Berlage sets his sights on a very similar target.

> A drive toward Unity in Plurality is taking command of things in general, a drive toward Order, toward Style. . . . The designer of today stands before an inviting prospect of artistic beautification, i.e. to pioneer the great architectural style of every future community. There is no fairer task.

Close as this may be to Muthesius, there are notable differences of approach. Berlage does not postulate any pressure of patriotic sentiment nor economic duress—these things are to happen because they are right, not because they are the price of survival. Further, there is no talk of *Durchgeistigung*, of spiritualisation, but rather, of socialisation (this seems to be another instance of the pre-Art Nouveau quality in Berlage's thought; his politics were of the left, and almost Positivist at times).

> As our new concept manifests itself, what spiritual idea shall serve as its foundation? Who can answer this? Christianity is dead, and only the preliminary stirrings can yet be felt of a new world-concept based upon the consequences of scientific progress. We need an ethical settlement, and in that connection there comes to the surface of the ferment of our times the question of Altruism. It comes to this—the individual or the Community? With the denial of traditional morality shall the individual alone be served, or, given the principle of equality, shall all?

Muthesius and Berlage agree on the supremacy of the community, but the latter has not the former's authoritarian streak, and for him the balance of individual and community was still to be settled. Nevertheless, he was in no doubt in which way things would go, he did his best work for communal patrons, and such work was the necessary end-product for him of his theories, which clearly envisage the architect as involved in society.

If one sets out those theories in short form—to manipulate space with walls within an order that gives a style proper to an emergent, irreligious society, one sees that this formula is also the one by which Berlage evaluated the work of Frank Lloyd Wright. He came upon Wright's work apparently unprepared in 1911, although the first Wasmuth volume had appeared in the previous year, and he was thus the third significant European theorist to discover Wright for himself. He had been preceded by Professor Kuno Francke, inspirer of the first Wasmuth volume, in 1909; and by C. R. Ashbee, who wrote the introduction to the second Wasmuth volume, and had visited Wright as early as 1901. The effect of the buildings he saw, and such Wright texts as he seems to have read, must have been to convince him that in Wright he saw a reflection of his own ideals. The sense of repose that he felt in the Martin House, was confirmed by Wright's statement that

> Simplicity and repose are the qualities that measure the true value of any work of art

and his admiration for Wright's straightforward use of walling by the Wrightian claim that

> The Wall was let alone from base to cornice or eaves.

As a result, the lecture he gave to the Zurich *Ingenieur- und Architekten-verein*, in March 1912, on his American experiences, pays due tribute to Richardson and Sullivan, but is dominated by Wright. In particular the Larkin Building excited his admiration, which should not occasion surprise since it has a good deal in common with his own *Beurs*. Internally both have large halls surrounded by galleries, executed largely in brick as internal facing, with an alternative material at points of structural importance —stone for the columns and the springing of the arches in his own work, reinforced concrete for the gallery floor slabs in Wright's, both serve group-functions, but Wright's had the advantage of being designed around the open office, which was new to Berlage, and, indeed, a recent emergent in American commercial organisation, rather than the time honoured business of the Stock Exchange, which was probably slightly suspect to Berlage's socialist mind. The outcome is one of the most generous and disinterested tributes paid by one architect to another in this century:[6]

> The building encloses only a single space, since, in accordance with the modern American concept, an office is not divided up into separate compartments. The boss sits at the same desk as his private secretary, whence he can supervise the great space in its entirety and the various open stories disposed as galleries around the central hall.
> It is a brick structure, and looks from the outside like a warehouse. Yet the interior is admirably illuminated, in spite of the corner stair-towers, like those of a church, which are lit from within. The galleries are illuminated by windows between the powerful pillars. . . .

[6] All these opinions of Berlage about Wright are taken from the lecture he gave on his American experiences in Zurich. The text of the relevant parts of this talk is given in H. de Fries, *Frank Lloyd Wright* (Berlin, 1926) and all the quotations from Wright that support them are from his article, which is discussed later in the chapter, *In the Cause of Architecture*.

Brickwork is the material of the interior as well, giving place to concrete for the floorslabs. The detailing naturally follows Wright's own unique style, and gives a wholly exceptional testimony of his original powers.
I came away with the conviction that I had seen a truly modern building, and filled with respect for a master who could create such a work, whose equal is yet to be found in Europe.

This was Wright seen as an ideal Berlagian architect, and this lecture and its subsequent reprinting was for many the most convincing intimation of Wright's qualities. But Berlage's own followers regarded Wright in a manner that Berlage's writings do not warrant. For them, after 1917, the Robie House outranked the Larkin Building as the prime example of Wright at his most masterly, and J. J. P. Oud speaks of it in the following terms

All the parts of this building, including the furnishings, were developed along mechanistic lines[7]

and Jan Wils took this valuation of Wright even farther[8]

People laughed at the Futurists, who want to demolish tradition and turn everything upside down.
They brushed off Marinetti as a lunatic, because he wanted to burn down Venice and rebuild it properly again.
And they shrugged up their shoulders when Wright said that the first task of the machine was to render all old work obsolete.

This assimilation of Wright to the Futurists is, in part, a mark of the generally syncretic trend of *de Stijl*, to which both Oud and Wils belonged for a time, but it is equally a testimony of the peculiar way in which Wright became known to the younger generation in Europe.

This emphasis on the mechanistic content of his work and theories might be supposed to stem from his lecture on *The Art and Craft of the Machine*, of 1901, but the text of this seems hardly to have been known in Europe before 1914. Instead, the answer seems to lie with two other documents: one was the essay *In the Cause of Architecture*, which Wright composed in 1908, and which was published with lavish illustrations in the *Architectural Record*; the other, which contained extensive quotations from *In the Cause*, was C. R. Ashbee's introduction to the second Wasmuth volume. The first Wasmuth volume was an *édition de luxe* of plans and rendered perspectives, large in format, unhandy to use, and expensive. The second was smaller, illustrated with photographs, and seems to have been much more influential. Like the reprint of Berlage's lecture, it did not go outside the canon of photographic illustrations established by *In the Cause*, so that, in spite of its late date it had no picture of the Robie House, which remained unknown and unappreciated except to those who had the patience to decipher its exciting features from the very uninformative illustrations in the first Wasmuth volume, or those, like Rob van t'Hoff, who had seen it with their own eyes. As a result, European ideas of Wright seem to have

[7] In *de Stijl*, Vol. 1, p. 41.   [8] In *Wendingen*, Vol. IV, p. 14.

146

been dominated at first by the Larkin Building and Unity Temple, the Coonley, Dana and Martin Houses.

Yet it is clear that, after 1917, the Robie House is the most admired and most imitated of Wright's buildings, and the reason for this seems to be that it, alone, with its bold forms and spectacular cantilevers, could give body to the image of Wright as a machine architect that Ashbee had built up in the second Wasmuth volume. This image of Wright was not accidental, and Ashbee is quite clear about his own intentions

> It is quite intentional that I do not dilate on the subject of Frank Lloyd Wright's interior architecture, for this does not appear to me to be the core of his creativity, nor is it really typical of him. To repeat it again, one recognises in his architecture the struggle for mastery of the machine, and that is the true province of his powers.

This view he supports with suitably mechanistic quotations from *In the Cause* and directs attention to it by acknowledging their source. Fourteen years later, when the Wendingen group published their album of Frank Lloyd Wright,[9] *In the Cause* (and two rather uninteresting pendants to it) was the only text by Wright himself that they reprinted. Thus the Wright that the young followers of Berlage knew was not the Wright of the vernacular and nature-worshipping mood of the introduction to the first Wasmuth volume (whom members of *de Stijl* would have despised, as will become apparent) but the Wright of

> Above all, integrity. The machine is the normal tool of our civilisation, give it work that it can do well; nothing is of greater importance. To do this will be to formulate new industrial ideals, sadly needed.

and

> The machine is here to stay. It is the forerunner of the democracy that is our dearest hope. There is no more important task before the architect than to use this normal tool to the best advantage.

or

> The old structural forms, which up to the present time have been called architecture, are decayed. Their life went from them long ago and new conditions industrially, steel and concrete, and terra-cotta in particular, are prophesying a more plastic art.

This is Wright comparable to the Futurists, and there was also Wright comparable to Berlage, who was equally comparable to Muthesius on occasions. The Wright/Berlage relationship filled in a gap in a spectrum of architectural ideas that ran from the Futurists at one extreme to the Rationalists and Academics at the other, and once that gap was filled the way was clear for the evolution of the syncretic aesthetic doctrines of *de Stijl*, in which elements of almost every corpus of pre-War theory are present.

[9] A special volume, outside the regular series, issued in 1925.

12: De Stijl: the Dutch phase

DE STIJL WAS one of two movements in Holland whose architecture was derived in part, at least, from the work or ideas of Berlage. The other movement, *Wendingen* or the Amsterdam School, was the more indebted to his actual work, which it evolved into a fantasticated handicraft style, eclectic rather than inventive, inclusive not exclusive in its attitude to forms and materials. *De Stijl*, on the other hand, was more indebted to his theories or, it might be better to say, his attitudes of mind, and set out to be Rationalist and disciplined, exclusive not inclusive, preferring a limited range of materials, forms and structural methods.

It is common practice to link the names of the two towns Rotterdam and Amsterdam to these two schools of thought, as if they were produced by some special local character of the citizens, but neither tendency is particularly localised as far as the distribution of its important monuments is concerned, and *de Stijl* might equally well be coupled with Utrecht on that score. What seems more relevant, is a discrimination based on matters of date—J. J. P. Oud, the dominating architectural figure of the early phase of *de Stijl*, was not born until 1890, and his earliest characteristic work, the rest-home *de Vonk* at Noordwijkerhout, was built in 1917, whereas Michel de Klerk, the equivalent figure in Amsterdam, was born as early as 1884, with his earliest characteristic work, the *Hillehuis*, built in 1911. This interval of six years seems to have been crucial: it meant that Oud's style matured, as will be seen later in this chapter, under the influence of Cubist and Futurist art, while de Klerk's matured in the long twilight of Dutch Art Nouveau.

However, in spite of this strict primacy of date, *Wendingen* (which was rather long-lived as twentieth-century movements go) did not become of international importance until the very beginning of the Twenties, when it established a short-lived liaison with Berlin Expressionists, and it is therefore proposed to deal first with the early phase of *de Stijl*, then with *Wendingen* and its international connections, and lastly with *de Stijl's* participation in the international Abstract Art Movement that over-ran all Expressionist tendencies after 1922.

For the purposes of this study it is proposed to divide the activities of *de Stijl* at 1921.[1] The exact date of such a division must always be arbitrary, because the change in the movement's character occupied more than twelve months, but the choice of date seems justified firstly, by the change in the format of the magazine *de Stijl* in that year, from a tall pocket-magazine format to a wide one better adapted to displayed features and large reproductions of works of art; and secondly by a wave of resignations of Dutch members of the group, which reached its peak in that year also; eight of the original ten members had disappeared by the end of the year.

The movement had never, in any case, been a close-knit fighting unit like Futurism; many of its members never met one another, and it seems that all they had in common was the acquaintance of van Doesburg, and, in most cases, a profound respect and liking for the painter Piet Mondriaan. The introduction to the first issue of the magazine (October 1917) can be read in a double sense.

> The object of this magazine will be to contribute to the development of a new consciousness of beauty. It aims to make modern man receptive to the new in creative art. It will oppose archaistic confusion—'Modern Baroque'—with the logical principles of a maturing style based on purer relationships with the spirit of our times and our means of expression. It will bring together present-day currents of thought about new creative activities—currents of thought that have developed independently though similar in essence. . . .

Although this was meant to be taken as the conflation of various '-isms' on an international scale, the fact remains that most of *de Stijl's* early members had worked in fairly complete isolation from one another until van Doesburg brought them together. Thus, among the architects, van t'Hoff only met Oud through the agency of van Doesburg, who, himself, had only come across van t'Hoff through a newspaper article about his houses at Huis ter Heide outside Utrecht. There was even a certain amount of suspicion existing between some of the members before the actual foundation of the group in 1917 and van der Leck, the painter, is reported as being unwilling to join if Oud and other architects were also to be admitted.

This is not to be attributed solely to personal causes. Over the early deliberations of the members broods the spectre of Berlage's version of *Gesamtkunstwerk*, in which painting and sculpture were to be subservient to architecture,[2] and van der Leck had no intention of being told what to do by architects. However, he contributed (under deception, he claims) one of the keynote articles to the first issue of *de Stijl*, in which he sets out a compromise position, accepting the Berlagian thesis in part, and then expressing its consequences on a *quid pro quo* basis, with painting and architecture in a sort of competitive partnership.

[1] This study of *de Stijl* is heavily indebted to Dr H. L. C. Jaffé's book *de Stijl 1917–1931* (Amsterdam, 1956) as all future studies of the movement will be, and also to the personal narratives given me by Rob van t'Hoff, Mart Stam and Walter Segal.
[2] As discussed in the previous chapter.

Painting has, in the cycle of time, separated itself from architecture, and developed independently, destroying old and naturalistic methods through experimentation. . . .
Nevertheless it always has need of some flat surface, and its ultimate aim is to work upon the useful, necessary surfaces created by the art of building. More than that, by its return to integration from isolation, it shall flavour the whole, and, by demanding suitable formal conceptions from architecture, it will regain its proper domain.

Though van der Leck resigned on discovering that the group contained architects after all, the position set out in these two quotations was, within limits, one that most members of the group could accept, even if, like Mondriaan they had reservations based on a sense that they were not yet ready for any *Gesamtkunstwerk*, as he wrote to van Doesburg

You should remember that my things are still intended to be paintings . . . not part of a building.

They felt, clearly, that their various arts had been refined, in isolation, to the point where their essences had been revealed, and been revealed as common to all the arts because geometrical and rectilinear. This common rectilinear character (so strongly felt by van Doesburg that he had thought of calling the magazine by some such title as *The Straight Line*, before opting for the Berlagian *de Stijl*) was to some extent the product of an almost anti-historical set of coincidences: on the one hand, the architects working on Berlagian and Wrightian precepts had arrived at a simple formula of plain vertical walls and flat roofs, free from decorative elements; on the other hand Mondriaan, and possibly other painters as well, inspired by the rectilinear mystical cosmogony of the theosophist Schoenmaekers, was on the point of arriving at an equally simple formula of rectangular patches of colour framed in horizontal and vertical lines, and free from figurative elements. Given this, it was suddenly and visibly possible, in Berlage's phrase, to have a style again (though not a style that Berlage himself would have liked). What is more, this style was to have practically all the social and cultural attributes that Berlage had postulated, and an even more openly Utopian slant. Between them, Mondriaan and van Doesburg created a fairly consistent image of a new world, based on the happenings and discoveries within their own small group and the outside world as they saw it. Mondriaan opened the first paragraph of the first article in the first issue of *de Stijl* with the assertion

The life of contemporary cultivated man is turning gradually away from nature; it becomes more and more an a-b-s-t-r-a-c-t life.

and practically every word in this simple-seeming statement is loaded with accessory meanings. The confrontation of *abstract* and *nature* is vital to the whole argument. From 1910, to the time this article was written, Mondriaan had been cautiously developing towards a purely abstract (non-figurative) style of painting, and in the process he had developed an elaborate and complex body of expository thought to go with it. The drift of all this theorising, heavily indebted to Schoenmaekers and also to writers like Kandinsky, was the common neo-Platonic idea, widely used by apologists of abstraction like Roger Fry,[3] that there was an ultimate reality lying behind the accidents of mere appearance, that painters should eschew the 'nature' of Realistic and Impressionist painting, which was entirely taken up with merely accidental qualities, and concentrate on the enduring absolutes of geometry, Schoenmaekers's *beeldende wiskunde* (i.e. creative mathematics) or Kandinsky's 'spiritual in art'.

The spirituality of Abstract art is insisted upon by van Doesburg in vaguely Hegelian terms

> It must be understood that all works which are wrought according to the spirit must diverge from the external forms of nature, and that they will diverge completely . . . when the spirit achieves perfect clarity.[4]

But, in the wider context of society and human culture, nature is also, for the *Stijlkunstenaar*, brute matter and brute man unredeemed by the spirit, which presumably is why Mondriaan specifies *cultivated man* as the enjoyer of a more and more abstract life, rather as Adolf Loos specifies advanced culture as the concomitant of freedom from ornament. But Mondriaan also specifies that his cultivated man be 'contemporary', and this introduces the progressivist-Utopian theme that runs strongly through early *de Stijl* theory. It will have been noted that van der Leck equated the naturalistic with the old; in the first Manifesto of *de Stijl* the signatories state

> 1. There is an old and a new spirit of the times. . . .
> 2. The War is destroying the old world and its contents . . , etc.

and, in general there is an almost Futurist sense of change and excitement in their writings, a sense that in their own time they will see a final break through from the old, corrupt world into a new and pure one. Almost inevitably, mechanisation figures largely in this vision, but not as something worth having for its own sake, or simply because it was new, as the Futurists saw it. For *de Stijl*, machinery, in separating Man from Nature hastened the spiritualisation of life. Van Doesburg wrote more than once

> The machine is, *par excellence*, a phenomenon of spiritual discipline. Materialism as a way of life and art took handicraft as its direct psychological expression. The new spiritual artistic sensibility of the twentieth century has not only felt the beauty of the machine, but has also taken cognisance of its unlimited expressive possibilities for the arts. . . . Under the supremacy of materialism, handicraft reduced men to the level of machines; the proper tendency for the machine (in the sense of cultural development) is as the unique medium of the very opposite, social liberation.[5]

[3] Fry made this point explicitly in his essay 'Art and Socialism', also reprinted in *Vision and Design*.
[4] *De Stijl*, II, p. 65.
[5] This version is from an essay left uncompleted at the time of van Doesburg's death in 1931, but close variants of it can be traced back to 1924, if not earlier, and make it clear that this particular concept of the cultural meaning of mechanisation was one to which he was very attached.

and again

> Every machine is the spiritualisation of an organism.

This substantial reversal of both Rationalist materialism and Futurist mechanolatry is extended by Mondriaan's views on the Modern city

> The genuinely Modern artist sees the metropolis as Abstract living converted into form; it is nearer to him than nature, and is more likely to stir in him the sense of beauty . . . that is why the metropolis is the place where the coming mathematical artistic temperament is being developed, the place whence the new style will emerge.

and the implied equation between Abstract art and machinery that runs through these passages receives support from the fact that both were also seen as instruments of something else that was built into de Stijl's programme: the depersonalisation of art. Individualism was part of the old world and the old spirit of the times, according to the first Manifesto, but the employment of reinforced concrete, seen as a machine material

> . . . removes the personal character from a building and thus tends towards a group art . . . with rhythmic inter-relationships of even the smallest structural parts, and no addition of decoration.

and, in his own eyes at least, a similar generalisation was the tendency of Mondriaan's paintings

> They unfold to us a world of universal beauty

It is interesting to note that this virtual equation between machinery and art was drawn without postulating a theory of Types or Norms as one of its terms, as Berlage or Muthesius might have done, or as the theorists of the Cubist tradition were to do in Paris. But, as H. L. C. Jaffé has pointed out, the well-known tag about absolute beauty, geometry and mechanical products, from Plato's *Philebus*, which so often appears in conjunction with the theory of Types, does not appear anywhere in de Stijl. Rather, they relied upon an implied analogy, which was brought to the surface only by Gino Severini, the ex-Futurist, who was a kind of corresponding member of the group, and proposed, in an early article under the symptomatic heading *Le Machinisme et l'Art—Reconstruction de l'Univers*

> The construction of a machine is analogous to the construction of a work of art

and

> we may conclude that the effect produced on the spectator by the machine is analogous to that produced by the work of art

From this summary of de Stijl attitudes to machinery and art, it will be clear that they had already crossed the watershed that divides the pre-War Futurist attitude to machinery as the agent of private, romantic, anti-Classical disorder, from the post-War 'Machine Aesthetic' that saw machinery as the agent of collective discipline and an order that drew nearer and nearer to the canons of Classical aesthetics. But it must also be recognised that this attitude, as it appears in *de Stijl* was also anti-Materialist and anti-Determinist, and, in view of the wide distribution of this and related attitudes in the Twenties, one should be very cautious of regarding the machine enthusiasts of that epoch as Determinists or Materialists, as is so often done. Their own writings will confirm the incorrectness of this reading of their intentions, since they almost always protest that 'the machine' is an instrument, not an objective of human existence. But it was the theorists of *de Stijl* who first transmogrified Futurism into this form, and they seem to have the best right to be considered the true founders of that enlightened Machine Aesthetic that inspired the best work of the Twenties.

If they transmogrified Futurism for their theoretical ends, they wrought an equal transformation of Cubism for their formal purposes, and the parallel processes by which this was done are typical of the conflation of Cubist practice and Futurist ideas that was the common inheritance of nearly all progressive movements after 1917. The sources of the art of van Doesburg and Mondriaan in pre-War Cubism were admitted by both of them, and can easily be traced in Mondriaan's paintings in particular. Although Mondriaan seems to have conceived of his *Nieuwe Beelding* as a genuine successor-style to Cubism, van Doesburg seems to have regarded his work more as a continuation of the abstracting processes that Cubism had initiated, and did not introduce a new word for his own art until he coined (or borrowed) *Elementarism* in 1926. Oud seems never to have been in doubt that the art practised by his painter-colleagues was a form of Cubism, even if he later came to believe it a corrupt form. This attitude of Oud's may well be the basis of subsequent confusion about a direct influence of Cubism on architecture. Such an influence is hard to find, and attempts to compare buildings of the 'International Style' with Cubist paintings, particularly those done in 1909–12 in Paris, are never very convincing. But if Cubism is read in Oud's extended sense, a sense that would easily cover the work of the Russian Abstractionists as well, then comparisons are possible and an influence admissible.

During the period that Oud was a member of *de Stijl*, however, influence was slight. Mondriaan and van Doesburg had developed their rectangular Abstraction to a fairly advanced degree, and had investigated many of its possibilities; their pictures were not yet restricted to a repertoire of coloured rectangles completely boxed in heavy black lines, and were still experimenting with overlapping rectangles, rectangles only partly boxed by lines, pictures based on free distribution of parts, and those composed on regular modular grids like the *Quadratur en Triangulatur* of Berlage and other followers of de Groot. They thus offered a very rich range of possible compositional techniques in one plane that architects could employ, while contemporary *de Stijl* sculpture, assembled, usually pyramidally, from juxtaposed or interpenetrating prisms, offered almost as many possibilities in three dimensions.

But very little of this made much direct impact on the buildings which characterise the early phase of *de Stijl*, and tend to follow Berlage where they do not follow Wright. No painterly influence on Robert van t'Hoff's house and summerhouse at Huis ter Heide is to be expected anyhow, since these had been commissioned, designed and completed before the group came into existence. Their appearance was conspicuously Wrightian, which was hardly surprising since their designer had actually been to Chicago to meet Wright, had seen the Unity Temple, the Robie House, etc. and seems to have been the member of *de Stijl* who introduced the others to Wright's work.[6] The second, larger house at Huis ter Heide is more important for its structure than for its tidy, symmetrically Wrightian exterior, for it was a pioneer concrete post-and-slab villa, designed at least as early as Le Corbusier's *Dom-ino* structure, though far less free in plan. Van t'Hoff was also designing furniture almost as early as this, and since some of it was built in Gerrit Rietveld's workshop, it may well have been van t'Hoff who introduced Rietveld both to Wright's furniture, and to his own preference for making each structural member a plain rectangular wooden element, visually discrete from even those to which it was attached.

Even in 1917–19 neither of the other two main *de Stijl* architects makes so clear an impression of maturity and control. In Oud's hostel 'de Vonk' and Wils's restaurant 'De Dubbele Sleutel' of 1919, with both of which van Doesburg was involved as colour-consultant, the structure consists of plain rectangular piers and walls of Berlagian brickwork, capped by thickish flat overhangs (not always concealing flat roofs) that come from Wright either direct or by way of Huis ter Heide. 'De Dubbele Sleutel', built on to the side of existing buildings is mildly asymmetrical, whereas the free-standing 'de Vonk' presents a strictly formal and axial appearance. It is surprising in retrospect how little of Oud's work of the period is anything but axial. The project for a small house in concrete of 1917 is symmetrical, as is the planning of much of his large-scale housing; the *Strand-boulevard* project of 1917, though it postulates an endless series of repetitive units, has each unit symmetrical, and of the two factory projects of 1919 one is

---

[6] According to van t'Hoff it would appear that Oud was ignorant of Wright's work (in spite of Berlage) until he was introduced by van Doesburg to van t'Hoff and saw the mass of material on Wright that the latter had brought back with him from the U.S. The story gains weight from the sudden manner in which the Robie House (which particularly impressed van t'Hoff) comes to the forefront of discussions of Wright's work, and displaces the Coonley and Isabel Roberts houses, which had dominated the scene under the influence of *In the Cause*, as described in the previous chapter. As to the situation with Rietveld, the instrumentality of van t'Hoff in bringing Wright to his notice is not doubted, but versions differ—though all, again agree that it was in connection with the furnishing of the house at Huis ter Heide.

symmetrical. The other, which is for Oud a remarkably free and diversified composition, has at least one passage of complex asymmetrical space-manipulation by means of projecting horizontal and vertical elements; sills, door-jambs, chimneys, balustrades, window-mullions, etc. that is unlike anything else in his own recorded work, and is as advanced for its day as the contemporary *de Stijl* interiors of Wilmos Huszar, or the series of chairs that Gerrit Rietveld was developing from 1917 onwards, though their full importance did not emerge till later.

The general caution of Oud's approach seems to have been an integral part of his character, and he felt so strongly the weight of responsibility that was placed upon his shoulders when he became city architect of Rotterdam at the very early age of twenty-eight, that he abstained from committing himself to many of *de Stijl's* activities (he signed none of the Manifestoes or petitions, for instance). Caution appears also in his more considered writings, which were published after he, and most of the other early members of the group, had resigned, but less so in his notes and captions in *de Stijl* before that date. Even so, the most interesting early contribution on architecture to the magazine, the first that breaks new ground in Holland—and indeed Europe north of the Alps—is Rob van t'Hoff's commentary to a drawing by Sant'Elia, which appeared in August 1919. Van t'Hoff had known Marinetti and other Futurists in London before the outbreak of the War, but had not met Sant'Elia—the photograph of the drawing was brought to his attention by van Doesburg, who had received it with other Futurist material from Italy, as a result, presumably, of his first attempts to establish international contacts as soon as hostilities had finished. It is of one of the *case a gradinate*, with external lift-tower and illuminated advertising signs on its parapet, and in view of the number of times it was reproduced (or re-reproduced from *de Stijl*) in Germany and elsewhere it must have become the very best known of all Sant'Elia drawings.

Van t'Hoff writes[7] first of Sant'Elia himself, however, and in terms that have been echoed ever since. He deplores the oblivion in which the 'unknown' architect has been lost, his early death, the shortage of ground-plans of his buildings and the fragmentary nature of his urbanistic vision. He also assumes from the horizontal banding of the wall surfaces that they have been plastered, which, he says, reveals a lack of clarity

However, the perfect management of this building taken as a whole, carried out in modern materials, so that we can consider it free from any adventitious effect, makes this work (and another to be reproduced later) worthy to be included in the new international trend in art. The aversion that Sant'Elia had for 'high class architecture' and Classicism with its decorative and academic approach, gives this work a freshness, a tautness and definiteness of expression, whereas most current art lacks this strength.

[7] *De Stijl*, II, pp. 114, 115.

At the end he reprints a cut version of the affirmations from the end of the Manifesto of Futurist Architecture, prefacing them with the pious hope

> May some of the following thoughts, e.g. that every generation (the buildings are in steel and concrete) shall have its own city, become dominant, and may we never diminish our appreciation for this architect who died so young.

As was so often the case with magazines of this kind, another Sant'Elia promised for publication at a later date did not materialise, but two by Chiattone did appear in due course, with a commentary by Oud, which characterised them as exhibiting the *Vaagheid der Romantiek* as against the *Klaarheid eener hoogere realiteit* of Sant'Elia. However, Oud rarely showed any interest in the work of any architect outside Holland, except Frank Lloyd Wright, and he tended to elaborate his theories upon the basis of his own practical experience, plus a view of the general trend of world art as it was represented to him by his colleagues of *de Stijl*. Or, to be more precise historically, as it had been represented to him by his former colleagues, for his larger writings date from 1921, the year in which he left the group, and onwards. But he stuck to the opinions he had formed then, and did not follow the later development of *de Stijl*—apparently because he did not want to develop or change his position.

> But to me the revealed line of development appears straight; and should it show itself devious, I stand by my right to believe it straight. This line is for me essential. . . .

The bulk of these more considered and more fully elaborated writings is made up of three essays which finally appeared together in one volume of the *Bauhausbücher* in 1926. The first of these (as it appears in this volume) deals with the history of Modern architecture in Holland (*Die Entwicklung der modernen Baukunst in Holland*) and was written in 1922–3. It establishes what was already becoming an orthodox family tree descending from Cuijpers through Berlage to himself; it anathematises the work of the Amsterdam school, and it relates his own work to that of a few select buildings abroad that seem to him *das Fundament . . . einer allgemeinen Schönheit, eines Stiles, zu ergeben*, which prove to be only Le Corbusier's Villa at Vaucresson, Gropius's remodelling of the *Stadttheater* at Jena, and Lönberg-Holm's design for the Chicago *Tribune* Tower. But, at that time, he would have been hard put to it to find anything even up to the standard of his own workers' housing at the Hook of Holland, which he also illustrates, without drawing on Amsterdam or Expressionist sources, and, within the fairly narrow limits of good and bad which he had set himself, he could indeed

> say this without Chauvinism, that present-day Dutch architecture has achieved importance

though even three years later its position of European leadership had already been lost.

The second essay, *Der Einfluss von Frank Lloyd Wright auf die Architektur Europas*, seems to have been written partly for this *Bauhausbuch*, and partly for the *Wendingen* volume on Wright which appeared in 1925. It does not contain much by way of appreciation of Wright that might not have been written by Berlage, except for some comments on the *de luxe* aspects of Wright's domestic work, to which reference will be made in the next chapter. There is however, an important attempt to sort out the meaning of the Wrightian and painterly contribution to younger Dutch architects' work that sheds light on what 'Cubism'—that is, the art of Mondriaan and van Doesburg—meant to him. It proved disappointing, he says, because formalism weakened its impact just at the time when its consequences promised to be of the greatest importance for the future of the art of building. Nevertheless

> Like the influence of Wright, Cubism played an important part in producing the characteristic forms that found expression in the aforementioned current of European architecture (*scil. de Stijl*)

and he was prepared to put a very high valuation on its contribution to the growth of the new architecture of his generation

> Cubism was an introspection—and a beginning. Trusting in the future, it imposed duties, where former generations, parasiting on the past, had taken liberties. The unintentional Romanticism of its vehement drive for co-ordination contained the inception of a new formal synthesis, an unhistorical Classicism.
> The need for number and measure, for cleanliness and order, for standardisation and repetition, for perfection and high finish; the properties of the organs of modern living, such as technique, transport and hygiene in the sphere of social conditions, mass-production methods among economic circumstances—all these find their fore-runner in Cubism.

It is clear that this version of 'Cubism' contains very little of what went on in Paris before 1914, but a great deal of what had preoccupied Werkbund and Futurist theorists, subsumed in the pure clean abstraction of *de Stijl* painting.

It was with ideas such as these already in his mind that Oud built out from basically Berlagian foundations the philosophy of architecture set out in *Über die zukünftige Baukunst und ihre architektonischen Möglichkeiten*. This essay is of the greatest interest because it was written in 1921, when he was in the process of breaking away from *de Stijl*, but, at that early date, must also be the first major theoretical pronouncement by any of the leading architects of the mainstream of development in the Twenties. He himself (in accord with his professed policy of sticking to his earlier ideas) was prepared to let it stand unaltered when it was reproduced in the *Bauhausbuch* in 1926, though it is clear from a set of aphorisms under the title *Ja und Nein* that had appeared in Wasmuth's *Monatshefte* in the previous year, that some of his ideas were under revision, and that he was also dissociating himself from concepts that his contemporaries had put in circulation. Thus

> I bow the knee to the wonders of technology, but I do not believe that a liner can be compared to the Parthenon.
> I long for a house that will satisfy my every demand for comfort, but a house is not for me a living-machine,

and it is hard to reconcile the endlessly repeated house-units of the Strandboulevard project, and his proposition of May 1918 that mass-production will make better aesthetic sense in mass-housing than in individual dwellings, with

> I await a style-defining crystallisation of form through the normalisation of building-elements, yet the mass-produced house seems too difficult to organise into collective assemblies.

Yet he allowed the text of *Zukünftige Baukunst* to stand. It opens with a sober celebration of the defeat of Academic and Ruskinian theory, and a restatement of Berlage's aesthetic of repose

> Life is struggle, but art in its highest form is victory, i.e. consummation.

Then follows an arraignment of the state of architecture as he found it, with its main fault identified as what the Futurists would have termed *Passatismo*

> Not only is the art of building not in advance of its time, it is not even abreast of it, and acts as a drag on the necessary progress of life . . . no longer aiming to embody the most desirable kind of dwelling in the most beautiful form, but offering to one and all a preconception of beauty which it places before all other considerations. . . . Thus it comes about that the products of technological progress do not find immediate application in building, but are first scrutinised by the standards of the ruling aesthetic, and if, as usual, found to be in opposition to them, will have difficulty in maintaining themselves against the venerable weight of the architectural profession.

He cites plate-glass, iron, reinforced concrete and machine-produced components as examples, but admits that no art is harder to reform than that of architecture. Against the chaos and empty formalism of this situation he sets a vision of *de Stijl's* abstract millenium

> In life, the unavoidable consequence imposes itself, nonetheless, with iron inevitability: Spirit overcomes Nature.
> Machinery supplants animal strength, philosophy replaces faith. The stability of old concepts of life is undermined, the natural concordance of their organs destroyed. New spiritual complexes are forged and free themselves from the old naturalistic ones, setting up an opposed equilibrium. . . .
> Only the art of building, that has the duty of reflecting the culture of its times, remains immune to this spiritual crisis.

The echoes of Sant'Elia here (cf. *New spiritual complexes are forged*, with *si sono relevati attegiamenti dello spirito*, etc.) are so clear that one is not surprised to find Futurism listed first among the movements that were not immune to the spiritual crisis, on account of its 'painterly reconciliation of space and time' (an idea owed to van Doesburg[8]). The other movement

---

[8] In his *Bauhausbuch* (Munich, 1924, No. 6) published under the title of *Grundbegriffe der neuen gestaltenden Kunst* and based on lectures given much earlier, van Doesburg had illustrated a very 'dynamic' Cubo-Futurist drawing of his own as a *raumzeitlich* reconstruction of a nude.

not immune was Cubism, in which he found

> through the analysis of natural form, the beginning of the transition from the natural to the spiritual, from the illustrative to the creative, from the closed to the spatial

and it is in these painterly activities that the salvation of architecture must lie since

> what it may not accomplish by its own powers may be achieved by the force of external circumstances, in addition to internal ones.

He counters the inevitable objection that architecture, unlike the free arts, is concerned with utility as well as beauty, by pointing out that in many useful objects where

> the ruling aesthetic plays a diminishing part in determining ultimate form . . . the drive for beauty in man is nevertheless so great that, as if by themselves, these objects achieve elementary aesthetic form over and above purely technical considerations

and his justificatory examples are, as might be expected, a conglobation of Futurist and Werkbund admirations

> . . . automobiles, steamers, yachts, men's wear, sports clothes, electrical and sanitary equipment, table-ware and so forth, possess within themselves, as the purest expressions of their time, the elements of a new language of aesthetic form, and can be considered as the point of departure for a new art, through their restrained form, lack of ornament and plain colours, the comparative perfection of their materials and the purity of their proportions—largely due to their new, mechanical methods of production.

All this encourages a drive toward Abstraction in architecture as well, but it is negative and does not have the aesthetic 'tension' of

> self-realisation in a great rhythmically balanced complex of interconnected, opposing but mutually-influenced parts, each of which supports the general aesthetic intention so that nothing can be added, nor taken away . . . and any alteration, even the smallest, results in complete destruction of the whole balance.

This appearance of Alberti (nothing added nor taken away) in the same paragraph as Berlage and so soon after Sant'Elia, is not difficult to parallel, in the quotations from Plotinus that appear in other *de Stijl* texts, or from Plato in equivalent writings from Paris, and it suggests that Oud's 'unhistorical Classicism' means here what similar ideas usually mean, Academic aesthetics without Academic detailing.

Where such an Albertian balance is lacking, Oud observed, the architecture of his day made up for it with decoration, in spite of the fact that

> Building without ornament affords the greatest possibilities for purity of architectural expression

and

> All decoration is inessential, mere outward compensation for inner impotence.

To account for the needless (as he saw it) duality of structure and ornament he has recourse to a familiar neo-Classical postulate, the primitive hut (which seems to be a close relation of the cave in which Adolf Loos supposed the first work of art to have been smudged)

> As soon as the first hut was built it was decorated, and the foundation was laid for centuries of subsequent anachronisms . . . and the muddling equation of Beauty and Decoration took shape

but now, with the abstract millenium at hand

> . . . a self-created architecture is possible at last, to which the other arts are no longer applied, and therefore no longer subordinated, but work organically with it

and this architecture (which would presumably have gratified van der Leck) would also have satisfied, in a complicated way, the ideal simplicity admired by Mondriaan, since

> . . . it endures no decoration, since it is in itself a complete space-creating organism, by which all decoration becomes individualisation, and therewith limitation, of the universal, i.e. the spatial.

This last sentence brings us close to the inner, inexplicable mystique of *de Stijl* at large, as well as of Oud in particular: the equation of individualism, decoration, handicraft and limitation (or closure) and its opposition to the matching equation of universalism, abstraction, machine-production and spatiality, makes sense as far as the first three terms of each set are concerned, but the last pair of terms, both in their connection to the rest of the set, and their opposition to one another, do not seem to follow, unless this spatiality/enclosure contrast is somehow to be derived from the mystical geometry of Schoenmaekers. Be that as it may, the implication that space is infinite space, not the enclosed *Raum* of Berlage, was probably vital to the integration of *de Stijl* into international Abstract art, for both Malevitsch and Lissitsky also regarded space in this manner.

The reader's sense that he has reached one of those core concepts that can only be discussed tautologically is reinforced at this point by the way in which Oud suddenly abandons generalities and turns to more practical matters, as if he had gone as far as he could along this road. On the practical side, Oud notes first the progressive invasion of all parts of building by mechanical methods, in spite of the obstacles put in their way, and in particular the impact of mechanical detailing:

> In contrast to handicraft details, that is those made by manual means—uncertain in form, proportion and colour—which elaborate endless variations on a dominant *motif*, it is the distinguishing feature of mechanical detailing that, reliably related in form and colour, it is perfectly similar to all other details of the same sort prepared at the same time.

Then he notes that new materials will not have any revolutionary effect where traditional formulae hinder their proper use:

> When iron came in, great hopes were entertained of a new architecture, but

it fell aesthetically-speaking into the background through improper application. . . .

Because of its visible solidity—unlike plate-glass which is only solid to the touch—we have supposed its destination to be the creation of masses and planes, instead of reflecting that the characteristic feature of iron construction is that it offers the maximum of structural strength with the minimum of material. . . . Its architectural value therefore lies in the creation of voids, not solids, in contrast to mass-walling, not continuing it.

similarly with glass

divided . . . into small parts by the customary glazing bars, it optically continues the solidity of the wall over the openings as well

and should therefore always be used in the largest possible sheets with the thinnest possible glazing bars and mullions.

He sees even more exciting possibilities in the use of reinforced concrete, which avoids the limitations imposed on brick by its modular sizes and its restricted spans over openings

Besides, the unfitness of other materials for the acceptance of tensile loading . . . hinders the construction of extensive horizontal spans and cantilevers. The combination of the necessary auxiliary materials such as wood and iron . . . with brick, is generally too heterogeneous to lead to satisfactory solutions in these sort of cases. If it is not plastered over, then neither a strict clean line in the brickwork nor a pure homogeneous plane is established, since the small units and the multiplicity of joins prevent this.

Against this, reinforced concrete offers a homogeneous coherence of supporting and supported parts, horizontal spreads of considerable dimensions, and the possibility of co-ordinating pure planes and masses.

This idea of using concrete to create a purely apparent unification of load and support shows how much aesthetic *parti-pris* lurks even in the practicalities of a man like Oud who left *de Stijl* because he felt its aesthetics were becoming too precious, but it is not unique, nor restricted to Holland, for one will find plaster freely used to create a fictitious homogeneity of breeze-block and concrete in much housing work by convinced Modernists in Germany, and of pot-tile and concrete in several houses by Le Corbusier.

In general the possibilities in reinforced concrete for creating buildings in which successive floors grow larger in plan as one ascends, and walls can be stepped forward, instead of being battered back in the common manner, give

on a constructive basis, the fundamentals for an art of building of an optically-immaterial, almost hovering appearance.

Then he turns to colour, the last important element in his architectural philosophy, and in this context handicraft materials are decried for an entirely fresh set of reasons, viz., that they are too *nuancé* and atmospheric in hue (which apparently smacked of Impressionism to Oud) and, worse still, their hues changed under weathering

so that what was originally a harmony could become a discord in a week; a discord that would strike the eye all the more clearly when pure painted colours have been used than where a more neutral tint is employed—a circumstance that probably explains the preference for dark green paint to set against the prevailing brick-grey of our country.

And so he comes to his conclusions

> All in all, it follows that an architecture rationally based on the circumstances of life today would be in every sense opposed to the sort of architecture that has existed up till now. Without falling into barren rationalism it would remain, above all, objective, but within this objectivity would experience higher things. In the sharpest contrast to the untechnically-formed and colourless products of momentary inspiration as we know them, its ordained task will be, in perfect devotion to an almost impersonal method of technical creation, to shape organisms of clear form and pure proportions. In place of the natural attractions of uncultivated materials, the broken hues in glass, the irregularity of finishes, the paleness of colour, the clouding of glazes, the weathering of walls, etc. it would unfold the stimulating qualities of sophisticated materials, the limpidity of glass, the shine and roundness of finishes, lustrous and shining colours, the glitter of steel, and so forth.
>
> Thus the development of the art of building goes toward an architecture more bound to matter than ever before in essence, but in appearance rising clear of material considerations; free from all Impressionistic creation of atmosphere, in the fullness of light, brought to purity of proportion and colour, organic clarity of form; an architecture that, in its freedom from inessentialism could surpass even Classical purity.

These are the words of a cautious man, who developed a middle-of-the-road reputation, was regarded as a Functionalist, and probably saw himself as one, and yet they announce the aim of replacing one kind of architectural illusionism (Impressionist atmospherics) by an even more deceptive one, in which greater materiality shall be disguised as decreased materiality; yet another warning that if the architecture of the Twenties is regarded in the purely materialistic terms in which it is commonly discussed, much of its point will be lost. Nowhere among the major figures of the Twenties will a pure Functionalist be found, an architect who designs entirely without aesthetic intentions, and once those intentions are admitted (as they commonly were, in so many words) then illusionism, particularly the illusion of weightlessness, or of structural homogeneity, follows hard on their heels.

13: Expressionism: Amsterdam and Berlin

IT WOULD BE altogether too facile to regard the various anti-Rationalist tendencies of 1914–23 as a revolt against the mainstream of development, or as a serious alternative 'school' to the emergent International Style. Though Twentieth-century architecture was undoubtedly impoverished formally by the demise of this manner of design, the resolute paring-down to one particular set of formal and structural solutions that took place in the early Twenties seems to have been a necessary phase of self-discipline and brain-cleansing before development could resume. It would, indeed, be better to regard *Wendingen* and Expressionist architecture as late outcroppings of attitudes to design that had been part of the main body of European architecture before 1914, but became increasingly unacceptable on formal grounds after 1918. And it should be emphasised that despite the tentative alliance of Amsterdam and Berlin in 1919, they were separate developments both in origin and character.

Since Amsterdam possesses the larger body of work, done over more than a decade, and was the instigator of the short-lived alliance, it will be dealt with first. The chief ornament of the school was Michel de Klerk (1884–1923) as already mentioned, and he, with Piet Kramer, the next most brilliant member of the Amsterdam school, did much of the detailing and interior work on van der Mey's *Scheepvaartshuis* in 1913. There, and at de Klerk's independent *Hillehuis* two years earlier, one can see emerging a distinctive style that might be called twentieth-century in accent, unrestrainedly eclectic in vocabulary, but nineteenth-century in its phraseology. Indeed the *Hillehuis* follows structural precepts that go back even further in Dutch town-house practice, but the *Scheepvaartshuis* follows, more or less, the structural precedents worked out in Berlage's office-buildings before the turn of the century. However, where Berlage's structures tend to be invested in a kind of neutralised Romanesque detailing by the time he came to design the *Beurs*, the detailing of these two pioneer works of the Amsterdam school is far from neutral in tone, and draws from a variety of sources, including Art Nouveau in general and Toorop in particular, Expressionist painting and carving, de Groot's mathematical exercises, from Berlage himself, and from Wright. As J. J. P. Oud observed at different times these last two are to be accounted the more important influences on the style, and this probably accounts for the strain of interest in exhibited structure (or pseudo-structure) that runs right through the decade of the school's greatest activity, also the tendency to use commonplace materials, like brick, tile-hanging and wood, in a manner that shows genuine affection, and such as Berlage could hardly have disapproved. Thus, on the *Scheepvaartshuis*, structural corbels made from several pieces of stone are allowed to appear, in spite of elaborate figurative carving, as corbels carved from several pieces of stone. Examples of this kind could be multiplied throughout the work of the school, and they emphasise the right of de Klerk and his connection to be regarded as the true heirs of certain aspects of Berlage and Wright, just as much as J. J. P. Oud and his connection were the heirs of other aspects. It was, no doubt, this common heritage that made it possible for Jan Wils, for instance, to pass from one side to the other without ceasing to write admiringly of Wright, and also made it possible for the Amsterdam and Rotterdam schools to fuse fairly painlessly into a national style once de Klerk was dead and van Doesburg was out of the country—though the process was no doubt facilitated by the existence, around 1925, of independent Wright/Berlagians like Willem Marinus Dudok, who subsequently became the hero-figure of middle-of-the-road Modernists.

However, the main characteristics of the Amsterdam School all lie in the direction of the physical manipulation of the building in the course of erection, rather than in intellectual decisions made beforehand: its vital expression is in its detailing, which is often representational and therefore its history is iconographical, rather than theoretical, and lies outside the scope of the present study. However, it served a useful irritant function in other people's theoretical writings, and not only acted as a standing example of individualistic licentiousness at which the moralists of *de Stijl* could point the finger of scorn, but also drew their attention to things that they might otherwise have missed in the work of Frank Lloyd Wright, for instance. Thus Oud, noting the misuse of Wright's example in Europe, draws attention to a vital aspect of his work that escaped comment elsewhere, and to which his own attention was almost certainly directed by the contrast between Amsterdam architecture and that of his own 'Cubist' connection.

> That which in Cubism—and it cannot be otherwise—is puritanical asceticism, spiritual self-denial, is with Wright exuberant plasticity, sensuous superfluity. What arises in Wright from the fullness of life to a degree of luxury that could only fit into an American 'High-life', withdraws in Europe to abstraction that derives from other ideals and embraces all men and everything.

If one substitutes 'Dutch middle-class' for 'American' one could equally well substitute de Klerk for Wright, for one of the aspects of his work, as in the Spaarndam housing, that has given offence to Rationalists ever since it was built, is the air of mild luxury it exudes, a luxury felt to be somehow improper to mass-housing. Another embarrassment concerning the Spaarndam housing is that it is difficult to make the favoured accusation of superficiality stick to it. Practically the whole Amsterdam School were *de facto* guilty of superficial 'façadism' in the work they did around the Amstellaan,[1] where they were called in simply to put by-law fronts on to contractor's housing, but on the Spaarndam, and in the triangular block that faces the Zaanstraat in particular, de Klerk cannot be made answerable for the crimes committed by his connection elsewhere. Inner and outer spaces, main and subsidiary buildings, public and private areas are related and integrated with a subtlety and understanding of effect that could not have been equalled in Holland in 1917, the year of its design, and that Oud himself probably could not have equalled at any time, even had he wanted to.

However, de Klerk's brilliance was of a somewhat improvisatory nature; the Amsterdam School, deprived of his constant example, began to decline from the moment of his death, because he left behind neither a workshop tradition nor a body of ideas committed to paper. *Wendingen*, Theo van der Wijdeveld's magazine, which was the official mouthpiece of the Amsterdam School, contrived to deduce no general principles from his work, and is, in fact, a disappointing vehicle of architectural theory. Its best achievements were its special numbers, and volumes *hors serie*, in honour of great men, including three on de Klerk, as a memorial after his death, one on Berlage, a small one on Eric Mendelsohn, and the double-number on Wright to which reference has already been made.

However, a general reading of *Wendingen* does serve to emphasise what other strains of architectural thought were current in the Amsterdam School besides the Berlagian. As has been noted, Jan Wils's equation of Wright with the Futurists appeared in *Wendingen*,[2] and the rest of his remarks are worth quoting because they underline a Futurist content in Amsterdam thought, informing and transforming a vaguely Berlagian social awareness, and a hint of Loosian rhetoric.

> And now it happened that a new strange sound was heard, the sound of exultant masses, liberated, aware of their strength, breaking the fetters of the past, sensing the sublime conquest of a new future; the sound of great vibrating machines and humming dynamos, that stand ready in their giant strength to lead, through unworthy generations, to the ultimate welfare and service of Mankind; the sound of droning propellers and whining sirens, and everything that comes in with the new age.
> Therein lies the strength of the present time, the new source of power. Not in contorted formlets, not in fear and trembling, not in sentimentality, nor in

[1] The explanation of the Amstellaan façades, on which hostile critics have relied so heavily in their attacks on the Amsterdam School, is given by J. P. Mieras in *Wendingen* (Amsterdam, 1923, VI, p. 3).

[2] 1919, VI, p. 16.

routine fishing in the ocean of old forms, but in convenience, amplitude, vastness and cleanliness shall the new art become the language of today.

The visual complement to this quasi-Futurist writing was Wijdeveld's *Groote Volkstheater* project. This would have altered a whole quarter of Amsterdam quite as drastically as anything that Marinetti could have done to Venice, since it would have obliterated most of the Vondelpark, partly under the theatre and its flanking wings, and partly under an enormous approach avenue that was to begin near the Leidseplein and enter the forecourt of the theatre at the point where it crossed an extension of the Emmalaan. Its length of almost a kilometre was to be flanked by skyscrapers up to thirty stories high, boat-shaped in plan with their major axes at right angles to the avenue. Though formally exciting, and impressive in scale, with its tower-blocks marching into the heart of five-storey Amsterdam, the scheme does not bear close examination, particularly in connection with such technical matters as foundations and circulation.

It seems doubtful if any member of the school, even de Klerk, was really capable of designing on this scale, and most of the energy of Amsterdam architects continued to go into residential work, either projected or completed. Outside de Klerk's designs, this residential work, particularly the villas, has a highly distinctive character—the partnerships of Vorkink Wormser, and Eibink and Snellebrand, not to mention such independents as Margit Kropholler, all produced work that was characterised by a most erudite eclecticism, and a literally plastic sense of plasticity. The formal borrowings included not only elements from Poelzig, Mendelsohn, Chiattone, and other sources that have since been loosely termed 'Expressionist', but also complete figurative envelopes—there is a well-known house by Kropholler shaped like a Noah's Ark, and van Doesburg once complained of another house (not traceable) in the form of a tram. The sense of plasticity, however, seems to have no antecedents, except possibly in Poelzig's studio practice, for it derives its marked character from the practice of doing the primary sketching of designs in three-dimensions and in soft plastic materials like clay and modelling wax. The resultant buildings though often quite compactly planned, give an impression of amoebic sprawl, with their curved plan-forms and walls of varying thickness, and were usually roofed with massive lids of thatch, which proves very amenable to design of this sort.

This mode of design lies a long way from the pure planes and masses praised by Oud, yet the material Oud envisaged as producing these pure forms, was admired by at least one of these designers of amoebic villas, Eibink, as suitable to his own mode of design. What is even more remarkable, in view of what is usually supposed about the superficiality of Amsterdam as against the structurality of *de Stijl*, is the fact that Eibink discusses this material—reinforced concrete—only as a structural means, and does not refer, as Oud does, to its visual character. For Eibink, the use of reinforced concrete is a means of liberating architecture from additive, inorganic, post-and-lintel design. As he wrote in *Wendingen* in 1919.

> For the character of concrete, i.e. its being cast in one piece, becomes an element of much richer meaning through reinforcement, since reinforced concrete facilitates the bringing of forces from all sides and directions into equilibrium at will. By this token, concrete changes from dead stuff to living organism . . . one builds no more in the restricted sense of assembling or piling elements together.

However, little concrete, if any, was used in these villas, so that in material as well as exterior plasticity, they represent the *Wendingen* group's closest approach to the work of Mendelsohn. A comparison of these villas with Mendelsohn's *Einsteinturm* is instructive, because it indicates the bases of the suggested alliance, as well as one of the differences on which it foundered. In both cases the exterior is conceived as if the building were composed of a soft plastic material that had been manipulated by a giant hand; in the case of the *Einsteinturm* and most of the villas the material is, in fact, brick cut and rendered over to resemble concrete, though the suggestion is present that the material actually is concrete. But the planning of the *Einsteinturm* is symmetrical, and based on an Academic apparatus of minor and major axes, whereas the villas are extremely a-formal and anti-symmetrical in plan, and represent one of the excesses of 'dynamism' that Mendelsohn could not accept in Amsterdam architecture.

The first approach to Mendelsohn came, in any case, from Wijdeveld,[3] not from the villa-designers, and was inspired by an exhibition of Mendelsohn's sketches at Paul Cassirer's gallery in Berlin in 1919. Though their creator, then thirty-two, was almost unknown, these sketches made a formidable impression at the time, and Wijdeveld invited Mendelsohn to come to Amsterdam to lecture to *Architectura et Amicitia* (the formal organisation of which *Wendingen* was the organ) and to assemble material for a special issue of the magazine. The impact of the sketches is not difficult to understand—though rooted in the work of pre-War masters like Poelzig and Olbrich, in much the same way that *Wendingen* was rooted in Berlage, they had an air of excitement and zest about them that was missing from the more placid work of Amsterdam. The difference seems mostly attributable to the difference of generation—in the direct sense that most of the *Wendingen* group were a little older than Mendelsohn anyhow, and in the less direct, but more important, sense of the point in Mendelsohn's career at which the War intervened. The Amsterdam architects preserved their links with the pre-War world and earlier masters unbroken, but not only had the War interrupted that continuity for everyone in Germany, but it had begun when Mendelsohn was only twenty-seven and only just established in practice. He had not, therefore, even any substantial body of pre-

[3] The narrative of events leading up to Wijdeveld's invitation is given by Arnold Whittick in his book on Mendelsohn, which also quotes the most interesting passages from his correspondence of the period.

War work of his own to look back on, and his wartime experiences had their effect on a mind not yet settled; a mind, like that of many of his German contemporaries, that was still far from settled five years after the Armistice, and he was to go on developing after most of the *Wendingen* designers had lost their drive.

As a result he handles his pre-War themes with a freshness they were losing, and with the advantage of having had four years in which to revise and revalue them without having to commit himself to anything more than paper sketches. Executed between 1914 and 1917 and then resumed in 1919 in a second series that continued for the rest of Mendelsohn's life, these sketches form a remarkable body of work by any standards, and the first set, alone, would be sufficient to establish him as one of the more remarkable architectural talents of the twentieth century. Though he himself provided little in the way of explanation of them, and subsequent critical exegesis by others has not been very helpful, it is possible to go some way in establishing their sources and their meaning. One of the most striking, for a car-body factory, is also one of the easiest to decipher. Reading between the illustrations to a lecture he gave in Berlin in 1919 (and later, in Amsterdam), one may identify the sources of the overhead gantry cranes in overhead railways that he had seen, and the dipylon end-structure in Olbrich's Darmstadt exhibition gateway of 1908. (Olbrich was an architect for whom he had a special regard, as the leader who might have delivered the *Wiener Sezession* from its own weaknesses.)

But whoever looks at this sketch cannot fail to be impressed by the way in which the building seems to strain forward along its major axis. This effect Mendelsohn called *dynamism*, but the word has broader connotations than the dynamism, inherent in certain forms, proposed in the Manifesto of Futurist architecture, and apparent as a kind of 'excelsior' in some of Sant'Elia's sketches. Mendelsohn's definition of dynamism varied, and although he seems at times to suggest that it is more than an expression of the internal pattern of stresses in a building, most of his direct definitions do not really go beyond such a concept, and in the case of the car-body factory he explicitly means only the expression of internal forces.

> This sketch of a bodywork factory derives its dynamism fully from the forces in its steel construction. The row of gantries, indicated as lattice trusses, draws the forms together sharply at the highest level, while at the same time the corner-blocks nod forward. That is, the loads transmitted through the gantries are absorbed by the tie-girder structures in the corner-towers.

Not the least important revelation of this passage is that it proves to deal with a structure in tension, a concept that seems to have had little interest for architects even after the War, let alone 1914 when this sketch was made. Only in Russia, after the Revolution, was there much enthusiasm for structures of this kind, and they seem to have been quite beyond the comprehension of the Dutch architects with whom Wijdeveld's invitation

2. Hendrikus
eter Berlage.
Iain Hall of the
eurs, Amsterdam,
fter 1900: a down-
o-earth
Lationalism,
lmost Gothic-
evival in character,
ecalling the virtues
f fifty years earlier.

3. Frank Lloyd
Vright. Office
lock of the Larkin
Company, Buffalo,
J.Y., 1905: an
chievement so far
ut of step with even
rogressive
rchitectural
hought at the time,
hat Berlage was
robably the only
Europeaan
rchitect who could
ppreciate it.

ABONNEMENT BIJ VOORUITBETALING BINNENLAND 4.50 BUITENLAND 5.50 PER JAARGANG. VOOR ANNONCES WENDE MEN ZICH TOT DEN UITGEVER.

DE STIJL

MAANDBLAD VOOR DE BEELDENDE VAKKEN. REDACTIE THEO VAN DOESBURG. UITGAVE X. HARMS TIEPEN.

ADRES VAN REDACTIE: KORT GALGEWATER 3 LEIDEN. ADMINISTRATIE: X. HARMS TIEPEN, HYPOLITUSBUURT 37 DELFT, INTERC. TEL. 729 EN 690.

1e JAARGANG.　　OCTOBER NEGENTIENHONDERDZEVENTIEN.　　NUMMER 1.

TER INLEIDING.

Dit tijdschriftje wil zijn eene bijdrage tot de ontwikkeling van het nieuwe schoonheidsbewustzijn. Het wil den modernen mensch ontvankelijk maken voor het nieuwe in de Beeldende Kunst. Het wil tegenover de archaïstische verwarring — het „moderne barok" — de logische beginselen stellen van een rijpenden stijl, gebaseerd op zuivere verhouding van tijdgeest en uitdrukkingsmiddelen. Het wil de huidige denkrichtingen betreffende de nieuwe beelding, die, hoewel in wezen gelijk, zich onafhankelijk van elkaar ontwikkeld hebben, in zich vereenigen.

De Redactie zal het hierboven omschreven doel trachten te bereiken door den werkelijk modernen kunstenaar, die iets kan bijdragen tot de hervorming van het aesthetisch besef en de bewustwording der beeldende kunst aan het woord te laten. Waar het publiek nog niet aan de nieuwe beeldingsschoonheid toe is, wordt het de taak van den vakman het schoonheidsbewustzijn bij den leek wakker te maken. De werkelijk moderne, — d. i. bewuste, kunstenaar heeft een dubbele roeping. Ten eerste: het rein-beeldende kunstwerk voort te brengen; ten tweede: het publiek voor de schoonheid der reine beeldende kunst ontvankelijk te maken. Hiervoor is een tijdschrift van intiemen aard noodzakelijk geworden. Te meer, daar de openbare kritiek in gebreke bleef het te kort aan schoonheidsontvankelijkheid voor de abstracte kunstopenbaring, aan te vullen. Tot dit laatste zal de Redactie de vaklieden zelf in staat stellen.

Dit tijdschriftje zal hierdoor een inniger contact scheppen tusschen kunstenaar en publiek en tusschen de beoefenaars der verschillende beeldende vakken. Door den modernen kunstenaar over zijn eigen vak aan het woord te laten zal het vooroordeel, als zou de moderne werkman volgens vooropgestelde theorieën werken, verdwijnen. Integendeel. Het zal blijken, dat het nieuwe kunstwerk niet voortkomt uit a priori aangenomen theorieën, maar juist andersom, dat de beginselen voortvloeien uit de beeldende arbeid.

Het zal zoodoende de mogelijkheid voorbereiden eener verdiepte kunstcultuur, gegrond op gemeenschappelijke belichaming van het nieuwe beeldende kunstbewustzijn. Zoodra de kunstenaars in de verschillende beeldende vakken tot de erkenning zullen komen, dat zij in principe aan elkaar gelijk zijn, dat ze eene algemeene taal te spreken hebben,

I

54. Theo van Doesburg and Wilmos Huszar. Opening page of the first issue of *de Stijl*, 1917. Huszar's logotype in the title is in a manner which was common to other painters of the *Stijl* group, and not far removed from:
55. Theo van Doesburg. *Black and white composition*, 1918: this in its turn can be related to fragments of Mondriaan's so-called 'Plus and Minus Compositions'—genuine stylistic unity underlay the foundation of *de Stijl*.

56. Rob van t'Hoff. Villa at Huis ter Heide, completed
1916: the first concrete-framed villa by a modern
architect, in a style derived from first-hand
acquaintance with the work of Wright.
57. Jan Wils. Restaurant, de Dubbele Sleutel, 1919:
Wrightian architecture in brick, derived at second hand
by way of Berlage's writings.

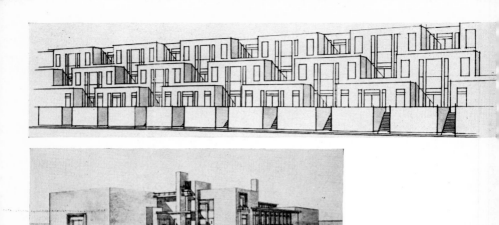

58, 59. J. J. P. Oud. Projects for Strandboulevard (seaside housing), 1917, and a small factory, 1919. The rectangularity of the forms, though different in character in each, is in contrast to 60, 61. Michel de Klerk. Post Office on the Zaanstraat, Amsterdam, 1917; and Theo van de Vijdeveld. Volkstheater Project, before 1921. Curvilinear plasticity and elaborately modelled surfaces of the Amsterdam school.

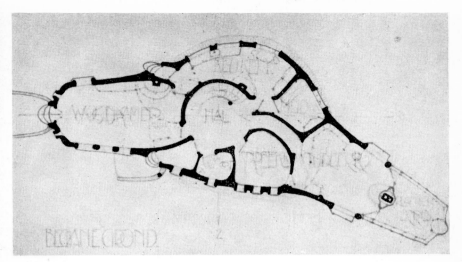

62. Eibink and Snellebrand. Project for a villa, 1920: freedom of planning among the younger members of the *Wendingen* circle was in advance of anything else in Europe at this time.
63. Eric Mendelsohn. The Einstein tower, Potsdam, 1919–1921: the canonical building of Expressionist architecture. Mendelsohn's Dutch friends never equalled it, he himself abandoned this style almost immediately.

64. Eric Mendelsohn. Project for a car-body factory, 1914
or later: although commonly written off as Expressionist
fantasy this project embodies important structural ideas
that Mendelsohn expounded much later, when describing
his concept of dynamism.

Eric Mendelsohn. Projects for a film-studio, above,
crematorium, below, and goods station, bottom; from
the same notebook as the car-body factory.

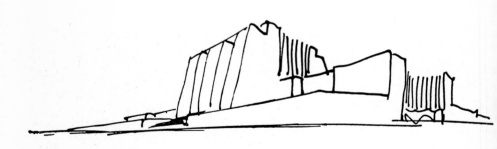

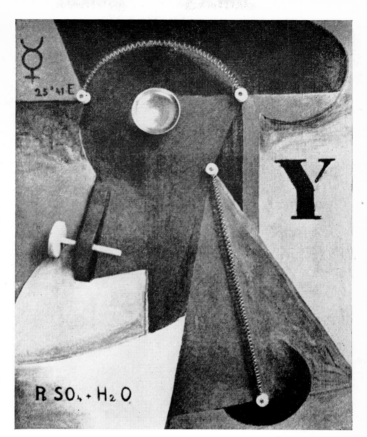

65. Aldo Fiozzi.
Valeurs Abstraits,
1920: this three-
dimensional collage
with scientific
pretensions by an
Italian dadaist gives a
fair idea of the width
of *de Stijl's* interests
in its second phase.
66, 67. Vladimir
Malevitsch. Funda-
mental Suprematist
Elements, 1914; and
Gerrit Thomas
Rietveld. Chair (first
version), 1917. The
central interests of *de
Stijl* remained
constructive, but
fused into an inter-
national Elementarist
aesthetic that had
been anticipated by
Malevitsch and
Rietveld.

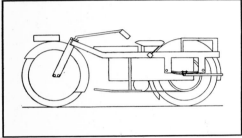

68, 69. Giaccomo Matté-Trucco. Rooftop test track of the Fiat factory, Turin, 1920-1923; and Werner Graeff. Project for a motor-cycle, 1922.

70. Mart Stam. Competition project for a glass and concrete office block in Königsberg, 1923: the use of Sant'Elian set-back façades (cf. fig. 4) is another demonstration of persistent Futurist influence on the *G*-group in Berlin.

71. El Lissitsky and Mart
Stam. 'Wolkenbügel' project,
1924: administrative blocks,
straddling important
thoroughfares on splayed legs
with external passenger lifts—
a highly sophisticated
descendant of Sant'Elia's
town-planning ideas, but see
also fig. 73 below.

72, 73. Wesnin Brothers. Project for the Leningrad *Pravda* offices, 1923, and El
Lissitsky 'Wolkenbügel' project, 1924. The *Pravda* building was regarded by
Lissitsky as a canonical building of Constructivism, and like his own first version
of the 'Wolkenbügel' had an upright and rectilinear structure.

74. Ladowski Psycho-
technical Laboratory,
model study for an
airport, 1923: extension
of the idea of Lissitsky's
abstract *Proun* object
into large-scale planning.

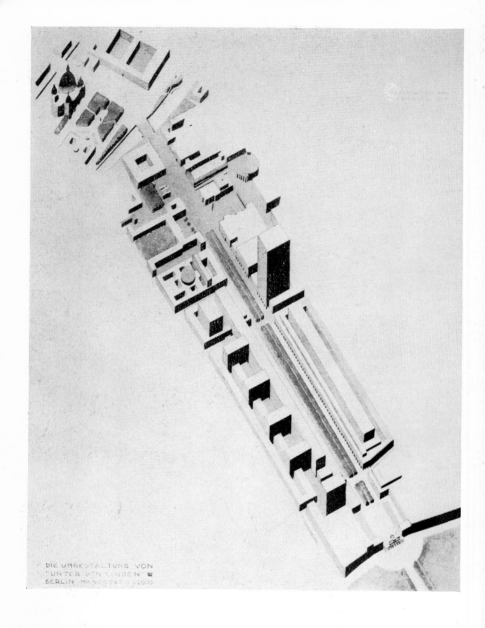

75. Cor van Eesteren (with Theo van Doesburg).
Prize-winning design for the reconstruction of
Unter den Linden, Berlin, 1925: a recombination of
the ideas of Elementarism with the academic
discipline of Elementary composition. The result, at
many points, anticipates the methods of grouping large
blocks that emerged in the 1950's.

76. Frederick Kiesler. *Cité dans l'Espace* (version shown in the Austrian Pavilion, Exposition des Arts Decoratifs), Paris, 1925: described by its designer as *architecture elementarisée*, it represents the fullest exploitation of Elementarist ideas of space.

77. Gerrit Thomas Rietveld. Schroeder House, Utrecht, 1925: the only large permanent structure to emerge from the period of greatest Elementarist activity: the balconies and roof structure extend into the surrounding space in a spectacular but orderly Elementarist manner.

179

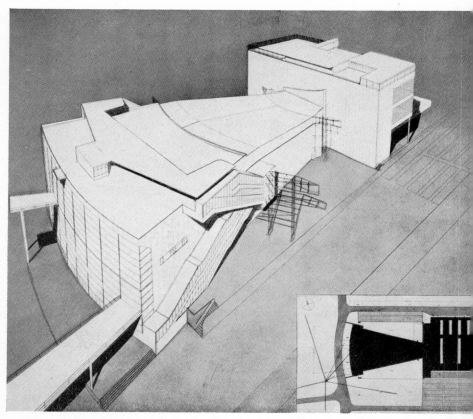

78. Marcel Breuer. Project for a theatre at Kharkov, 1930: Bauhaus schemes of the late twenties, such as this, show the supercession of Dutch Elementarist influence by that of the Russian constructivists.

79. Mart Stam. Chair in steel tube and webbing, 1926; and Marcel Breuer. Chair in steel tube with caned back and seat: again it was under Russian influence that Mart Stam produced the design that liberated chairs from Rietveld's Elementarist *impasse*, and made possible the Breuer type that has become a 'twentieth-century classic'.

brought Mendelsohn in contact. Whatever their feelings about him, and it is clear that Mendelsohn was well received, it is equally clear that he had grave misgivings about what he saw. Instead of warming toward the dramatic plasticity of the *Wendingen* circle, he reacted away from it, toward Oud and his connection in Rotterdam, though he was as far from accepting their position as he was from accepting Amsterdam's. In a letter to his wife he opted for a middle attitude.

> Certainly the primary element is function, but function without sensibility remains mere construction. More than ever I stand by my programme of reconciliation . . . Rotterdam will pursue the way of pure construction with a deathly chill in its veins, and Amsterdam will be destroyed by the fire of its own dynamics. Function plus dynamics is the challenge.

Although he speaks of his reconciliatory programme as something he stands by, and therefore already in existence, the evidence of his sketches and completed buildings suggests that it may not have been in existence very long, for it is clear that the Dutch visit preceded a major upheaval in his manner of conceiving buildings, which finally emerges, as in his factory at Luckenwalde or the Sternfeld House, completely stripped of its bulging plastic forms, disciplined down to straight-edged, square-arrised forms, mostly horizontal and vertical in disposition. This period of transition was completed by 1923, when these two buildings were also completed, but had begun as early as 1920 when the designs for the hat factory at Luckenwalde were put in hand, and its transitional character is manifested by its extensive use of oblique and diagonal forms, tapered columns and beams; forms and structures to which he was not to revert for almost three decades, leaving this factory as unique in his work of the Twenties as it is remarkable in the quality of its design.

However, it is extremely difficult to find any direct reflection of all this tumult of ideas in his few published writings, just as he never describes himself by the epithet most commonly coupled with his name and work; Expressionist. He uses the term once, but in such a way as to imply that it is simply another extremist position (like Constructivist) that he cannot accept, and he was introduced to *Wendingen* readers as an Expressionist by implication, and that is all. On the other hand, it must be noted that in 1919 he expressed opinions that could be construed as Expressionist

> The inner excitements of our time, its impulse toward new departures in all provinces of our common life, compel the artist to bring himself forward in his work and represent his own will

But the artist is to do this in the context of his community

> But, more and more, his personality is taken up with the rule of responsibility to the new community, his path more strictly mapped out as his own demands become greater

and architecture is more conditioned by its community responsibilities than other arts

> As ever, architecture has the power of most visibly recording the formal urges of a period, so today the outcome of this battle (*scil.* against past styles) lies in the hands of the people as a whole.

The introduction of philosophical and art-historical concepts of this order is not quite unique for the period, since van Doesburg also employs ideas like *Zeitgeist* and *Wille zum Stil*, but it is certainly unusual in architectural writing by architects, and it is followed by an equally unusual piece of disguised Semper (or Berlage)

> When forms break down, they are replaced by fresh ones, that have existed all the time, but only now come to the fore.

but the occasion for this rediscovery of lost forms is one on which most of his contemporaries were agreed

> For the special conditions of architecture, the way in which the *Zeitgeist* reshuffles our aims is significant: new tasks through the changed building needs of Transport, Economy, Religion; new constructional possibilities through new materials, glass, iron, concrete.

However, if this is familiar ground, his illustrations of good new structure are unfamiliar, and may be epitomised by his selection of an aircraft (in itself common post-Futurist practice) of an obviously aviomorphic type, the Rumpler *Taube*, with its dove-like wing plan, instead of the regular Euclidian forms of the biplanes preferred by his contemporaries of the other persuasion. Also in contrast to them is his sharp criticism of Bruno Taut's 1913 *Stahlwerksverband* Pavilion for disguised Hellenism, and even sharper criticism of the *Turbinenfabrik*, where, he says, Behrens

> papers over the expressiveness of the hall with the formality of a many-faceted temple-pediment, belittles the plastic fullness of the corner-towers with horizontal jointing grooves, distorts and contradicts their static content . . . claps part on part, building on building, whereas organic construction signifies unbreakable relationships, consistent growth and uninterrupted contours.

This puts him a very long way from the architects in the mainstream of German development, with their additive structures and their general reverence for Behrens, but it leaves him still within reach of the opinions of Eibink, noted above. But with the lecture he gave in 1923 to *Architectura et Amicitia*, he moves out into a world of his own, although both text and illustrations show that he was well-informed on the work of his contemporaries in France, as well as Holland and Germany. The quality of his new opinions, which were to be the last he committed to print for a long time, can best be given by the following passage of almost continuous quotation (and, in reading it, scorn at his views on Relativity should be tempered by the reflection that of all the aesthetic theorists who have mangled Einstein's opinions, Mendelsohn alone knew Einstein well at first hand as a person)

> Since the recognition that the two conceptions hitherto kept separate by Science—Matter and Energy—are only different conditions of the same basic

stuff, that nothing in the Universe is without Relativity to the Cosmos, without connection with the whole—since then Engineers have abandoned the theory of dead material, and given themselves to the dutiful service of Nature. In the most elementary conditions they find regularly-related connections, and their previous arrogance gives way to joyful participation in creative process. The machine, so far the subservient agent of uncreative exploitation, becomes a constructive element in a new living organism. We owe its existence somewhat to the generosity of some unknown agency, as it might be the inventive pleasure of some constructional genius, but at the same time it originates as a necessary by-product of progress, as need dictates. Its real task is this; to satisfy the many changing relationships between population figures and increased demand, between industrialisation and rising consumption, to bring itself to order and control its own effects.

Men of our time, out of the excitement of their high-speed life, can only find compensation in relaxed horizontal forms. Only through a drive for effectiveness can we master our unrest, only at top speed will we conquer our haste. Then will the spinning world stand still.

Unthinkable that this conquest, this mastery of natural elements be given up. But the problem is; to make school-room learning of it.

The child learns to telephone, and the grand order of number crumbles, great distance dwindles to a little walk.

Technology is Handicraft, Laboratory is Workshop, the Inventor is Master.

The echoes of Futurism in the concluding sentences are confirmed by the illustrations that accompany them, but there is little else here that can be related to other contemporary streams of architectural thought, not even to his Berlin School contemporaries in their Expressionist phase. Indeed there is not much that can be related to his own architectural practice, although the matter/energy relationship is clearly related to the explanation of dynamism quoted earlier, which comes from the same lecture. In any case, the lecture was given in the year in which the period of violent transition in his architecture ended, and should, perhaps be treated simply as attempted verbalisation of the plastic ideas implicit in the very violent sketches of that phase. His work does not cease to develop, but, although curved forms reappear, they are not the soft organic curves of his early work, but segments of circles, and they usually manifest themselves as sharply arrised structural slabs. Walls remain vertical, surfaces hard and shiny, he uses glass as lavishly as his other German contemporaries, and he becomes a distinguished contributor to the body of work produced by the Berlin School, marked out only by a slightly more personal idiom than most of them employed.

By the time he finally moved away from what, for want of a better term, must still be called Expressionism,[4] in 1923, other Berlin architects, like

[4] Attempts to define Expressionism have been avoided so far because the term has always been so loosely used as to defy definition. The ideas quoted here can be construed as Expressionist only because they put forward a concept that is commonly associated with the work of painters like Kokoschka and Nolde, and sculptors like Barlach, but it is very doubtful if this idea of self-expression was very widely entertained even by artists such as these whose style has later become the touchstone of Expressionism. Again and again, since the word was first put into circulation around 1911, it has been used to signify, purely and simply, work that is

Gropius and Mies van der Rohe, had also begun to abandon what little they had taken up of it; Hugo Häring, whose Garkau farm buildings are one of the masterpieces of the Expressionist phase, began to drop from the foreground, and only Hans Scharoun was to maintain a persistently irregular attitude to design. The dividing line between the two epochs is given by the interval of time that separates the *Friedrichstrasse* and Chicago *Tribune* skyscraper competitions, both of which called up remarkable enthusiasm and inventiveness among the progressive architects of Northern Europe, including some of the best work of the outgoing, shortlived anti-Rationalist phase, and equally good work from the protagonists of the alternative approach, based on abstract, constructive art—the approach that finally made the International Style truly international.

not old-fashioned, but does not conform to the current progressive norms of the time. There is practically no other sense in which the term can be made to stick to the work of Poelzig, which seems never to have been intended to express anything personal at all, and Mendelsohn is nearly always found to be expressing something about the nature or contents of the building. Since the expression of the function of the building is taken to be one of the touchstones of the non-Expressionist approach, we may suspect that we see here, as in so much twentieth-century architectural polemics, one of those situations where an aesthetic standpoint is defended by accusing the other party of abandoning a theoretical position that is, in fact, common ground to both sides.

14: De Stijl: the International phase

THOUGH IT IS impossible to draw a hard and fast line between the Dutch and International phases of *de Stijl*, in terms of theoretical writings or artistic productions, the change in membership between 1920 and 1922 is very marked indeed, and gives a fair picture of the transformation that was in process. By the beginning of 1922 van der Leck, van Tongerloo, van t'Hoff, Wils, Oud and Kok had left, and Huszar was about to leave, while Mondriaan, established in Paris since 1919, was no longer a directly effective member, though he did not resign finally until 1925. Severini had also lost contact, so that van Doesburg himself alone remained of the original membership. The new men who filled the gaps were very different from those who had left.

Only two of them were Dutch, two were imaginary, one was German, one was Russian. The Dutch pair were Gerrit Rietveld, who had been a member since as early as 1918, but only now came to prominence, and Cor van Eesteren, whom van Doesburg enrolled in Weimar in 1923. Both have gained fame as architects though Rietveld seems to have entered the group as a furniture-maker, and van Eesteren, far from being a convinced Modernist when he met van Doesburg, was on his way to take up a Rome scholarship. The two imaginary members were both pseudo-persons of van Doesburg[1] in his Dadaist mood, I. K. Bonset and Aldo Camini, and it was over these signatures that he made most of his purely literary contributions to *de Stijl*. The German was Hans Richter, a former Dadaist who had turned to abstraction independently of the Dutch Movement, and the Russian was El Lissitsky, the apostle of Constructivism to Western Europe. The adherence of Lissitsky was brief, though important, and his place was taken by two other members of the Berlin *G* group, Frederich Kiesler, the Austrian theatrical designer, and Werner Graeff, an ex-student of the Bauhaus who was later connected with the Werkbund. The fourth and most celebrated member of *G*, Mies van der Rohe, never became a

---

[1] Even 'van Doesburg' was a pseudonym—his real name was C. E. M. Kupper.

member of *de Stijl*, and van Doesburg's attitude to him is not clear.[2]

The varying background and activities of these new members are worth noting, because they emphasise the degree to which the second phase of *de Stijl* differs from the first. No longer constrained by the exigencies of War and restricted communications to *faire école* on the narrow stage of Dutch art, van Doesburg could exercise his talents on a European scale. From 1919 onwards he travelled extensively, much as Marinetti had done, visiting most of the active centres of progressive art in Germany, as well as Prague, Paris, and certain other towns in France. In the process he established contact with most of the leading figures in art whose ideas were at all sympathetic to his, and the magazine, whose distribution became increasingly international, reflects this new situation not only in a new format, but in an increasing diversity of contents as well. Whereas, in the days of Oud and Mondriaan, it had exhibited the fairly consistent doctrine discussed in chapter 12, it now embraced Dadaism, late Futurism, Russian trends such as Constructivism and Suprematism, and the various Parisian trends that were associated with Léonce Rosenberg's *Effort Moderne* connection, as well as the new emergents in Berlin. It also published creative literary work, commonly Dadaist or Futurist in tone, and not all of it signed Bonset or Camini, but contributed or quoted from outside sources.

However diverse these various tendencies may appear, they all had one or more aspects in common with what *de Stijl* had already thought or done, and they extend and develop van Doesburg's attitude to art and architecture, without causing any major break or disturbance. Thus from the Futurists, with whom he made direct contact even before the War was over, he gained confirmation of his mechanolatry, and the idea of a liberated typography, which begins to appear in *de Stijl* in 1920. He also established contact with the *Valori Plastici* group, and thus with de Chirico, perhaps the most surprising of his new connections, though he discusses de Chirico's paintings in terms of space, machinery and other themes that were already familiar. By March 1920 he was in touch with the *Section d'Or* group and *L'Effort Moderne* in Paris, whose interests in Cubism, and machinery, and generally intellectual and progressivist attitude would obviously appeal to him, and an eulogy of *L'Esprit Nouveau* appeared in *de Stijl* in February 1921. In the next two months he began to reprint Dadaist texts, which seem to have appealed to him by their extremism, their disgust with tradition and the past, and, most likely, their positive,

[2] He is supposed to have invited Mies to submit material, somewhere in the early Twenties, for an exhibition at *L'Effort Moderne*, but no work of his appeared in that organisation's magazine (which bore the same name). From what one knows of Léonce Rosenberg, who edited the magazine and ran the gallery, this would have been an incredible omission if he had been aware of Mies's work—illustrations of designs by Kiesler, for instance, began to appear as soon as they were available to him. It is also worth noting that no work of Mies appeared in *de Stijl* either, until 1928.

if perverse attitude to Rationalism. The films of Richter and Eggeling were noticed in July of the same year—their Abstraction and 'space-time' qualities would obviously appeal—while the October issue contained a reproduction of a painting by Fernand Leger, the first photograph of a motor-car to appear in its pages, quasi-Futurist poetry by Nicholas Beaudouin, the *Aufruf zur elementaren Kunst* and quotations from a book by the German architectural writer, Adolf Behne. The far ranging eclecticism and *joie de vivre* of this period is nicely symbolised by Aldo Fiozzi's *Valeurs Abstraits* which was reproduced in January 1921—a Dadaist three-dimensional collage with a French title, made by an Italian ex-Futurist, bearing the alarming 'scientific' injunction $R SO_4 + H_2O$. Yet the most significant item to appear, as far as future developments were concerned, was the *Aufruf zur elementaren Kunst*, whose importance will be discussed later.

This phase of extension and exploration in van Doesburg's career reaches its climax in 1922, the year in which he published his most extended personal statement of aims, found himself confronted by the problem of the Bauhaus, by the personality of Lissitsky, with whom he helped to organise the Düsseldorf Congress of Progressive Artists, and with whom (and others) he signed the foundation Manifesto of the Constructivist International. The statement of aims is, in a good Berlagian tradition, the reprint of a lecture given in Berlin, Jena and the Weimar Bauhaus late in 1921, under the title of *Der Wille zum Stil*, and much of what he had to say under this equally Berlagian heading was not very new. He rehearsed such established *de Stijl* themes as the anathema on Individualism and Expressionism, the opposition of nature and spirit, the analogies of mechanical and artistic design, but in a new and rather laconic tone of voice, of a sort that had been prophesied by Marinetti and, indeed, sound rather Marinettian

> All that we used to designate as Magic, Spirit, Love, etc. will now be efficiently accomplished. The idea of the Miraculous, that primitive man made so free with, will now be realised simply through electric current, mechanical control of light and water, the technological conquest of space and time.

This laconic tone reaches its apotheosis in another document of 1922, the Foundation Manifesto of the Constructivist International, which contains the following remarkable disclaimer

> This International is not the result of some humanitarian, idealistic or political sentiment, but of that amoral and elementary principle on which science and technology are based.

But beside these old sentiments in a new voice (though one suspects that even the sentiments may have been shocking at the Bauhaus) *Der Wille zum Stil* does introduce two new themes of importance. One is the Machine Aesthetic as such, the other is Elementarism. Of the former, van Doesburg says

> Since it is correct to say that culture in its widest sense means independence of

Nature, then we must not wonder that the machine stands in the forefront of our cultural will-to-style. . . . Consequently, the spiritual and practical needs of our time are realised in constructive sensibility. The new possibilities of the machine have created an aesthetic expressive of our time, that I once called 'the Mechanical Aesthetic'.

Since his examples are, among others, locomotives, cars, aeroplanes, etc. he is not contributing anything very new except the blanket term to describe the visual qualities that these objects had in common. But this blanket term does appear to be a genuine innovation, dating back to an article in the *Bouwkundig Weekblad* earlier in 1921, which is the former occasion to which he refers. Conceivably the Futurists may have already been in possession of the term before this, though Bragaglia's Manifesto on the subject did not appear until 1925. Furthermore, a note in *de Stijl* by Enrico Prampolini seems to imply that for him, at least, the word was a northern discovery, made at the time of the Düsseldorf Congress which he attended. The passage in which this occurs is worth noting, because it also seems to imply that the Futurists consciously handed on the torch of mechanistic aesthetics to those, north of the Alps, whom Prampolini groups as Constructivists (van Doesburg, Richter, Lissitsky, Eggeling and Moholy-Nagy)

> We today—who have hymned and exalted the suggestive powers of the machine as inspiration and fixed our sensations and plastic emotions in pioneer plastic works—we see the first outlines of the new machine aesthetic sketched on the glowing horizon . . . the first plastic expressions vouchsafed by a mechanical cosmogony

The conjunction of 'the mechanical aesthetic' with 'constructive sensibility' and of 'a new machine aesthetic' with a list of artists termed 'constructivist' is symptomatic, if no more, of a growing feeling, which has much later been codified as a definitive credo, that the art proper to a mechanical age is Russian Abstract art, loosely termed Constructivist. As applied to the work and theory of the year under review, the term is a confusing one, since it has to stand for two opposing tendencies in Soviet art—the idealistic approach of Gabo and Pevsner, later termed Constructivist, but at that time, perversely enough, though like so many other Idealistic creeds, known as *Realist*, and the other, anti-Idealist and anti-art, approach of Lissitsky and his connection, which Lissitsky probably dubbed Constructivist in the same year of 1922. However, as far as the discussions and writings of 1922 are concerned, the term Elementarist seems much more to the point, since it was used by many of those involved (but not by Gabo and Pevsner, who were not involved anyhow), was derived from the ideas of Malevitsch, like many of the aesthetic practices, and genuinely identifies what the various parties had in common.

Whatever the initial debt of the Elementarist idea to the Academic tradition (cf. chapter 1) the word *elements* appears to have been in use in a more or less Elementarist sense by Malevitsch by about 1915, when he conceived of his Suprematist paintings as being composed of *fundamental suprematist elements*[3]—simple geometric forms that are the basic units of his composition. In this he may appear to stand very close to Guadet, but in his sculpture and in the developing Elementarist tradition at large, an element is only a structural part of any volume that really registers in the composition, and is usually restricted to a plain rectangular shape in itself—in van Doesburg's Elementarist paintings the 'elements' are the areas of colour, or the frames around them, but not the coloured forms as a whole, and in such examples of Elementarist architecture as Rietveld's House at Utrecht, the elements are the structure of the building, and not, as they would be with Guadet, its functional volumes.

The idea of Elementarism seems to have reached Germany either directly by way of Lissitsky when he came from Moscow in 1921, or in a more roundabout way that included Puni and Moholy-Nagy. It is unlikely that Lissitsky would not have known of such a concept if it were current, but it must be noted that the *Aufruf zur elementaren Kunst*,[4] to which reference has already been made, was signed by Puni and Moholy-Nagy, as well as the ex-Dadaists Hausman and Arp, and seems to be the earliest record of the word. This *Aufruf* contained the most succinct yet misleading definition of Elementarism that ever appeared

> Elementary is the art that does not philosophise, but is built out of its own proper elements alone.

which is not so much a tautology, as an equation that could be rephrased (given the necessary background knowledge) in the form: Elementarism equals art made of Malevitsch's elements minus Malevitsch's aesthetic philosophy, for the Elementarists' elements did not, as the Suprematists' did, carry a load of empathetic values,[5] but were simply units of structure and space-division. This absence of symbolic or mystical overtones is in line with van Doesburg's new laconic manner, but probably derives from the two Dadaists among the Elementarists, both of whom had been members of the Zurich Dada group, with its notorious contempt for metaphysics and 'spiritual values'.

Though the paintings of Moholy-Nagy afford the earliest conscious examples of Elementarist art, and Kiesler's *Cité dans l'Espace* (discussed later in this chapter) is the most spectacular example of *Architecture Elementarisée* as he himself called it, the most striking example of an Elementarist structure was conceived and built before the word existed—the

---

[3] The dates of Malevitsch's early paintings, like those of many other pioneers of Abstract painting, have been rendered extremely suspect by the activities of critics eager to prove that their own choices were the 'first' to produce Abstract art. The date given here is the latest reasonable alternative.

[4] This Elementarist manifesto was reprinted in *de Stijl*, IV, p. 156.

[5] Thus, Malevitsch's drawings of the War years often have titles such as 'Sensation of Universal Space', 'Sensation of Flight', and so forth.

earliest version of Gerrit Rietveld's arm-chair, which was illustrated in *de Stijl* in 1919, but seems to have been designed as early as 1917. Curiously enough, the germs of this conception must have come from Wright, as represented to Rietveld by van t'Hoff. The form, a 'Morris chair' with a high plank back, is Wrightian, as is the use of plain machine-cut rails, such as Wright had valued in his own furniture as

> The straight-line clean-cut forms that the machine can render far better than would be possible by hand.[6]

But, to this Wrightian origin, had been applied precisely that type of European abstracting thought that Oud had identified as Wright's opposite. The functions of the chair have been analysed, discriminated, reduced to their 'essentials'—the sitting and enclosing functions are served by four planks (back, seat and two sides) that are visually separated from one another, from the two planks (arms) that serve to support the occupant's arms, and from the network of plain rails that serves the supporting functions, and maintain the various elements in their correct relative positions in space.

The phrase 'positions in space' is advisedly used here—immediate commentary on this chair in the pages of *de Stijl* has two themes; the inviolate and unmutilated condition of each structural member, none of which is mortised or rabbeted by another, and the spatiality of the total structure. Rietveld himself insists that

> above all, the whole stands free and clear in space

and van Doesburg goes further, and having acclaimed such furniture as 'the abstract-real sculpture of our future interior', devoted to it in volume III of *de Stijl*, a curious poem, in which its mechanistic and spatial qualities are contrasted with those of a painting by de Chirico

> In the 'Solitude' of de Chirico.
> In the foreground mathematical man—space-master, space-mastered
> With every plane, angle and point around at or near him
> a spatial measurement *symbolised*
> > SPACE ANATOMY
> and in contrast to mathematical man caught in his space web
> a sober open space with a factory and a right-angled pipe at hand
> Rietveld's chair: unwilful but inexorable effect on empty space
> and in contrast:
> > FUNCTION
> > > TO SIT
> > > > CHAIR
> material necessity set against rich, continuous and vast creation of open space.
> CHAIR
> Silent eloquence of a machine

or, in other words, the chair is, and affects, what the painting can only represent or symbolise, a functional structure in three-dimensional space. It

---

[6] This, again, from *In the Cause of Architecture*.

is clear that in this context the concept of space is considerably more than of a void containing objects, and it seems to come nearer to a three-dimensional grid—something more than the continuum discussed in chapter 4, in that it appears to contain a regular, measurable, imaginary structure, an idea that may have been put into circulation among *de Stijl* by the Futurist Azari in his note on the Futurist Aerial Theatre, which describes aircraft

climbing around an invisible spiral staircase . . . gymnastics on the invisible trapezes of the atmosphere

and clearly implies some form of structure in space, if only the co-ordinates of a three-dimensional graph. Something similar is implied in the universal geometry of horizontals and verticals that Mondriaan took over from Schoenmaekers, while the key concept in Mondriaan's view of space (as expressed in his essay *Le Néoplasticisme*), of the rectangle as a form

. . . where lines cross or touch tangentially, *but do not cease to continue* (his italics)

is given visible substance by the structural elements of Rietveld's chair, where the lines, embodied as the rails of the structure, do indeed form rectangles by touching tangentially, and continuing an arbitrary distance beyond the point of interception. Space in Elementarist art is, indeed, continuous and open, and the work of art is a structure that makes its rectangularity manifest by giving body to its grid-lines and the planes and volumes between them, and this is still true even when the grid, as in some van Doesburg paintings of the mid-Twenties, has been skewed out of the vertical.

Though such concepts were to be put to very effective use at the Bauhaus later in the decade, they seem to have been unknown there at the time van Doesburg first came in contact with it—an encounter that, for a variety of reasons, was a conspicuous disappointment to him. The facts of the case have been effectively obscured by a highly circumstantial version of events put about by his widow, according to which Gropius and van Doesburg met at the house of Bruno Taut in 1919, and Gropius there made van Doesburg the offer of a teaching post at the Bauhaus. When he arrived in Weimar to take this up (as late as 1921, for some unexplained reason) he was refused the post by Gropius. This version is denied by the other side, and regarded as improbable by those who knew both men, but the truth is still hard to come at, and the oscillations of van Doesburg's attitude are not easy to explain. It is true, however, that his first attacks do not begin until after he had visited Weimar, in the May 1922 issue of *de Stijl*. On the other hand, they consist of the kind of observations that a convinced anti-Expressionist *Stijlkunstenaar* could have made without having been crossed by the Bauhaus administration—confronted by Itten's Freudian pedagogy, by the *Vorkurs* with its preoccupation with natural materials, and remembering the newly completed *Sommerfeld* house outside Berlin, it would need very little more to provoke van Doesburg to the magnificent jibe

191

As the church is a parody of Christianity, so is Gropius's Bauhaus in Weimar a parody of the new creativity . . . not only here, but elsewhere (e.g. the anthroposophical art-humbug of Dornach) the new artistic expression degenerates to a sort of ultra-baroque.[7]

Yet he had reasons to be friendly to the Bauhaus: he had a friend, Lyonel Feininger established there from an early date, an old admiration and a new acquaintance—Kandinsky and Moholy-Nagy—both joined the staff in this period, and the programme of the school had always been as anti-individualistic as his own. He had welcomed the foundation of the Bauhaus in 1919, and in 1924, after he had left Weimar and moved to Paris, he spoke in favour of the school and against its detractors. It is worth noting too, that only on one other occasion did a hostile note on the Bauhaus appear in *de Stijl*, and not over van Doesburg's own signature, and that, apart from these two instances, the hostility seems to have been largely retrospective, if not actually posthumous. Conceivably he had expected to galvanise staff and students alike by his lecture, only to find that to the student body he was just another visiting eccentric,[8] and so conceived a disappointment at the lack of results that had grown into a resentment by the time that he tried to rewrite the history of Modern art, in 1927, as the history of the universal and exclusive influence of *de Stijl*.[9] He was, almost certainly, the first of the Abstractionists who helped to alter the Bauhaus outlook, but he was only the first, and the real credit for the alteration must go to Moholy-Nagy (of whom he was reported to be jealous).

At all events, his quarrel with the Bauhaus was less that it was too arty, as some of his younger colleagues seem to have thought, than that it had opted for the wrong kind of art. An outright rejection of 'art', in this context, is generally credited to the *G* group, but although their views on the subject were tough, they shaded off from a hard core of rejection towards less absolute attitudes, and even the determinism of its most determined anti-artists had qualifications. The hard core is represented by Mies van der Rohe, taking his stand on something very like nineteenth-century Rationalism (see chapter 19) and declaring

We reject all aesthetic speculation, all doctrine, all formalism

but the slogans and polemical paragraphs that speckle the newspaper-sized pages of *G* give a more liberal, though equally emphatic, impression. An overall artistic creativity was permitted, even if the separate 'arts' were despised.

[7] *De Stijl*, V, column 71 (after the magazine changed over to a wide-page format, the type continued to be set to the old width, two columns to a page, each column numbered separately).

[8] On visiting eccentrics at the Bauhaus, including van Doesburg, with an alternative date for his lecture, see Helmut von Erffa's article 'Bauhaus First Phase' in the *Architectural Review* (London, August 1957).

[9] This extraordinary performance, which van Doesburg appears to have had in mind for some time beforehand, appeared in the jubilee number of 1927, which was, of course, *de Stijl's* tenth, not twenty-fifth, birthday.

The opposition between the new creativity (in art) and the old, restricted art, is principal. We do not intend to bridge it over, but to deepen it

and this, clearly, is simply a rewording of the regular *de Stijl* contrast between old art and new.

Similarly, the interpretation of mechanical determinism has to be wide enough to include something almost mystical. Werner Graeff, reputedly the most tough-minded of the group, who is supposed to have left the Bauhaus in disgust, can be found asserting

Uninfluenced by the methods of mechanical technology, the new and greater technology begins—the technology of tensions, invisible motions, action-at-a distance, and speeds unimaginable now in 1922.

This appears to be Futurism reworded, and it is to be noted that in the same issue of *G* an extended and enthusiastic review of Lindner and Steinmetz's *Ingenieurbauten* (cf. chapter 5) has to take second place to pictures (the first of many in many different publications all over Europe) of Giacomo Matte-Trucco's Fiat factory at Turin, with its test-track for cars on the roof, the most nearly Futurist building ever built. It is clear that *G* opinions were very various in origin,[10] but they have one constant theme— elementary creativity, elementary means of creation, the elementarism that had been brought to Berlin by Lissitsky.

Born in 1890, Lissitsky was one of the great 'ideas-men' of the Modern Movement. He may have had little to contribute that was original, but his impact, as the chief agent in bringing Russian developments to the attention of architects in Western Europe was of great importance. Not only did he bring fresh ideas of Cubo-Futurist extraction to minds that were already prepared for them by other similar developments, but he also enjoyed a prestige of a kind also enjoyed by an Ehrenburg, a Mayakowsky, a Prokofieff, as a species of ambassador at large of the new Soviet culture that appeared to many at that time almost as Futurism made fact. In addition he was endowed with an extremely persuasive, though quite unspectacular personality, and, in Western Europe at least, he gave far more than he received—there is, for instance, no perceptible *de Stijl* influence on him, but his influence upon even van Doesburg is made clear by the fact that in 1922, almost a complete issue was given over to his ideas, and another issue made over in its entirety to reproductions of his graphic work.

Both writings and pictures were devoted to the concept of *Proun*, which was in many ways, his most characteristic contribution to the common pool of Abstractionist ideas. *Proun* is merely a Russian word for 'object' but in Lissitsky's hands it takes on a number of specialised collateral meanings, like the word *abstract* in Mondriaan's usage. *Proun* occupies[11] a

[10] *G*1 was the more productive of slogans and ideas, *G*2 of illustrations of executed works and projects by the group's members.
[11] These quotations are from the version of *Proun* that appeared in *de Stijl*, V, column 82.

specific place in the history of creative design

> . . . the halting place on the road of development of the new creativity, planted
> in soil manured by the corpse of painting and its artists.

Even pure painting is classed among the dead

> . . . though here the artist began his own transformation—from the imitator of
> objects to the creator of a new world of objects

and this is a rejection of the 'non-objectivity' of Malevitsch, to whom he
was otherwise somewhat indebted. In this new world of objects, *Proun*
was to be the seminal object

> *Proun* begins on the flat plane, goes on to the construction of three-dimensional
> models, and beyond that to the construction of every object of our common
> life.
> Thus *Proun* supersedes painting and its artists on the one hand, the machine
> and its engineers on the other; proceeds to the construction of space, organises
> its dimensions by means of its elements, and creates a new, manifold yet
> unified, image of our nature.

Proun, in fact, is a sort of aesthetic prototype for something very like a
gigantic Berlagian *Gesamtkunstwerk*, complete with its own version of
Eenheid in Veelheid. The emphasis on space-manipulation as the primary
function of *Proun* is perhaps the newest thing, apart from the claim to
hegemony over technology, in the *Proun* programme, but the actual approach to the consideration of space, if one may judge by what Lissitsky
wrote later about the 'psychotechnical laboratory' run by his associate
Ladowski, was cast in the rather Academic framework of 'Mass, space,
plane, proportion, rhythm'.

Some further aspects of *Proun* seem self-contradictory; thus, Lissitsky
condemns in one place

> . . . The narrow, limited, isolated and dismembered disciplines of Science

yet he seems to be able to accept elsewhere in the same document an almost
Choisyesque Rationalism

> Material becomes form through construction.
> Contemporary demands and economy of means need one another
> . . .
> *Proun* is creative formation (mastery of space) by means of economical construc-
> tion with revalued materials.

But this last is, on examination, a most important proposition, for it is one
of the beginnings of the idea that the formal disciplines of the Modern
Movement are in some way the product of a philosophy resembling that of
nineteenth-century Rationalism. Whether or not they were so produced is
not the point at this juncture, but the art and the writings of Lissitsky were
probably the first to bring them together. As for Lissitsky himself, this
Rationalistic approach was what he later called 'Constructivism', and under
this name became more or less the official credo of Soviet architecture in
the Twenties (although his ideas had been suppressed in painting in 1921).

The pioneer Constructivist structure was, for him, the *Leningrad-Pravda* building projected by the brothers A. and W. Wesnin in 1923

> The building is characteristic of an age that thirsts after glass, iron and concrete. All the accessories that a metropolitan street imposes on a building—illustrations, publicity, clock, loudspeaker, even the lifts inside—are all drawn into the design as equally important parts and brought to unity. This is the aesthetic of constructivism.[12]

The description suggests, the drawings confirm, that this is a Futurist conception, subjected to the order of what Oud would have called an 'unhistorical Classicism', almost a square in plan, and almost a pure prism in bulk, with rather diagrammatic structure of stanchions and girders, to which all the mandatory 'accessories' including the lifts are tacked on as independent elements, in the Guadetesque sense of an element as the embodiment of a function, not in the Elementarist sense of an element as an atomic unit of structure or space-division. In Wesnin and in Lissitsky, as much as in Oud or in Le Corbusier, one can see that reabsorption of new concepts into traditional disciplines that made the creation of architecture possible, even at the cost of theoretical contradictions.

But before this could be done, the new ideas had to be made familiar and universal, and perhaps the most important outcome of 1922, and its encounters between van Doesburg and Lissitsky, was, for this reason, the Düsseldorf Congress of Progressive Artists. Though this was, to judge from the accounts given of it, little more than a fraternal assemblage of kindred spirits and a certain amount of more or less orderly discussion, its consequences for the arts of design were far greater than were those of the more widely publicised congresses of 1921 (Paris and Weimar, both Dadaist dominated). Chiefly this was due to its genuinely international character, for it brought together not only *de Stijl* and the *G* group, its effective instigators, but also the Futurists from Italy, *L'Effort Moderne* from Paris, the *MA* group of Hungarian expatriates, Victor Bourgeois's *Sept Arts* connection from Brussels, various Dadaists and other independents. It thus covered progressive Abstractionists from France, Belgium, Holland, Switzerland, Germany, and Russia, and also opened up lines of communication with Austria, Hungary and Eastern Europe. It created an international awareness of a continent-wide Abstractionist-Architectural Movement, it made that Movement aware of itself, and thus made its members and groups aware of one another, so that questions of primacy and influence become almost insoluble from 1922 onwards—to judge from *de Stijl* and *L'Effort Moderne*, for instance, any new thing would get in one magazine as soon as it got into the other, and ideas became common property as quickly as they were printed and the magazines posted.

The new state of affairs was formally recognised, so to speak, by the formation of a Constructivist International to whose Foundation Manifesto

[12] From Lissitsky's book *Russland* (Vienna, 1930, p. 13).

195

reference has already been made, and whose signatories were van Doesburg and Lissitsky themselves, Hans Richter and Max Burchardt (Germany) and Karel Maes (Belgium). As an operative body, this international was only a gesture, and soon evaporated—partly because it was not really needed when communications were good enough to keep the various Abstractionists in touch, and partly because its moving spirits left Germany and lost personal touch with one another in 1923. Lissitsky, shortly followed by his *protégé* Mart Stam, transferred to Zurich (on account of his health—he was consumptive), where he soon founded a new review *ABC* closely modelled on the short-lived *G*; and van Doesburg, with his wife and new-found disciple Cor van Eesteren, moved to Paris at the invitation, it is said, of Léonce Rosenberg. His subsequent activities become more and more involved with Paris and its art-world, though he and van Eesteren achieved a major *coup* when van Eesteren won the competition for the replanning of *Unter den Linden* with a scheme that is an ingenious recombination of ideas from van Eesteren's Academic training, *de Stijl* sculpture, and some of the projects executed in Ladowski's 'psychotechnical laboratory' in Moscow, but later published in *ABC*.

About the same time, there was a further wave of recruiting for *de Stijl* which included such unconformable personalities as Antheil the composer, and the sculptor Constantin Brancusi—the latter having been taken on, seemingly, to replace Mondriaan, who resigned in 1925, as honorary figure-head to the movement. However, before these events took place, van Doesburg, van Eesteren and Rietveld issued a new Manifesto, *Vers une Construction Collective*,[13] which reveals, in the very first word of its title, the immediate impact of Paris. It is a curious document, with its eclecticism, its pretensions (and they are no more) to scientific objectivity, but it is important because it brings together a number of ideas that were to remain current, in association, for some time

1. Working collectively we have examined architecture as an unity created by all the arts, industry, technology, etc. and find that the consequences give a new style
2. We have examined the Laws of Space and their infinite variations (that is, the contrast of spaces, their dissonances, their complements, etc.) and we find that these variations can be regulated to a balanced unity
3. We have examined the Laws of Colour in space and continuity, and find that a balanced relationship of these elements will finally give a new and positive unity
4. We have examined the relationships of Space and Time, and find that the manifestation of these two elements through colour gives a new dimension
5. We have examined the reciprocal relationships of measure, proportion, space, time and materials and have found the definitive method for building them into unity
6. We have, by the destruction of enclosure—walls, etc.—removed the duality of interior and exterior

[13] This appeared in *de Stijl*, VI, columns 91, 92, under the title '$- \square + = R_4$', and in November of the same year (1924) in *L'Effort Moderne* under its regular title of *Vers une Construction Collective*.

7. We have established the true place of colour in architecture, and we declare that painting without architectural construction (that is, the easel-painting) has no further reason for existence

8. The era of destruction is completely finished, a new era begins, of *Construction*

The incantatory effect of the repetitions and partial repetitions of the middle passages of this document cannot conceal the fact that the lack of anything new to say has been made good by saying things that other people have said before, even as far back as Georges Seurat, whose laws of colour-harmony have been barely rewritten to give these 'Laws of Space'. Similarly, there is nothing very new in the other main van Doesburg document of this period, the 'manifesto' *Tot een Beeldende Architectuur* of 1924. However, one or two of the numbered propositions are worth citing, for the way in which they crystallise certain ideas that were current in Elementarist circles. Thus there is the Lissitskian

4. The new architecture is functional; that is, it is developed out of an accurate setting forth of practical demands, which it establishes in a comprehensible plan

—but Lissitskian with the proviso that it may also owe a good deal to Paris, both in the use of the word *functioneel* (probably for the first time in that sense in a Northern language) and in the emphasis on plan. In a later proposition there is also an attempt to formulate the aesthetic behind the sprawling, space-invading plans, and balcony-broken elevations of Elementarist buildings, thus

11. The new architecture is anti-cubic; that is, it does not seek to fix the various functional space-cells together within a closed cube, but throws the functional space-cells . . . away from the centre of the cube towards the outside, whereby height, width, depth + time tend towards a wholly new plastic expression in open space.

De Stijl as a generating influence was practically finished by 1924–5, yet some of the most indicative works of art generated by that influence were produced in those two years. Rietveld's Schröder House, at Utrecht was, and remains, the only Elementarist structure to be built in permanent form. It owes a good deal to Oud's factory projects of 1919, and the play of spaces and planes on the outside has very little relation to the interior, but the bold display of horizontal and vertical slabs, steel stanchions and hand-rails, the window-frames, eaves and other 'proper elements' on the outside do form a sort of habitable Elementarist structure on the scale of man. At the same time Kiesler, who joined *de Stijl* in 1923, when Lissitsky left, was elaborating a completely open spatial aesthetic on a rectangular grid, which was fully and properly seen by the world at large at the Paris exhibition of 1925, when it occupied a large part of the Austrian Pavilion, under the name of *La Cité dans l'Espace*. It was a suspended construction of wooden rails and flat planes forming and occupying the rectangularities of a spatial grid in the regular Elementarist way, but to judge from Kiesler's notes of the subject in *de Stijl*, VII, it had also some of the properties of *Proun*

> A system of tension in free space
> A change of space into urbanism
> No foundation, no walls
> Detachment from the earth, suppression of the static axis
> In creating new possibilities for living, it creates a new society

In creating this space-structure, he had reached the end of the possibilities of an aesthetic, as Malevitsch had done in 1918 with his *White on White*, and subsequent exhibition structures have achieved a similar extreme position to *Le Cité dans l'Espace* without ever being able to go any further. It represents the ultimate condition of the ideas of *de Stijl* and Elementarism, and the road of progress lay in side-stepping them, or replacing their merely analytical approach by a synthetic one.

This process was put in hand by Mart Stam, who delivered the design of chairs from the similar Elementarist impasse into which Rietveld had led it in 1919. Both Marcel Breuer and Le Corbusier produced chairs which were, in terms of their overall conception, Rietveld's chair reworked in fabric and steel. Fabric replaced the planks of the seats and arms, steel tube replaced the wooden rails of the supporting structure, and though side-tubes were needed to keep the fabric in shape and in tension, the backs and seat were clearly conceived as quite separate from the supporting parts, as they had been in the original Rietveld model. Both of these chairs were also armchairs, and where Mart Stam set his foot on the road of development was in undertaking the design of an upright chair. Here, the back and the seat could be made co-planar with the horizontals and verticals of the supporting structure, the separate side-tubes could be eliminated and the fabric could be stretched directly over opposite members of the structural frame, which could, itself, be reduced to a single loop of tube, bending the front legs under to form long feet, extending to the back of the chair, and thus eliminating the need for back legs.

This was how Stam conceived his chair late in 1924, but for lack of technical resources the earliest models had to be made of lengths of straight tube joined by elbow-pieces, thus losing the springiness inherent in the design. However, in 1925, the preparations for the Weissenhof exhibition brought him once more into contact with Mies van der Rohe, who had access to the necessary pipe-bending technicians, and in 1926 the Stam chair was realised, as was an alternative by Mies, which set out to exploit the spring possibilities of this design to the full by treating the whole of the front legs as a continuous curved spring (though this made it difficult to get in and out of). The design won immediate acceptance and the proliferation of such integrated designs for steel tube chairs was so rapid and universal that it soon appeared almost an anonymous, automatic creation of the *Zeitgeist* like Choisy's flying buttress. But one should observe that there existed parties with a definite interest in spreading this idea, and there is a patent disingenuousness in the attempt of del Marle (an ex-Futurist in close touch with *de Stijl*) to excuse his own obvious cribbing of the Mies chair, by saying in *L'Effort Moderne* in 1927

> For practically a year we laboured, my faithful craftsman and I, upon its possibilities.
> Parallel to us, Mies van der Rohe, Marcel Breuer, Mart Stam.
> Steel, so modern a material, and the Rationalism that commands its use, together give all our realisations a family face. Should the credit go to Mies van der Rohe or to Breuer? Plagiarism? NEVER. Rationalism engenders a collective art.

This is altogether too knowing, and a little too quick off the mark in scouting the idea of plagiarism, but it has an interest besides its disingenuousness. It could only have appeared plausible at a time when it was general practice to suppress or ignore the actions that generate history (such as Stam's invention of the integrated chair) and make history the generator of the actions, and so far had this tendency gone by the time that van Doesburg assembled the material for *de Stijl's* tenth anniversary number in 1927, that even the things that its members and contributors had undoubtedly done were being attributed to the activities of the *Zeitgeist*,[14] and he made himself and the movement look ridiculous by overcompensating, with wild claims to influence on Malevitsch, Le Corbusier, Mallet Stevens and others.

The truth, almost inevitably, lies between the two. The spirit of the times in the plastic arts was largely the creation of an interaction of Cubist forms and Futurist ideas, as was *de Stijl*, as were most of the movements it encountered or allied itself to. Much of *de Stijl's* importance lay in its being first in the field with an organised body of ideas, a magazine and an energetic impresario. By this early leadership it was to be enabled to give an international unity to a number of diverse groups, and, through Lissitsky, bring the Russian contribution to the notice of Europe. Paradoxically, it was Russia that offered the way of deliverance from the limitations of *de Stijl's* own aesthetics, as has been noted in connection with Mart Stam, but as must also be recognised in connection with van Doesburg himself, whose new style, which he developed in the middle Twenties, was not only called by him Elementarist (though it differed from structural Elementarism) but also depended on a diagonal mode of composition that he clearly derived from Ladowskian aesthetics by way of Lissitsky, and has a history in the Russian Movement that goes back to paintings done by Malevitsch during the War. Van Doesburg and Hans Arp used this mode of composition, as well as Arp's newly developed 'biomorphic' abstraction in the decoration of the *Aubette* café and cinema in Strassburg in 1927–8, but Russianism on an even bigger scale can be seen in some Bauhaus projects of the late Twenties, such as Breuer's scheme for a theatre at Kharkov or

[14] Mondriaan was no help here; by 1926 he had begun to speak of *de Stijl* in the past tense, and say that its existence or otherwise as a group was unimportant, sufficient was the fact that a new art now existed, etc.

Gropius's design for a civic centre in Halle, which are very different to the neat asymmetrical groupings of boxes they had done earlier under van Doesburg's and Moholy-Nagy's influence, for their boldly exposed lattice girders and other structures bear witness to the influence of architectural Constructivism.

Section four

PARIS: THE WORLD OF ART AND LE CORBUSIER

Apollinaire, G: *Les Peintres Cubistes,* Paris, 1913.
Gleizes, A: *Du Cubisme,* Paris, 1920
Cocteau, J: *Le Rappel à l'Ordre,* Paris, 1923.
Ozenfant & Jeanneret: *Après le Cubisme,* Paris, 1919.
     La Peinture Moderne, Paris, 1926.
Gauthier, M: *Le Corbusier,* Paris, 1926.
Le Corbusier: *Oeuvre Complète,* vol. I, Zurich, 1946.
    Vers une Architecture, Paris, 1923.
    Urbanisme, Paris, 1926.
    (Note, the quotations from these last two works which appear in the following pages are taken from Frederick Etchell's standard English translations—*Towards a New Architecture,* and *The City of Tomorrow*—wherever possible.)
Periodicals
 L'Esprit Nouveau, 1919–1925.
 L'Effort Moderne, 1924–1927.
 L'Architecture Vivante, 1923 onwards.
 Journal de Psychologie Normale et Pathologique
 (special issue, No. 23, 1926, on aesthetics and the arts with essays by Ozenfant, Le Corbusier, Pierre Urbain).

15: Architecture and the Cubist tradition

SO POWERFUL WAS the *mystique* of reinforced concrete in Paris by about 1920 that many French writers have accepted the idea that the new architecture of the Twenties was in some way caused by this one material, rather than facilitated by it. This acceptance of Choisy's view of technique as a prime cause of style, was doubtless encouraged by the dominating position of Perret as the sole innovator of consequence in the years immediately before the War, but Rob Mallet-Stevens is speaking in the most general terms when he declares, in 1925,[1]

> Abruptly, everything changed. Reinforced concrete appeared revolutionising the processes of construction . . . science creates a new aesthetic, forms are profoundly modified.

Indeed, he goes so far as to attribute the lag in architectural development as between Europe and America (dates were not his strong point) to an American preference for the wrong material, iron.

> Reinforced concrete supervened. The Americans resisted this mode of construction for a long time, and iron reigned supreme in their art of building.

The position here adopted by Mallet-Stevens clearly accepts reinforced concrete as something which had imposed itself, just as Choisy supposed the flying buttress to have imposed itself, and this imposition he accepted as a sufficient explanation of the new aesthetic, the profoundly modified forms. However, at a distance of almost forty years in time, it is clear that the modes of employing reinforced concrete were already extremely various, ranging from the careful Classicism of Perret to the bold vault-work of Freyssinet, and that none of these varieties was, in practice, employed by the younger architects who made the French contribution to the mainstream of the International Style. In particular, they avoided vaults, and curved forms in section generally (which even Perret employed), but frequently made use of curved forms in plan. Though they paid frequent lip-service to the achievements of their immediate elders, their only real inheritance from these pioneers of reinforced concrete was Perret's preference for

[1] This, also, is from *Wendingen's* special number on Frank Lloyd Wright!

trabeated structural frames. It is clear that their choice of an architectural idiom must have been affected by influences outside the Rationalist and Academic traditions, and at least two of these influences are easy to identify. One is the actual business of building in Paris, its finance, its patronage, its vernacular traditions, which will be dealt with in the next chapter; the other influence is that of the Cubist tradition in the visual arts.

This Cubist tradition was, itself, part of that larger and paradoxical tradition of being anti-traditional, that goes back, in painting, at least to Courbet, parallel with an innovating tradition in Rationalist architectural thought that goes back to Labrouste. Both traditions were regarded, with varying justification, as anti-Academic, but Cubism, more than any previous phase of the pictorial revolution, presented aspects that could be approximated to those of Rationalist architectural theory. This could not be done directly with either the works or the recorded utterances of the founding masters, Picasso and Braque, in spite of their occasional use of architectural subject-matter, but already (by 1912) in the work of Gris there was sensibly the employment of structural grids and proportional systems. However, it was from the 'intellectual' wing of Cubism, the *Groupe de Puteaux*, exhibiting as the *Section d'Or*, that the most productive line of development was to stem.

This group centred around the Duchamp brothers: Marcel, Gaston (who used the *nom-de-pinceau* of Jacques Villon) and Raymond (who hyphenated Villon on to his legal surname). There are some striking, though probably accidental resemblances between tricks of draughtsmanship employed by Sant'Elia, and some employed by Jacques Villon, and Raymond had architectural leanings, while Fernand Leger, who was also a member of the group, had drawing office experience. However, the one surviving record (a photograph of a model and some interiors) of the Cubist architecture of Raymond Duchamp-Villon suggests that his ideas lay a long way from the progressive trends of the time of its conception, 1912. It is little more than the routine structure of a symmetrical villa in the Mansardic tradition[2] tricked out with fans of prismatic mouldings instead of Rococo (or even Art Nouveau) details. The fact that this no more than superficially Modern design was deemed worthy of illustration in Apollinaire's *Les Peintres Cubistes* suggests that the Movement as a whole was thoroughly out of touch with forward ideas in architecture—a point that is worth making in view of what has been so often said or implied about the connections between Cubism and the International Style.

As has been said elsewhere, it is only in conjunction with Futurist ideas that Cubism was able to make any significant contribution to the mainstream, but the particular conjunction achieved by Marcel Duchamp, the member of the *Groupe de Puteaux* who is most important in this connection,

---

[2] A model of the façade was reproduced in Guillaume Apollinaire's *Les Peintres Cubistes* (Paris, 1913).

is very different to that found in the circle of *de Stijl* or the Elementarists. The peculiar slant given to Cubo-Futurist aesthetics by Duchamp is present as early as a work that has been discussed already as a possible source of Futurist pictorial methods, the 'Coffee Mill' of 1911. Whereas in the work of Picasso and Braque by 1911 the 'decomposition' of subject-matter had been brought to an advanced stage in the interests of certain purely pictorial and personal preoccupations (violent imagery, controlled space-illusions, etc.), Duchamp decomposes the 'Coffee Mill' in order to reveal its mechanics, as in an exploded view in an instruction manual—there is even an arrow showing which way to turn the crank. He has shifted attention from the business of picture-making to an examination of the *innerste Wesen* of the picture's subject-matter, though his reasons for doing so are less likely to be those of Werkbund Rationalists than those of Futurist anti-Traditionalists.

In the next phase, both wings of Cubism work to eliminate the distinction between picture and subject-matter, but in opposite directions. Picasso and Braque, by applying pieces of the subject-matter directly to the picture surface (collage) eventually arrive at a form of picture which is not a representation, but a thing to be valued in its own right, or, in Ozenfant's words[3]

> The emotion no longer comes from an extrinsic object reproduced or painted on the canvas, but from within the picture: *tableau-objet*.

But if Picasso and Braque had sacrificed their subject-matter for the sake of the picture, Duchamp now did the other thing, and sacrificed the picture for the sake of the subject-matter. The 'Bicycle Wheel', of 1912, was exactly what it claimed to be, and being mounted in such a way that it was free to turn, presented Futurist motion in actuality, not painted illusion. The most celebrated, and instructive of his *ready-mades*, however, was the 'Bottle-rack' which he exhibited in New York in 1914. This was an *objet-objet*, so to speak, of the purest type, without the side interests presented by the rotation of the 'Bicycle Wheel'. The subject-matter becomes, without any transformation or qualification, the object presented for the public to view—the shocking effect it had was less concerned with iconography (somewhat similar functional objects were familiar in Cubist still-lifes) than with the elimination of too many stages of the traditional process: subject-artist-painting-public.

But the other aspect of this unconventional gesture is of greater historical importance, even if of less interest to Duchamp himself. His intention may have been to deflate the status of 'art', in the Marinettian manner, but the status he conferred on a simple, mass-produced object by having it exhibited in an art gallery went far beyond anything the Futurists or the Werkbund had achieved up to that time. This was the first time (or, at least,

[3] In the *Journal de Psychologie Normale* (Paris, 1926, p. 295).

the first occasion of consequence) that an ordinary engineering product had, in physical fact, been translated to the realm of art. It seems that for Duchamp himself the gesture was self-sufficient, and self-justifying, but for lesser men it was necessary to produce justificatory arguments. One such was readily available in the New York circle with which Duchamp was connected—Plato's proposition in the *Philebus* that absolute beauty resides in geometrical and manufactured objects

> . . . understand me to mean straight lines and circles, and the plane or solid figures which are formed out of them by lathes, rulers and protractors; for these I affirm to be . . . eternal and absolutely beautiful.

G. H. Hamilton has noted[4] three uses of this quotation in the circle around Alfred Stieglitz, to which Duchamp belonged: applied to Picasso in 1911; to Cubism, Futurism and pure Abstraction in 1913; and again in 1913 by Duchamp's old associate from Puteaux, Francis Picabia, in discussing his own paintings, which were almost Abstract at that time, but, under Duchamp's influence, soon also turned to Mechanistic satire on 'art'.

Although the intention of both these artists remained satirical in an elevated way, it would, clearly, be possible to rephrase this interconnection of Abstract art, machine design, and absolute beauty in an equally elevated, but more serious way. This they were unlikely to do in New York at that time, but other members of their connection in Paris were to achieve this standpoint at a later date, as soon as they disposed of a theory of Norms of Types, like that current in Germany and Holland. At this point, it is worth noting just how much Parisian theorists had in common with their Dutch counterparts, since it is upon these common holdings that much of the ultimate unity of the International Style was to depend. They had a common Cubo-Futurist background, though differently interpreted; they had a common tendency to vaguely Platonic ideas (though the *Philebus* quotation does not appear in *de Stijl* at all), and they shared Gino Severini, whose analogies between art and machinery appeared in the *Mercure de France* in the same year (1917) as they appeared in *de Stijl*. Actual similarities of opinion will be noted in due course, the immediate interest of Severini in this Parisian context lies in another direction.

He was the first to call for a return to order—a return in the literal sense of a turning back, from Cubism to Classicism,[5] to central perspective and normally-constituted objects. The result, in Severini's paintings of the Twenties, is mere decorative prettiness, but he helped to bridge the gap between painting and architecture, in which the Classical strain and the appeal to the past were equally current in the early post-War years. In this Classicising connection, however, the writing of another member of the *Groupe de Puteaux*, Albert Gleizes, is of greater consequence. For him, as

---

[4] In an article on John Covert in *College Art Journal* (New York, Fall 1952).
[5] He published a book entitled *du Cubisme au Classicisme* in Paris in 1921.

for some of the younger architects, the recovery of Classical discipline was a step to something beyond Classicism.

> When the ultimate effort has been made, it will not be Classicism they rediscover, but the tradition, pure and simple; that which used to permit a strict and hierarchical collaboration in the creation of works of impersonal art.

Here two concordances with Dutch ideas immediately strike the eye. One, concerned with *Gesamtkunstwerk*, is fully confirmed by Gleizes elsewhere; the implications of *collaboration* and *hierarchisée* are supported by

> La peinture et la sculpture sont fonction de l'architecture.

an idea which was common property but, in the case of Gleizes, could be derived from Charles Blanc[6]

> Leaving their common cradle in architecture, two arts have freed themselves in succession from the maternal womb; sculpture first, painting later.

The other Dutch concordance lies in the concept of an *Œuvre d'art impersonelle*, on which his ideas are almost Mondriaanesque.

> Cubist paintings are impersonal . . . beauty is no longer seizable chance, but unavoidable.
> While works of painting have hitherto been so fugitive that they could not be duplicated . . . these, now, can be multiplied to infinity, whether by the artist who created them, or by scrupulous intermediaries . . . with paintings so that no copy is more 'original' than another, the selling price will drop of its own accord.

The implication, that only works whose qualities are completely determinate can be accurately reproduced, suggests (and the text elsewhere confirms) that Gleizes is thinking of reproduction by hand, since most mechanical means would have to be such (e.g. photographic) that they could reproduce accidental effects as well. However, he speaks also of *autres moyens d'ordre mécanique*, and thus implies that the benefits of mass-production, or mass-reproduction, will only be conferred on the buying public by objects which he elsewhere describes as conceived

> . . . following well defined, but nevertheless very simple laws

This idea, that only geometrically simple designs are cheap to mass-produce, was common property by the end of the Twenties, and has remained current ever since. But it was not Gleizes who gave it currency, and its wide distribution is due to those who combined it with a theory of types and with the idea of the *objet-objet*, the Purists.

Though a number of artists in Paris around 1922 exhibited broadly Purist tendencies, the Purists proper were only two, Amedée Ozenfant and Charles Edouard Jeanneret. They first met in 1918, through the agency of Auguste Perret, to whom Jeanneret, later to be known as Le Corbusier, had been a draughtsman in 1908–9. Later, in 1910–11, he had been in Germany to study the Werkbund and German design at the suggestion of

[6] *Grammaire des Arts de Dessin* (Paris, 1867, p. 509).

206

his master at the art school of his native Chaux-de-Fonds. This trip brought him in contact with the ideas of Muthesius and thus with the theory of types. In 1913 he heard Berlage lecture on Wright, which seems to have started an interest in the aesthetics of machine products, an interest which ripened into an admiration for the simple geometrical forms of early air-craft and automobile design during the years following his establishment in Paris in 1917, in connection with the Voisin company. Thus, by the time he met Ozenfant, when they were both aged thirty-three, he had behind him a career rich, already, in experience of practically everything except painting as a pure art, while Ozenfant who seems hardly to have stirred outside the world of art, was better versed in the recent history of Cubism than anything else. The difference of background is startlingly manifest in the paintings they exhibited at their first Purist exhibition, in 1919. Jeanneret's have the studious simplicity of schoolroom exercises in rendering regular geometrical solids, which is all that they are, whereas Ozenfant's have the strained quality of a sophisticated and romantic talent, which indeed he possessed, being disciplined into simplicity for the sake of an intellectual programme.

Given this peculiar combination of talents, well-informed on both the recent developments in painting and on recent developments in technology, it is not surprising that the Manifesto *Après le Cubisme*, which appeared as the catalogue to this first exhibition, should read like a continuation of the Classicised Cubo-Futurism of Severini and Gleizes—indeed such a pro-gramme is consciously explicit in the magazine *Sic* which appeared in 1916, and with which, as with another short-lived periodical *L'Elan*, Ozenfant had been connected. If *Après le Cubisme* is tamer in its layout than either of these magazines, it is also far more stimulating reading than the writing of either Severini or Gleizes. The main drift of the argument depends on the unity, later doubted by both authors, of art and science.

Nothing justifies us in supposing that there should be any incompatibility be-tween science and art. The one and the other have the common aim of reducing the universe to equations. We shall prove that pure art and pure science are not watertight domains. They have a common mind . . . art and science depend on number.

From this they derive the proposition

The aim of pure science is the expression of natural laws through the search for constants. The aim of serious art is also the expression of invariants.

The negative aspects of the *invariant* bring the Purists fairly close to *de Stijl* theory once more, for among the propositions which appear at the end of *Après le Cubisme* (like the affirmations at the end of a Futurist Manifesto) is one which reads

The work of art must not be accidental, exceptional, impressionist, inorganic, protestatory, picturesque, but, on the contrary, generalised, static, expressive of the invariant.

But the positive aspects of this concept of *l'invariant* tend in a quite different direction as might be expected, because not only does it subsume the *lois axiales de l'œuvre d'art*, but it could be extended to cover also the *objet-objet*, which becomes platonised by the Purists as the *objet-type*, or *objet-standard*. By this is implied an absolute object—house, bottle, guitar, etc.—beyond the reach of the accidents of personality, perspective or time, and also mass-produced. Here, the Purists diverge also from the position adopted by Duchamp five years earlier: his 'Bottle-rack' was mass-produced because no other kind of bottle-racks existed, and its metaphysical overtones were almost accidental

> The ready-mades may be unique as a concept, but they are not necessarily unique as examples. For instance, the original 'Bottle-rack' was lost and replaced by another.[7]

This represents a very drastic revision of the status of the work of art, but it follows after the original gesture of exhibition. With the Purists, however, even though the issue was prejudged, the choice of a certain class of objects as the subject-matter of their painting was preceded, not followed, by a variety of metaphysical, aesthetic and other arguments—arguments which originally appeared in *L'Esprit Nouveau* (and were later reprinted in *La Peinture Moderne*). *L'Esprit Nouveau* was the last but one and by far the most substantial of a series of attempts to found a Cubist magazine in Paris, and its success was largely due to the fact that it transcended the merely parochial interests of the School of Paris and became a magazine of general progressive culture. Besides the two Purists whose interests were already very wide, it had, in its early stages, a third founding director, Paul Dermée, the poet. Even without his participation, however, the magazine continued to embrace fields as diverse as architecture, painting, sculpture, product design, music, literature, philosophy, psychology, politics and economics. It enjoyed the support (unreliably) of certain commercial interests[8] (Voisin, Pleyel, etc.) and by running for nearly six years, from late 1919 to the middle of 1925, it proved itself more durable than any other Modern-Movement periodicals except *Der Sturm* and *de Stijl*, while in terms of sheer wordage and illustrations reproduced, it beats even these.

Even the name of the magazine had connections that promised the widest scope. As has already been noted, the phrase *l'esprit nouveau* had been employed by Choisy in a context that was likely to recommend it to others demanding a *rappel à l'ordre*, in architecture. But the phrase *rappel à l'ordre* is notoriously a Cocteauism, and in 1919 Jean Cocteau was also in possession of *esprit nouveau*, in the sense of a *Zeitgeist*:

[7] According to H. and S. Janis, in Robert Motherwell's book, *The Dada Painters and Poets* (New York, 1951, p. 311).

[8] Firms who rendered the magazine this sort of aid received not only large areas of advertising space as such, but frequently received free puffs in the editorial matter.

L'esprit nouveau agite toutes les branches de l'art.[9]

The Purists were in fairly close touch with Cocteau during the early Twenties (he contributed an article on the *Groupe de Puteaux* painter, Roger de la Fresnaye, to the magazine) but the traditional derivation of the name is via Dermée from Guillaume Apollinaire, who was using the phrase *l'esprit nouveau*, to describe a kind of Futurist imperative to progress, in the months preceding his death in 1920. At all events, it was a slogan that gratified the sensibilities of several aspects of the Parisian *avant-garde*, and carried implications that ranged from the Futurist to the Classicist, as did the contents of the magazine itself, which, however, resisted any forward-looking movements that seemed to spell disorder—its immediate response to Freudian psychology, for instance, was derisive.

The arguments which lead up to the concept of the *objet-type*, or *objet-standard*, represent a fairly thorough-going fusion of the Futurist, Cubist and Classicising themes, and they start with a hostile assessment (as in *Après le Cubisme*) of the state of Cubism in 1919. They declare the bankruptcy of

Cubism Limited, proprietors of a patent process

though they declare their admiration for its earlier products. The bankruptcy they attribute to the Cubists' insistence on their *droits au lyrisme*, which had caused their work to become too disorderly and too personal to be in accord with the spirit of the times, which demanded order and impersonality. The precise nature of their version of the spirit of the times is established by means of a very revealing reworking of existing techniques used by the Futurists. Thus, the illustrations to the chapter headed '*Formation de l'Optique Moderne*', begin with a purely Futurist set of images—a car, New York by night, the skeleton of an airship hangar, the equipment of a dentist's surgery—but then follow two final images that were, indeed, foreshadowed by Marinetti's *Manifesto of Geometrical and Mechanical Splendour*, but belong much more to the Purists' insistence on number, classification and order—a calculating machine and a filing system. The important characteristics of the new times, as they saw them were first: Economy

> The gait of present civilisation, its future, its character, depend on awaited discoveries, new formulas that provoke ever more economical mechanisms, permitting us to use energy in more efficient ways, thus giving our potentialities, and consequently our minds, a superior liberty and higher ambitions

second: The separation of techniques and aesthetics

> Mechanisation has diverted from our hands all work of exactitude and quality, and has delegated it to the machine. Our situation appears more clearly thereby: on one side, technical knowledge remains with technology (mechanisation) while, on the other, the plastic question remains untouched. . . . Mechanisation,

[9] Although *Le Rappel à l'Ordre* did not come out in book form until 1923, this particular observation appeared in print in 1919.

having resolved the problems of technology, leaves the problem of art intact. To refuse to recognise the step that has been taken is to impede the progress of art toward its pure and proper ends.

third: The dominance of simple geometry

> If we go indoors to work . . . the office is square, the desk is square and cubic, and everything on it is at right angles (the paper, the envelopes, the correspondence baskets with their geometrical weave, the files, the folders, the registers, etc.) . . . the hours of our day are spent amid a geometrical spectacle, our eyes are subject to a constant commerce with forms that are almost all geometry

Art was to be judged by the degree in which it was compatible with these characteristics of the times, and most art was found to be so incompatible that

> one is baffled by an inexplicable spectacle; practically everything proceeds by anti-geometry . . . so that one deduces that these are the works of some improbable race living outside time, in countries where other laws seem to reign than those that we have recognised, and are suited to our faculties of perception[10]

However, the reasons why geometry is the touchstone of probity are double: not only is it the thumb-print of modern technology, but it is also the manifestation of perennial laws governing art, justified by the past not the present

> It is in the past that the axial laws of the work of art are found, time alone proving their durability, their *sine qua non.*

and on the same page, the name of Phidias is cited, not for the first or last time, as an ultimate term of reference in aesthetic value.

This double status of geometry, as something both new and perennial, is comparable to the status of abstraction in *de Stijl* theory, and one might be tempted to regard the two terms as almost interchangeable, particularly since their associated ideas come so close. Thus

> The vertical and the horizontal are—among the sensorial manifestations of natural phenomena—verifications of one of the most directly apparent laws. The horizontal and the vertical determine two right angles, out of the infinity of possible angles, the right angle is the *angle-type*; the right angle is one of the symbols of perfection

contains nothing to which Mondriaan could not have subscribed, and elsewhere in *La Peinture Moderne* one can find Impressionism denounced, nature suspected, handicraft despised, universality and internationalism approved. The Purists' quarrel with *de Stijl*, which was fundamental though not reciprocated, concerned the question of representation. Purist compositions were built up, not of abstract forms, but of representations of objects.

---

[10] Fernand Leger carried this comparison between art and machinery even farther in *L'Effort Moderne* for February 1924, contrasting the formal disorder and nuanced colours of the *Salon d'Automne*, with the precise and simple geometry, the unmodulated 'local' colours of the exhibits in the *Salon d'Aviation*, with which it shared the Grand Palais in 1921. He also commented pityingly on the pathetic awe with which the technicians, having slipped through the partition, viewed the works of art—but failed to observe that he must have presented an analogous spectacle to them.

These can no longer be the abstract or conventional symbols of writing or mathematics, which escape those who do not know the code, but facts conditioned in such a manner as to stir our senses effectively, and also to interest our minds.

Thus, for example, a negative demonstration is furnished today by a whole movement in painting recently born in Holland, which appears to us to have withdrawn completely from the necessary and sufficient conditions for painting (intelligibility and perceptual apparatus) using only certain geometrical signs bounded by the rectangle.

One might, by an art stripped bare, strive for purity of expression; yet the means chosen must permit one to say something, and that worth saying.

As to what was worth being said, the Purists were prepared to admit of any theme that might be proposed, but for themselves, true heirs of Puteaux, they accepted a restriction to a limited range of *objet-types*. This acceptance was as explicit in their writings as in their paintings, and is formulated, in *La Peinture Moderne*, at the end of a remarkable eulogy of mass-produced utensils. Purism, the authors state, desires to go beyond the purely ornamental pleasures of abstract art, in order to offer *une emotion intellectuelle et affective*

> That is why Purism begins with elements chosen from existing objects, extracting their most specific forms.
> It draws them for preference from among those that serve the most direct of human uses; those which are like extensions of man's limbs, and thus of an extreme intimacy, a banality that makes them barely exist as subjects of interest in themselves, and hardly lend themselves to anecdote.

But these objects which *figurent le mieux l'objet-type*, were endowed with an almost moral importance as products of extreme economy.

> Purism has brought to light the *Law of Mechanical Selection*. This establishes that objects tend toward a type that is determined by the evolution of forms between the ideal of maximum utility, and the satisfaction of the necessities of economical manufacture, which conform inevitably to the laws of nature. This double play of laws has resulted in the creation of a certain number of objects that may thus be called standardised. . . . Without prescribing any theme, Purism has so far limited its choice to these objects

As they appear in Purist paintings—an appearance which is of importance for the effect it had upon the formal usages of the architecture produced by Jeanneret in his 'Le Corbusier' *persona*—these simple objects, mostly bottles, carafes, glasses and smoker's equipment, are presented, not in central perspective, but in a side-elevation convention closely based on that of engineering drawing, but with a form of pseudo-plan shown for the tops of open vessels (more rarely for their bases) which are presented as quartics, or circles. The avoidance of perspective was programmatic, firstly to eliminate accidents

> Ordinary perspective in its full theoretical rigour, gives only the accidental appearance of objects[11]

[11] This is quoted from one of the essays in *L'Esprit Nouveau* that was somewhat modified when transferred to *La Peinture Moderne*, and the phrase does not exist, as such, in the book, though it clearly belongs to its argument.

and secondly, because such an elimination of the accidents of perspective was held to be particularly necessary in the representation of types. This idea can be traced back, before the War, to Maurice Princet, an actuary who was friendly with Braque and Picasso, and is reported to have asked

> You represent by means of a trapezium a table as you see it, distorted by perspective, but what would happen if you took it into your head to represent a *table-type*. You would have to set it up in the picture-plane and revert from a trapezium to a true rectangle. If this table was covered in objects equally distorted by perspective, the same movement of correction would operate for each of them. Thus, the oval of a glass would become an exact circle. . . .[12]

As they appear in aesthetic theory—an appearance that affected both Le Corbusier's architecture and his views on furnishing—these simple objects can be related to the ideas of at least one other influential thinker, Paul Valéry, also a Classicist fascinated by mathematics. It will be noted that the Purists say that the double play of laws (function and economy) *has resulted*, in the perfect tense, in the creation of a certain number of standardised objects. That is to say, their *objets-type* stand at the end of a completed process (a remarkable attitude for two authors who had gone out of their way to indicate that the whole basis of life was undergoing a technical revolution) and a similar view of a terminated process is found in Valéry's almost contemporary *Eupalinos, ou l'architecte*

> Phaedrus: There are some admirable tools, neat as bones.
> Socrates: They are self-made, to some extent; centuries of use have necessarily discovered the best form, uncountable practice achieves the ideal, and there stops. The best efforts of thousands of men converge slowly towards the most economical and certain shape.[13]

However, there is evidence that the Purists did not believe, in practice, that the process was finished. In discussing the *maison-outil*, or *maison-type* in his architectural writings of the same period, Le Corbusier emphasises that its form is not, as yet, functional, economic or settled. In their paintings too, the Purists practised selection over and above that exercised by industry and commerce, refusing to admit to their range of subject-matter certain objects (such as imitation cut-glass tumblers) that persisted in the catalogue illustrations that were their sources, in defiance of the pseudo-Darwinian Law of Mechanical Selection—they were quite prepared, in fact, to finish a process that would not finish itself.

What is interesting in this situation is that, as has been seen, most of the ideas deployed by the Purists can be traced back to 1913 and beyond—the object, the type, the platonic, mechanistic and geometric preferences had all been current before the War, but no one then, had been able to weld

[12] This question has achieved a slightly legendary status in the history of Cubism, but was not committed to print until it was quoted by André L'hote, as late as 1933, in *L'Amour de l'Art* (Paris, 1933, No. 9, p. 216).
[13] In the definitive texts of *Eupalinos* (e.g. Professor Stewart's translation) this exchange does not appear, and it is quoted here from the headpiece to Pierre Urbin's essay in the *Journal de Psychologie Normale*.

them into a coherent aesthetic philosophy which, as in Le Corbusier's ✗
hands, could embrace buildings, the objects that furnished and equipped
them, and the works of art that embellished them. Partly this must have
been due to the excessively tumultuous condition of Cubist circles before
1914 but even more it was probably due to the emergence of a sudden
early maturity in many branches of machine design immediately after 1918.
The Purists' vision of a mechanical and geometrical environment was there
for all to see, with even greater force than the earlier vision of the Futurists.
Much of the elementary platonic geometry exhibited by the machinery of
the Twenties was far from inherent in the nature of mechanical design, but
the product of personal and local aesthetic choice, and therefore transient
—technology was not on the verge of achieving *formules definitives*, as
Pierre Urbain believed, but was shortly to get on the move again. But the
temporary halt and stabilisation of design persisted long enough to convince
those who were ready to be convinced that the perennial laws of geometry
were about to drive accident and variability from the visual world, that the
equipment of daily life was about to achieve final and typical form.

Among those who were convinced was Jeanneret-Corbusier, who gave
so much weight to the importance of the stabilised, finalised, mass-produced *objet-type*, that his last word on architecture in 1923, the last illustration in *Vers une Architecture*, was a plain English briar-pipe, offered
without explanation or justification, but with the clear implication that this ✗
was the standard to which architecture should aspire. However, the evolution of his ideas on the *maison-type* was conditioned, warped and finally
frustrated by the market in which he hoped to build it, the building world
of Paris whose characteristics in the Twenties were so exceptional that they
must be described before we turn to the *maison-type* itself.

16: Progressive building in Paris: 1918-1928

THE SITUATION FACING Le Corbusier, or anyone else hoping to erect Modern buildings in Paris in the Nineteen-twenties, was stimulating, frustrating, and complicated.[1] Intellectually architects might find themselves aspiring to build on a grand scale for a new mechanised society, but economically and socially they would often find themselves driven to erect small buildings of specialised type for a class of patrons they suspected as representatives of a dead social order. Hence their hatred of the established architectural order, of the *École* and the *Académie*—hence too their private feuds and passionate attachments to this master or that. The combination of intellectual abundance and physical restriction is one of the most striking features of this situation.

Intellectually, the climate of ideas could hardly have been richer, and remained so till the end of the decade. Extremist movements may have been short-lived, but they were replaceable. Futurism remained an active force until about the middle of the decade, the survivors of the heroic age of Cubism were still present. The freedoms of Dadaism may have proven unsubstantial, but they were succeeded after 1922 by the more organised programme of liberation of the Surrealists. Purism may have expired in 1925, but van Doesburg was at hand to provoke a ferment of Abstractionist activity toward the end of the decade. *L'Esprit Nouveau* may have expired with its parent movement, but *L'Effort Moderne*,[2] last of the Cubist magazines, had already been appearing for almost two years, and there was also, by 1925, a magazine devoted specifically to progressive architecture, *L'Architecture Vivante*,[3] edited by Albert Morancé and Jean Badovici.

These two last-named publications are important for their internationalism, giving considerable space to Dutch, German and Russian design,

---

[1] Outside Le Corbusier's *Œuvre Complète*, and similar publications about André Lurçat and Michel Roux-Spitz, the documentation of the buildings of Paris in this period is thin, and the coverage by periodicals almost non-existent. This chapter is therefore very deeply indebted to the personal reminiscences of Ernö Goldfinger, Pierre Vago and André Lurçat.

[2] Began to appear in 1924. [3] Began to appear in 1923.

and reprinting articles by van de Velde, Oud, Mondriaan, van Doesburg, Loos and others. Furthermore, the range of personalities that a young architect could adopt as a master was widening. Perret and Garnier were both established in Paris by now, as was Adolf Loos, and there were soon new buildings by all three of them to admire—Perret's church at Raincy, Garnier's town hall at Boulogne-sur-Seine, and Loos's house for Tristan Tzara in the Avenue Junot. Only Perret was officially (or unofficially) available as a teacher, and even Loos recommended his disciples to study under him in preference to any of the younger Moderns or himself.

You come to Paris to learn French, not Esperanto.

However, although Perret's school in the Palais de Bois was a formally constituted *atelier* of the *École des Beaux-Arts*, official discrimination against his students was such that they had to finish their course under some other master if they hoped to be *Diplomé*. This is typical of the official attitude to even middle-of-the-road progressive design, but the paucity of official or municipal commissions for younger architects has another reason beyond this. In contrast to the situation in Germany, where progressive architects, at least after 1925, could almost count on employment from progressive official bodies in such work as the design of large housing schemes, work of this scale and nature was unusual in France in the Twenties. Apart from the 'new town' at Villeurbane, and a privately sponsored settlement at Pessac, designed by Le Corbusier, there is little that can be compared with German activity. Michel Roux-Spitz was the nearest to a young Modernist to receive any official work, and that at the very end of the decade, while Henri Sauvage's block of flats in the Rue des Amiraux is as unusual in being a large, modern apartment house as it is in being patently derived from Sant'Elia's *case a gradinate*.

But the range and source of foreign influence in Paris went far beyond the presence of Loos. The city, as the artistic capital of the world, was full of students and artists from overseas, and many of its key figures had foreign backgrounds. To speak only of architects, Le Corbusier's outside connections have already been mentioned, but he had also travelled as far afield as Turkey, while Robert Mallet-Stevens was of Belgian extraction, had a long-standing connection with England, and a professed admiration for Mackintosh. Yet the biggest single source of outside influence on younger Paris architects at this time was undoubtedly the *Exposition des Arts Décoratifs* in 1925. This has its place in the history of Western taste, in any case, as the source of the popular jazz-modern style that was for some time a rival to the International style, but Mallet-Stevens and the Purists were also involved in it, the former in the design of an entrance and some Cubistic concrete 'trees', the latter, after much backstage intrigue, in the erection of the *Pavillon de l'Esprit Nouveau*, which will be discussed in a later chapter.

From abroad there came a Dutch Pavilion in an overwrought but not untypical Amsterdam idiom, designed by J. F. Staal, a British Pavilion that could have been designed by a Frenchman (in fact, by Easton and Robertson), while an Austrian Pavilion designed by Josef Hoffmann, but containing Keisler's *Cité dans l'Espace*, which has already been described, brought Elementarist design to Paris for the the first time on a large enough scale to be appreciated as architecture, and had a visible influence on the garden elevation of Le Corbusier's Villa at Garches, designed in the following year. But the pavilion which seems to have made the biggest impact was that from the USSR. At such a time it could hardly have gone unnoticed however it had been designed, but Melnikov's deceptively simple structure in wood must have looked as if it had been deliberately conceived to excite and annoy. Its general form was a glass-walled parallelogram, with a broad processional staircase, partly open to the sky under the truss-work of the roof. This staircase, which brought the visitor up to first-floor level and then down again, traversed the plan on its longer diagonal, thus giving the pavilion a form of symmetry, but not one that was listed among the Academic recipes—thus provoking the Beaux-Arts aesthetician Borislav-lievitch to a violent attack, occupying three pages of the journal *La Construction Moderne*. Younger and less prejudiced visitors, however, would probably agree with Lissitsky's estimate of it[4]

> . . . the project aims at the loosening up of volumes through the free disposition of the staircase. . . . The building is honestly built of wood, not on the Nationalist log-cabin principle, but in a Modern carpentry technique. It is transparent, the colours are pure. No false monumentality but a new sensibility.

All in all, this was a promising environment for younger architects to develop a new architecture—except in the matter of patronage. This came, when it did come, from a small, if cosmopolitan, section of Paris society which was already sufficiently sophisticated visually to accept architectural forms that, however Functional and Rational, were as unconventional as those of Cubist and Futurist art. In other words, the clientele of Modern architecture was composed of artists, their patrons and dealers, and a few casual visitors to the architectural section of the *Salon d'Automne*. The consequence was, firstly, that they would nearly all require at least one large, well-windowed north-light room, to use as a studio or gallery, secondly that their private lives were apt to be so eccentric as to put anti-typical demands on functional planning, and thirdly that, although a few were as munificent as the Princesse de Polignac, most of them were of only moderate means and needed very economical structures. In addition, buildings of this kind, for a patronage that was often foreign in extraction, seemed often to attract randomly spiteful application of the town-planning by-laws by the *Préfecture de la Seine*.

[4] *Russland*, p. 13.

The general consequence was that the bulk of Modern architecture in Paris in the Twenties consisted of one particular *maison-type*, the studio- *X* house, twisted out of recognition by random or personal factors. Thus the pure studio-type appears far more frequently in Le Corbusier's projects than in his built work, and André Lurçat, the most prolific builder of studios, only on one occasion approximates really closely to the type, in a house in Boulogne-sur-Seine, late in the decade. Yet, if the type was obscured, it was never absent from architects' thoughts for long, and often coloured their designs for buildings with quite different functions. The existence of the type dates back to the previous century, when it could often be found in its pure form of a long, narrow house, its dimensions fixed by the normal dimensions of a Paris building plot. Since it was usually hard up against other buildings on either side, its windows were all on the ends, those on the more northerly end usually being amalgamated into one single expanse of glass, often two stories high and spreading from wall to wall to light the studio.

The two-storey studio can also be taken as a given feature, often with a storage or sleeping balcony across the back of it, reached by a spiral stair or cat ladder, especially where studios were stacked up in multi-storey blocks, as they are at the foot of Montmartre. In these cases any other necessary rooms were usually at the back of the studio, but in single-studio houses they were more often underneath. The difficulty of spanning the width of the studio with beams strong enough to support further rooms on top was one of the main factors in planning the accommodation this way up, but even when reinforced concrete had obviated this difficulty, this arrangement remains the custom—though Perret, for instance, inverts it in the Orloff house, and has a ground-floor studio. The other form of section, with the smaller rooms behind the studio was the particular preference of Le Corbusier, who continued to use the long narrow plan with double-height studio and sleeping balcony even in his designs of the Fifties (as the flats at Marseilles) even in buildings that were not studio-houses (where the high room becomes a living room) and even in buildings that were not on long narrow sites (as the single house at Weissenhof) and did not need to have their fenestration confined to their end-walls.

There was a sharp divergence in the way in which architects faced the problem of the studio-house façade. The north-light window gives on to the street much more often than a statistical average would lead one to expect, and thus has to share the elevation with an entrance, probably garage doors and one or more small windows. Perret and his followers employ a strongly accentuated exposed frame, and distribute the various openings within it in such a way as to create at least an illusion of symmetry. The others, Mallet-Stevens, Lurçat, Le Corbusier and their followers, who were responsible for something like four studios out of every five in the Twenties, exploit the difference in size and function of the openings to create an asymmetrical pattern of holes pierced in a flat white surface,[5] on which an all-over rendering has been spread to obliterate the distinction between support and load, frame and fill.

For this they could plead the support of tradition—not the tradition of the professional architects, but that of the vernacular buildings of the Paris region, for the city still affords many examples of unpretentious utilitarian buildings, with windows of various sizes set asymmetrically in white-rendered walls. Attention had been drawn to such buildings by the paintings of Utrillo, which take them as their prime subject-matter, and by the Cubo-Futurist magazine *Sic* which exhorted its readers in 1916

> Aimons la maison neuve
> Aimons la maison blanche

which, judging from the elaborate surface finishes preferred by professional architects of the period, can only refer to whitewashed vernacular buildings.

But Le Corbusier, at least, had other reasons for admiring whitewashed architecture, reasons that seem to be involved with his own experiences as a painter, and his theories about the beauty of banality. In reviewing the architectural section of the *Salon d'Automne* of 1922 in *L'Esprit Nouveau* he wrote, complaining of a preoccupation with *de luxe* materials.

> If the house is entirely white, the design of things stands out without possible transgression, the volumes of things appear clearly, the colour of things is explicit.

So far, he could be a painter extolling the virtues of working on a white ground, but he pursues the theme to the point where whitewash becomes a sort of *couleur-type*, with folkloristic overtones.

> Whitewash is absolute; on it, everything stands out, inscribes itself absolutely; it is sincere and loyal. Whitewash is the riches of poor and rich, of all men— just as bread, milk and water are the riches of the slave and the king.

Thus, the vernacular architecture of Paris provokes him to reflections that reach deeply into his experience and theories, but it also provoked him to conceive something more specific: the project for the *Maison Citrohan*. This simple house is almost a pure *studio-type*, but he provides for it a derivation as characteristically unexpected as it is deeply indebted to the authority of the vernacular[6]

> We were eating in a little cabbie's restaurant in the middle of Paris. There was a bar (zinc), the kitchen at the back, a garret-floor divides the height of the

[5] In the Rue du Belvedere, Boulogne-sur-Seine, and in the villa Seurat, off the Rue de la Tombe-Issoire, the Perret solution, and that favoured by the younger Modernists can be found almost next door to one another.

[6] This is wisdom after the event, not a contemporary record of his feelings, and did not appear in print until Volume I of the *Œuvre Complète*, p. 31. The windows in question had tall narrow panes which can still be found on older industrial buildings all over the Paris area, as well as on the electricity sub-stations built in the early Twenties.

premises in two, the front opens directly on the street. Simplification of sources of illumination—just one big bay at each end; two lateral bearing walls, a flat roof on top; a veritable box that could usefully become a house.

while the fenestration of *Maison Citrohan*, like that of the bulk of the studio-houses standing in Paris at that time (1920) drew on another vernacular tradition.

We had observed that the glazing of factories in the Paris suburbs let light in and kept thieves out without any difficult joinery. And was very attractive aesthetically, judiciously used.

But *Citrohan* is an admitted pun on *Citroën*, and raises a problem that can only be discussed in the context of Le Corbusier's first book over that famous signature, *Vers une Architecture*.

17: Vers une Architecture

LE CORBUSIER'S FIRST book on architecture, which was to prove to be one of the most influential, widely read and least understood of all the architectural writings of the twentieth century, was put together in the last months of a long pause in his architectural activity—the articles in *L'Esprit Nouveau*, from which it was contrived, had all appeared by January 1922, some months before that year's *Salon d'Automne* brought him in contact with the client for whom he built his first Modern house, the little villa at Vaucresson. So great was the change that had come over his architectural ideas in this pause, from 1917 to 1923, that he has subsequently suppressed the work of the earlier phase, though in 1921, before the *Citrohan* project had taken its final form, he was still sufficiently pleased with the last of these early works, a house at Chaux-de-Fonds, to have it published at length in *L'Esprit Nouveau*, and to use it to make a point in *Vers une Architecture*.

Indeed, for a house of 1917, it was nothing to be ashamed of. It shows a similar kind of brisk, up-to-the-minute eclecticism to that of Gropius's Werkbund Pavilion at Cologne, three years earlier, though one of its stylistic sources may have been the reasons for its later suppression from the Corbusian canon. He records that the client, seeing a project of Perret's among a portfolio of Le Corbusier's own designs said

Faites-moi quelque chose de semblable
(Make me something like that)

and the resultant building, though far from *semblable*, is unmistakably Perretesque in its general conception, which may well have been an embarrassment to him after he changed his attitude to Perret in 1923. However, the design has other sources as well; the *Beaux-Arts* tradition has been laid under tribute for much of the detailing, the overall massing bears a striking (if coincidental) resemblance to Philibert del'Orme's gate-house at Anet, though the treatment of the apsidal wings seems indebted more directly to Hoffmann's Villa Ast, and the general layout of the interior is markedly Wrightian, a double-height living room, with an access-balcony serving the bedrooms, forming the central volume of an open cruciform plan, in the manner of the Roberts House of 1907. This may have been a source of embarrassment to him, for his attitude to Wright was rather ambivalent. He knew Berlage too well not to be acquainted with Wright's work, and told Sigfried Giedion that he had actually heard Berlage's lecture of 1913, but when Wijdeveld asked him to contribute to the special issue of *Wendingen* devoted to Wright, he is reported to have replied 'Connais pas cet architecte'.[1]

Even if he was not pleased with the aesthetics of this house, its technical qualities should have continued to gratify him. It has flat roofs draining to internal run-off pipes, a device which was, even in 1926, of great consequence to him as a way of avoiding the disastrous results of ridge-melting and eaves-freezing of pitched roofs under snow, a serious menace to building in Chaux-de-Fonds. Further, it shares with van t'Hoff's villa at Huis ter Heide the distinction of being the first concrete-framed villa in Europe, and its mode of construction was of the greatest technical interest. The frame and roof-slabs were put up between the end of August and the onset of the winter's snows, at which point building-work in Chaux-de-Fonds normally ceased, but with the roofs already up, it was possible to proceed with building right through the winter—albeit at the cost of using warmed bricks and anti-freeze in the mortar.

But all this was to be put away when he conceived the *Citrohan* project

> With this house we turned our backs on the architectural ideas of the Academic schools—and the Modern ones too.

As has been said, the invented name *Citrohan* was a conscious pun

> To avoid saying 'Citroën'. In other words, a house like a car

a concept that introduces two other important lines of thought besides those that have already been discussed in connection with this project. On the one hand there was the cut-to-the-bone aesthetic of *'Outillage'*, of equipment as against furniture; on the other hand was the dream of a mass-produced *maison-type*, and in 1919, when the basic form of the *Maison Citrohan* was taking shape in his mind, this dream appeared to be on the point of realisation. The Voisin Company, at the termination of its war-time aircraft contracts (like other aircraft companies after the Second World War) tried to keep its plant occupied by breaking into the housing business. At least two prototypes of the *Maison Voisin* were built, one plain, one fancy, and neither of them very distinguished architecturally, though they present the technical peculiarity (presumably derived from aircraft practice) that their roof-trusses span the longer dimension of the rectangular plan, not the shorter, and the gables, in consequence, are on the sides, not the ends of the house.

[1] This is reply as André Lurçat gave it me. Wijdeveld's own version is given by N. Pevsner in the *Architects' Journal* (London, 4 May 1939, p. 732).

Le Corbusier himself will not admit to any part in their design, but his description of them[2] shows that they lay very close to his own ideas.

> Up till now it seemed that a house must be heavily attached to the soil, by the depth of its foundations, the weight of its thick walls. . . . It is no trick that the *Maison Voisin* is one of the first to mark the exact reversal of this conception. The science of building has evolved in a shattering manner in recent times. The art of building has struck root firmly in science.
>
> The statement of the problem by itself indicated the means of realisation, powerfully affirming the immense revolution on which architecture has embarked. When the art of building is modified to such an extent, established aesthetics of construction are automatically over-thrown.

Thus far, Choisy up-to-date. Next, having posed the problem of post-War building in terms of a shortage of skilled labour overwhelmed by an almost unlimited demand for houses, he adopts a more Futurist tone.

> . . . impossible to wait on the slow collaboration of the successive efforts of excavator, mason, carpenter, joiner, tiler, plumber . . . *houses must go up all of a piece, made by machine tools in a factory, assembled as Ford assembles cars, on moving conveyor belts.*
>
> Meanwhile, aviation was achieving prodigies of serial production. An aeroplane is a little house that can fly and resist the storm.
>
> It is in aircraft factories that the soldier-architects have decided to build their houses; they decided to build this house like an aircraft, with the same structural methods, lightweight framing, metal bracers, tubular supports.

A house built like an aeroplane would be a very fair realisation of the kind of architecture that Sant'Elia had demanded, built of light-weight replacements for brick, stone and wood, and a knowledge of Sant' Elia's views probably lies at the back of the enthusiastic tone of this passage, but his concluding remarks seem to return to his desire for simplicity and normality; he appears to specify for this house an *habitant-type*.

> These lightweight houses, supple and strong as car-bodies or airframes, are ingenious in plan: they offer the comforts a wise man might demand. To inhabit such houses one needs the mind of a sage, animated by *L'Esprit Nouveau*. A generation is coming to birth that will know how to live in *Maisons Voisin*.

Although the *Maison Voisin* itself does not appear in *Vers une Architecture* (nor do Perret's studies for mass-production houses, in spite of the fact that they had appeared in *L'Esprit Nouveau*), the idea of the *maison fabriquée en série*, the *maison-outil*, the *maison-type*, and various other isotopes of the *machine à habiter* are very much in evidence. However, they appear only in certain parts of a book whose parts are so curiously related that the effective significance of the concept can only be disentangled by taking the argument completely apart, and scrutinising the pieces separately.

No great violence is thereby done, because *Vers une Architecture* has no argument in any normal sense of the word. It has, instead, a series of rhetorical or rhapsodical essays on a limited number of themes, assembled side by side in such a way as to give the impression that these themes have

[2] The account of the Voisin house will be found in *L'Esprit Nouveau*, No. 2, p. 211.

some necessary connection. All but one of these essays had appeared in *L'Esprit Nouveau*, though not quite in the order of the book, and most of them are *reproduit tel*, page for page. Two main themes can be distinguished at once, and can be roughly labelled Academic and Mechanistic. All the essays can be put under one or other of these headings in terms of their main subject-matter, and they are grouped in the book in a manner which emphasises this distinction. Thus, the Academic material comes in two compact blocks, the first labelled '*Trois Rappels à MM les Architectes*', dealing with Surface, Volume and Plan, followed immediately by one on '*Tracés Régulateurs*'. The second block, headed '*Architecture*', contains three essays devoted to 'The Lesson of Rome', 'The Illusion of Plans', and 'Pure Creation of the Mind'.

The Mechanistic essays are fitted around these two blocks as follows: first (in the book, but not in the magazine) '*Esthétique de l'Ingenieur*'; next, after the '*Rappels*', a section of three essays under the heading '*Des Yeux qui ne Voient pas*', dealing with Liners, Aircraft, and Automobiles; and finally, after '*Architecture*', the chapter on mass-production houses, and an entirely new one entitled '*Architecture ou Revolution*'. As will be seen, although the book opens on a Mechanistic note, the chapters which actually deal with the virtues of machinery are firmly sandwiched between two sections whose main function is to rehearse the more Abstract and Classical —*large et sévère*—ideas of the Academic tradition, so that the reader who goes straight through the book gets the impression that he is being conducted through an orderly argument in which machine-design stands as a necessary intermediate stage between certain Abstract fundamentals of design and the glories of the Parthenon. This impression is reinforced by a judicious intermixture of themes in the illustrations and captions. Thus, Plan and Surface are illustrated by photographs of grain silos and American factory buildings respectively, while Pure Creation has its photographs of the Parthenon and the Propylaea captioned with phrases such as

> Voici la machine à émouvoir

or

> All this plastic machinery is realised in marble with the rigour that we have
> learned to apply in the machine. The impression is of naked, polished steel.

This interfusion of the Mechanical and the Classical achieves a kind of apotheosis in the chapter on Automobiles. Here on a pair of facing pages the reader finds, at the top, the Basilica at Paestum on the left, the Parthenon on the right, and, below, a Humber of 1907 and a Delage of the early Twenties. On reflection the reader realises that this is supposed to be read from page to page, implying an equivalent progress between Humber and Delage and between Paestum and Acropolis, but the immediate response seems always to be to read down the page, thus producing an image of contrast, like Marinetti's between a racing car and the *Nike* of Samothrace.

The four illustrations together are clearly intended to be read in some such sense, as well as that of progress in design, and this is hardly surprising, for other versions of the Marinettian image were current in Paris at the time. Thus, in February 1922, Francis Picabia mangled it[3] to suit his own ends as

> Tristan Tzara . . . has decided to put his top hat on a locomotive: obviously, that is easier than putting it on the *Victory* of Samothrace

and in 1927 a reader of *L'Effort Moderne* complained

> Walking down the Champs Élysées, I saw, on a car displayed in the premises of a motor manufacturer, a radiator cap representing a miniature *Victory* of Samothrace,[4] looking completely ridiculous, and quite contrary to the precise, simple and logical order of the car itself.

But Le Corbusier's intention is not to present a *contradiction d'esprit* between the Mechanical and the Classical. Quite the other way about, he proposed, following the line established by Severini and Gleizes, to establish an analogy, if not an equivalence between the two

> This precision, this cleanliness in execution go farther back than our reborn mechanical sense. Phidias felt in this way; the entablature of the Parthenon is a witness.

and throughout the book, Classical architecture and Machine design are represented as having in common such ideas as 'selection applied to a standard', and the paring away of accidents from a type.

Bearing this supposed analogy or equivalence in mind, we can now turn to the content of the individual essays, taking first those on Academic themes, because they reveal Le Corbusier's aesthetic processes. The three *Rappels* are united by the proposition

> Mass and surface are the elements by which architecture manifests itself. Mass and surface are determined by the plan. The plan is the generator.

and the first chapter, on Volume (Mass), opens with the much-quoted statement

> L'Architecture est le jeu savant, correct et magnifique des volumes assemblés sous la lumière.
> (Architecture is the masterly, correct and magnificent play of masses brought together in light.)

Typically, this contains a proposition so commonsensical as to be self-evident—architecture is a play of volumes appreciated by the eyes—into which are injected the intangibles *savant, correct et magnifique*, and the loaded word *assemblés*. If, as seems likely, it is the *assemblage* which has to be *correct*, etc. then we appear to be dealing with something like Guadet's *composition* (which can be confirmed by examination of Le Corbusier's other writings and his buildings) and, in that case, the three intangibles

[3] In the pamphlet *Pomme du Pin*, which he published in St Raphaël in 1922.
[4] This must, almost certainly, have been a Rolls-Royce.

are not beyond interpretation. *Correct* implies a standard of judgement, or a body of rules, *Savant* that this standard or those rules are known and understood, and *Magnifique* that they are applied, probably, with talent or imagination. But the precise nature of the rules is left ambiguous—early in the chapter they appear to consist in the employment of the regular Phileban solids

> . . . cubes, cones, spheres, cylinders or pyramids are the great primary forms which light reveals to advantage . . . these are *beautiful forms, the most beautiful forms.*

whereas at the end of this same chapter, when he discusses American grain silos more specifically, the rules appear to be the laws of nature

> Not in pursuit of an architectural idea, but simply guided by the results of calculation (derived from the principles which govern our universe) and the conception of a living organism, the engineers of today make use of primary elements and, by co-ordinating them in accordance with the rules, provoke in us architectural emotions, and thus make the work of man ring in unison with the universal order

This paragraph is crucial to this part of the argument, and to a great deal else in the book. The *formes primaires* of the earlier quotation are rendered fully Guadetesque by becoming *éléments primaires* (easy enough with grain silos, where the functional components approximate so closely to the Phileban solids) co-ordinated *suivant les règles*. But a new ambiguity enters —are these *règles* to be equated with the *principes qui gèrent notre univers?* Though there is no external reason why they should be, it seems necessary to Le Corbusier's argument that some such equivalence be accepted by the reader, otherwise the accordance of the non-architectural forms of the silos with his own aesthetic preferences may be no more than a coincidence.

A somewhat similar procedure is followed for Surface, illustrated by views of concrete-framed factories to exemplify the *formules d'atélier* 'accuser la forme' and 'modeler la surface', but the chapter on Plan is different. Here silos and factories fail him, and he falls back on illustrations from Choisy's *Histoire*, Garnier and Perret. The familiar illustrations from Choisy make the connection between plan and the total form of a building very visible, but they do not, in themselves, make it clear to what extent the plan creates the form, and to what extent it derives from the form and the techniques used to create it—i.e. bay-widths that can be spanned, thickness of wall required to support various kinds of roof. Le Corbusier does not even allude to this second possibility—for him there is no question of the primacy of plan.

> The plan is at its basis. . . . The plan bears within itself a primary and pre-determined rhythm. . . . The plan carries in itself the very essence of sensation.

This hammering of the importance of the plan echoes, if it does not repeat in detail, the weight attached to the elegancies of the paper pattern of a building's plan at the *École des Beaux-Arts*, where, following Guadet, the elements of a building being of conventional form and structure, their distribution on plan did largely determine the appearance of the exterior. But Le Corbusier seems also to have had in his mind the idea of plans as a species of *Secret Professionel*, for this idea appears in the writings, very much under his influence, of Pierre Urbain, who speaks[5] of the lay public as being

> . . . rarely in a position to understand the influence of its own needs on the architecture of its time, since they affect above all *the plan*, and only a professional education of a sufficiently advanced standard permits one to judge that, or even to read its disposition.

In any case, having declared the determining influence of the plan, Le Corbusier then undermines his case by offering in the next chapter an almost independent aesthetic order for the elevations—*Les Tracés Régulateurs*. So strongly does he feel about them that he not only declares them to be good and necessary, but makes an appeal to history as well

> But the past has left us proofs, iconographical documents, steles, slabs, inscribed stones, parchments, manuscripts, printed matter. . . .

Unfortunately his use of historical evidence is sloppy in the extreme, and so this chapter shows him in a bad light. Lines inked on photographs of the Porte Saint Denis and the façade of Notre Dame are an inaccurate version of Blondel's diagram in the first instance, and over a foot thick to scale in the second; those on photographs of the Capitol at Rome and the Petit Trianon are more convincing because they demonstrate nothing that one does not feel, as Choisy did about Serlio, to have been impossible to demonstrate by simple numbers. Where he relies on book-learning he inspires even less confidence: he has patently misunderstood Choisy's reconstruction of the façade of the arsenal of the Piraeus and believes it to be a copy of an original Greek drawing, while one of the two diagrams of Achemenid domes that he reproduces out of Dieulafoy is so inaccurately drawn as to suggest that he had not understood the form of the building.

Nevertheless, the drift of these first four Academic chapters is clear enough: he prefers an architecture of geometrical forms so elementary that the main art of design lies in their distribution in plan, and in the distribution of the incidents on their surfaces. The second Academic group takes up a different theme: that Functionalism is not enough.

> Architecture goes beyond utilitarian needs.
> You employ stone, wood and concrete, and with these materials you build houses and palaces. That is construction. Ingenuity is at work. But suddenly you touch my heart, you do me good, I am happy and I say 'This is beautiful'.
> That is Architecture. Art enters in.

Each chapter of this section is concerned with spiritual qualities in some way, the third specifically so. The first, 'The Lesson of Rome', praises the ancient Romans for their devotion to the regular Phileban Solids, and for

[5] Also in the special issue of the *Journal de Psychologie Normale*.

their sense of order; from mediaeval Rome it singles out Santa Maria in Cosmedin for its abstinence and simplicity, and the architecture of its ambones (to which his attention had probably been directed by Choisy's account of the liturgical furniture in San Clemente); from Renaissance Rome he singles out Michelangelo, whom he places on a level with Phidias at the summit of human achievement, and in a justly celebrated passage he praises St Peter's for its

> . . . gigantic geometry of harmonious relationships . . . the mouldings are of an intensely passionate character, harsh and pathetic.

Finally, he denounces *la Rome des Horreurs*, Rome from Vignola to Victor Emmanuel, and concludes

> The Grand Prix de Rome and the Villa Medici are the cancer of French architecture.

The next chapter, 'The Illusion of Plans', continues this attack on the *École* but, as might be expected in view of the earlier chapter in praise of the plan, the attack is not radical.

> In a great public institution, the *École des Beaux-Arts*, the principles of good planning have been studied, and then, as time has gone by, dogmas have been established, and recipes and tricks. A method of teaching useful enough at the beginning has become a dangerous practice.

The particular dangerous practice to which he objects is an excess of emphasis on the plan as a work of art in its own right, and chiefly, star-planning for its own sake. Against this he insists that

> A plan proceeds from within to without

and then, contrariwise, gives an account of the interior volumes of the Green Mosque at Brousa in the opposite direction, as seen by a visitor proceeding from the outside inwards. However, this little exercise in the description of a building's interior, as actually seen, gives a useful clue to the meaning of an obscure and over-wrought chapter. In the descriptions of real buildings and actual archaeological sites it is clear that when he says *plan* what he usually means is a sequence of interior volumes as the visitor actually experiences them, and when he says *axis*, he means the route by which they are traversed, or a vista along which they can be seen

> The axis of the Acropolis runs from the Piraeus to Pentelicus, from the mountain to the sea

and this, taken in conjunction with some very perceptive evaluations of the visual siting and walkable topology of the Acropolis, the Forum at Pompeii, and Hadrian's villa, seems to reveal a revival in very personal and rather mystical terms

> l'axe est dans les intentions. . . .

of Choisy's Picturesque evaluations of some of the same monuments—

in fact, Choisy's illustrations of the Acropolis appear once more in this chapter.

The third part of 'Architecture', 'Pure Creation of the Mind', consists chiefly of reproductions of some extremely good photographs of ancient Greek architecture, supported by a text and captions that make two points. Firstly against Functionalism, and also against such associated nineteenth-century concepts as Naturalism, as in the following, dubiously based on personal observation

> Certain writers have declared that the Doric column was inspired by a tree springing from the earth, without a base, etc. . . . . It is most false, since the tree with straight trunk is unknown in Greece, where only stunted pines and twisted olives grow. *The Greeks created a plastic system* . . . so pure that it gives almost the feeling of a natural growth. But nonetheless, it is entirely man's creation. . . .

This coincidence of the natural and the human is attributed to a

> concordance avec l'axe qui est en l'homme

which returns us to the subject of the previous chapter.

The second point which is made is that which, almost alone, relates the Academic chapters to the Mechanistic half of the book. The point is made, obliquely at the very beginning of the chapter

> Profile and contour (i.e. Modénature) are the touchstone of the Architect. Here he reveals himself as artist or mere engineer.

and yet, in spite of this lower valuation placed upon engineers, his standard terms of praise in the captions to detail photographs of the *modénature* of flutings, echinoi, guttae, etc. are drawn from engineering.

> The curve of the echinus is as rational as that of a large shell. The section of the cornice is as tight as an engineer's outline.

The intention is clear: contemporary technology is to be held up as an example to contemporary architecture in decline from Greek standards of *moralité dorique*. This is explicit from the opening words of the first chapter of the book

> The engineer's aesthetic and architecture—two things that march together and follow from one another—the one at its full height, the other in an unhappy state of retrogression

and this unfavourable comparison is rubbed in again and again throughout the first chapter.

> There exists in France a great national school of architecture, and there are, in every country, architectural schools of various kinds, to mystify young minds and teach them the obsequiousness of the toady.
> Our engineers are healthy and virile, active and useful, balanced and happy in their work. Our architects are disillusioned and unemployed, boastful or peevish.
> Architects, emerging from the schools, . . . enter in the town in the spirit of a milkman who should, as it were, sell his milk mixed with vitriol or poison.

Besides this elevation of the engineer to the status of a noble savage of

. Raymond
uchamp-Villon. *La
illa Cubiste* (model of
çade), 1912: the
plication of Cubist-
yle forms in place of
aditional decoration.
. Charles Edouard
anneret (Le
orbusier). *Peinture*,
20. Programmatic
urist painting with
jects projected
cording to Princet's
eory of types.

229   F.M.A.

82. Charles Edouard Jeanneret (Le Corbusier). Still-
life, 1924. Developed Purist painting, bringing
together a number of the familiar objects prized by the
Purists.
83. Mass-produced French glass and china, composed
into a still-life by Jeanneret or Ozenfant; the forms
reappear in the painting above, except those of the 'cut-
glass goblet' at left.

84. Henri Sauvage. Flats in Rue des Amiraux,
Paris, 1924. Futurist in derivation, from Sant'
Elia's *case a gradinati*, this block is rare in Paris
at the time for its size and its wide frontage.
85. K. Melnikov, Russian Pavilion at the
Exposition des Arts Décoratifs, Paris, 1925, the
first sight of the new Russian architecture in
the West.

86. André Lurçat. Studio house in Rue de Belvedere,
Paris, 1926. The function, site and form are all typical
of the basic building type that was the mainstay of early
modern architecture in Paris.
87, 88. Studio flat in the Boulevard Rochechouart,
Paris, and a saddler's shop near the Place du Tertre,
Paris; the raw materials, functionally and formally, of
the modern studio house vernacular.

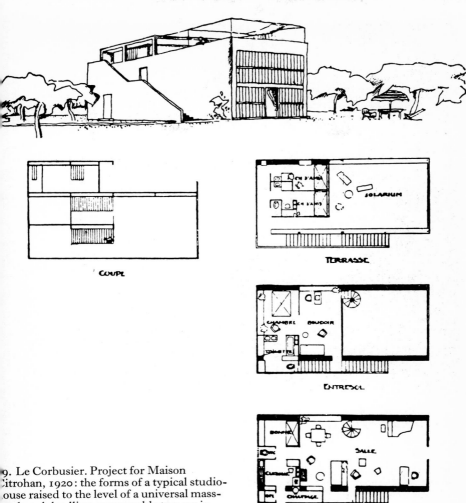

COUPE

TERRASSE

ENTRESOL

REZ DE CHAUSSÉE

9. Le Corbusier. Project for Maison Citrohan, 1920: the forms of a typical studio-house raised to the level of a universal mass-produced dwelling, comparable to a car in price and availability.

90, 91. Charles Edouard Jeanneret (Le Corbusier). Villa in La Chaux de Fonds, Switzerland, 1916: the last work of Le Corbusier's first career as an architect, comparable in its brilliance of technique and eclecticism with Gropius and Meyer's Werkbund Pavilion of 1914 (cf. figs. 29 and 30).

92. Page opening from Le Corbusier, *Vers une Architecture*, Paris, 1923; with a typography and economy reminiscent of Choisy's *Histoire*, Le Corbusier here made his most telling and influential comparison of architecture and machinery; the progress of the Greek Temple and the progress of the automobile.

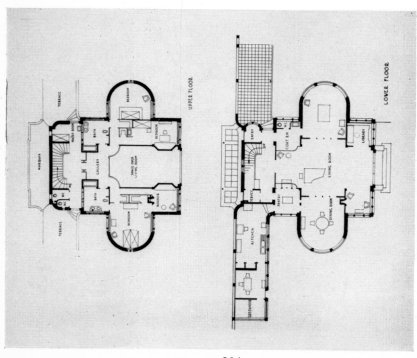

Parthénon, de 600 à 550 av. J.-C.

Le Parthénon est un produit de sélection appliquée à un standart établi. Depuis un siècle déjà, le temple grec était organisé dans tous ses éléments.

Lorsqu'un standart est établi, le jeu de la concurrence immédiate et violente s'exerce. C'est le match ; pour gagner, il faut

Humber, 1907.

Cliché de La Vie Automobile.

Cliché Albert Morancé.

Parthénon, de 447 à 434 av. J.-C.

faire mieux que l'adversaire dans toutes les parties, dans la ligne d'ensemble et dans tous les détails. C'est alors l'étude poussée des parties. Progrès.

Le standart est une nécessité d'ordre apporté dans le travail humain.

Le standart s'établit sur des bases certaines, non pas arbi-

Delage, Grand-Sport 1921.

93. Le Corbusier. Exterior of the *Pavillon de l'Esprit Nouveau*, Exposition des Arts Decoratifs, Paris, 1925: this half of the pavilion was one unit from the Immeuble-villas project—each unit was, effectively, a Maison Citrohan and a garden terrace.
94. Le Corbusier. Interior of the *Pavillon de l'Esprit Nouveau*, Paris, 1925: furnished with equipment from manufacturers' catalogues (cf. fig. 83).

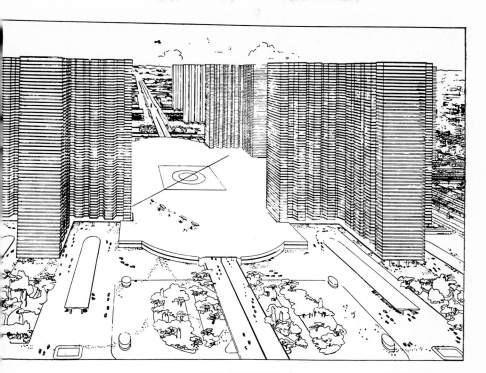

95. Le Corbusier. Central station area of project for *Une Ville Contemporaine*, 1921–1922: the Futurist dream of multi-level circulation and towers, regularised in terms of Beaux-Arts geometry and German-style glass towers (cf. fig. 106).
96. Le Corbusier and Pierre Jeanneret. Ozenfant House (present state), Paris, 1922: the first building of Le Corbusier's second career as an architect.

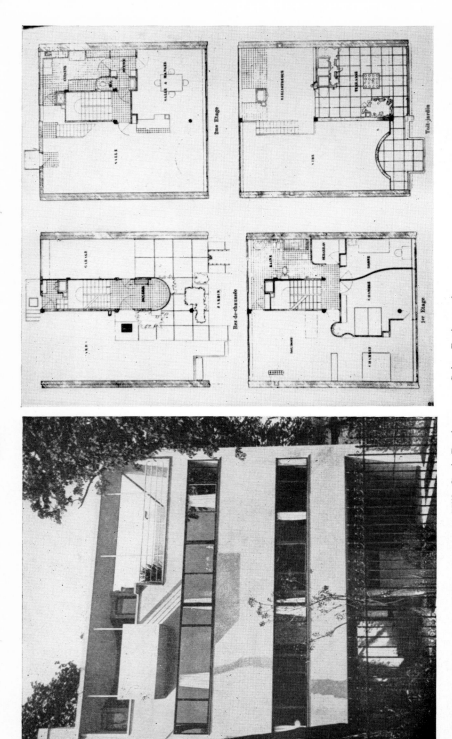

97, 98. Le Corbusier and Pierre Jeanneret. Villa Cook, Boulogne-sur-Seine, Paris, 1926: together with the Palais du Peuple of the same year, this 'vraie maison cubique' with its square plan, section and elevation, ingenious curved walls, open ground floor and 'fenêtres en

238

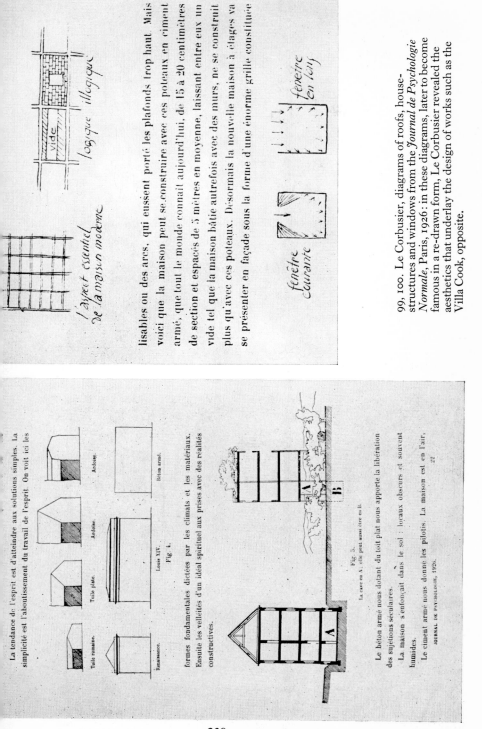

La tendance de l'esprit est d'atteindre aux solutions simples. La simplicité est l'aboutissement du travail de l'esprit. On voit ici les

Tuile romaine. Tuile plate. Ardoise. Ardoise.

Renaissance. Louis XIV. Béton armé.

Fig. 4.

formes fondamentales dictées par les climats et les matériaux. Ensuite les velléités d'un idéal spirituel aux prises avec des réalités constructives.

Le béton armé nous dotant du toit plat nous apporte la libération des sujétions séculaires.

La maison s'enfonçait dans le sol : locaux obscurs et souvent humides.

Le ciment armé nous donne les pilotis. La maison est en l'air,

22

JOURNAL DE PSYCHOLOGIE, 1926.

Fig. 5.
La cave en A, elle peut aussi être en B.

lisables ou des arcs, qui eussent porté les plafonds trop haut. Mais voici que la maison peut se construire avec ces poteaux en ciment armé, que tout le monde connaît aujourd'hui, de 15 à 20 centimètres de section et espacés de 5 mètres en moyenne, laissant entre eux un vide tel que la maison bâtie autrefois avec des murs, ne se construit plus qu'avec ces poteaux. Désormais la nouvelle maison à étages va se présenter en façade sous la forme d'une énorme grille constitue

l'aspect essentiel de la maison moderne

logique illogique

vide

fenêtre courante

fenêtre en long

99, 100. Le Corbusier, diagrams of roofs, house-structures and windows from the *Journal de Psychologie Normale*, Paris, 1926: in these diagrams, later to become famous in a re-drawn form, Le Corbusier revealed the aesthetics that underlay the design of works such as the Villa Cook, opposite.

101, 102. Le Corbusier and Pierre Jeanneret. *Les Terrasses*, Garches, 1927–1928: the most complete demonstration of Le Corbusier's aesthetics of 1926, formal, classicizing in elevation, free in plan in spite of the regular grid of columns, violent in the penetrations from floor to floor.

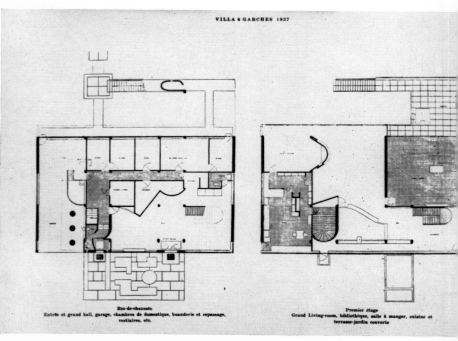

VILLA à GARCHES 1927

Rez-de-chaussée
Entrée et grand hall, garage, chambres de domestique, buanderie et repassage, vestiaires, etc.

Premier étage
Grand Living-room, bibliothèque, salle à manger, cuisine et terrasse-jardin couverte

design, in the tradition of Marinetti and Loos, and a pre-statement (in the magazine a restatement) of the theme:

> The purpose of construction is to make things hold together; of architecture to move us.

This first chapter introduces the concept of the house as an *outil*, and with it an eulogy of the morality of scrapping that is an extension of the Futurists' 'Our houses will last less time than we do'.

> A question of morality. Lack of truth is intolerable, we perish in untruth. Architecture is one of the most urgent needs of man, for the house has always been the indispensable and first tool that he has forged for himself. Man's stock of tools marks out the stages of civilisation . . . the result of successive improvements, the effort of all generations is embodied in them.

Having thus combined the ideas of Choisy and Paul Valéry, Le Corbusier makes the point that the generations have collaborated in these successive perfectionings chiefly by throwing away the products of their forefathers

> We throw the out-of-date tool on the scrap-heap: the carbine, the culverin, the growler and the old locomotive. This action is a manifestation of health, of moral health, of morale also; it is not right that we should produce bad things because of a bad tool, nor is it right that we should waste our energy, our health and our courage because of a bad tool; it must be thrown away and replaced.

But houses, for various reasons, have not been scrapped and replaced.

> Architects work in 'styles' or discuss questions of structure in and out of season: their clients, the public, still think in terms of conventional appearance, and reason on the foundation of insufficient education. Our external world has been enormously transformed in its outward appearance and in the use made of it, by reason of the machine. We have gained a new perspective and a new social life, but we have not yet adapted the house thereto.

Here one may distinguish two major concepts: the establishment of perfected objects (types) by scrapping; and the creation of a new mechanised environment in which neither the stylistic interests of the *Beaux-Arts*, nor the structural Rationalism of the *Polytechnique* are of any service. In both these concepts technology stands simultaneously as a critique of present conditions and a standard of emulation for the future, and it occupies the same two positions not only throughout the rest of this chapter, but also throughout the rest of the argument, particularly in the section *Des Yeux Qui Ne Voient Pas*.

In the first of these chapters, on Liners, it is used to establish the true style, as he saw it, of the times. It opens with a flurry of polemics against a school of designers, whose public advocate was Guillaume Janneau, who had committed the unforgivable crime of using *Tracés Régulateurs* to create old-fashioned 'stylistic' (*scil.* Classicised Art Nouveau) decoration. Since he maintained that

> Architecture has nothing to do with the various 'styles'.

he found himself forced to suggest what it did have to do with, and, like Mondriaan, Oud, and many others he has to propose, first, that and secondly that this style is to be found in a list of objects that are (almost inevitably) a conglobation of Futurist and Werkbund preferences, though slanted toward *objets-type*

> Our modern life . . . has created its own objects, its costume, its fountain pen, its eversharp pencil, its typewriter, its telephone, its admirable office-furniture, its plate glass and its 'Innovation' trunks, the safety razor and the briar pipe, the bowler hat and the limousine, the steamship and the airplane.

The reasons why these *objets-type* fix the style is clear enough, they fit in so well with his Phileban preferences, though Le Corbusier soon squelches any hope that he might admit to this by saying in the next chapter

> The lesson of the airplane is not primarily in the forms it has created

though one cannot help noticing that he selects aircraft of regular Phileban, not to say Palladian, forms, and when he comes to discuss the benefits of streamlining, does so only in so far as it applies to airships and cars.

Thus, although the main business of these three chapters is, he claims, *manières de penser*, and not with formal problems, the illustrations constantly reaffirm his aesthetic admirations, adorning rather than advancing the argument. Thus, though the chapter on automobiles is professedly concerned with the virtues of standardisation and the benefits of competition, it is not illustrated by any vehicles that could be considered standardised (except in the low-level sense of all having a wheel at each corner) or successfully competitive in either commerce or sport. The function of most of the illustrations is to maintain a kind of running visual sermon on aesthetic probity, just as he reads one on *moralité dorique* into the stones of the Parthenon. At the same time they provoke him to thoughts of the following order: about liners

> If we forget for a moment that a steamship is a machine for transport and look at it with a fresh eye, we shall feel that we are facing an important manifestation of temerity, of discipline, of harmony, of beauty that is calm, vital and strong. A seriously-minded architect, looking at it as an architect (i.e. a creator of organisms), will find in a steamship his freedom from an age-long but contemptible enslavement to the past.

about aircraft

> The problem of the house has not yet been stated.
> The airplane shows us that a problem well stated finds its solution. To wish to fly like a bird is to state the problem badly, and Ader's *Bat* never left the ground . . . to search for a means of suspension in the air, and a means of propulsion, was to put the problem properly:[6] in less than ten years the whole world could fly.

[6] It is worth noting that he does not discuss the problem of penetration in this context, nor that of controls—that is, he states the problem of aviation as Chanute or Lilienthal stated it, but whether he did so with knowledge of their work is not clear. Ironically enough the Ader *Bat* was proved to be just capable of flight before *L'Esprit Nouveau* had ceased publication, and the fact was noted in its pages, with-

> Let us display then, the Parthenon and the motor-car so that it may be clear that it is a question of two products of selection in different fields. . . . And what then? Well, it remains to use the motor-car as a challenge to our houses and our great buildings. It is here that we come to a dead stop. 'Rien ne va plus.' Here we have no Parthenons.

However, '*Des Yeux Qui Ne Voient Pas*', viewed as a whole, is chiefly notable as the main vehicle for Le Corbusier's ideas on house design. These ideas are professedly of only technical import

> The standard of the house is a question of practical and constructive order.

under the much-quoted rubric (which, however, never appears in the body of that chapter)

> La maison est une machine à habiter.
> (The house is a machine for living in.)

and they are summed up, in their purely technical aspects, in the *Manuel de l'Habitation* (which appears at the end of the chapter on Aircraft) with its famous slogans

> Demand a bathroom looking south, one of the largest rooms in the house. . .
> Demand bare walls . . . built-in fittings to take the place of much of the furniture.
> If you can, put the kitchen on top of the house to avoid smells. . . .
> Demand concealed or diffused lighting.
> Demand a vacuum-cleaner.
> Teach your children that a house is only habitable when it is full of light and air, when the floors and walls are clear.
> Take a flat that is one size smaller than what your parents accustomed you to. . . .

This document is clearly (and admittedly) addressed more to the lay public than to architects, and may be regarded as a kind of prospectus of life as it would be led in the mass-produced houses he had envisaged, for the closing words of the footnote at the end of the chapter are

> . . . construire en série des machines à habiter

and clearly refer forward to *Maisons en Série*.

But before the reader reaches this chapter, he is presented with the three that make up '*Architecture*', and has had it hammered into him that Functionalism is not enough. If he has been persuaded by what has gone before, the reader will, presumably, take it that the projects that are repro- duced in *Maisons en Série* are more than functional, are architecture. But, in fact, Le Corbusier's closing remarks on the subject suggest that they are not, as will be seen later. The bulk of the chapter is occupied by a survey of the author's own projects in the field of mass-production housing, space for a very full coverage having been created by the sup- pression of the two pages devoted to Auguste Perret that had appeared in

out any comment beyond that it contributed to the glory of France as the pioneer country of aviation! The question of penetration, or streamlining, is discussed later in *Vers une Architecture*, but without reference to airplanes!

L'Esprit Nouveau. The schemes can be characterised by the constructional methods employed: *Dom-ino* (concrete post and slab), *Monol* (mass-walling in various materials and segmental concrete vaults) and *Citrohan* (side walls and concrete joists). The culmination comes with the *Immeubles-Villas*, in which dwelling units, each consisting of a modified *Citrohan* house with a garden court alongside it, are assembled into gigantic blocks five or six houses high, and up to twelve units long, facing inwards on to garden courts and with complicated multi-level services and roads running between the backs of neighbouring pairs of blocks. Food, drink and domestic service were to be provided on an hotel basis, car-parking underground, below the gardens and sports fields.

The scale, the town-planning assumptions, the way of life envisaged for the inhabitants are Futurist, while the idea of villas assembled into well-ventilated dwelling blocks condenses two of the architectural necessities noted by Marinetti in *Le Futurisme*. But Le Corbusier differs from the Futurists in maintaining (and, in the changed post-War circumstances, he was probably right) that while the techniques, the mechanisms and the social necessities for such an architecture existed already, the people were not ready for it

> The right state of mind does not exist

and were still devoted to

> this solidly built thing which sets out to defy time and decay, and which is an expensive luxury by which wealth can be shown.

This, to him, was a decisive blockage to progress, which could not get under way until established architectural prejudices had been eradicated

> If we eliminate from our hearts and minds all dead concepts in regard to the house, and look at the question from a critical and objective point of view, we shall arrive at the House-machine (*maison outil*), the mass-production house, healthy (and morally so too) and beautiful in the same way that the working tools and instruments that accompany our existence are beautiful

But this eradication of prejudice would only facilitate the building of houses that possessed the beauty of tools,[7] and in this context this should logically mean that they would be less than architecture. But this does not seem to be what Le Corbusier intends to mean, and we find ourselves faced with an ambiguity similar to that in an earlier chapter between the laws of nature and the rules of art. This ambiguity is deepened in the closing chapter, which was written as a concluding and unifying *coda* to the disparate pieces which make up the book. Its title is '*Architecture ou Révolution*', but since it deals almost entirely with the technical reform of dwellings it ought, logically again, to have been called '*Construction ou Révolution*', and

---

[7] In later editions of *Vers une Architecture*, apparently realising that he had left a crucial hole in his argument at this point, he added the words 'Beautiful also with all the animation that the artist's sensibility can add to severe and pure functioning elements'.

far from truly uniting the main themes, architectural and mechanical, of the book it introduces an entirely new one, the social pressures resulting from the quantitative and qualitative deficiencies of housing in France. Since it is a plea for more housing it might, one supposes, be construed as a plea for architecture in the low-level sense of more work for architects, and it may have been so read in the Twenties when young architects were work-starved. But its explicit theme is the inadequacy of housing as then standing or as then conceived, for a mechanised society, with new needs, and new psychological drives, such as that *esprit de corps* that could be found in the factories, but had no counterpart in social life outside. The solution demanded is

> . . . an amelioration, of historical importance

in the construction, planning and equipment of houses, and the chapter closes, and with it the book, on a fine rhetorical note of reforming zeal.

> Disturbed by the reactions which play upon him from every quarter, the man of today is conscious, on the one hand, of a new world which is forming itself regularly, logically and clearly, which produces in a straightforward way things which are useful and usable, and on the other hand he finds himself to his surprise, living in an old and hostile environment. . . .
> There reigns a great disagreement between the modern state of mind, which is an admonition to us, and the stifling accumulation of age-long detritus.
> The problem is one of adaptation, in which the realities of our life are in question. Society is filled with a violent desire for something which it may obtain or may not. Everything lies in that; everything depends on the effort made and the attention paid to these alarming symptoms.
> Architecture or Revolution.
> Revolution can be avoided.

Taken out of context, or even kept within the context of this chapter alone, this appears to be a statement of social protest purely, but put into the context of the book as a whole, it appears to be a statement of protest against the employment of the wrong style—the disaccord that is really at stake is between two or more sets of geometrical forms, and this is suggestively underlined by the last illustration, the briar pipe. This was an object that had already been cited as an example of the natural style of the times, and brought into the hours of *repos* something of that geometrical order which Le Corbusier acclaimed as characteristic of the hours of work.

It was also a familiar and reassuring object, and therefore also underlines the tone of reassurance to architects that runs through the whole book. Viewing the work as a whole, one sees that even if it has no argument, it has at least a motto-theme, which may be summarised as follows: architecture is in disorder now, but its essential laws of Classical geometry remain. Mechanisation does not threaten these laws but reinforces them, and when architecture has recovered these Classical laws and made its peace with machinery, it will be in a position to redress the wrongs of society. In this Le Corbusier was probably well in accord with the mood of the times as it existed, even if he did not quite accord with that mood as advanced architects themselves understood it, for it should be noted that whereas the original title *Vers une Architecture*, simply says 'Towards an Architecture', and implies, from internal evidence in the book, an absolute or essential architecture, which had always existed and had merely been mislaid, the titles of the English and German translations are *'Towards a New Architecture'* and *'Kommende Baukunst'* respectively, and put an entirely different slant on the matter, though not one that is entirely unsupported by the text. In any case, it was precisely this rediscovery of the old in the new, this justification of the revolutionary by the familiar, that ensured the book its enormous readership, and an influence, inevitably superficial, beyond that of any other architectural work published in this century to date. It enabled men, regarding the author's undoubtedly revolutionary buildings, to find in them justifications for their most ingrained prejudices—it is noticeable that its influence has been greatest where the French *Beaux-Arts* tradition is strongest. Its great success, however, has not only overwhelmed better-reasoned and more genuinely revolutionary works by other authors, but has also reduced the attention given to other, and better-reasoned books by Le Corbusier himself, which are the subject of the next chapter.

18: Le Corbusier: town-planning and aesthetics

BY 1926, THE year when Le Corbusier committed to print his next impor- (A)
tant theoretical statements, he had become something of an established
figure in the world of Paris architecture. The middle-of-the-road magazine *La Construction Moderne* included him in a list of celebrities whose
views on the housing crisis they canvassed; he had some half dozen
schemes completed or in construction, and even his personal appearance
was a subject of comment, for he endeavoured to present himself as an
homme-type of the age, in the dark clothes, bowler hat, pipe and bow tie of
an engineer. But what had established him, more than anything else, was
the *Pavillon de l'Esprit Nouveau*, erected with the powerful and necessary
backing of Charles de Monzie, Minister of Fine Arts, at the *Exposition des
Arts Décoratifs*.

Though the exhibits designed by Kiesler and Melnikov were, in some
ways, more advanced aesthetically and structurally, this pavilion had the
advantage of completeness, it envisaged a whole way of domestic life down
to its minor details. The structure was, effectively and allowing for an
existing tree on the site, a full-scale mock-up of one unit of the *Immeuble-
Villas*, complete with its adjoined terrace, furnished with *objets-type* and
Purist works of art. It created an entirely homogeneous visual setting, a
creation of a single mind, so that one is tempted to compare it to those
interiors completely designed by such masters of the previous generation
as van de Velde or Mackintosh, but there is an extremely important difference. Only the structure is a work of design by the mind that created
the environment, the rest was claimed to be a work of selection almost
in the Duchamp manner from standard products, *objets-type*, already on
the market, and the homogeneity of the whole came largely from the
adaptation of the structure to an aesthetic derived from certain classes of
objets-type, and the rejection of any standard products that did not answer
this aesthetic. Although certain distortions of intention appear in this
process, and some objects had to be diverted from their original functions,
e.g. laboratory vessels as flower-vases, the resulting interior owed much of
its impact to the directness with which mass-produced equipment, such

as Thonet and Maple chairs, could fulfil aesthetic functions that were supposed, even in progressive circles, to require the services of cabinet makers. Even the paintings on the walls were of the type then supposed to be capable of mass-reproduction in the sense intended by Albert Gleizes, and annexed to this *appartement-type* was a species of rotunda housing large-scale dioramas of Le Corbusier's two town-planning schemes of the period. Thus, the pavilion, taken as a whole, gave visual form to all the main themes of the articles on design that had appeared in *L'Esprit Nouveau* (which ceased publication at the time of the exhibition) and were at different times reprinted in book form: painting: *La Peinture Moderne*; architecture: *Vers une Architecture*; product design: *L'Art Décoratif d'Aujourd'hui*, a polemical work of only local interest, and town-planning, *Urbanisme*, which is among his best worked-out books of the period, but not among the most influential.

It opens with an *Avertissement* full of aphorisms and slogans whose import is familiar from *Vers une Architecture*

> A town is a tool.
> Towns no longer fulfil this function. They are ineffectual, they use up our bodies, they thwart our souls.

or again

> A city!
> It is the grip of man on nature.

and yet again

> Geometry is the means, created by ourselves, whereby we perceive the external world and express the world within us.

but if these given grounds are familiar, the procedure of the argument is not. The first chapter opens by picking upon what seems at first to be only a detailcon sideration in town planning, straight roads versus curved. But this is the fundamental consideration for Le Corbusier. In attacking Camillo Sitte he is attacking what he considers to be a philosophy of disorder and mere aesthetics; serpentine roads he dubs *Le Chemin des Ânes*, straight roads *Le Chemin des Hommes*, apparently because he is under the impression that to travel in straight lines is to reveal the ability to reason and a sense of purpose peculiar to *homo sapiens*

> L'homme marche droît parcequ'il a un but

a statement which is equally true, given a reasonably flat surface, of donkeys that have an end in view. All he is doing, in fact, is restating his familiar aesthetic prejudices in a new rhetorical form, but this particular preference gives a basic inclination to the whole argument of the book—before all else, the *Ville-outil*, the *ville-type*, will be rectilinear. Even before the beginning of this chapter, at the end of the *Avertissement*, he had reproduced one of those nemonic charts of regular geometrical forms that used to appear in the back cover of arithmetic exercise books (and not only in France) and the *Débat Général* of the seven opening chapters rarely strays outside the terms of reference laid down by this chart. Right angles and the Phileban solids are praised, and a curious diagram underlines the value he attaches to these forms. It balances, on one side 'classicisme', epitomised by triangle, square, sphere, etc. against 'barbarisme', characterised by verticals, zigzags and, it should be noted, a sculpture by Rob van t'Hoff and a diagram of a Gothic *chevet*, with a caption that says, *inter alia*

> One is a symbol of perfection, the other of effort only. All the same, one is of a more elevated order than the other, for one is complete and the other is only an attempt.

A matching diagram, over the page, shows a rising line of Culture crossing a descending line of Barbarism at 1453 (*Prise de Constantinople*) with the façade of *Notre Dame* on one side of the intersection, and the Perrault front of the Louvre on the other—an overwhelmingly clear statement of his Classicist preferences, that introduces a *Définition du Sentiment Moderne*. This begins with what is effectively a second caption to the diagram described above

> Our modern culture, acquired by the West, has its roots set deep in the invasions which extinguished antique culture. After the check of AD 1000 it began to build itself again slowly through another ten centuries. With a primitive but admirably ingenious equipment invented in the Middle Ages it inscribed certain points of great splendour in the eighteenth century. . . . Where the eighteenth century defined the fundamental principles of reason, the nineteenth century, by a magnificent effort, gave itself up to analysis and experiment, and created an equipment which was entirely new, formidable, revolutionary and destined to revolutionise society. . . .

So far (as so often with Le Corbusier) compressed Choisy, and he makes no attempt to prove that his *Sentiment Moderne* arises from all this in any consequential manner, but merely asserts that it can now be felt.

> We are the heirs of that effort, we are aware of our modern feeling and we know that an era of creation is about to commence. . . .
> This modern sentiment is a spirit of geometry, a spirit of construction and synthesis. Exactitude and order are its essential condition. . . . This is the passion of the age. With what astonishment do we regard the disordered and spasmodic impulses of Romanticism! A period when the soul was thrown back on itself in such an effort of analysis that it was as though a volcano were in eruption. No longer do we get these eruptions of overcharged personality. The amplitude of our means impels us toward the general, and to an appreciation of the simple fact. In place of individualism and its fevered products, we prefer the commonplace, the everyday, the rule to the exception. The everyday, the rule, the common rule seem to us now the strategic base for the journey towards progress and the beautiful. A general beauty draws us in, and the heroically beautiful seems merely theatrical. We prefer Bach to Wagner. . . .

This breaks no new ground, but it sets out his justifications of the typical, of the generalised *situation-type* in a more concise form than can be found elsewhere, and it is worth noting that while he sets up Bach, the Pantheon, Babylonian and Roman planning and *le Roi Soleil*, as objects of admiration and insists that

> We love the *solution*, and we are uneasy at the sight of failures, however grandiose or dramatic

he nevertheless follows this with an almost Futurist appreciation of the grandiose drama of the emergent tendencies, still lacking solution, of the times

> Throughout the world we see the array of mighty powers, both in the industrial and the social spheres; we see, emerging from chaos, ordered and logical aspirations, and we feel that they are in harmony with the means of realisation at our disposal. New forms come to birth; the world adopts a new attitude. The old prejudices crumble and crack and totter. . . . An indescribable quiver is passing through everything; it is putting the old machine out of gear; it is the motive force and aim of the age.

The Futurist tone of this passage is the more remarkable in that the very next chapter is a flat refutation of the Futurist theory of *caducità*, of the idea that works of art should be perishable. Le Corbusier distinguishes, along familiar lines, works of art from works of technology, and insists that only the latter are perishable, in a most remarkable chapter, under the heading of *Perennité*. He opens by rephrasing his earlier praise of engineers in such a way that they are demoted from the status of noble savages to that of a species of perfected, but sub-human Rationalists

> The industrial achievements of our own age which impress us so profoundly today are created by placid and modest men, whose thoughts are limited and direct, engineers who do their additions on squared paper . . . yet these men can bring those of us who have something of the poet in us to the very extreme of enthusiasm and emotion.

Against the products of reason, which he declares to be expendable and fallible, he sets the products of passion, which he claims are as permanent as human nature is permanent

> . . . reason is an open account stretching to infinity in which each successive stage is registered. . . . Human passion, since man was man, has been constant . . . the gauge by which we can measure the permanence of human creations.
> The activity of the mind continues unendingly, in an ascending curve; it creates its implements; and this we call progress. The components of passion remain constant, coming between two limits which the ages have not altered.

On this basis, he can do two things: (*a*) he can advance a criticism of the beauty of machinery that reverses the Futurist position, and (*b*) he can call in question the aesthetic status of some of the most admired works of civil engineering. On the first count, he opposes the Futurist position that machines are beautiful in so far as they are not the products of 'art' by proposing that the intervention of 'passion' is vital

> Let us attempt to formulate the standards of mechanical beauty. If one could admit that mechanical beauty was a matter of *pure reason*, the question would be settled out of hand: mechanical creation could have no permanent aesthetic value. Each piece of mechanism would be more beautiful than what had preceded it and would inevitably be surpassed by its successors. And so we should

get an ephemeral beauty, soon out of date and despised. But in practice things do not happen so; man's sensibilities intervene even in the midst of the most rigorous calculation . . . intervention of an individual taste, sensibility and passion.

yet in spite of this he inconsistently maintains that the nature of machinery remains perishable even in conception

The foaming locomotive, the rearing steed that evoked the hasty lyricism of Huysmans, is rusting iron on the scrap-heap. The cars of the next *Salon* require that Citroen write off the model that has been all the rage. But the Roman aqueduct endures. . . .

This brings him to his second count.

The Roman aqueduct endures, the Coliseum is piously conserved, the Pont du Gard lives on. But will the emotion produced in us by Eiffel's Pont de Garabit endure?

The work of Eiffel has often been taken as a touchstone of Modernity, and it is maintained that only true 'Moderns' can admire it. Le Corbusier's attitude to the Eiffel Tower is as hesitant as to the Pont de Garabit, and in a caption to a photograph of the Tower (albeit titled *Hommage à Eiffel*) he postpones judgement on it to the Greek Kalends, more or less

. . . when the city is built on the same grand scale, then we shall be in a position to go into the question of the permanence of the Eiffel Tower.

But in captioning the Pont du Gard he relapses without hesitation into the rhetoric of the *École*

Le Pont du Gard. Romain. Classé au Panthéon de la gloire.

The hesitant attitude toward the work of so great an engineer, whose reputation has proven highly durable, may be due, among other things, to a distrust of the non-Phileban forms of Eiffel's work—a distrust that was fairly general among Parisian aestheticians when confronted with splay-legged lattice structures of any kind, as in this comment, by a caption-writer (who elsewhere revealed himself a mechanical ignoramus) in *Cahiers d'Art*, on a German coaling gantry.

The work of the engineer, pure in its origins, begins gradually to be adulterated by aesthetic pursuits. The crane which is seen on this page is soaked in romantic Expressionism. It would be a great pity if engineers refused to recognise that their work is not meant to communicate emotions, but with a view to rigorously defined utilisation. Emotion comes by super-addition when the work exactly fulfils the function for which it is destined[1]

While it is doubtful if Le Corbusier would subscribe to the old-fashioned type of Functionalism revealed in the last sentence of this quotation, any more than he would pass so ill-informed a judgement on what appears to be an exemplary piece of engineering design, it is interesting to record

[1] Unsigned caption in *Cahiers d'Art* (Paris, 1926, No. 5, p. 114). This writer's qualifications to pass judgement on works of engineering may be gauged by his further statement, lower down the same page, that turbine ships need no funnels.

that he did share the caption-writer's suspicion of engineers who had aesthetic ideas 'above their stations'.

> When a man's passion for creation has taken form, his work will endure through the ages.
> But this is a dangerous judgement, for shall we see engineers trying to turn themselves into men of aesthetic sensibility? That would be a real danger. . . . An engineer should stay fixed, and remain a calculator, for his particular justification is to remain within the confines of pure reason.

Works of engineering are not to be ranked with works of art, lacking the sanction of time, nor engineers with artists, lacking the sanction of passion —and since the city was intended to last, it too must be a work of passion

> But it is the city's business to make itself permanent, and this depends on considerations other than those of calculation. And it is only Architecture which can give all the things that go *beyond* calculation.

Between this taking up of position on the grounds of geometry and perenniality, and the actual excursions into town planning that make up the second half of *Urbanisme*, there are interposed a series of disorderly chapters (disorderly in sequence rather than argument) from which, however, the following important points can be extracted. Firstly, the concept of standardisation is rephrased in such a way that it does not restrict the 'passion' of the town planner, by taking over (with acknowledgements) an idea from the Abbé Laugier

> 1. Chaos, disorder and a wild variety in the general layout (that is, a composition rich in contrapuntal elements like a fugue or a symphony).
> 2. Uniformity in detail (that is, reticence, decency, 'alignment' of details).

which is exemplified later by reference to *les villes dites 'd'art'*

> The basis of all this is the existence of a standard. So in Rome, in Venice; all dwelling-houses are stuccoed; in Siena they are of brick; the windows are to one scale, the roofs to the same pitch and covered with the same tiles; the colour is uniform.

Secondly:

> Il faut planter des arbres!

an idea which also seems to derive from his experience of cities of art (he mentions Turkey in particular) as well as a day-to-day familiarity with Haussmann's town planning. Thirdly; two chapters and a supplement of newspaper cuttings *reproduit tel*, are devoted to an exposition of the increasingly critical condition of vehicular circulation in the great cities of the world. This exposition still carries weight, not only because the crisis is now general to all cities, but also because his means of presentation, ranging from statistical curves to comic drawings, give both quantitative and personal force to his argument. Fourthly; the means to do something to ameliorate this condition, and other ills of great cities. Here, following Futurist precept again, he corrects the proposition of Choisy, only twenty-five years earlier, that the present state of *outillage* in building was substantially that of the Gothic or even prehistoric periods. He contrasts the navvying equipment used as recently as in Haussmann's public works in Paris, with the fully mechanised system of mixers, conveyors and telpherage employed in pouring the concrete of the Barrage de Barberine, in the Alps, but he also underlines the inadequate use made of current techniques by a further contrast, between the 3000 hand-made kilometres of the Wall of China and the 140 machine-cut kilometres of the Paris Métro, on which work was still proceeding in the Twenties.

This, appropriately, concludes the *Débat Général*, and brings him to the second part of the book, in which the various ideas he has brought forward are applied to actual town-planning schemes. The manner in which he approaches the problem is entirely characteristic. In direct contrast to Sant' Elia, whose town-planning ideas grew out of a specific topographical location, Milan Central Station, or to Tony Garnier, whose *Cité Industrielle* stood on a site which, though ideal for his purposes, had the characteristics and limitations of natural topography, Le Corbusier starts on a blank sheet of paper, and rejects even imaginary accidents of site.

> Proceeding in the manner of an investigator in his laboratory, I have avoided all special cases, and all that may be accidental, and I have assumed an ideal site to begin with.

Although this seems to imply a curious view of scientific method, the approach is not an unexpected one. He elaborates first a *solution-type*, in the abstract, its real life application can wait. This particular *système préconise* was first developed in 1921–2, and shown at the *Salon d'Automne* of the latter year, under the title *Une Ville Contemporaine pour 3 Millions d'Habitants*. It will be noted that he called it a *contemporary* city, and was offended when it was termed a city of the future, insisting that it could be, and ought to be, built at once.

Upon the unrestricted plane of his ideal site, the planning makes a pattern of unmistakable *Beaux-Arts* extraction, with major and minor axes, star intersections of orthogonal and diagonal roads, and the rest of the apparatus. As in Garnier's *Cité*, industry is dismissed to the outskirts

> In a decent house the servants' stairs do not go through the drawing-room— even if the maid is charming (or if the little boats delight the loiterer leaning on the bridge).

but in contradistinction to Garnier, the circulation-planning, however diagrammatic, is generous and appears free from bottle-necks. At points of maximum traffic-pressure, the means of achieving adequate circulation surface are Sant' Elian (if they do not go back beyond him to Tony Moilin) and at the centre of the city, there are no fewer than seven superimposed levels. Of these, the uppermost is an aircraft landing-deck, thus repeating a suicidal device from Sant'Elia, of asking aircraft to land between ranks of tall buildings, and the Sant'Elian source of this particular device seems underlined by the fact that the main central station is under-

253

neath. The contrast between the *Beaux-Arts* pattern of the plan as a whole and the Futurist quality of the section is very striking, and is heightened by the Futurist tone in which Le Corbusier discusses the sky-scraper office-blocks that cluster so dangerously close around the landing deck

> And actually these skyscrapers will contain the city's brains, the brains of the whole nation. They stand for all the careful working-out and organisation on which the general activity is based. Everything is concentrated in them: apparatus for abolishing time and space, telephones, cables and wireless; the banks, business affairs and the control of industry; finance, commerce, specialisation. The station is in the midst of the skyscrapers, the tubes run below them and the tracks for fast traffic are at their base.

The skyscrapers themselves are unique in his work, and unlike any of the subsequent designs for tall slabs and towers that have come from his hand. To judge from the observations he passed on them when they first appeared in *Vers une Architecture*, they were originally worked up from ideas of Auguste Perret's, but the master's own version, when it finally appeared, had Classical detailing, and bridges spanning from tower to tower several stories up—and was rejected by Le Corbusier as *Futurisme bien dangereux*! The form which he himself gives to these towers is a cross in plan, with each arm massively pleated, so that many rooms have three exterior walls, and these walls are entirely glazed. He dates the first sketches for this project as early as 1920, so that they are contemporary, within a few months, to Mies van der Rohe's earliest Friedrichstrasse project, which also has walls of glass, prismatically folded. No necessary connection between the two projects need be postulated, beyond a common source in German ideas of the pre-War period, particularly since Le Corbusier had gone out of his way to denounce, in 1921, the strong vertical emphasis that such a façade would give, as an error peculiar to German architecture.

> One simple fact condemns the lot; in a building one lives floor by floor (*on vit par étage*) horizontally not vertically. The German palaces are just lift cages. . . . The *Louvre* and *Bon Marché* shops are in horizontals and they are right and the German architects are wrong.[2]

The other main class of accommodation envisaged for the *Ville Contemporaine*, seems to consist entirely of middle-class housing, of the *Immeubles-villas* type, grouped either in hollow squares as they had appeared in *Vers une Architecture*, or *à redents*, that is, in setbacks that advance and retreat symmetrically on either side of the street, a device that does much to account for the elegant abstract pattern of the overall plan.

Whatever reservations one may entertain about the use of *Beaux-Arts* formulae and other aesthetic predeterminations, *Une Ville Contemporaine*

---

[2] In *L'Esprit Nouveau* (1921, No. 9); the buildings he had in mind were, for instance, Messel's Wertheim store and similar neo-Gothic structures, and, on another count, the neo-Classical work of Behrens, which he had come to hate as German militaristic propaganda, particularly the Embassy in Petrograd.

remains a remarkable achievement and a measure of Le Corbusier's powers. Since it was exhibited in a definitive form as early as 1922, it was only four years later than the definitive publication of Garnier's *Cité*, which did not appear until 1918, but in spirit a whole generation has grown up between the two, and it has clear advantages of boldness and adequacy over Garnier's project. Over Sant' Elia's design it has an equally clear advantage of completeness—it is a whole city, not a series of tactical exercises in solving isolated problems, and over contemporary German projects, such as the Rococo elaborations of Camillo Sitte worked out by Bruno Taut under the influence of Finsterlin, it has clear advantages of order, comprehensibility and feasibility.

In the *Pavillon de l'Esprit Nouveau*, Le Corbusier exhibited this scheme in one diorama, and, facing it, another diorama in which he attempted to apply the *système préconise* to an actual city, as the *Plan Voisin de Paris*. At once its weaknesses begin to appear—the destination of the two great motor roads that form the *axe primaire* and the *axe secondaire* of the plan is never resolved and they disappear off the map, north, south, east and west. Symmetry, as such, has to be compromised—the towers stand mostly along the *axe secondaire*, northwards from Chatelet, the *Immeubles-villas* mostly along the *axe primaire*, well to the west, north of the Tuileries and the Champs Élysées, and separated from the business towers by the central station, which has no buildings of any importance on top of it.

It was immediately noted, when the Plan Voisin was exhibited in 1925, that it would involve the demolition of most of historical Paris north of the Seine, since it occupies a sector extending from the Place de la Republique to points west of the Gare St Lazare, and extending as far north as the Gare de l'Est. Within this pair of overlapping rectangles a few recognised monuments were to be preserved, not always on their original sites, though the Place Vendôme, which Le Corbusier greatly admired, was to be left intact and in place. He was clearly conscious of the shocking effect that such a project was likely to have, even in progressive circles, and he set out to block two lines of protest in advance, one, by pointing out that the small site-area and large capacity of high-rise developments would make it possible to accommodate many without dispossessing more than a few by demolitions, and another by some ingenious guess-work about the finance involved. However, these financial proposals involved the welcoming of foreign, even German, capital investment in the centre of Paris, and he only succeeded in further offending the kind of patriotic Traditionalists whom the whole project was most likely to alarm.[3]

Yet he himself clearly felt that he stood firmly in a tradition that had

[3] Gauthier's biography of Le Corbusier gives a good account of the polemical campaigns launched against him by the factions of Mauclair, Umbdenstock and others.

native roots in Paris, both intellectually and historically. The concluding words of the text of *Urbanisme* are against revolution for its own sake

> Things are not revolutionised by making revolutions. The real revolution lies in the solution of existing problems.

and they are faced by a final illustration: an engraving of Louis XIV commanding the construction of the Invalides, with the caption

> Homage to a great town-planner—This despot conceived great projects and realised them. Over all the country his noble works still fill us with admiration. He was capable of saying, 'We wish it', or 'Such is our pleasure'.

to which he adds parenthetically, as if he feared to alarm progressive sentiment

> (ceci n'est pas une déclaration de 'Action Française'.)

The reader, reflecting on these two first books of Le Corbusier, cannot fail to note how little they contain in the way of positive statements about the detail aesthetics of architecture, about the way that a building should look. The *Maison Citrohan*, its derivatives and multiples, are justified only in terms of function and construction, in spite of all that was said about Functionalism being less than architecture; the towers of the *Ville Contemporaine* were little more than diagrams, with whose aesthetics he was professedly out of sympathy. It seems likely that it was not until about the year 1925 that he had any settled aesthetic opinions on the subject, for his work of the early Twenties is variable and manifestly tentative. The Villa at Vaucresson, commissioned by a client who had been impressed by the *Citrohan* project, shows him in two minds about symmetry, and has one asymmetrical façade and one conventional one, though without any really axial qualities in the internal planning; the Ozenfant House had a saw-toothed roof, such as he was never to repeat again; the LaRoche-Jeanneret houses had a sprawling, picturesque plan, such as he also never repeated, and was, in fact, a symmetrical project with one limb amputated. All these works contain good, or even brilliant, parts, but none has the ease or assurance of the house at Chaux-de-Fonds. That quality begins to be recovered in his works of 1925–6 and may be exemplified by the dormitory wing of the Palais du Peuple, near the Gobelins manufactory, and the Maison Cook, in Boulogne-sur-Seine.

The first initiates a series of hostel-type structures that he put up in the Twenties and Thirties, a plain rectangular block of four identical dormitory floors, served by a connecting stair at one end, the whole raised on pilotis above a diminutive garden little larger in area than the plan of the block itself. The roof is flat and without visible excrescences, though it was originally intended to sport a pergola at the garden end, commanding a view over the Parc des Gobelins. Since the staircase is partly buried in the adjoining *Palais* (*sic*: a converted warehouse) all that one sees is the pure elevated rectangle of the dormitory, with extremely elegant fenestration, repeated identically from floor to floor, drawn on the unmodulated 'blanc de chaux' of the flat façades.

The Maison Cook is a more complex affair, though justifiably described by the architect himself as 'La vraie maison cubique'.[4] Both in plan and on its main elevation, it consists of compositions within an almost exact square. Although the main elevation has an open terrace to one side of the highest floor, a concrete 'sun-shade' is carried across in front of this to maintain the rectangular format, and although the main salon, also at this level, is of double height, this fact is not demonstrated on the street side, which emphasises, rather, that 'on vit par étage'. The block is on pilotis again, leaving an almost unobstructed ground floor from party-wall to party-wall, and on the two main floors there are fenêtres en longueur, also spanning from wall to wall, the central structural column being set back behind them to give an uninterrupted run of glass. On plan, this mode of composing within a predetermined rectangular format is even more striking because of the use of curved forms, a usage that also appears in the Guiette house at Antwerp (designed in the same year) and the large and complicated villa at Garches for Charles de Monzie, which must have been put in hand soon after this, and appears to draw heavily on the Maison Cook as a prototype. Not only is the mode of composing with rectangular and curved elements within a rectangular field of predetermined dimensions very similar to the mode of composing his paintings, but many of the curved shapes, whatever their functional justification, appear to derive from the forms of the objets-type in the pictures as well.

This group of buildings and projects designed by him around this time has a very strongly characterised style of plain square silhouettes, white rendered walls with the absolute minimum of relief (balanced by a tendency to punch large holes right through them into the interior), compact rectangular plans featuring the use of curved walls and free-standing columns, long horizontal strips of window, flat roofs, and pilotis (or a clearly differentiated basement floor) to lift the main block clear of the ground. In his well-known writings, the justifications of these various usages appear only after the event—sometimes long after it—but there is a document of the exact period, that has largely escaped attention, yet provides a fairly extended explanation of his intentions in the employment of this particular style.

Since it appeared in a learned publication—a special issue of the Journal de Psychologie Normale et Pathologique devoted to the arts and aesthetics—it is free both of the rhetorical tone of persuasion used in L'Esprit Nouveau, and also of the polemical pressures of monthly journalism. The consequence is an essay (partly worked up from a lecture given earlier at the Sorbonne) that differs in method from his other writing of the period

---

[4] It is not quite a strict cube, since the width is a little less than the other two main dimensions.

and differs also in the frankness with which it is prepared to discuss purely aesthetic considerations. It opens with a display of juggling with dictionary definitions of art, architecture, and so forth, from which he emerges with two definitions-by-differentiation of the art of architecture. Firstly by differentiation of two bodies of architects, whose aims are

> For the first, to introduce into architecture the concept of ornament, and the presence of fixed rules, settled methods, settled procedures. For the second, the rules are *to be* fixed, the methods *to be* settled, the procedures *to be* discovered.

and secondly by differentiating two extremes of procedure

> There are, in the flux of ideas that comprise these definitions, the two poles of architecture, which are: to construct buildings (realm of technique); and to embellish them and make them glorious, delightful, etc. (realm of sentiment).

The first distinction is clearly meant to separate the academics from the progressives, the second to continue the distinction between technology and aesthetics. However, having repeated his determination to separate them, he also insists on the necessity of their simultaneous presence

> Technicité et sentiment, synchronisme insécable

but throughout this argument, he frequently insists on the primacy of techniques.

> I have said that the technical consideration comes first before everything and is its condition, that it carries within it unavoidable plastic consequences, and that it leads sometimes to radical aesthetic transformations

This is clearly Choisyesque and echoes of Choisy are fairly frequent in the early pages, notably a definition of the nature of walling in reinforced concrete construction that repeats both the meaning and to some extent the actual words of Choisy's definition of the nature of walling in Gothic.

> What was once a load-bearing organ, has become a simple infilling

But, as elsewhere, Choisy's limitations are transcended by Le Corbusier's Futurist sense of the recent mechanical revolution, which he now recognises to have disturbed sentiment as well as technology

> It makes him travel twenty, fifty times as fast as before, makes him produce a hundred times as much as before, offers him sights and interests a thousand times as varied as before. At that rate we can safely say that the age is new, and the individual out of orbit.
> That which constituted the very basis of mind, the exact site of permanent things that gave an eternal-seeming basis to the endeavours of the mind and man's way of life—that site is upset, no longer precise nor immediate.

From this he deduces, in particular, the need to evolve new plans to suit new needs

> Now, the *art of constructing buildings* is different, different methods on different plans. We must start again from Zero.

an apparent echo of Sant'Elia (*si ricomincia da capo*) that is partly sustained in the ensuing observation

... for nothing more exists of the ancient values: a wall no longer needs to carry weight, a house has every interest in being off the ground (on pilotis) and not directly on the earth; a house no longer needs a pitched roof, can be made in a factory.

Here, it will be observed, he is, almost for the first time, discussing the shape and construction of a house, frame-built, flat-roofed, on pilotis. But against these new possibilities he sets the permanence of human reactions

Past, present, future, it is plainly the reactions of the same man to the same agents of stimulation ... and our sensations are types, related to forms, lines and colours.

Here again we seem to have an echo of Charles Blanc's belief that various forms have a regular relation with human responses, but in the case of Le Corbusier this idea had probably been reinforced by the 'research' of Charles Henry, the academic aesthetician whose findings had been published extensively in *L'Esprit Nouveau*. In any case, we are faced once again, as so often in his early writings, with an ambiguity—in this case amounting to a contradiction, between two lines of thought, between two concepts of order, between the supposedly progressive and changeable nature of technology and the supposedly eternal and immutable nature of aesthetics. But this time he recognises the dichotomy, and also recognises that something must be done about it.

Insofar as the house has repudiated *en bloc* the traditional baggage of forms, lines and colours, we too find ourselves here forced to start again from zero, and to make a fresh choice in conformity with that sense of harmony that, at all times, balances the equation of reason and passion.

That is to say, a technological revolution has devalued the old repertoire of architectural forms, so we must now select a new set of forms, still answerable to the existing rules of aesthetics. Nothing could be farther from the Functionalist-determinist attitude with which Le Corbusier has been so often credited—what is revealed here, and confirmed by his other writings *passim*, is an attitude in which aesthetics, not function, are both determined and determining.

At this point, his argument reaches a dead stop, his first main point has been made, and he takes off again on an entirely different and unexpected tack. He now sets out in tabular form five *Éléments Objectifs de Discussion sur le Phénomène Architecturale*

1. Architecture: to construct a shelter
2. Shelter: to put a covering over walls
3. Covering: to span an opening and leave clear space
4. Light the shelter: to make windows
5. Window: to span an opening

and, as is immediately obvious, this list puts very close limits on the way in which architecture can be discussed. It never allows architecture out of the realm of *technicité*; it postulates the existence of walls, roofs and windows; and it defines windows in a tendentious manner, in order to be certain of arriving at the form of window to which the author was already committed—*la fenêtre en longueur*. Elements (3) and (5) define a covering and a window in identical terms, as the spanning of an opening, and not only does this imply that these two spans ought to be the same, i.e. effected by the same structural member, but that changes in the manner of spanning openings should bring with them changes in the form of windows. Before the existence of reinforced concrete, windows

> . . . could not usefully be widened, because that would have necessitated flat vaults that were too long and difficult to build; or arches that would have pushed the ceilings too high. But now a house can be built of reinforced concrete uprights . . . leaving total voids between them. . . . What good is it, I ask, to fill this space up again, when it has been given me empty? What use is a window, if not to light the walls? It was thus that I came to admit that a *fenêtre en longueur*, equal in size to a window *en hauteur* is superior to it, since it permits the illumination of the flanking walls.

There follows, after this, the discussion of walls as *remplissage* in a concrete frame, which is, in fact, a justification of his usages in fenestration, since there the distinction between frame and fill can be seen, whereas his solid walling tends to use an overall rendering to obliterate this distinction. Next comes a justification of flat roofs on functional grounds, supported by a lengthy piece of autobiography about the disastrous behaviour of the pitched roof on his early cinema at Chaux-de-Fonds, where the snow melted from internal heating on the high parts of the roof, and the water ran down until it encountered the unthawed snow at the eaves plate, whereupon it ran back down the inside of the walls. This he claims, is avoided on a flat roof laid to fall toward the warmed centre, as in the villa at Chaux, and

> If this is the only solution to extreme cases, we can be sure it is the *solution-type* for all cases.

—a most remarkable declaration from one who had earlier refused to argue from *le cas d'espèce*.

In any case, the main argument in favour of flat roofs is aesthetic, and is developed in the latter part of the essay, which is largely a transcript of his lecture at the Sorbonne.

> What I wish to show, is that there is an established hierarchy of different states of minds, and that certain of them are, perhaps, superior to others. This, at all events, I allow myself to affirm since it is for me a certainty: mind manifests itself through geometry. From this I deduce that when geometry is all-powerful, mind has made progress over preceding periods of barbarism . . . arrived at a period of intellectual clarity such as the Renaissance, it arrives also at the all-powerful horizontal, the horizontal that closes the composition at its crown.

or, put more bluntly, a parapet concealed the pitched roof behind.

> Now, we dispose today of the means to pursue this magnificent ascent towards geometry, thanks to the invention of reinforced concrete, which offers us the most pure mechanism for orthogonal composition.

and the employment of such pure mechanisms carries within it, he asserts, perfection.

But the perfections of geometry can be carried further: *tracés régulateurs* can be used to give eternally valid aesthetic order to the technically valid openings in the wall that are dictated by *le plan nouveau*, and it is worth noting that this particular argument is argued back from a predetermined rectangular block to the final disposition of the functional openings

> . . . first the general cube of the building affects you fundamentally and definitively . . . you pierce a window, open a doorway; immediately, relationships arise between the spaces so defined. . . . It remains only to polish your labours by introducing the most perfect unity, ruling the work and regulating the various elements; *tracés régulateurs* take over.

The accompanying sketches confirm the method, which could equally have been deduced from the buildings of the period: a given, unmodulated cube is pierced by openings that are then pulled into their final positions by a simple system of diagonals. Since the essay was published Le Corbusier has shown drawings of the actual *tracés* used on a number of the buildings of the late Twenties, all depending on the creation of an harmonious pattern within the limits of a given rectangular façade. The simplicity of the method, usually deriving from a single diagonal and lines parallel or normal to it, was apparently programmatic, for at this point in the argument Le Corbusier turns aside to upbraid Berlage (not named but clearly implied)[5] for his close-spaced grids of *Quadratur en Triangulatur*, of which he says

> That is no longer a *tracé régulateur*, but the weave of a canvas.

Simplicity is also the justification advanced for another usage, which had at that time some significance as a slogan against the *École des Beaux-Arts*, the suppression of cornices, but simplicity is not to be pursued as an end in itself

> It would be desolating to find ourselves capsized into a fashion for simplicity. . . . If it is simplicity derived from great complexity and richness, all is well; but if it is only poverty that is expressed . . . nothing is gained, no progress made.

and simplicity of this complex and rich order can only arise from mental discipline and, particularly, the discipline of mathematics.

> . . . but that simplicity demands, on the contrary, great constructional exactitude, absolute precision of intention and reasoning; above all it demands the contributions of proportion, of mathematical relationships; it aims to provoke that enjoyment of mathematical order that is one of the most lawful aspirations of the modern frame of mind.

Licite, the lawful aspirations of the modern mind—this is an extraordinary note on which to end a paper by one so widely regarded as a transgressor of laws, as the arch-revolutionary of twentieth-century architecture. But

[5] He describes 'un confrère d' Amsterdam, homme de haute valeur, ayant derrière lui une carrière glorieuse de précurseur', and clinches the identification by some thumb-nail versions of diagrams from the *Grundlagen*.

the fact remains that the real revolution lay in his completed buildings, and the main interest of this paper lies in the way in which it does, fairly and completely, describe most of the outstanding characteristics of those buildings. On the technical side, they were to be frame-built, walled in light materials, largely glazed, flat-roofed, raised on stilts; on the aesthetic side they were to be simple and cubic, topped by a horizontal line and without a cornice, with the openings in the walls distributed according to simple geometrical recipes. Only two indirect connections between these two sets of postulates can be observed, however: the identical definition of window and covering, which requires, in frame construction, a particular kind of window opening, and thus, to some extent, a particular kind of façade composition; and the primacy accorded to the plan, which cannot, one would think, be divorced entirely from either the structural frame or the fenestration and thus ought to provide a link between technique and aesthetics. And yet Le Corbusier's two great country houses of the end of the Twenties, at Garches and at Poissy, both make nonsense of this supposition by employing what he later termed '*le plan libre*'. At Garches, wall to wall fenestration runs across the whole of the front and two thirds of the rear façade, without any apparent respect for the daylighting needs of the rooms behind, while at the Villa Savoye at Poissy a standard band of fenestration runs right round the main floor of the house, and the only regard it pays to what is behind it is to remain unglazed where it gives on to open courtyard and not on to closed room-space. In both houses the frame is an absolute three-dimensional grid which exists independently of the planning of the various floors—not only do stray columns pass through some rooms in seemingly awkward places, but in some instances walls that could comfortably have filled-in the spaces from column to column, have apparently been deliberately joggled out of line to leave the structure in clear distinction from the partitioning.

But this device appears to reveal a fundamental streak in his psychological make-up. The difference between frame and wall must be made manifest at all costs, even at the cost of common-sense logic, just as in his writings it is clearly more important for him to make his ideas manifest than it is to make them logical. But in this, there is no doubt that he succeeded, more than any other architectural theorist of the time. His illogicalities have always been common knowledge, but his ideas have been accepted in spite of that—or more likely, because of that. He has put into circulation a body of formal devices and emotional attitudes that are so intricately entangled in his own mind, and have become so much a part of the common currency of the Modern Movement, that it is rarely observed how little necessary connection they have with one another. But it is worth noting here that the most persuasive of his writings, and the most persuasive of his formal usages, come from epochs almost a decade apart. The formal usages were given currency mostly by buildings completed between 1930 and 1933 and the ideas came almost exclusively from *Vers une Architecture*, of 1923. The same decade encompassed, near enough, the rise and fall of the International Style in Germany, a development in which the synchronisation of theory and practice was never seriously in doubt, and therefore presents a very different picture to the historian.

Section five

BERLIN, THE BAUHAUS, THE VICTORY OF THE NEW STYLE

Scheerbart, P: *Glasarchitektur,* Berlin, 1914.
Taut, B: *Die Stadtkrone,* Jena, 1919.
   Ein Wohnhaus, Stuttgart, 1927.
   Modern Architecture, London, 1929.
   (German Version; *Die Neue Baukunst,* Berlin, 1929.)
(no author given): *The Tribune Tower Competition,* Chicago, 1923.
Wingler, Hans M: *Das Bauhaus, 1919–1933,* Cologne, 1962.
Gropius, Gropius and Bayer: *Bauhaus 1919–1928,* New York, 1938
       (for the English texts of Bauhaus documents
       quoted in the pages that follow).
Gropius, W: *Internationale Architektur,* Munich, 1925.
   Bauhausbauten Dessau, Munich, 1930.
Kandinsky, W: *Punkt und Linie zu Fläche,* Munich, 1925.
Klee, P: *Pädagogisches Skizzenbuch,* Munich, 1926.
Johnson, P: *Mies van der Rohe,* Museum of Modern Art, New York,
     (2nd edn.), 1953.
Behrendt, W. C: *Der Sieg des Neuen Baustils,* Stuttgart, 1927.
von Senger, A: *Krisis der Architektur,* Zurich, 1928.
Schnaidt, C: *Hannes Meyer,* Teufen, 1965.
Hilbersheimer, L: *Internationale Neue Baukunst,* Stuttgart, 1927.
   Grosstadt-Architektur, Stuttgart, 1927.
   Hallenbauten, Stuttgart, 1928.
   Beton als Gestalter, Stuttgart, 1928.
Korn, A: *Glas im Bau und als Gebrauchsgegenstand,* Berlin, 1929.
Platz, G: *Die Baukunst der neuesten Zeit,* Berlin, 1927.
Mendelsohn, E: *Amerika,* Berlin, 1928.
   Russland-Europa-Amerika, Berlin, 1929.
Giedion, S: *Bauen in Frankreich, Eisen, Eisenbeton,* Leipzig, 1928.
Moholy-Nagy, L: *Von Material zu Architektur,* Munich, 1929.
     (English translation: *The New Vision, Documents of
     Modern Art: Vol. 3,* George Wittenborn, New York,
     1949, from which most of the quotations in the follow-
     ing pages are taken.)

19: The Berlin school

IN SPITE OF the appearance of notable Modern buildings in cities such as Dessau and Stuttgart, the main power and strength of the German contribution to mainstream Modern architecture came from Berlin—indeed, most of these notable buildings in other towns were the work of architects with, at least, Berlin connections.[1] As the second artistic capital of Europe, after Paris, it was clearly likely to produce work of interest, but it contained, in addition, a remarkable group of architectural talents. No other centre in the early Twenties could have boasted, as Berlin could, more than a dozen progressive architects of more than average competence, sufficiently resilient in mental constitution to take in their stride a major aesthetic revolution, from Expressionism to Elementarism, and to design in either style with equal vigour and assurance. Yet Bruno Taut, Mies van der Rohe, Erich Mendelsohn, and Walter Gropius, were as typical of the Berlin architecture of 1919 as of 1926, their contributions to the second phase were as notable as to the first, and all but Mendelsohn did as much to make the skyscraper typical of Expressionism as they did to make the *Siedlung* typical of the Elementarist phase that runs into the International Style.

The theories of Erich Mendelsohn have been discussed in an earlier chapter, those of Gropius will be discussed in the next: for the moment we are concerned with Bruno Taut and Mies van der Rohe. As a mirror of the ideas current in his time, rather than as an original thinker, Taut is of the greatest interest: at the end of the Twenties he contributed to the group of encyclopaedic works on Modern architecture the only one in a 'popular' vein; in the course of the decade he produced a number of minor pieces of documentary interest, and at its very beginning he produced what is, historically, his most important book, because it is one of the few major documents of the Expressionist phase that can be set beside Mendelsohn's lectures—*Die Stadtkrone*.

This book, written in 1919 and dedicated, understandably, to the *Fried-*

---

[1] The next three chapters are, again, much in debt to the personal memoirs of survivors of the period—Mart Stam, Artur Korn, and Walter Segal—and to Sybil Moholy-Nagy's book about her husband, *Moholy-Nagy* (New York, 1950).

fertigen, the Peaceable, is primarily concerned with town planning, but in a manner contrary in intention, if not in effect, to anything produced outside the Berlin Expressionist circle. It is, in part, a polemic against advanced town planning as it then stood, with its emphasis on residential planning, zoning and Garden City ideals. These, according to Taut, do not produce a complete city but a *Rumpf ohne Kopf*—urbanisation without an emphatic central feature. Such a feature, a *Stadtkrone*, was for Taut a symbolic public building making a bold silhouette against the sky, visible from all over the city, much as an oriental pagoda or minaret, or a Gothic spire could be seen to dominate the surrounding buildings—indeed, the whole tone of the book is summed up by its frontispiece, a reproduction of Van Eyck's St Barbara seated before her Gothic tower.

His own positive suggestions envisage a city of more or less radial plan, at little more than Garden City densities, focused on an agglomeration of public buildings disposed biaxially in a central rectangle, and capped by a glass tower, usually shown in his sketches with the sun rising or setting behind it. It is worth noting that Le Corbusier's *Ville Contemporaine* would have presented a somewhat similar appearance, though designed from a diametrically opposed point of view, for the glass tower of Taut's ideal city has a very different derivation. It appears to have been, by months or only minutes, the first of a number of glass-tower projects that ornamented Berlin architectural thought around 1920, but it is the only one that can be shown to derive directly from an inspiration that can only be suspected in the case of the others—Paul Scheerbart's book *Glasarchitektur*.

Taut and Scheerbart had known one another before 1913 (Scheerbart died in 1915) and whether or not Taut's glass pavilion at Cologne in 1914 was inspired by Scheerbart, it was certainly dedicated to him,[2] just as *Glasarchitektur*, which appeared in the same year, was dedicated to Taut. *Die Stadtkrone* opens and closes with longish quotations, architectural in theme, from Scheerbart's 'Hippopotamus Novel' (*Nilpferdroman*) *Immer Mutig*, and is shot through with his faith in glass as a building material and sensitivity to its visual qualities.

The appearance of such a person as Scheerbart, best known as an eccentric writer of fantasticated novels verging on what would now be called science-fiction, in the annals of anything so intimately bound up with the more aseptic side of Modern architecture as glass walling, may occasion surprise, but his passionate faith in glass and hatred of masonry

> Glass brings us the new Age
> Brick-culture does us nothing but harm[3]

---

[2] According to Konrad Werner Schultz, who devotes nearly two pages to influences bearing on the glass architecture of the Cologne Exhibition in his book *Glas in der Architektur der Gegenwart* (Stuttgart, 1929).

[3] This was quoted by Taut in a book about his own private house, *Ein Wohnhaus* (Stuttgart, 1927), and seems to be the last trace of Scheerbart in his work, literary

were backed by a sharp sense of the practicalities of using the new material, while the possible impact of the book on architects of a *sachlich* turn of mind was heightened by its very sober typography, quite unlike the Yellow-Book style of Scheerbart's novels. In spite of the clearly Art Nouveau aesthetic of detailing and decoration that runs through the book, in spite of its Futurist visions of a night landscape criss-crossed by railways ablaze with coloured lights, illuminated motorboats, liners, and the glazed water-side palaces of a new Venice, Zeppelins cruising overhead picking out the shapes of the Alps with coloured searchlights, and glass-walled hotels gleaming on every mountainside—in spite of all this he had a shrewd appreciation of the problems of condensation, heat-loss, etc. that would arise with all-glass walling, as well as a clear sense of the possibilities of metal and concrete structure in combination with glass.

Indeed, technically, his vision anticipates a great deal that was to come about in the Twenties, including such concepts as a new relationship of house to garden through the use of glass walls and movable partitions. In general, Taut does little more than skim off the superficial possibilities that Scheerbart suggests, but others, on whom the influence is too diffuse to be easily demonstrated (because they had the War years in which to digest the book and forget about its author) take it much deeper. In the case of the Bauhaus, which went further than anyone else in research into light and transparency, there are both strong possibilities and strong hints of a direct influence. The first proclamation of the Weimar Bauhaus, which may even have been roughed out in Berlin, has on its cover a woodcut by Lyonel Feininger showing the entirely Scheerbartian conception of a Gothic cathedral topped by beacon lights, while, inside, it has Gropius writing of 'a building like a crystal symbol' and calling for the elimination of snobbish differentiation between hand-workers and brain-workers, just as Scheerbart, in the passages from *Immer Mutig* that appeared in *Die Stadtkrone*, had prophesied

Kings walk with beggar-men . . . artisans with the men of learning.

Scheerbartian ideas could easily have been in Gropius's mind at this time since he was busy recruiting his first Bauhaus staff from the circle of *Der Sturm*, which had published *Glasarchitektur*, and was in close touch with both Bruno Taut and his brother Max.

Also in close touch with the two Tauts at the same time was Mies van der Rohe, whose possible connections with Scheerbart are as intriguing as they are undemonstrable. It seems inconceivable that his two projects for glass-skycrapers, one for the Friedrichstrasse Station competition (1919) and the other for an unspecified site (1921) should owe nothing to the prophet of glass, especially in view of the care lavished on investigating their

or architectural. The house itself, designed some two years previously, is probably the last building with identifiable Scheerbartian qualities built by anybody.

optical qualities as reflectors and refractors of light, and their conspicuously Expressionist forms, which would have fitted them admirably for the role of *Stadtkronen*, but the fact remains that when Mies came to discuss them in print (in Bruno Taut's magazine *Frühlicht*) he did so in terms that are almost the opposite of Scheerbart's romanticism.

> Skyscrapers reveal their bold structural pattern during construction. Only then does the gigantic steel web seem impressive. When the outer walls are put in place, the structural system which is the basis of all artistic design, is hidden in a chaos of meaningless and trivial forms. . . . Instead of trying to solve new problems with old forms, we should develop the new forms from the very nature of the new problems.
> We can see the new structural principles most clearly when we use glass in place of the outer walls, which is feasible today since in a skeleton building these outer walls do not actually carry weight. The use of glass imposes new solutions. . . .
> I discovered by working with actual glass models that the important thing is the play of reflections, and not the effect of light and shadow as in ordinary buildings.

The tough tone, the fascination with skeletal structure, belong to a different world to Scheerbart's, the world of Lissitsky, Werner Graeff and the *G* group which was to be formed within less than twelve months of this being written.

Also, between the Friedrichstrasse competition and the writing of these words, Berlin architects had involved themselves in two other sky-scraper competitions, and had drastically overhauled their ideas in the process.

Many entries for the Friedrichstrasse had clearly Scheerbartian inspirations—elaborately faceted glass towers, or towers with curvilinear glass pavilions at their feet—but the Koenigsberg competition and that for the Chicago *Tribune* Tower produced work of a different order. Some confusion surrounds both competitions because of designs that were completed, but not submitted, yet were subsequently published. Thus the Koenigsberg competition is now remembered chiefly for a design that seems never to have been submitted—Mart Stam's concrete-framed, glass-clad reworking of the Sant'Elian theme of set-back floors and projecting lift-towers, while the Chicago *Tribune* is remembered now for a whole group of designs that were unnoticed, unplaced or unsubmitted.

While the most discussed,[4] and most admired, of all the entries was Eliel Saarinen's, placed second and since deservedly forgotten, the competition attracted interest and entries from all over Scandinavia and the German-speaking world. In a modified Wrightian style there were designs from Bijvoet and Duiker (unplaced) and Lönberg-Holm (unsubmitted), both making much of overhangs and cantilevered projections, and in the new, tough Berlin style of severe framed structures in glass and reinforced concrete, there were entries from Max Taut (unplaced) and Ludwig

---

[4] Typical of the discussion at its best are Irving K. Pond's contributions to *Architectural Forum* (New York, 1921, pp. 41ff., 179ff.).

Hilberseimer (unsubmitted), the latter representing an extremity of stark *Zweckarchitektur*, unrelieved by imagination or aesthetic intent.

Between these two groups, stylistically, lies the most interesting German entry, the only one to keep the name of the Chicago *Tribune* alive in the history-books: Gropius and Meyer's. The design is of double importance historically; it marks the recovery by Gropius of the strong line he had pursued before 1914, and had lost in such Expressionist experiments as the Weimar monument, the Sommerfeld and Otte houses; but it also signals the emergence of the characteristic features of the second phase of Berlin architecture. It puts vigorous emphasis on function and structure, by means of a formal vocabulary derived partly from an appreciation of engineering structure, and partly from the Elementarist aesthetics of the Dutch and Russian Abstractionists. Its top-heavy silhouette and fly-away balconies seem chiefly Russian in extraction (though the block form can be at least paralleled in Mendelsohn's *Carmelkrone* drawings of the same year) while the factory-pattern fenestration over the whole block picks up the rhythm of the elevations of the old *Tribune* printing works at the back of the site in such a way as to integrate it fully into the design—an expression of sympathy with engineer-architecture that can be found in no other entry for the competition, and would probably have been beyond the aesthetic capacity of anyone not trained in the Werkbund factory aesthetics of 1910–14.

This was also practically the last of the skyscraper projects, and with the increasing availability of real work, *Stadtkrone* pipe-dreams recede from the foreground of architectural thought in Berlin, and the accent of design becomes, whatever Le Corbusier may have said to the contrary, predominantly horizontal. At the same time, leadership of the school tends to pass from the Taut connection to that of the *G* group. However, the school remained professionally coherent, no schism between Expressionists and Elementarists appeared. Men changed their attitudes but not their friends and in 1925 they regularised their solidarity by forming the *Ring*, whose membership included at different times Gropius, Mies van der Rohe, Bruno and Max Taut, Erich Mendelsohn, the Luckhardt brothers, Hans Scharoun, Hugo Häring, Hans Poelzig, Artur Korn, Richard Doecker, Otto Bartning, Hilberseimer and others—the complete circle of progressive Berlin architects irrespective of their stylistic preferences.

With the waning of the influence of the ex-Expressionists, with Gropius largely taken up with the affairs of the Bauhaus, and Mendelsohn deeply involved in his connection with various large Jewish trading houses, the leadership of the *Ring* went almost automatically to Mies van der Rohe, and he fulfilled this role with increasing authority as the decade grew older. That authority among his fellow architects, whom he overtops as surely as did Le Corbusier those of Paris, seems to have depended less on great force of personality or dazzling originality, than on sheer unshakeable merit as a designer. In whatever style circumstances or inclination led him to design, he was outstanding, possibly because he was, he claimed, indifferent to style.

As with many who profess such an indifference, his work, and particularly his sketches, showed in the early Twenties an almost excessive susceptibility to formal influence, but with the proviso that everything that he absorbed was transmuted. Thus, he emerges from his encounters with Stam and Lissitsky as less original than either, but a more convincing designer than both. His accession to the tough-minded school of design, of which they, and Werner Graeff, were the main propulsive force, is marked by a design as important as Gropius and Meyer's *Tribune* project, and for similar reasons: a concrete office block of dominantly horizontal design.

Not a frame structure, it was envisaged as a post-and-slab (or, since the posts were rectangular in section, tapered and connected by beams under the slab, a portal-frame-and-slab) construction, but with a structural and functional peculiarity that seems to have some connection with Wright's Larkin Building. Hilberseimer describes it thus

> Here, the floor-plate is turned up vertically at the end of the cantilevers and becomes the outer wall, serving as a backing to the filing-cabinets which have been transferred to the outer wall from the inner space for the sake of a better-arranged layout

but makes no reference to the fact that the filing systems of the Larkin building were similarly arranged (a device that Mies could have known through Berlage). He also describes the arrangement of the fenestration in a manner reminiscent of Le Corbusier's '*on vit par étage*'

> Above the filing lies a continuous band of window rising to the floor above, without supports or masonry. By this means the ranging of the floors (one above the other) is most energetically emphasised.

However, Hilberseimer makes no reference to elements of other styles that linger in this building—the axial planning and disposition of the entrance, and the fact that each floor cantilevers out a little further than that below, giving an almost Expressionist silhouette.

The degree of caution revealed here, retaining such parts of past disciplines as are necessary to stabilise new adventures in design, is still present even in the most 'revolutionary' of Mies's projects, the brick villa of 1923. Much has been made of certain superficial resemblances between the plan of this design and paintings by van Doesburg, but it is a richer and more complex concept than that. The slabs of brick that form the structure can be regarded as 'elements' in Kiesler's sense, disposed in an 'unending space' such as Lissitsky might have specified. The relationship of these brick slabs to the volumes they do not completely enclose can indeed be likened to the bars of dark paint that do not completely enclose the areas of colour in van Doesburg's painting 'Rhythm of a Russian Dance', but this loose relationship of house to surroundings might equally well have a Scheerbartian inspiration, just as the carefully preserved purity of the wall slabs has an unmistakable origin in Berlage. Above all, the massing of the composition belongs to an older tradition than the Elementarist approach noted by Barr and others. Although the plan itself is perhaps the first real advance on Wright's Prairie houses, the elevations are less up-to-date in a way than those of some Dutch Wrightians, for there is a complete lack of consequential overhangs. Instead, the elevations pyramid back to a taller central block—the silhouette is that of a *Stadtkrone* in miniature, or of picturesquely grouped neo-Classical villa, and reveals the strength of Mies's *Schinkelschüler* inclinations even at this late date.

The caution continues through the group of brick buildings, actually executed, that stem from this project. In the Wolf House at Guben something of the pyramidal massing is retained, even in 1926, and the brickwork shows an almost Dutch prettiness in the use of bond-patterns and the use of Dudok-like re-entrants on vertical arrises. The Monument to the Communist 'martyrs' Karl Liebnecht and Rosa Luxemburg, built in Berlin in the same year, has closer affiliations with Abstract art in the massing of its projecting rectangular volumes, but it also presents an appearance of Expressionist cragginess, and its surface of twisted and overburned bricks calls to mind the textured upper storey of Mendelsohn's double villa on the Carolingerplatz, Charlottenburg. It is only in the Lange house at Krefeld, as late as 1928, still in brick, that anything like the entirely tough tone of his earlier writings and associates really comes to the surface. The street front of this house in particular gives an impression of studied gracelessness, in spite of its warm colours, although further inspection will show that a most refined sense (if not system) of proportion relates the parts. Even here, where his manner of design reaches an extreme point, the facts of the building cannot quite be equated with the toughest of his theoretical propositions of the *G* epoch

> We reject all aesthetic speculation, all doctrine, all formalism

or

> We refuse to recognise problems of form; we recognise only problems of building.
> Form is not the aim of our work, only the result
> Form by itself does not exist
> Form as an aim is formalism, and that we reject.

The 'problems of building' that he was prepared to recognise were structure, planning disciplines, industrialisation of methods—in general, the sort of problem that would attract the attention of Werner Graeff and others who found the Bauhaus too 'arty'. Nevertheless, it is interesting that out of this rather negative approach there does emerge a positive and even familiar philosophy of design: *Zeitgeist* plus Rationalism equals *Raumgestaltung*.

> Greek temples, Roman Basilicas and mediaeval cathedrals are significant to us as the creations of a whole epoch, rather than as works of individual architects....

They are pure expressions of their time. Their true meaning is that they are symbols of their epoch.

Architecture is the will of the epoch translated into space.

If we discard all romantic conceptions, we can recognise the stone structures of the Greeks, the brick and concrete construction of the Romans and the mediaeval cathedrals, all as bold engineering achievements. . . .

Our utilitarian buildings can become worthy of the name of architecture only if they truly interpret their time by their perfect functional expression.

Whatever the personal and literary influences bearing on this attitude, there was a growing social pressure, quite outside the *G* connection, that drove his ideas, and those of other Berlin architects, in this Rationalist and Functionalist direction in the middle of the Twenties. From about 1924 onwards, progressive organs of local government in different parts of Germany began to commission and build designs for large-scale, low-cost housing developments, and a surprisingly large proportion of this work went to comparatively extreme Modernists—the *Ring* were heavily engaged in the suburbs of Berlin until after 1930. Given the financial condition of the country at the time, these *Siedlungen* had to be built down to the most stringent budgets, and a ruthlessly rational approach was required to extract the maximum possible performance from materials, machinery, and every square meter of built floor space and occupied site area. Research into economy and maximum performance was carried to its farthest point in this period by Ernst May and his team at the Municipal Building Department at Frankfurt am Main, who developed special building techniques, and special furniture and equipment in order to hold down costs and speed up the work of building. Unusually, for a programme of this kind, the architectural quality of the buildings was high, and the quality of the planning has become a by-word, particularly the Römerstadt scheme. Although Berlin architects did not dispose of an equivalent research organisation[5] their work does not lag far behind that of May's office, and the actual architectural quality of their work is very similar to his.

That quality can be fairly simply described: most such developments were in three- to five-storey blocks of some length, strung out along access roads; their structure was of bricks or, more likely, cinder-blocks and almost always rendered over, the windows smallish, their precise size being determined usually by minimum daylighting standards. Any aesthetics these lengthy façades might boast had to be fought for, and had to be expressed from the given elements. In practice this meant that the colour of the rendering might be changed for the 'basement' or 'attic' stories, that rhythmic and proportional effects might be contrived from the disposition of the fenestration, and that the corner of a street, or other given inter-

[5] It is worth noting that Gropius's main papers on mass-housing, which contributed so much to world thought, contributed little to German thought on the subject, since they did not appear until 1929 and 1931, by which time the work of May, in particular, and various *Ring* architects had already given an empirical and partly statistical basis to mass-housing work in Germany.

ruption, such as the need to provide local shops, might provide the opportunity for some three-dimensional relief. The generally high standard of at least the façades of these developments is a major achievement of the German architecture of the Twenties, but this achievement has its ironical aspect, for, since these low cost developments also constituted the bulk of the Modern architecture that could be seen around Berlin, they gave rise to the legend (backed by a certain amount of Corbusian wishful thinking) that Modern architecture is, by its nature, a cheap style of building.

Even so, the participation of Mies van der Rohe, with his well-known preference for de luxe finishes, etc. in the business of *Siedlung* building still comes as something of a surprise, yet his small development on the Afrikanische Strasse, and the related block at Weissenhof, are by far the most distinguished of all such buildings architecturally, though their effect depends almost entirely on the size and spacing of the window-openings.

The block at Weissenhof was one of the best known and most widely discussed buildings in the period, partly because of its inherent qualities, and partly because of its situation. In 1925, the Deutscher Werkbund invited Mies to take charge of the overall planning of what was to be their first major exhibition since Cologne, a group of residential buildings, some permanent, some transient, on the small hill of Weissenhof, overlooking Stuttgart, to be opened to the public in the summer of 1927. Since time was short, and most of the buildings would still be in the process of design when the overall plan was complete, the town-planning problem was one of permissive discipline, giving an ordered relationship to a number of blocks whose very bulk was still indeterminate at this early stage.

The solution was not the academic one of driving an array of axes across the site and letting the buildings square up to them as best they could— the site was too small, too irregular in outline and too beset with topographical accidents for that. Instead, Mies organised his anticipated volumes across the rise of the hill in the form of what might nowadays be termed a 'terrain-sculpture'—a related sequence of rectangular blocks and connecting terraces, organised somewhat in the manner of the brick villa project of 1923, with his own block of flats serving as a *Stadtkrone* at the highest point. This highly original concept, the first new contribution to three-dimensional town planning since Sant'Elia, had to be sacrificed in part to local preferences and financial stringencies (the terraces were replaced by conventional road access, which broke up the continuity of the sculptural whole) but even so, a good deal of the initial concept survived, and can still be appreciated in aerial photographs taken at the time.

It is hardly necessary to record that Mies made no written pronouncement about this remarkable piece of planning; instead, he explained his intentions at Weissenhof in two apparently contradictory statements about the problem of residential design. The contradiction, though striking, is in fact superficial, and it will be seen that the libertarian sentiments of the first do not rule out the special case discussed in the second.

> The problem of the modern dwelling is primarily architectural, in spite of its technical and economic aspects. It is a complex problem of planning and can therefore only be solved by creative minds, not by calculation and organisation. Therefore, I felt it imperative, in spite of current talk about Rationalisation and Standardisation, to keep the project at Stuttgart from being one-sided or doctrinaire. I have therefore invited leading representatives of the Modern Movement to make their contribution to the problem of the modern dwelling.

One cannot but notice the deviation from the earlier tough tone which appears in this statement. However, it returns, almost in the language of 1922 in the other statement

> Today the factor of economy makes Rationalisation and Standardisation imperative for rental housing. On the other hand the increased complexity of our requirements demands flexibility. The future will have to reckon with both. For this purpose skeleton construction is the most suitable system. It makes possible Rationalised building methods and allows the interior to be freely divided. If we regard kitchens and bathrooms, because of their plumbing, as a fixed core, then all other space may be partitioned by means of movable walls. This should, I believe, satisfy all normal requirements.

Although his block of flats at Weissenhof did not have what would normally be called movable partitions, it did have a skeleton frame (though this was invisible on the outside), it did treat the kitchens and bathrooms as fixed cores, and did arrange each of the twenty-four main flats differently in plan. Mies here gave the most striking and convincing demonstration of the concept of the flexible plan that had been seen up to this date, even though most of the theoretical pronouncements on the subject had come from Le Corbusier.

Comparison with Le Corbusier is both apt and proper at this point, for, quite apart from his achievements as a town planner and a flat planner at Weissenhof, Mies also effected an even bigger feat there; he made the Modern Movement visibly international. Le Corbusier, Oud, Stam and the Belgian, Victor Bourgeois all contributed buildings to the scheme; Oud and Stam in the form of terraces of small cottages, Le Corbusier a double house and a *Maison Citrohan*, and Victor Bourgeois a single house slightly apart from the rest of the exhibition. However, visitors to Weissenhof could not but notice that the buildings designed by non-Germans were quite at home with their close neighbours designed by members of the *Ring*, and that a conspicuous harmony of style pervaded the whole *Siedlung*. This manifest international coherence had a double significance: on the one hand it made Modern architecture the target of chauvinist critics all over the world, whether they were Nazis, the Mauclair connection in France, or the wilder followers of Frank Lloyd Wright; on the other hand, following the lead established by Gropius' book *Internationale Architektur*, it led Alfred H. Barr to apply to mature Modern architecture of the mainstream that stylistic label that has adhered to it ever since—'The International Style'.

Yet, in spite of these international overtones, Weissenhof was primarily a manifestation of *Ring* architecture, and, apart from the four non-German designers mentioned above (and for Stam 'non-German' is a dubiously valid epithet) the remaining eleven were mostly Berliners by professional domicile, birth or attachment—Mies himself, Gropius, Hilberseimer, the Tauts, Scharoun, Doecker, Behrens, etc. The style to which the foreign designs conformed was the style of Berlin by sheer pressure of numbers. No other city at the time could have mustered, as Berlin could by this date, over a dozen convinced Modernists of recognisable talent. Paris might have produced four, the whole of Holland about the same number, the rest of the world another eight or so. In terms of the growth of the Modern Movement, Germany's greatest contribution was the sheer quantity of men and buildings produced by Berlin, but in terms of the subsequent distribution of that Movement across the Western world, Germany's two great contributions are an institution that was an entirely Berlin conception, albeit located elsewhere, the Bauhaus, which will be discussed in the next chapter, and a spate of encyclopaedic books, discussed two chapters hence, of which the most important, Moholy-Nagy's *Von Material zu Architektur*, was itself a Bauhaus product.

20: The Bauhaus

ALTHOUGH THE BAUHAUS has become so established a symbol of Modernity that the adoption of its methods is a recognised sign that a school has 'gone Modern', it had many roots in the past. It was formed by the fusion, in 1919, of two existing institutions in Weimar, one an Academy of Fine Arts with a tradition that reached back into history, the other a *Kunstgewerbe* school founded by Henry van de Velde after he came to Weimar in 1903 at the behest of the last Grand duke of Sachsen-Weimar, at the beginning of that wave of enthusiasm for improved design that also produced the Werkbund. From both institutions Gropius inherited buildings, a few members of the pre-War staffs, and, to begin with, what might be termed the 'goodwill'.

Though his action in fusing the two schools was a pioneering gesture, it was not an original idea. Something of the kind had been in van de Velde's mind even before he came to Weimar, and while he was there proposals came from the Academy for closer relationships between the two schools. At the level of practical experiment, Poelzig at Breslau had instituted craft workshops in the Academy even before 1914, and in the same period Richard Meyer ran art classes in the *Kunstgewerbe* school at Hamburg.[1] The ground was thus prepared well before Gropius took over the two schools in Weimar, and his action realised a concept that was already current in progressive circles. Over and above this, the staff he gathered round him in the first years of the Bauhaus could hardly be called new men possessed of dangerous new ideas. They were recruited mainly through two overlapping connections that had existed before the War—*Der Sturm* in Berlin, and his friends in musical circles in Vienna. Most of the men produced in this way had been born before 1890, their art and their reputations had begun to mature before 1914.

Most of them were also painters, in spite of the fact that the Bauhaus was intended to train for all branches of design, culminating in architec-

---

[1] On the subject of attempts to bring the Academies and the *Kunstgewerbe* schools closer together, see Nikolaus Pevsner, *Academies of Art* (Cambridge, 1940, pp. 274, 275).

ture. And all, in the public mind at least, were Expressionists. This last point not only alarmed the citizens of Weimar, and laid the foundations of that hostility that was eventually to make Gropius's position untenable, but it also imposed certain strains on the internal orientations of the school itself. It was, clearly, inevitable that Gropius should have to rely on men and connections established before the War, but later staff-student tensions and minor 'palace revolutions' were equally inevitably engendered by the need for the older generation with pre-War ideas to adapt themselves to changed circumstances. Although the outwardly visible change in Bauhaus policy is associated with the visits of van Doesburg, and the admission of Moholy-Nagy to the staff in 1923, the Bauhaus had, in fact, been in process of transformation almost from its foundation and was to remain so until its dissolution in Berlin in 1933. Much of its historical interest lies in the manner in which it reflects the changing aspect of German architectural thought in the Twenties, though its ultimate historical significance will always lie in the effect it had on international architectural thought in the Thirties and Forties.

The Scheerbartian qualities of the first Bauhaus Proclamation have already been mentioned. Lyonel Feininger, who designed the cover, was a member of the *Sturmkreis*, and the medium he employed, a woodcut, was one of the favourites of Expressionist artists. The text of Gropius's statement is entirely in character with the cover.

> The complete building is the ultimate aim of the visual arts. Their highest function was once the decoration of buildings. They exist, nowadays, in an isolation from which they can be rescued only by the conscious joint efforts of all craftsmen. Architects, painters and sculptors must recognise once more the nature of buildings as composite entities. Only then will their works be permeated with that architectonic feeling which has become lost in the art of the salons.

So far, this is not very different from the line taken by, say, Berlage before 1910, but the next two paragraphs have a more specifically Expressionist quality.

> Architects, painters and sculptors, we must all turn to the crafts.
> Then there will be no 'professional art'. There is no essential difference between the artist and the craftsman: the artist is a craftsman raised to a higher power. In rare moments of illumination, unbidden by conscious will, the Grace of Heaven may cause his handicraft to blossom into art. A groundwork of craft-discipline is essential to every artist.
> Let us create a new guild of craftsmen, without the class-snobbery that tries to erect a haughty barrier between artist and craftsman. Let us conceive, consider and create together the new building of the future that will bring all into one single integrated creation: architecture, painting and sculpture rising to Heaven out of the hands of a million craftsmen, the crystal symbol of the new faith of the future.

What cannot fail to astonish in this statement is that a person like Gropius, grounded in the Werkbund and the office of Behrens, in touch with *Der Sturm* and its emphasis on Futurism, should be capable at this time of

277

making no reference whatever to machinery, and should take his stand solely on the Morrisian standpoint of inspired craftsmanship. It was not until 1923 that the Bauhaus was to show any outward interest in mechanised production, and the problems of designing for it. By that time, its teaching methods had become inseparably bound up with craftsmanship—a point that its apologists found sufficiently embarrassing to need explanation.

Yet this craftsmanly inclination was to be one of the main strengths of the Bauhaus method of education, because it made possible the elaboration of an unacademic teaching system that could not, at that time, have been based upon a mechanistic approach. Handicraft, as a teaching discipline, implies 'learning by doing' rather than learning by reading or listening to lectures, and this, however its methods and intentions may have been modified by different teachers at various times, became the 'Bauhaus Method' and ultimately the norm for advanced architectural training all over the world. The idea of 'learning by doing' is probably owed chiefly to Fröbel, as Frederick Logan has pointed out,[2] but it may well owe a great deal also to the established methods of *Kunstgewerbeschule* workshop instruction, and the basic innovation of the Bauhaus—implicit in the way the school was formed in the first place—lay in the introduction of these handicraft methods into Fine Art instruction. The other great innovation was the determination to cleanse every incoming student's mind of all preconceptions and to put him, so to speak, back into Kindergarten to start again from scratch. This was effected through the *Vorkurs*, or preliminary course, which has acquired such fame that it has come to be regarded as the essence, even the entirety, of the Bauhaus Method.

The conception and early elaboration of the *Vorkurs* was the work of Johannes Itten, a Swiss painter with pedagogical interests, whom Gropius had met through his musical connections, and Georg Muche, a young *Sturmkünstler*. The aims of the course were set out in specific terms only in 1922, when the first flurry of excitement had died down a little and something like an Itten-system could be said to exist. On the occasion of an exhibition of works by Bauhaus 'apprentices' and 'journeymen' Itten wrote an introduction to the catalogue which reads, in part

The course is intended to liberate the student's creative power, to give him an understanding of Nature's materials, and to acquaint him with the basic principles which underly all creative activity in the visual arts. Every new student arrives encumbered with a mass of accumulated information which he must abandon before he can achieve perception and knowledge that are really his own. If he is to work in wood, for example, he must have a 'feeling' for wood. He must also understand its relation to other materials . . . combining and composing them to make their relationship fully apparent.
Preparatory work also involves exact depiction of actual materials. If a student draws or paints a piece of wood true to nature in every detail, it will help him to understand the material. The work of old masters, such as Bosch, Meister Francke or Grünewald also offers instruction in the study of form, which is an

[2] In the *College Art Journal* (New York, Fall 1950, p. 36ff.).

essential part of the preliminary course. This instruction is intended to enable the student to perceive the harmonious relationship of different rhythms and to express such harmony through the use of one or several materials. The preliminary course concerns the student's whole personality, since it seeks to liberate him, to make him stand on his own feet, and makes it possible for him to gain a knowledge of both material and form through direct experience.

As a matter of principle, each apprentice has to do his own designing. . . .

The underlying assumptions of this document can best be brought out by making flat contrasts between it and the common assumptions of Academic teaching. An obvious one is that the laws of form are to be found in the works of German primitives, not in the Classics, but more important ones are: the idea of vocation to a material or technique, not to a function in society; the liberation of innate abilities, not the acquisition of methods; the cultivation of intuitive sensibility, not the acquirement of knowledge; and, most significant of all, the destruction of previous training, not its exploitation, the intention to return incoming students to the noble savagery of childhood. To have gone so far against established precedent without moving forward into a mechanised culture, meant that Itten had to go right outside the general body of Western, Rational thought, and under his influence Bauhaus students involved themselves in the study of mediaeval mystics like Eckhart, and Eastern spiritual discipline such as Mazdaznan, Tao and Zen. The alarm of the citizens of Weimar, city of Goethe, can easily be understood, as can the contempt felt by the tough-minded connection in Berlin.

No document now exists that gives a contemporary estimate of the place of the *Vorkurs*, its handicrafts and intuitive approach to materials, in the total Bauhaus curriculum of these early years: Gropius's *Idee und Aufbau des Staatlichen Bauhauses Weimar* did not appear until 1923, when changes in the Bauhaus staff and methods were already under way, and his own design methods had passed the point of decision marked by the Chicago *Tribune* Project. Indeed, the great value of this document lies in the fact that it gives an extended survey of his opinions just at the time when he, and the Bauhaus, were entering their period of greatest mastery and greatest certainty about their position in the life and thought of the time. If it seems to spend too much time labouring well-worn themes, it is invaluable among the literature of the period for its moderate tone and Rational exposition.

It opens with sweeping historical generalisations, through which a version of Itten's mysticism can be perceived.

The dominant spirit of our epoch is already recognisable although its form is not yet clearly defined. The old dualistic world-concept which envisaged the ego in opposition to the universe is rapidly losing ground. In its place is rising the idea of a universal unity in which all opposing forces exist in a state of absolute balance.

Then follows a brief survey of the recent history of design, viewed from the standpoint of the Werkbund: the decadence of architecture as the unifying agent in creating a *Gesamtkunstwerk*, the failure of the Academies and the

279

decay of folk art, the need for *Durchgeistigung*

> Only work which is the product of an inner compulsion can have spiritual meaning. Mechanised work is lifeless, proper only to the lifeless machine . . . the solution depends on a change in the individual's attitude toward his work

the isolation of the creative artist and the famine of industrial designers, concluding with an extraordinarily self-satisfied estimate of the achievement of the nineteenth-century reformers.

> Ruskin and Morris in England, van de Velde in Belgium Olbrich, Behrens and others in Germany, and finally the Deutscher Werkbund, all sought and finally found the basis of a reunion between creative artists and the industrial world.

In view of this belief that the older masters were right, it is not surprising to find that in spite of much emphasis on intuition and innate ability, he conceives the process of artistic creation in terms that Muthesius might have proposed, as *Raumgestaltung*.

> The objective of all creative efforts in the visual arts is to give form to space . . . through his intuition, through his metaphysical powers, man discovers the immaterial space of inward vision and inspiration. This conception of space demands realisation in the material world. . . .
>
> In a work of art the laws of the physical world, the intellectual world and the world of the spirit function and are expressed simultaneously.

This insistence on the spiritual emphasises, if emphasis were needed that Gropius, at the time that he was setting up the second order of Bauhaus teaching, the order of strict geometry and analysis, was far from being the Materialist or Functionalist he is commonly thought to have been—indeed, the Bauhaus had no Functionalist phase until Hannes Meyer took over on Gropius's retirement.

The most curious feature of *Idee und Aufbau*, however, appears in the next section, where he discusses the actual educational programme. Here, in spite of what has been said earlier in favour of unity and against dualism, he accepts a division of the teaching discipline into two halves, *Werklehre* and *Formlehre*, corresponding, in a general sense, to the curricula of the two schools that had been telescoped to form the Bauhaus. Later, to justify *Formlehre* he draws a musical analogy that, if anything, deepens the division.

> The musician who wants to make audible a musical idea, needs for its rendering not only a musical instrument but also a knowledge of theory. Without this knowledge his idea will never emerge from chaos. . . . A corresponding knowledge of theory . . . must again be established as a basis for practice in the visual arts.

This division of the teaching programme into two parallel parts, was to be accompanied by three-fold division in time: first the *Vorkurs*, lasting six months; next, three years' instruction in a particular craft (metalwork, pottery, weaving, woodwork, etc.) under regular articles of apprenticeship, ending, for the successful student, with his *Gesellenbrief* or Journeyman's

Diploma; and lastly, a variable period of instruction in architecture, research, etc. ending in a Master's Diploma.

It should be pointed out that Gropius aimed to close the central division between *Werklehre* and *Formlehre* by the appointment of studio-masters who were equally proficient on both sides, but in the end could only find such 'ambidextrous' talents among his own *Gesellen*, Marcel Breuer, Josef Albers, Herbert Bayer—all products of the first, Expressionist period.

The justification of *Werklehre* involves Gropius in a revealing justification of handicrafts as a teaching discipline

> The Bauhaus believes the machine to be our modern medium of design and seeks to come to terms with it

he begins, betraying a major change of orientation since the Proclamation of 1919.

> But it would be senseless to launch a gifted apprentice straight into industry without preparation in a craft. . . . He would be stifled by the materialistic and one-sided outlook predominant in factories today. A craft, however, cannot conflict with the feeling for workmanship which, as an artist, he inevitably has, and it is therefore the best opportunity for practical training.

This view of the crafts, as a buffer between sensitive spirits and the harsh realities of mechanised production, naturally aroused the scorn of tough-minded students, even inside the Bauhaus, but Gropius had another, and more substantial justification.

> The teaching of a craft is meant to prepare for designing for mass-production. Starting with the simplest tools and least complicated jobs, he gradually acquires ability to master more intricate problems and to work with machines, while at the same time he keeps in touch with the entire process of production from start to finish . . .

and this became a sort of article of faith with the Bauhaus, and may be found repeated, almost word for word, by Moholy-Nagy in 1928.

Gropius's views on *Formlehre* are even more noteworthy, because they indicate a shift of opinion, as compared with Itten, away from Irrationalism and Mediaevalism toward a more Rational, International and even Academic position. One should note, to begin with, that his quarrel with the 'Academies' seems to have been chiefly that they had failed to conserve, or produce, a body of theory about aesthetics

> The academies, whose task it might have been to cultivate such a theory completely failed to do so

and he then goes on to outline a body of ideas which is quite Academic in its outlook, in the sense that most of the ideas can be paralleled in Blanc's *Grammaire*, though unlikely to have come from it direct

> Forms and colours gain meaning only in so far as they are related to our inner selves. . . . Red, for instance, evokes in us other emotions than does blue or yellow, round forms speak differently to us than do pointed or jagged ones. The elements which constitute the grammar of creation are its rules of rhythm, of proportion, of light values, of full or empty space.

Although he makes no value judgements here as between one sort of forms and another, there is very little, barring the references to space, to set this apart from the ideas entertained by Le Corbusier at the same time, and though the Phileban solids are not mentioned by Gropius in this document, they were mentioned very shortly afterwards by Moholy-Nagy as being of special value to the Bauhaus.

> It is characteristic of that moment that Moholy-Nagy who saw me at Jenaer (Glasfabrik) while I changed my earlier cylindrical milk jugs into drop-shaped ones, said to me 'Wagenfeld, how can you betray the Bauhaus like this? We have always fought for simple basic shapes, cylinder, cube, cone, and now you are making a soft form which is dead against all we have been after.'[3]

Here were wide grounds for later agreement with French ideas, agreement that helped to create the International Style, and there were other grounds as well, notably an acceptance by Gropius of the imperatives of Futurism. In spite of the fact that the Bauhaus did not teach certain subjects that might have been thought essential to a Machine Age architecture

> . . . construction in steel and reinforced concrete, statics, mechanics, physics, industrial methods, heating, plumbing, technical chemistry.

echoes of Futurist rhetoric ring clearly in some passages of *Idee und Aufbau*.

> Architecture during the last few generations has become weakly sentimental, aesthetic and decorative . . . this kind of architecture we disown. We aim to create a clear, organic architecture whose inner logic will be radiant and naked, unencumbered by lying facings and trickery; we want an architecture adapted to our world of machines, radios and fast cars . . . with the increasing strength and solidity of the new materials—steel, concrete, glass—and with the new audacity of engineering, the ponderousness of the old methods of building is giving way to a new lightness and airiness.

After this, implications of agreement with other post-War movements follow naturally: with Mendelsohn

> A new aesthetic of the horizontal is beginning to develop

and with *de Stijl*

> At the same time the symmetrical relationship of the parts of the building and their orientation towards a central axis is being replaced by a new conception of equilibrium which transmutes this dead symmetry of similar parts into an asymmetrical but rhythmical balance.

Idee und Aufbau concludes, after references to the need for standardisation, to unity in diversity and to collaborative *Gesamtkunstwerk*, with something that might have been expected to appear earlier—a statement of the relationship of the Bauhaus to education in general. This, while making the expected bow to the Montessori tradition and to 'learning by doing', con-

[3] This story, told by Wilhelm Wagenfeldt in a letter to Nikolaus Pevsner is the nearest thing to confirmation of the stories that circulate about students being severely reprimanded, even expelled, at the Bauhaus for not designing Rationally in the right 'Rational style'.

tains one revealing and surprising statement—surprising in the context of its time, and of what the Bauhaus is often supposed to have been.

> Its responsibility is to educate men and women to understand the world in which they live, and to invent and create forms symbolising that world.

This again shows how far Gropius stood at the time from any Functionalist ideas of formal Determinism, though his contemporaries appear to have seen his position quite differently

> At present, under the influence of these Constructivist ideas, reliance is placed in industry and the art of the engineer, falling at once into an 'Engineering Romanticism' grave enough to disturb somewhat its positive orientation; at all events, I hope that a new Academicism delighting in square Stylisation and relying on an unenlightened play of mechanistic forms, will not be the fruit of this art school, unique today in its Radicalism[4]

The proof of freedom from formal Determinism is in the history of the Bauhaus itself and in the revolution in aesthetics that manifested itself around 1923. Though the change-over from Expressionism to Elementarism was probably not regarded by many of the staff as the adoption of a better set of symbols for their times, it appears that some at least of the students saw matters in this light. In any case, while the replacement of the *Vorkurs* of Itten and Muche by that of Moholy-Nagy and Albers marks the point of crisis in this development, it was *only* the *Vorkurs* that was affected by this change of staff, and other departments of the school made the change of style without sackings and resignations.

Apart from Itten and possibly Gerhard Marcks, who was in charge of the pottery workshop, it does not appear that any of the staff were particularly committed to the old order, and there can be little doubt that it was the adaptability of men like Muche, who transferred to another section, and the uncommitted position of men like Klee and Kandinsky, both of whom ran the *Vorkurs* for short periods during the crisis—it was this that saw the Bauhaus through a period of revolution that ought, on the face of things, to have torn it apart.

Out of these men of transition, it is Paul Klee who emerges with the greatest distinction, and the greatest historical interest in this connection because of his *Pädagogisches Skizzenbuch*, a transitional document that fits neatly into the gap between Itten's method and Moholy's. The notes and sketches that form the *Skizzenbuch* are an edited selection from the papers he accumulated in the course of his teaching experience in 1923 and 1924, and the effect of the editing is to give a clear picture of a very definite view of the nature of practical aesthetics. Klee visualises the process of design as beginning with a point which moves, thus producing a line, which moves, thus producing a plane, which moves, thus creating a volume. A somewhat similar idea can be found in Kandinsky's *Punkt und Linie zu Fläche*, but

[4] Paul Westheim, in an article on the state of the arts in Germany in *L'Esprit Nouveau*, No. 20.

whereas Kandinsky couches his argument in high-level Abstractions, Klee starts with the actual experience of making marks on paper, and remains within sight of practicalities, thus conserving the less spiritual parts, at least, of Itten's craftsmanly approach.

But Klee's book also contains a good deal of the international Abstract body of ideas that had begun to appear in Gropius's thought by this time, and he disposes of Academic ideas like rhythmic proportion and the colour-wheel. Also, he speaks in favour of a fairly determinate type of draughts-manship—by implication in the first part of the *Skizzenbuch*, but explicitly in a lecture[5] he delivered in Jena in 1924, when he said

> Where the possibility of measurement is in doubt, line cannot have been used with absolute purity.

Where Klee's transitional position becomes crucial, more than simply interesting, is in his concept of space. Though he was no physicist, a number of drawings concerning the motion of bodies through space in the *Skizzenbuch* suggest that he had a better intuitive grasp of both the Newtonian and Einsteinian concepts of space than had some of his contemporaries who made great play with them in their writings. At the same time, however, certain other drawings and some paintings done by him show that he also commanded another conception of space sufficiently close to that of the Elementarists to make their ideas readily acceptable to any students who had passed through Klee's hands. In drawings of about 1920, such as *Ideal Menage, Lily* and *Zimmerperspektive*, he draws rectilinear objects as if they were transparent, e.g. all twelve edges of a cube would be visible at once, but without serious deviations from central perspective, and with the objects more or less orthogonally disposed. This gives a very strong impression of space conceived as a regular, measurable, rectilinear continuum, as in Kiesler's *Cité dans l'Espace*, and must have helped to clear the way for Moholy-Nagy's persistent handling of space in this way in his courses.

Related, though by no means identical, concepts of space can be seen in Oskar Schlemmer's book *Die Bühne im Bauhaus* but, although Schlemmer was one of those whom Itten had introduced to the staff and had been at the Bauhaus since 1921, he too was one of the adaptables, and his book, like Klee's, was a symptom of the new order, for the series of *Bauhaus-bücher* in which both appeared, was a brain-child of Moholy-Nagy, and is one of the characteristic products of the second phase of Bauhaus activity.[6] If that phase is to be given a definitive beginning, then it must be 1923. In

[5] The text of this lecture has been published in English as *On Modern Art* (London, 1948).

[6] It would, perhaps, be more accurate to say that the Bauhaus sponsored, rather than published, these books, since all came out under the imprint of the Albert-Langen-Verlag in Munich, while very few publications indeed appeared directly under the Bauhaus imprint at Weimar or Dessau.

that year Itten went and Moholy came, *Idee und Aufbau* gave the teaching programme the shape it was to retain until Gropius left, and the exhibition which provoked Gropius to write this document, not only had the clearly second-phase title of *Art and Technology; a new Unity* (Gropius also gave a lecture under this title) but its main feature, the house *Am Horn*, contained furniture and fittings, designed by Marcel Breuer, Alma Buscher, Erich Brendel and others that show almost to the month the change of attitude in the carpentry shop—there even exists a photograph of the dressing-table by Breuer in which reflections in its circular and oval mirrors have clearly been deliberately contrived to resemble the overlaps and transparencies of one of Moholy-Nagy's paintings.

From this point forwards the establishment of the Bauhaus Method in the form later spread across the world, seems to have been rapid. The division between *Werklehre* and *Formlehre* was being progressively eliminated by the appointment of new staff, and the school in general was acquiring a more homogeneous and less eccentric tone. At the same time, things became more businesslike in every sense of the word: closer ties with manufacturing industry were established, and Bauhaus designs were increasingly used, while at the same time there was a concomitant decline in mysticism, metaphysics and the fancy dress that went with it

> In accordance with Gropius's opinion that the artist of today should wear conventional clothes.

From about 1924 onwards, the products and buildings designed at the Bauhaus also begin to exhibit a recognisable Bauhaus Style—and this must be said even though Gropius and others have denied that there ever was such a thing. Admittedly, style as such was not cultivated, but the forms that were created to symbolise the world in which the *Bauhäusler* found himself showed, naturally enough, considerable unanimity, and the repertoire of Phileban forms, space-grids, glossy synthetic finishes and tweedy natural ones, the use of steel and glass and the evolution of a basically *de Stijl* manner of typography—all these added up, through constant repetition, to a genuinely unified style.

However, in less generalised terms, there are three main monuments that epitomise the second phase of the Bauhaus: The *Bauhausbücher* as a venture in publishing, Moholy-Nagy's own *Bauhausbuch* as a *summa aesthetica* of what the school stood for, and the new buildings at Dessau into which the Bauhaus moved in 1926. Moholy's book *Von Material zu Architektur* is of such importance to the present study that it will form the main subject of the next chapter, but it was only one of a most remarkable series of books, fourteen in all, that appeared between 1925 and 1930. Gropius and Moholy were the co-editors of this series, which seems to have had (perhaps not consciously) a double objective—to explain the Bauhaus to the world, and to make available to the public that was interested in the Bauhaus those other texts which they felt supported or extended their views.

Thus, titles that deal specifically with the Bauhaus itself include Klee's *Pädagogisches Skizzenbuch* and Schlemmer's *Die Bühne im Bauhaus*, one on the Haus am Horn under the title *Ein Versuchshaus* by Adolf Meyer, *Neue Arbeiten* surveying recent work (1925) by staff and students, compiled by Gropius, two by Moholy himself—*Malerei, Photograhie, Film* and *Von Material*—and Gropius's own description of the new buildings at Dessau, under the title *Bauhausbauten Dessau*. On the other side, beginning with the hard case of Kandinsky's *Punkt und Linie*, which did come from inside the Bauhaus but is more profitably read as a personal document from one of the pioneers of abstract art, the *Bauhausbücher* give a unique international coverage of the art of their time. The very first *Bauhausbuch* of all was Gropius's own *Internationale Architektur*, an avowedly popular survey of Modern architecture from all over Europe which now has the added historical significance of filling in the background of architectural knowledge against which the new buildings at Dessau must have been designed.

However, the other *Bauhausbücher* are not surveys, but personal statements by artists of note: van Doesburg's *Grundbegriffe der neuen gestaltenden Kunst*, Mondriaan's *Neue Gestaltung* and Oud's *Holländische Architektur*, to which reference has already been made, gave a very full coverage to those aspects of Dutch theory that would interest the 'Bauhaus Public'. The Russian and Elementarist viewpoint was reinforced by Malevitsch's *Die gegenstandslose Welt*, which came out in 1928 at the same time as the *Bauhausbuch* reprint of Gleize's *du Cubisme*—these two presumably being intended to support Moholy's own *Von Material zu Architektur* which appeared at the same time. But equally revealing of Bauhaus atmosphere and its changes were the titles that never saw the light of day, even though they had been promised in the first flush of enthusiasm—a *Merzbuch* by the Dadaist Kurt Schwitters, something on the *MA-gruppe* by Lassak and Kallai, a book on Russia by Adolf Behne, a book with the promising title of *Bildnerische Mechanik* by Paul Klee, two issues of a *Bildermagazin der Zeit*, an untitled book by Le Corbusier, and a treatise on Futurism by Marinetti and Prampolini. It is not difficult to see why some of these were not published—the book by Le Corbusier was presumably rendered superfluous by Hildebrandt's translation of *Vers une Architecture*, that on Russia by a spate of publications on the subject about 1927, but one cannot help wondering if the disappearance of the Dadaist and Futurist titles may not have been due to that increasing sense of respectability among German Modernists that is expressed in Gropius's desire that students should dress conventionally. Even without these missing titles however, the *Bauhausbücher* represent one of the most concentrated publishing campaigns of books on Modern art, as well as one of the most varied. They mark the emergence of the Bauhaus from Expressionist provincialism into the mainstream of Modern architecture, and the new buildings at Dessau show that the school had moved into a position of undisputed leadership.

The need for these buildings arose through the continuing hostility of the authorities and the public of Weimar, who, in general, found Elementarism no more reassuring than Expressionism. Though local opposition was countered by international support, even from former critics like van Doesburg, the position of the school had been rendered untenable by Easter, 1925, and an offer of re-establishment from the progressive mayor of Dessau, Fritz Hesse, was too good to be overlooked. All the staff except Gerhard Marcks, last of the 'old guard' and all but a few of the students supported Gropius, and the school moved more or less entire, as a going concern, to its new home at Dessau. Though housed in temporary quarters for over a year, they were able to move into the new buildings by December 1926, when they were formally opened.

These buildings were the first unmistakable harbinger of an International Style—the style that existed at Weissenhof in 1927, but had not existed at Paris in 1925—and they were created in an atmosphere of awareness of international developments that is made very clear by Gropius's *Bauhaus-buch*. Its contents cover his own work and his immediate architectural ancestors in the Werkbund, including van de Velde, they include also projects by Mart Stam, the Wesnin brothers in Moscow, Matté-Trucco's Fiat factory, Dutch architects of the *de Stijl* and Wrightian persuasions, Wright himself, Mendelsohn, Korn and other Berlin contemporaries, several Czech architects who failed to establish themselves but were highly regarded in Germany at the time, and Guevrekian and Le Corbusier from Paris. Affinities, sometimes very close affinities, can be observed between the Bauhaus buildings and many of these designs, but never outright borrowing as in the Cologne Pavilion of 1914.

At Dessau, Gropius's work seems to be informed by aesthetic determinations which are at last the match of his social and technical convictions. He seems less influenced by fashion as a consequence, and is able to make genuinely original contributions to the formal usages of the growing International Style. The planning, for instance, whatever its remote debts to the Picturesque, Constructivist and Elementarist traditions, is like nothing else of the period in its centrifugal organisation—by comparison the work of a Mies or a van Doesburg appears timidly conventional in its tendency to centralisation and pyramidal composition. Equally new and rare is the mode of vision—the emphasis in *Bauhausbauten Dessau* is first and foremost on a set of air views of the buildings, an attitude that cannot be paralleled at the time outside the mind of Malevitsch as later revealed in *Die Gegenstandslose Welt*. The three-dimensional quality of the planning is also remarkable, with two stories of the school bridged across a road, a much more radical conception than the mere corridor bridges of Serafimov and Kravets's gigantic light industry centre at Kharkov, whose design must already have been under way.

Indeed, this central, bridged section of the Bauhaus building casts light

287

on aspects of Gropius that are at variance with the commonly held views of him. The bridge was not forced on him by topography (as the great glazed walls were, allegedly, forced on him by a gift of plate glass) for the road which traverses the site was not there when he took over the land, and was not usable until some time after the buildings were completed. The decision to arrange the circulation and the buildings in this way appears to have been an almost abstract decision made on an ideal terrain. Almost abstract, rather than completely abstract, because behind the architectonic decision lies a rather surprising social one—the road that divides the site also divides the buildings into two distinct halves in spite of the bridge; on one side the Bauhaus, on the other the *Fachschule* of the city of Dessau, each with a separate entrance, almost suggesting that the 'arrogant barrier of snobbery' had once more been erected between artist and craftsman.

In spite of this—perhaps because of it—the Bauhaus remains a masterpiece of the new architecture. Indeed, it was the first really great work in the style, exceeding in subtlety and originality the few works that were comparable with it in size, such as Mart Stam's van Nelle factory in Rotterdam,[7] exceeding in size the few works that rivalled it in aesthetic quality, such as the early work of Le Corbusier. It stands beside those works completed by Le Corbusier in 1926—the Cook house and the Palais du Peuple wing—and Mies van der Rohe's block-model for Weissenhof as the first proof of the maturity of the new architecture. That maturity was confirmed at Weissenhof when the buildings were seen, and seen to be internationally unanimous in style, and with its international maturity the style became explicable, to some extent, in verbal terms, with the result that Weissenhof triggered off a spate of books by German authors that aim to deal encyclopaedically with the materials, the history or the aesthetics of the new style.

[7] The normal attribution to the firm of Brinckmann and van der Vlugt is legally accurate, but Mart Stam headed the design team within the office that produced the main block, and that part is, apparently, entirely his own in inspiration—it has obvious affinities with the Koenigsberg project, in spite of the different structure—and largely his in detail.

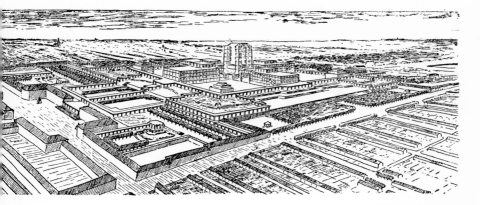

Bruno Taut. City centre from *die Stadtkrone*,
9: central buildings of a projected city piled up
a visual symbol or landmark.
Lyonel Feininger, woodcut from the cover of
first Bauhaus proclamation, 1919. Here, as in
ut's *Stadtkrone*, the emphasis on towers and
t seems to derive from Scheerbart's
sarchitektur.
Eric Mendelsohn. Dye-vat and drying
er, hat factory at Luckenwalde, 1921–1923:
plain and elegant Functional forms mark the
of his Expressionist architecture.

106. Mies van der Rohe. Glass tower project for the
Friedrichstrasse station competition, Berlin, 1919.
Mies's two projects for glass-walled skyscraper office
blocks are the last great manifestations of the
Scheerbartian glass-dream, and the first important
products of the skyscraper enthusiasm that gripped
Berlin architects in the early Twenties.

107. Gropius and Meyer. Skyscraper project for the *Chicago Tribune* tower competition, 1922: an important transitional building in the evolution of Berlin architecture away from Expressionism, it was also the only *Tribune* competition entry that picked up the structural module of the existing printing works at the back of the offices.

108. Mies van der Rohe. Project for a concrete office block, 1922: in spite of the quasi-Expressionist outward stepping of the floors, the dominantly horizontal conception marks the entry of the second phase in Berlin architecture.

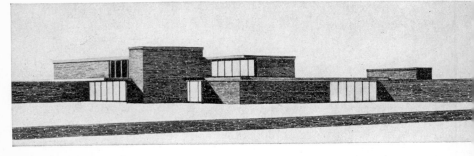

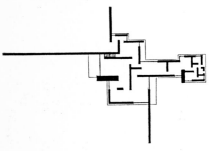

109, 110. Mies van der Rohe. Project for a brick villa, 1923: one of Mies's most celebrated conceptions, spreading into the surrounding space like one of Lissitsky's 'Prouns'.

111, 112, 113. Mies van der Rohe. Wolf House, Guben, 1926: Monument to Karl Liebknecht and Rosa Luxemburg, Berlin, 1926; Lange House Krefeld, 1928: the evolution of a brick architecture from Dutch detailing and Expressionist roughness towards a studied purity relying on the richness of the materials employed.

114. Bruno Taut. 'Gehag' housing, Berlin-Britz, 1927: low cost mass-housing of the sort that established the unique character and standing of the Berlin school.

115. Mies van der Rohe. Block-model of housing and landscaping at the Weissenhof-Siedlung, 1925: town planning seen as a sculptural continuum.

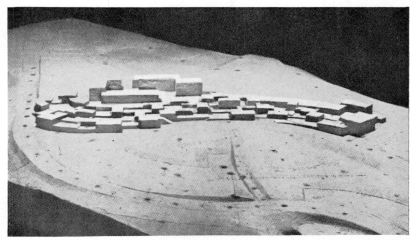

116. Mies van der Rohe. Block of flats, Weissenhof-Siedlung, Stuttgart, 1927: an exterior building-envelope of perfect regularity concealing a number of differently-arranged flats.

117, 118. Bauhaus 'Vorkurs'. Studies of pictorial composition and collages of various materials, executed under Johannes Itten: in spite of his Expressionist tendencies, Itten's use of techniques like collage prepared the way for later developments in the Vorkurs.

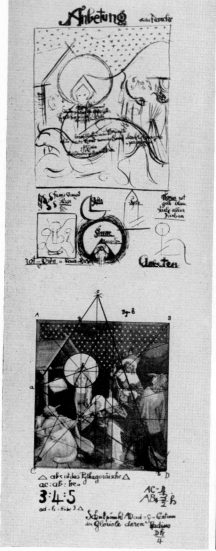

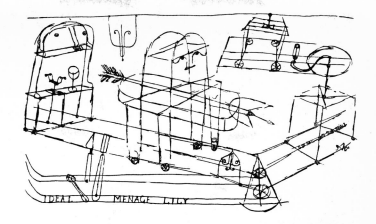

IDEAL MENAGE LILY

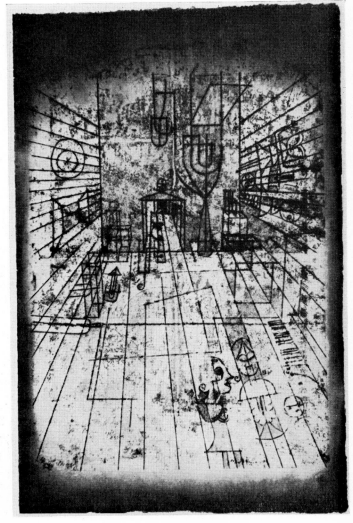

120. Paul Klee.
Ideal Menage Lily, 1920,
Zimmerperspektive,
1920: Klee's drawings,
though created outside
the Elementarist
tradition, and seeming
sometimes to satirize its
mechanolatry (Ideal
Menage), still suggest a
very similar conception
of space to that of, say,
Moholy-Nagy (fig. 126).

295

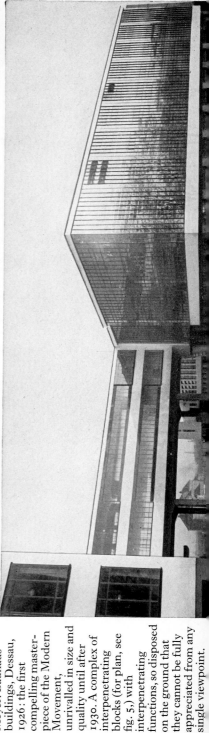

121, 122. Gropius & Meyer. Bauhaus buildings, Dessau, 1926: the first compelling masterpiece of the Modern Movement, unrivalled in size and quality until after 1930. A complex of interpenetrating blocks (for plan, see fig. 5.) with interpenetrating functions, so disposed on the ground that they cannot be fully appreciated from any single viewpoint.

296

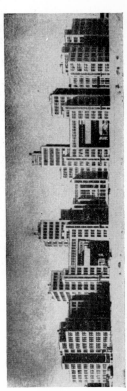

123, 124. Brinck-
mann and van der
Vlugt (designer,
Mart Stam). Main
block of van Nelle
factory, Rotter-
dam, 1927, and
Serafimov and
Kravets, State
Light Industry
Centre, Kharkov,
1926–1930: these
two works from
the extremes of
the Elementarist-
Constructivist
territory were the
only contem-
porary works of
the Modern
Movement to
rival, or exceed,
the scale of the
Bauhaus
buildings.

125. View of New York (the Graybar Building) from
Bruno Taut, *Die Neue Baukunst*: throughout the
Twenties, the U.S.A. continued to offer Europeans,
and especially German writers, an image of the
Futurist city made real.

126. Airshaft of a ship, from
Moholy-Nagy, *Von Material zu
Architektur*, 1928: Moholy, like Le
Corbusier, goes to engineering for
demonstration of his theories—here,
the creation of 'functional' space.
127. Laszlo Moholy-Nagy. Enamel,
1922: one of three versions of a
painting ordered and 'painted' by
telephone in Berlin; like Duchamp's
'Ready-mades', an extreme gesture
towards mechanized art.

abb. 68 die "kaaba" in mekka

foto: gaday team

ein haragestalteter meteor — eine exakte stereometrische figur von eigenen dimensionen — wird zum gegenstand der anbetung, zur kultstätte.

das erste stadium:

1.

die blockhafte plastik:

der materialblock, der seine masse im klaren, unangetasteten volumen zeigt (dolmen in karnak), pyramiden (abb. 67); ferner: naturmonumente; meteoriten: kaaba in mekka (abb. 68); kristallinische blöcke (abb. 69—71).

98

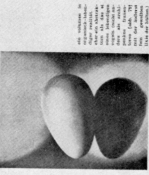

abb. 69 stereometrische figuren, die proelemente der volumengestaltung

foto: herbert bayer

abb. 70 constantin brancusi 1926
plastik für blinde

ein volumen in organisch-lebendiger realität. aber ein abstraktum als das ei eines lebendigen vogels (nicht außen als architektonischer frauentorso (abb. 79) mit der aufbewahrten gewollten linie der haltes.)

99

128. Page opening from Moholy-Nagy, *Von Material zu Architektur*, 1928: one of the most sophisticated products of the Elementarist tradition. *Von Material* puts typo-

129, 130. Mies van der Rohe. Pavilion of the *Deutscher Werkbund*, International Exhibition, Barcelona, 1929: a summation of the possibilities and symbolising powers that underlay the German side of the International style, gathering up traditions that ran back through the Elementarists, the G-group, Berlage, Wright and Schinkel.

131, 132, 133. Le Corbusier and Pierre Jeanneret. *Les Heures Claires*, Poissy-sur-Seine, 1928–1930: the summation of the Latin stream in the International style—a post-Futurist villa, planned around a central ramp, raised on stilts for vehicle circulation, and set down, a pure aesthetic object, in an abstract landscape.

34. Richard Buckminster Fuller. 'Dymaxion' house project, 1927–1930: conceived at the time that the International style was crystallising into a set of forms symbolising the Machine Age, this project for a house of light metals and plastic, planned radially around a core of mechanical services, established a radical technological criticism of the International style as mechanically inadequate.

135, 136, 137. Walter Gropius, Body for Adler Cabriolet, 1930:
Sir Charles Burney, Streamlined cars, 1930: Buckminster
Fuller, Dymaxion ground-taxiing unit, 1933: the end of the
First Machine Age in design can be demonstrated in its
symbolic machine, the automobile. Gropius' Adler, though
handsome, is mechanically backward when compared with the
streamlined, rear-engined harbingers of the next phase.

21: Germany: the encyclopaedics

THE ATMOSPHERE OF 1927 is best given by a book-title that could hardly have been imagined a year earlier—*Der Sieg des neuen Baustils*, Walter Curt Behrendt's contribution to the body of literature on Modern architecture that is explanatory rather than propagandist in aim, though even he fell victim to an old-established exasperation of the propagandists

> When will clients finally realise the spiritual discrepancy between their Louis Seize interiors and their Rolls-Royce cars?

But the victory of the new architecture was real and international—sufficiently so for 1928 to witness the first attacks on it as an 'International Style', for in that year Alexander von Senger published his *Krisis der Architektur*, directed against Modern architecture as a whole, but based entirely on quotations from Le Corbusier's books and from *L'Esprit Nouveau*, which is described as

> . . . this neo-Jacobin review, Le Corbusier's organ, the synthesis of Russian, German and Austrian tendencies, is furthermore, nothing but a disguised Bolshevik propaganda magazine.

The mainstream of Modern architecture had found its International Style, and so had its opponents, for whom von Senger's tone and tactics were to become the norm. But the attitude of the numerous German books that appeared after Weissenhof is not defensive, and their aim is to consolidate the victory of the new style by effecting broad surveys of its materials, its history, its aesthetics. In this context, Ludwig Hilberseimer stands out for his industry, if for no other reason, and is one of the most characteristic figures of the epoch. His career, to this date, had not been outstandingly busy or successful in architecture, but now, under the aegis of Hannes Meyer, he founded a town-planning department at the Bauhaus, and in two years produced four books that give a remarkably full coverage of the Modern Movement as it then understood itself.

In one of them he surveyed the new architecture as a movement covering most of Europe, *Internationale Neue Baukunst*, which illustrated the work of some seventy European architects (and four Americans), and proved his judgement to be remarkably sure—very few of the architects whose work he included have subsequently dropped out of professional esteem, and in at least one case—that of Sant'Elia—subsequent re-appraisals have fully justified his inclusion. Some of his other choices have proven almost clairvoyant: Alberto Sartoris and the Figini-Pollini partnership had hardly a building to their credit at the time that Hilberseimer's book was written.

Two of the other books he wrote at this time were surveys of particular building types—using that term fairly loosely, to cover both *Hallenbauten*, which dealt with auditoria, markets, etc. and *Grosstadt-Architektur* which surveyed public and semi-public buildings of a metropolitan scale. His fourth book, and the most interesting of this group, deals with a particular material, concrete.

Its title, *Beton als Gestalter*, gives a false impression of it, and suggests that it belongs to a current of thought which was becoming increasingly prevalent at this time, tending to interpret the International Style in purely Rationalist terms, as the product of the materials and techniques employed. Lissitsky may well have started this tendency in German-speaking circles, for Hannes Meyer who took it into the Bauhaus had come under his influence, and it is noteworthy that the young Italian architects who formed the like-thinking *Movimento Italiano per l'Architettura Razionale* had also come under Constructivist influence. It is also noteworthy that they were not anti-Traditionalists, and this neo-Rationalist movement in general found considerable reinforcement in the past, as in such studies of the nineteenth century as Giedion's *Bauen in Frankreich*, which will be discussed later.

But Berlin played no great part in this development, which was largely the work of 'provincials' from Switzerland, Italy, and the Anglo-Saxon countries. Though Berlin writers had plenty to say about the new materials at this time their tone was not Rationalistic. Thus, in *Glas im Bau und als Gebrauchsgegenstand*, Artur Korn, whose architecture at this time had taken a very tough, almost *G*, quality, nevertheless writes of glass in an almost poetic tone, laying particular stress on its aesthetic qualities. Indeed, his book begins with an almost Scheerbartian apotheosis of mediaeval stained glass, and then goes on

> Nothing has been lost of the riches of those earlier creations, but it has been reworked in new materials for new functions. A new world of glass has been opened that concedes nothing to the windows of the Gothic world in beauty.
> But we have secured a great advance over them . . . in making an independent glass skin. No more wall and window, even though the window might be the dominant part—this window is the wall itself, this wall is itself the window.
> And therewith a development is consummated, something absolutely new over and above all that the past can show: the denial of the outer wall that for thousands of years had to be made of solid materials—stone, wood or something similar. In this new dispensation the outer wall no longer makes itself visible.
> The interior spatial depths, the form-giving structural frame are in evidence, appearing through the glass wall which itself is only hinted at, only barely to be appreciated through reflected light, distortion and mirror effects.

And therewith appears the truly unique quality of glass compared to all materials hitherto in use: It is there and it is not there.
It is the great mystery membrane, delicate and strong at the same time.

The words 'there and not there' are to be interpreted in more than one sense, for he cites examples of transparency (the Bauhaus), reflectivity (Mies's glass towers) and of the use of non-reflecting glass as an invisible barrier against the weather (a shop designed by himself and his partner Konrad Weitzmann). But his attitude, if poetically inclined, remains practical: he does not philosophise.

Hilberseimer does; and the introduction to *Beton als Gestalter* is a reflective essay on the relationship of architecture as an art to science and technology. His opening paragraph rejects at once both the Rationalist determinism of the nineteenth century and the science-as-spiritualisation of *de Stijl*

> The scientific spirit of the nineteenth century had for its ultimate goal the conquest of the forces of nature. The rapid perfection of scientific methods of research and their technical aids led in every field to unexpected results and caused, for a whole epoch, an over-estimation of the possibilities of technology. The dangers that lurked here for the *Geisteswissenschaften*, through the connection of material conclusions with immaterial conceptions—these dangers can fortunately be avoided with the disciplines grouped as 'Technology'. The discoveries and inventions in this province can be compared directly with reality, and be corrected accordingly

This separation of the spiritual sciences from physical science and technology is remarkable for the time at which it was written, but—since he clearly includes aesthetics among the spiritual sciences—it also involves him in some rather perilous reasoning. Having defined the relationship of technique and architecture thus

> . . . that technique is never more than a means for the art of building, that technique and art are profoundly different.

after having praised engineers for perfecting concrete construction

> unrestricted by aesthetic preconceptions and free from nostalgia for things outside their technique.

he is in a strong position in discussing the quality of buildings where conscious aesthetic intention is apparent, but badly placed where it is not. Thus, he is well placed to castigate Auguste Perret and Martin Elsässer for dressing up their concrete in period style, or Rietveld who is blamed for indulging in *Konstruktivismus* and *artistisches Spiel*, those who disguise the economical aims of reinforced concrete construction with gratuitous mass, and even Gottfried Semper

> who wished to hear of iron used only to increase the tensile strength of mass construction

and not as a visible architectural element in its own right.

But he is badly placed to evaluate a class of buildings that have had peculiar standing in the eyes of Modernists ever since Muthesius—engineering structures.

> If we categorise constructions and projects conceived in the spirit of reinforced concrete construction as architecture, then the aesthetic rules connected with and derived from stone building will no longer serve. For a new sense of space has become effective, a new relationship of support and load that has radically affected the optical aspect of buildings.
>
> Out of mental convenience all this has been given out as 'Neue Sachlichkeit' or simply technology, without, to be sure, anyone having any standards for where technique leaves off and creativity begins. Certainly, purely technical construction is still not architecture, but even in the field of so-called technological building it would still be difficult to draw a line between the creative and the uncreative. And besides, many of these buildings are of an astonishing architectonic quality, powerful originality and primitive architectural feeling.

He offers no solution to this dilemma, except possibly a marginal reference to the concept of *Einheit von Aussen- und Innenbau* as a key to the new architecture, but his closing paragraph suggests that he has little faith in any deductive formulation of rules of judgement.

> Aristotle justly observed that art runs ahead of its theories. The creator is intuitive —the work comes spontaneously from his hands according to its own rules. All science, all research, all perception cannot replace the naive certainty of the artist. The new therefore can be judged neither by the old rules nor by these deduced rules. . . .

Such reasonable doubt, anti-Rationalist but not irrational, seems not to have been shared by those who, in the same two or three years sought to fix the position of the Modern Movement in history. Either they did not recognise the emergence of a specifically new architecture, and gave blanket treatment to all Twentieth-century architecture, progressive or otherwise. Or, alternatively, they recognised a new architecture, but saw it as a continuation of the Rationalist tradition of the previous century. The first attitude made it possible to bring Modern architecture within the scope of existing series of art-historical publications—three volumes of the *Blauen Bücher* edited by Walter Müller-Wulckow and dealing with Factories, Housing, and Public Buildings respectively, put Modern German architecture into an established semi-popular series of picture-books, while Gustav Platz's compendious *Die Baukunst der neuesten Zeit* elevated it to the level of the Propyläen-Verlag, and thus to the highest levels of commerical art-historical publishing.

Works that recognised the emergence of a new architecture but linked it back exclusively to restricted aspects of the nineteenth century also appeared at both the popular and specialist levels. The most influential of the former class was undoubtedly Bruno Taut's *Modern Architecture*, which appeared in a German edition as *Die Neue Baukunst in Europa und Amerika* in the same year (1929). The German edition was scantily provided with plans and sections, the English edition was entirely innocent of them, but this, on Gropius's word, was apparently considered proper to works intended for a wide readership. However, the book has some subsidiary interests besides the overriding one of being the first large popular work on the Modern Movement to appear in English. It gave importance to the work of the Expressionists[1] and of the Amsterdam School at a time when their reputations were declining, and its attitude to America is fairly typical of a general tendency of the time.

During the Twenties the attention of German architects began to wander from the work of Wright, to which it had been directed by Berlage and the Wasmuth publications, to the other America, the skyscraper America admired by the Futurists and Le Corbusier. Taut's attention has not wandered very far, only to a handful of New York buildings, such as the Graybar Building (seen in a purely Futurist context with the elevated railway cutting across its base) and the grain silos that had already been canonised by the *Ingenieurbauten* tradition, but other German architectural observers had been almost completely diverted. Both Mendelsohn and Richard Neutra had gone to the USA with the intention (or at least the main intention) of meeting Wright and Sullivan, but in Mendelsohn's *Amerika* and *Russland Europa Amerika* it is the skyscraper image that dominates and in Neutra's *Wie baut Amerika?* it is the techniques of skyscraper building in steel that occupy his attention.

But *Modern Architecture* also puts the new style firmly in a line of descent from a few selected aspects of nineteenth-century design, even to the extent of pronouncing that

> With the outbreak of the War, the history of Modern architecture may be considered closed

and, quite consistently with this view, he pays no attention to the Cubist, Futurist and Abstractionist Movements that had helped to forge the formal language that he himself was using by this time. In this, however, he was supported, influenced even, by a book from which some of his illustrations were taken, a book that has had a wide and curious influence on the Modern Movement's view of its own history—*Bauen in Frankreich*; *Eisen, Eisenbeton*, by Sigfried Giedion. The title suggests the book's aim quite concisely—to systematise and bring up to date the view of nineteenth-century engineering construction advanced by Muthesius and by Meyer in the early years of the century, by including the reinforced concrete work done under the aegis of Perret and Freyssinet since their time. It is important because it helped to give the International Style a sense of international ancestry but it did so in a biased manner. The commitment of the book is to the Rationalist side, but the author was also an art historian trained under Wölfflin. His art-historical training tends to make him assume that things that look alike must have some historical connection; his Rationalist inclination, however, tends to make him overlook purely aesthetic determinants

[1] Taut pays tribute particularly to Olbrich, August Endell, and Poelzig but—in spite of devoting half a page and two illustrations to the Glass Pavilion at Cologne—he is completely silent on Scheerbart.

of style, and between the two, a whole section of the history of Modern architecture is mislaid. Yet there is much about the book that commands respect.

His estimate of the historian's position in the relativistic world of twentieth-century thought is commendably honest.

> The historian too stands in time, not above it. He has lost his pedestal in eternity. . . .
> Past present and future are for us an uninterruptible process. However, we do not live backwards but forwards. Though the past strengthens us with the assurance that our wills are not limited and individual, the future, come what may, appears of greater consequence to us.

Out of these concepts of a responsibility to the developing present, of the imperturbable continuity of history, and of a corporate will (or *Zeitgeist*) he evolves an attitude that inexorably condemns him to an incomplete view of the rise of the International Style.

> The task of the historian is to recognise beginnings and—despite all the debris that overlays them—to bring out the continuity of development . . . out of the vast complexity of a past period to expose those elements that became points of departure for the future.

As will be seen, these two last statements give a programme with a strong element of *parti-pris* in it. Any historian is liable to view the past according to the preoccupations of his own time, but Giedion makes this a deliberate, not accidental, approach and the emphasis on continuity leaves him at liberty to overlook anything that he does not wish to deal with, as being mere 'dèbris'.

As a result, the history of iron and reinforced concrete is discussed primarily from the viewpoint of one who had only 'discovered' Modern architecture four years before he began to write this book, at the time of the *Bauhauswoche* of 1923, and had taken over the preoccupations of the times as if they were the preoccupations of the whole Movement. He makes direct comparisons of nineteenth-century engineering structure and twentieth-century architecture, frequently reinforcing them with massive black arrows. Free-standing columns in the *Réserve* of Labrouste's *Bibliothèque St Geneviève* are confronted with free-standing columns in Le Corbusier's *Maison Cook*; the frame structure of Saulnier's *Chocolat Menier* factory is confronted with the frame of Mies van der Rohe's Weissenhof flats; the glazed walling of Eiffel's *Grande Galerie* for the 1878 Exposition in Paris with the glazed walling of the Bauhaus; and the lifts of the Eiffel Tower with the suspended railways of Mart Stam's scheme for the redevelopment of the Rokin. To these comparisons are added an apotheosis of the *École Polytechnique* as one of the ultimate sources of the new architecture, and a list of 'prophetic' quotations from Théophile Gautier, Anatole de Baudot, César Daly, Octave Mirbeau and others—texts from holy writ that Le

Corbusier was quick to employ in his own defence during the wrangles over the League of Nations competition.

Much of this had involved solid, if indiscriminate, research work and uninhibited revaluations of familiar structures like the Eiffel Tower, but conspicuously missing from the argument is the 'dèbris' that had accumulated since and made things like free-standing columns and glazed walling of importance to architects, the whole revolution in architectural theory that had been going on from 1908 and was barely completed two decades later when *Bauen in Frankreich* was published. Yet the text of the book reveals at many points that Giedion's own viewpoint was largely shaped by that revolution: the caption, headed *Umgestaltung der Erdoberfläche*, to a picture of industrial landscape outside Marseilles shows a Futurist interest in multi-level circulation and Sant'Elia's 'reordering the earth's crust'; he refers to *Konstruktivismus* in the nineteenth century, and at one point he uses a phrase whose extraction is manifestly Doesburgian:

die Elemente für eine kollektive Gestaltung schaffen.

While, clearly, Giedion's terms of reference did not necessarily require him to recognise every beginning, and while he has subsequently repaired the omission in his later book *Space Time and Architecture*, the absence of the theoretical and aesthetic 'débris' from *Bauen in Frankreich* has given most of its readers the impression that the International Style is directly descended from the *Grands Constructeurs* of the nineteenth century, and is purely Rational and Functional in its approach. Such an idea was sympathetic to many architects at the time, and it was of particular usefulness to apologists of the style in Anglo-Saxon countries where, despite the efforts of Geoffrey Scott, firmly established Ruskinian prejudices made argument from moral, rather than aesthetic grounds, more effective. Yet, by a fortunate historical irony, when men in those countries set out to train young architects in the supposedly Functionalist disciplines of the new architecture, the only pedagogic textbook available to them, the book that made the Bauhaus method available to the world, was almost exactly opposite in bias, was sophisticated on just those subjects where Giedion was naïve, and by a further historical irony, was the work of the typographer of *Bauen in Frankreich*, Moholy-Nagy.

At first sight there might appear to be a more than superficial connection between the two books—Moholy has a warm footnote reference to *Bauen in Frankreich*, and the title of his Book, *Von Material zu Architektur* might suggest that this too is a work of the Rationalist persuasion. In fact, the *von . . . zu* does little more than indicate the order in which the subject-matter of the book is tackled, but this title may well have been chosen with one eye on the way advanced architectural opinion was running, since it was originally promised as *Von Kunst zu Leben*, and republished in English as *The New Vision* late in the Nineteen-thirties when the tide of opinion had changed again. This last title was, in any case, the truest, for what Moholy sets out is something that Le Corbusier might have termed a *formation de l'optique moderne*. It is almost exclusively concerned with visual and formal problems, and deals with them in a resolutely Modern manner, its examples, precepts and standards being drawn almost entirely from within the Modern Movement itself.

In this it reflects a great deal of its author's personality and background. Born in 1895, Laszlo Moholy-Nagy was a clear decade younger than the pioneers in either architecture or the plastic arts, and grew up in a world in which Modern art existed already. His early imagination was coloured by an agency that had come into the world at about the same time as himself, the illustrated magazines, to such an extent that he was overcome with disappointment on finding that Szeged, the nearest town of any size to his boyhood home in Hungary, had no skyscrapers. An injury received a few months after that which carried off Sant'Elia, and in the same battle zone though on the other side, kept him out of most of the later fighting in the War, and gave him time to investigate Modern art, although his formal training, like Marinetti's, was in law. By the time he arrived in Berlin, early in 1921, starving but a little ahead of other Abstractionists from Eastern Europe, he had undergone the education of a Modernist, revolutions and all, in compressed form.

Although he kept up his Hungarian connections, and represented the Hungarian, expatriate *MA-Gruppe* at the various congresses (Weimar Düsseldorf, etc.) of the period, he was soon deeply involved in the turbulent artistic culture of Berlin. His authorship of the *Aufruf zur Elementaren Kunst* has already been mentioned, and he was in touch with Lissitsky from the time of the latter's arrival, also with Gabo, Schwitters and Arp, with the *Stijl* and *Sturm* connections. But once a certain amount of Futurist rhetoric had been worked out of his system, his devotion was almost exclusively to the Russian connection, and from some point in 1921 onwards, his work depends on Malevitsch's Suprematist elements of circle, cross and square, at least for its point of departure, often for its entire formal repertoire. From a slightly earlier date he had begun to interest himself in 'Modern' techniques like collage, and 'Modern' materials like transparent plastics, not merely because they were new but because a consuming interest in light, as the ultimate *malerische Element*, felt by other young painters beside himself, could not be satisfied with traditional means.

However, his most spectacular excursion into Modern methods had quite another stimulus, and quite a different import, and must rank with Duchamp's 'Bottle-rack' as a major gesture towards a revision of the relationship between artist, subject, and public in a mechanised society. At his one man show at the *Sturm* gallery in 1922, Moholy exhibited a group of Elementarist compositions including three of identical design but differing size, of whose creation he gives the following account[2]

> . . . in 1922 I ordered by telephone from a sign factory five paintings in por-
> celain enamel. I had the factory's colour chart before me and I sketched my
> paintings on graph-paper. At the other end of the telephone the factory super-
> visor had the same kind of paper divided into squares. He took down the dic-
> tated shapes in the correct position.

This intrusion of a whole industrial organisation and a telephone service into the accepted conventions of artistic creation has clearly the same kind of Dadaist significance as Duchamp's elimination of artist and painting from those conventions with the 'Bottle-rack', though Moholy was, ap-parently, more conscious of the positive aspects of his action and the claims they made for the status of mechanical methods. And where Du-champ's apologists tended to explain his intentions in a platonic sense, Moholy was prepared to do this for himself—his esteem of the Phileban solids has been noted, and apropos the 'telephone paintings' he later wrote

> But my belief is that mathematically harmonious shapes, executed precisely
> are filled with emotional quality, and they represent the perfect balance be,
> tween feeling and intellect.

If, as seems possible, he felt this way at the time that these paintings were executed, then they are not to be categorised with the tough-minded arte-facts of the *G* connection—indeed, that party in Berlin seems to have regarded Moholy's *Vorkurs* at the Bauhaus as being just as deplorably 'arty' as Itten's.

Nevertheless, it is noteworthy that the first task assigned to him when he joined the Bauhaus in 1923 was the reform of the metal-working shop, which suggests that he was regarded as particularly equipped for techniques and materials of that kind, and he only took over the *Vorkurs* later in the same year, in collaboration with Josef Albers, who had been allotted to the preliminary course a little earlier. Exactly how much of the *Vorkurs*, as it found its way into *Von Material zu Architektur*, is due to Albers and how much to Moholy is now difficult to assess, but it is clear that the latter soon became the dominant personality, and not only in the *Vorkurs*, for he seems to have risen rapidly to a position of eminence second only to that of Gropius as an exponent of Bauhaus ideas and a shaper of Bauhaus policy. Thus, although the editorship of the *Bauhausbücher* was ostensibly shared by himself and Gropius, the titles and authors represent so closely his own syncretic interests that one may suspect that they were largely his own choice—as if he wished all the Bauhaus public to have the same broad ground in the modern '-isms' as himself.

Such a wish clearly underlies, in part, the organisation of the subject-matter of *Von Material zu Architektur*. Though Moholy disclaims that it

[2] This account of the telephone paintings is taken from the autobiographical fragment *Abstract of an Artist*, which appeared as a supplement to the second American edition of *The New Vision* (New York, 1949).

is 'lexikalisch' in its treatment of materials and methods, it is encyclopaedic in its coverage of the Modern Movement, and illustrates, apart from Bauhaus products, works by Schwitters, Marinetti, Picasso, Brancusi, Archipenko, Barlach, Belling, Pevsner, Schlemmer, Vantongerloo, Servranckx, Rodin, Rodchenko, Cocteau, Gabo, Lipchitz, Le Corbusier, Stam, and Eiffel. It also discusses at less or greater length the following movements: Abstraction, Dadaism, Futurism, Constructivism, Tactilism, *merzbild*, Cubism, neo-Plasticism, Realism, Surrealism, Purism, Pointillism, and Impressionism, and the following extensions of the visual culture of educated Europeans: photography, microphotography, crystallography, kinetic sculpture, films, illuminated advertising, montage and primitive art.

This wide-ranging visual erudition and sharp appreciation of the environment of urban living are difficult to parallel, except possibly in the art and writings of Boccioni, but Moholy has the advantage over Boccioni in his ability to draw this mass of information and experience into a quite compact and orderly body of theory—the first orderly body of theory to be drawn out of, rather than put into, the Modern Movement. The first impression gained on reading the book is that for Moholy art started in 1900. There are a few references to the art of the past—the Pyramids and the Kaaba at Mecca to make a point about Phileban forms, a Leonardo and a Giambologna to make another point about sculpture—but his view does not really extend back beyond the Eiffel Tower. He harks back to neither the geometry of Greece, nor the masonry of the Middle Ages, he is not interested in temples and cathedrals, his theories are to derive their authority from the present condition of culture, not from history.

The first part of the book is accordingly devoted to a discussion of the relationships between individuals, their mechanised environment, and the process of education. The line of argument was, by 1928, an established Bauhaus thesis, concerning the need to educate complete personalities not narrow specialists, and the flavour of the discussion is adequately given by some of the paragraph-headings

The future needs the whole man
Not against technology, but with it
Man, not the product, is the aim
Everybody is talented
The responsibility for putting this into effect lies with all of us
Utopia?
Education has a great task to fulfil here

and this task of education is outlined thus

We need Utopians of genius, a new Jules Verne; not to sketch in broad perspective an easily grasped technical utopia, but the very existence of future men whose basic laws of being respond to instinctive simplicity as well as the complicated relationships of life.
Our educators have the task of ordering development towards the healthy exercise of our powers, to lay the foundations of a balanced life even in the earliest stage of training.

He then pays tribute to the educational pioneers whose work preceded the Bauhaus—a register of names and movements that is a history in itself, and the concluding paragraphs of section I seek to fix the place of the Bauhaus in this picture of society, culture and education—and to explain once more the reasons for handicraft training in a mechanised society.

Whatever the educational method outlined in the other three sections of *Von Material zu Architektur* may owe to the pioneers whom Moholy had listed in the first section, it has three very clear debts to sources nearer home: To Itten's original *Vorkurs*, to Klee and Kandinsky, and to Malevitsch. The debt to Itten is clear and fundamental—the emphasis on learning by doing and on the nature of materials. Moholy's original contribution here is in changing over from the idea of an intuitive grasp of the 'inner nature' of materials to an objective, physical assessment of their ascertainable properties of texture, strength, flexibility, transparency, workability, etc.

The debt to Klee and Kandinsky lies in the *von . . . zu* organisation of the book. Both of their *Bauhausbücher* had started from a consideration of points, and proceeded from them to lines and thus to planes, at which level Kandinsky leaves off, though Klee goes on to volume and space. In Moholy's non-draughtsmanly view, point and line were simply aspects of planes, which he would call surfaces, but from that level onwards he proceeds in step with Klee, albeit handling ideas in a manner that was utterly different in every way from that of the *Pädagogisches Skizzenbuch*. Malevitsch is his predecessor in visual erudition, in close critical analyses of Cubist paintings, and in emphasis on such things as the views down from, and up to, aeroplanes.

The first point in which Moholy transcends all his predecessors is in his phenomenal command of the non-artistic visual experiences of his time. Words cannot convey the impact made on the eye by the original edition of this book, its emphatic typography, its businesslike layout, and the range of its illustrations, from neat diagrams and models of Bauhaus equipment, through reproductions of original works of art, and scientific documentary photographs, to extraordinary agency pictures of such things as dumps of old motor-tyres, airships, sporting events, street-scenes, film sets, and a celebrated sequence, illustrating a point about texture, of a cat's fur in negative, an old man's skin and a mouldy apple. Brought up on illustrated magazines, Moholy communicates in this book something of the visual richness of a magazine-culture and brings it to bear upon the problem of visual education. For these images, however striking in their own right or in juxtaposition are not, so to speak, a *musée imaginaire*,[3] they support and explain the educational system that is expounded in the three main sections of the book. Section II begins with the tactile qualities of materials, and

[3] Any more than are the illustrations—sometimes even more bizarre—in Amedée Ozenfant's almost exactly contemporary book *The Foundations of Modern Art*.

illustrates the famous tactile-machines that were devised for th
gation at the Bauhaus and then goes on to consider the other aspc
surfaces of materials that can be physically appreciated and physi
manipulated, culminating in the use of surfaces as a screen for the projection of patterns of light. Section III also culminates in the use of light, as
the ultimate means of creating sculptural volume, but the road that leads
to it is interesting for the way in which it shows his methodical mind at
work.

He begins with the 'Block-like', a term which includes any unmodelled or
unpierced solid of recognisable geometrical form. These recognisable forms
are, as might be expected, the Phileban solids, but later in the section he
produces an extended list of forms, in order to encompass also non-
Phileban solids encountered in science and technology.

> Until a short time ago,[4] geometrical elements, such as the sphere, cone, cylinder,
> cube, prism and pyramid, were taken as the foundation of sculpture. But
> biotechnical elements have now been added. . . .
> These biotechnical elements formerly entered more particularly into techno-
> logy, where the functional approach called for maximum economy. Raoul
> Francé has distinguished seven biotechnical elements: crystal, sphere, cone,
> plate, strip, rod and spiral (screw); he says that these are the basic technical
> elements of the whole world. They suffice for all its processes and are sufficient
> to bring them to their optimum condition.[5]

However, these extensions to the repertoire of regular forms occur somewhat later in the argument, after he has proceeded from pure blocks to
modelled blocks and thence to pierced blocks, from standing sculpture to
balanced and kinetic sculpture or mobiles, and just before he tackles the
problem of the creation of virtual volumes by the movement of lights in
space (fireworks, illuminated advertising). By this point he is already
entangled with the subject of Section IV, Space, but before tackling space
he sets out, in a neat table, the *Formlehre* that has been covered so far

> A general systematisation of the elements (of artistic creation) is based upon
> the relations of
>   1. Known forms, such as
>   mathematical and geometrical shapes
>   biotechnical elements
>   2. New forms, such as
>   free shapes
> The production of new forms may be based on
>   1. relations of measurement (golden section and other proportions)
>   position (measurable in angles)
>   movement (speed, direction, thrust, intersection, telescoping interlocking,
>   penetration, mutual interpenetration)

[4] Just how short that time had been since these Phileban solids had been so highly
esteemed, may be judged by comparing this statement with Moholy's letter to
Wilhelm Wagenfeldt, quoted in the previous chapter.
[5] Francé, whose ideas had been discussed earlier in the book, was not, it seems,
an authority of standing in the field, but the author of works of popularisation on
scientific subjects.

2. differing aspects of material
   structure
   texture
   surface treatment
   massing
3. light (colour, optical illusions, reflected light, mirroring)

The relationships of forms may become effective as

1. contrasts
2. deviations
3. variations
   shifting and dislocation ⎤
   repetition   ⎬ and their combinations
   rotation   ⎥
   mirror images   ⎦

With this behind him, he turns to space, which for him is so much the stuff of architecture that the terms are interchangeable. He sees the play of space as the distinguishing characteristic of Modern architecture, so that the possibility of confusion in nomenclature as between large sculpture and small architecture which existed in older cultures when architecture too was only the manipulation of volume, no longer exists. The nature of this space is defined by him in various ways—at the beginning of Section IV he lists forty-four adjectives that have been used to describe aspects of space, and then cites a minimum definition

Space is the relation between the position of bodies.

This scientific definition he will accept only as a point of departure, and from it he approaches his subject on a number of lines. Firstly, as an aspect of functional organisation

The elements necessary to the fulfilment of the function of a building unite in a spatial creation that can become a spatial experience for us. The ordering of space in this case is no more than the most economical union of planning methods and human needs. The current programme of life plays an important role in this, but does not entirely determine the type of space created.

Visual justification of this concept of functional space is provided by a view up an airshaft, in which the stairs and landings are all pierced to promote better air-flow, and at the same time create quite accidentally the kind of play of space that would attract an Elementarist. Further explanation can be found in the caption to another illustration.

The concept 'façade' is already passing from architecture. No place remains in buildings for that which is not adapted to some function: to the development of the front (balconies, advertising) is added the exploitation of the roofs (garden terraces, landing grounds).

This last view of a building engaged functionally with the surrounding space on every side is clearly Futurist, and there are further descriptions of spatial manipulation which confirm that his attitude is both Elementarist and Futurist in approach. On the Elementarist side

Out of cosmic space a 'piece of space' is cut by means of a, sometimes complicated-seeming, network of limiting and interpenetrating strips, wires and sheets of glazing, as if space were a divisible compact substance. Thus, modern architecture is founded on a full interpenetration with outer space

and on the Futurist side

The organisation of this space-creation will be accomplished thus: measurably, by the limits of physical bodies, immeasurably by dynamic fields of force, and space-creation will be the confluence of ever-fluid spatial existences.

Though the last quotation is a very toned-down version of Boccioni's 'field theory', most of the illustrations to this section thunder with Futurist rhetoric, even to the extent of being faked to heighten the effect, as where a flight of five Swedish seaplanes has been obviously collaged on to a view of a multi-level traffic intersection in San Diego, Calif.

No other document of the period gives so graphic or so encyclopaedic a view of what the architect can do with space, but it is emphasised that he does not work upon space as a private aesthetic game

The experience of space is not a privilege of the gifted few, but a biological function

and this brings in the most interesting aspect of Moholy's view of space: experienced space, and the linked concept of 'biological'.

We must acknowledge that in every respect, space is a reality of our sensory experience.
Man becomes conscious of space . . . first through the sense of sight.
The experience of the visual relations of bodies may be tested by movement, by changing one's position, and by the sense of touch. Further possibilities for the experience of space lie in the acoustical and balancing organs.

Much of the importance of this view lies in the way in which it inverts earlier ideas on the subject. Just as he had inverted Itten's idea of the 'inner nature' of materials and replaced it by an emphasis on their ascertainable physical properties, so Moholy replaces the idea of space entertained by say, Geoffrey Scott, as something affecting the inner nature of man by a symbolic *Einfühlung*, with the idea of space as something affecting the sense organs of men by direct physical *Erlebnis*. Scott would have taken the part played by the sense organs as a mere means to the greater end of aesthetic experience, but for Moholy the mechanics are what matters, and are the aesthetic experience itself.

Architecture—the ordering of space—is justified in Moholy's eyes in so far as it furthers the ascertainable biological needs of man, and where the book has a weakness in the eyes of a reader of today is in never coming to grips, in detail, with those needs. At the time at which it was written, they could probably be taken for granted since the subject was in the air, at least in the negative sense of minimum standards of sanitation, daylighting, floor-space, ventilation, etc. and anyone familiar with slums such as those that were still being cleared at Frankfurt am Main, would know what Moholy had in mind when he quoted the *grausam wahren Spruch* of the low-life illustrator Heinrich Zille

318

You can kill a man with a building just as easily as with an axe.

Even so, the concept of 'The Biological taken as the guide in everything' is clear in general outline, and it leads him to a restatement of a principle that tended to be overlooked in the Twenties

> Today it is a question of nothing less than the reconquest of the biological fundamentals. Only then can the maximum use be made of technical advances in physical culture, nutritional science, dwelling design and the organisation of work

summed up in the slogan already quoted

> Man, not the product, is the aim.

His attitude emerges as a kind of non-Determinist Functionalism, based no longer on the bare logic of structural Rationalism, but upon the study of man as a variable organism. Though he probably accepted ideas like Le Corbusier's *besoins-type*—Giedion's use of the word *Existenzminimum* is another of the same family—his system was built on more liberal foundations than these, and was capable of interpretation and reinterpretation in a wider context than that of the International Style. For this reason, if for no other, it occupies the unexpected position of being at the same time the first book entirely derived from the Modern Movement, and also one of the first to point the way to the next steps forward.

22: Conclusion: Functionalism and Technology

BY THE MIDDLE of the Thirties it was already common practice to use the word *Functionalism*, as a blanket term for the progressive architecture of the Twenties and its canon of approved forerunners that had been set up by writers like Sigfried Giedion. Yet, leaving the shortlived *G* episode in Berlin on one side, it is doubtful if the ideas implicit in Functionalism—let alone the word itself—were ever significantly present in the minds of any of the influential architects of the period. Scholiasts may care to dispute the exact date on which this misleading word was first used as the label for the International Style, but there is little doubt that the first consequential use was in Alberto Sartoris's book *Gli Elementi dell'architettura Funzionale*, which appeared in Milan in 1932. Responsibility for the term is laid on Le Corbusier's shoulders—the work was originally to have been called *Architettura Razionale*, or something similar, but, in a letter which is reprinted as a preface to the book, Le Corbusier wrote

> The title of your book is limited: it is a real fault to be constrained to put the word *Rational* on one side of the barricade, and leave only the word *Academic* to be put on the other. Instead of Rational say *Functional*. . . .

Most critics of the Thirties were perfectly happy to make this substitution of words, but not of ideas, and *Functional* has, almost without exception been interpreted in the limited sense that Le Corbusier attributed to *Rational*, a tendency which culminated in the revival of a nineteenth-century determinism such as both Le Corbusier and Gropius had rejected, summed up in Louis Sullivan's empty jingle

> Form follows function

Functionalism, as a creed or programme, may have a certain austere nobility, but it is poverty-stricken symbolically. The architecture of the Twenties, though capable of its own austerity and nobility, was heavily, and designedly, loaded with symbolic meanings that were discarded or ignored by its apologists in the Thirties. Two main reasons emerge for this decision to fight on a narrowed front. Firstly, most of those apologists came from outside the countries—Holland, Germany and France—that had done most to create the new style, and came to it late. They thus failed to participate in those exchanges of ideas, collisions of men and movements, congresses and polemics, in which the main lines of thought and practice were roughed out before 1925, and they were strangers to the local conditions that coloured them. Thus, Sigfried Giedion, Swiss, caught only the tail end of this process in 1923; Sartoris, Italian, missed it almost completely; Lewis Mumford, American, in spite of his sociological perceptiveness, was too remotely placed to have any real sense of the aesthetic issues involved—hence his largely irrelevant tergiversations on the problem of monumentality.

The second reason for deciding to fight on the narrowed front was that there was no longer any choice of whether or not to fight. With the International Style outlawed politically in Germany and Russia, and crippled economically in France, the style and its friends were fighting for a toehold in politically-suspicious Fascist Italy, aesthetically-indifferent England, and depression-stunned America. Under these circumstances it was better to advocate or defend the new architecture on logical and economic grounds than on grounds of aesthetics or symbolisms that might stir nothing but hostility. This may have been good tactics—the point remains arguable— but it was certainly misrepresentation. Emotion had played a much larger part than logic in the creation of the style; inexpensive buildings had been clothed in it, but it was no more an inherently economical style than any other. The true aim of the style had clearly been, to quote Gropius's words about the Bauhaus and its relation to the world of the Machine Age

... to invent and create forms symbolising that world.

and it is in respect of such symbolic forms that its historical justification must lie.

How far it had succeeded in its own terms in creating such terms, and in carrying such symbolism, can best be judged by examining two buildings, widely held to be masterpieces, and both designed in 1928. One of them is the German Pavilion at the Barcelona Exhibition of 1929, a work of Mies van der Rohe, so purely symbolic in intention that the concept of Functionalism would need to be stretched to the point of unrecognisability before it could be made to fit it—the more so since it is not easy to formulate in Rational terms precisely what it was intended to symbolise. A loose background, rather than a precise exposition, of the probable intentions can be established from Mies's pronouncements on exhibitions in 1928

The era of monumental expositions that make money is past. Today we judge an exposition by what it accomplishes in the cultural field.
Economic, technical and cultural conditions have changed radically. Both technology and industry face entirely new problems. It is very important for our culture and our society, as well as for technology and industry, to find good solutions. German industry, and indeed European industry as a whole, must understand and solve these specific tasks. The path must lead from quantity towards quality—from the extensive to the intensive.

Along this path industry and technology will join with the forces of thought and culture.

We are in a period of transition—a transition that will change the world.

To explain and help along this transition will be the responsibility of future expositions. . . .

The ambiguities of these statements were resolved in the Pavilion by architectural usages that tapped many sources of symbolism—or, at least sources of architectural prestige. Attention has been drawn to echoes of Wright, of *de Stijl* and *Schinkelschüler* tradition, in the Pavilion, but its full richness is only apparent when these references are rendered precise. All three of these echoes are, in practice, summed up in a mode of occupying space which is strictly Elementarist. Its horizontal planes, which have been likened to Wright, and its scattered vertical surfaces, whose distribution on plan has been referred to van Doesburg, mark out one of Moholy's 'pieces of space' in such a way that a 'full penetration with outer space' is effectively achieved. Further, the distribution of the columns which support the roof slab without assistance from the vertical planes, is completely regular and their spacing suggests the Elementarist concept of space as a measurable continuum, irrespective of the objects it contains. And again, the podium on which the whole structure stands, in which Philip Johnson has found 'a touch of Schinkel', extending on one side a good way beyond the area covered by the roof slab, is also a composition in its own right in plan because of the two pools let into it, and thus resembles the patterned base-boards which form an active part in those Abstract studies of volumetric relations that came from the Ladowski-Lissitsky circle, and, like them, appears to symbolise 'infinite space' as an active component of the whole design.

To this last effect the materials also contribute, since the marble floor of the podium, everywhere visible, or at least appreciable even where covered by carpeting, emphasises the spatial continuity of the complete scheme. But this marble, and the marbling of the walls, has another level of meaning—the feeling of luxury it imparts sustains the idea of transition from quantity to quality of which Mies had spoken, and introduces further paradoxical echoes of both Berlage and Loos. These walls are space-creators, in Berlage's sense and have been 'let alone from floor to cornice' in the manner that Berlage admired in Wright; yet, if it be objected that the sheets of marble or onyx with which they are faced are 'decoration hung on them' such as Berlage disapproved, one could properly counter that Adolf Loos, the enemy of decoration, was prepared to admit large areas of strongly patterned marble as wall-cladding in his interiors.

The continuity of the space is further demonstrated by the transparency of the glass walls that occur in various parts of the scheme, so that a visitor's eye might pass from space to space even where his foot could not. On the other hand the glass was tinted so that its materiality could also be appreciated, in the manner of Artur Korn's *There and not There* paradox. The glass of these walls is carried in chromium glazing bars, and the chromium surface is repeated on the coverings of the cruciform columns. This confrontation of rich modern materials with the rich ancient material of the marble is a manifestation of that tradition of the parity of artistic and anti-artistic materials that runs back through Dadaism and Futurism to the *papiers collés* of the Cubists.

One can also distinguish something faintly Dadaist and even anti-Rationalist in the non-structural parts of the Pavilion. A Mondriaanesque Abstract logical consistency, for instance, would have dictated something other than the naturalistic nude statue by Kolbe that stands in the smaller pool—in this architecture it has something of the incongruity of Duchamp's 'Bottle-rack' in an art exhibition, though it lives happily enough with the marble wall that serves as a background to it. Again, the movable furniture, and particularly the massive steel-framed chairs flout, consciously, one suspects, the canons of economy inherent in that Rationalism that del Marle had proposed as the motive force behind the employment of steel in chairs; they are rhetorically over-size, immensely heavy, and do not use the material in such a way as to extract maximum performance from it.

It is clear that even if it were profitable to apply strict standards of Rationalist efficiency or Functionalist formal determinism to such a structure, most of what makes it architecturally effective would go unnoted in such an analysis. The same is true of the designs of Le Corbusier, whose work, while often extremely practical, does not yield up its secrets to logical analysis alone. In his *Dom-ino* project for instance, he postulated a structure whose only given elements were the floor slabs and the columns that supported them. The disposition of the walls was thus left at liberty, but some critics have logically extrapolated also that this left Le Corbusier at the mercy of his floor slabs. Nothing could be farther from the truth as far as his completed buildings are concerned which, from the villa at Chaux-de-Fonds onwards, have their floor slabs treated in a most cavalier fashion, and much of their internal architecture created by breaking through from one storey to another. Conversely, if there is a building in which the horizontal slabs are absolute, it is Mies's Barcelona Pavilion—the pools merely diversify the surface of the podium, nothing breaks through the roof slab and nothing rises above it; the whole building is designed almost in two dimensions, and this is true of much of his later work as well.

In the case of the other building of 1928 which it is proposed to study here, Le Corbusier's house, *Les Heures Claires*, built for the Savoye family at Poissy-sur-Seine and completed in 1930, the vertical penetrations are of crucial importance in the whole design. They are not large in plan but, since they are effected by a pedestrian ramp, whose balustrades make bold diagonals across many internal views, they are very conspicuous to a person using the house. Furthermore, this ramp was designed as the preferred route of what the architect calls the *promenade architecturale* through the various spaces of the building—a concept which appears to lie close to that almost mystical meaning of the word 'axis' that he had employed in *Vers une Architecture*. The floors connected by this ramp are strongly characterised functionally—*on vit par étage*—the ground floor being taken up with services and servants, transport and entrance facilities, and a guest room; the first floor given over to the main living accommodation, virtually a week-end bungalow complete with patio; and the highest floor a roof garden with sun-bathing deck and viewing platform, surrounded by a windscreen wall.

This, of course, is only the functional breakdown; what makes the building architecture by Le Corbusier's standards and enables it to touch the heart, is the way these three floors have been handled visually. The house as a whole is white—*le couleur-type*—and square—one of *les plus belles formes*—set down in a sea of uninterrupted grass—*le terrain idéal*—which the architect has called a Virgilian Landscape. Upon this traditional ground he erected one of the least traditional buildings of his career, rich in the imagery of the Twenties. The ground floor is set back a considerable distance on three sides from the perimeter of the block, and the consequent shadow into which it is plunged was deepened by dark paint and light-absorbent areas of fenestration. When the house is viewed from the grounds, this floor hardly registers visually, and the whole upper part of the house appears to be delicately poised in space, supported only by the row of slender pilotis under the edge of the first floor—precisely that species of material-immaterial illusionism that Oud had prophesied, but that Le Corbusier more often practised.

However, the setting back of the ground floor has further meaning. It leaves room for a motor-car to pass between the wall and the pilotis supporting the floor above; the curve of this wall on the side away from the road was, Le Corbusier claims, dictated by the minimum turning circle of a car. A car, having set down its passengers at the main entrance on the apex of this curve, could pass down the other side of the building, still under the cover of the floor above, and return to the main road along a drive parallel to that on which it had approached the house. This appears to be nothing less than a typically Corbusian 'inversion' of the test-track on roof of the Matté-Trucco's Fiat factory, tucked under the building instead of laid on top of it, creating a suitably emotive approach to the home of a fully motorised post-Futurist family. Inside this floor, the entrance hall has an irregular plan, but is given a business-like and ship-shape appearance by narrow-paned industrial glazing, by the plain balustrades of the ramp and the spiral staircase leading to the floor above, and by the washbasin, light fittings, etc. which, as in the *Pavillon de l'Esprit Nouveau*, appear to be of industrial or nautical extraction. On the main living floor above, the planning shows less of that *Beaux-Arts* formality that had appeared in the slightly earlier house at Garches, but is composed much as an Abstract painting might have been composed, by jig-sawing together a number of rectangles to fit into a given square plan. The feeling of the arrangement of parts within a pre-determined frame is heightened by the continuous and un-varied window-strip—the ultimate *fenêtre en longueur*—that runs right round this floor, irrespective of the needs of the rooms or open spaces behind it. However, where this strip runs across the wall of the open patio it is un-glazed, as is the viewing window in the screen wall of the roof-garden, a fulfilment, however late and unconscious, of Marinetti's demand for villas sited for view and breeze. The screen wall, again, raises painterly echoes: in contrast to the square plan of the main floor; it is composed of irregular curves and short straights, mostly standing well back from perimeter of the block. Not only are these curves, on plan, like the shapes to be found in his *Peintures Puristes*, but their modelling, seen in raking sunlight, has the same delicate and insubstantial air as that of the bottles and glasses in his paintings and the effect of these curved forms, standing on a square slab raised on legs is like nothing so much as a still-life arranged on a table. And set down in this landscape it has the same kind of Dadaist quality as the statue in the Barcelona Pavilion.

Enough has been said to show that no single-valued criterion, such as Functionalism, will ever serve to explain the forms and surfaces of these buildings, and enough should also have been said to suggest the way in which they are rich in the associations and symbolic values current in their time. And enough has also been said to show that they came extraordinarily close to realising the general idea of a Machine Age architecture that was entertained by their designers. Their status as masterpieces rests, as it does with most other masterpieces of architecture, upon the authority and felicity with which they give expression to a view of men in relation to their environment. They are masterpieces of the order of the Sainte Chapelle or the Villa Rotonda, and if one speaks of them in the present, in spite of the fact that one no longer exists and the other is squalidly neglected, it is because in a Machine Age we have the benefit of massive photographic records of both in their pristine magnificence, and can form of them an estimate far more plastically exact than one ever could from, say, the note-books of Villard d'Honnecourt of the *Quattro Libri* of Palladio.

But because of this undoubted success, we are entitled to enquire, at the very highest level, whether the aims of the International Style were worth entertaining, and whether its estimate of a Machine Age was a viable one. Something like a flat rebuttal of both aims and estimate can be found in the writings of Buckminster Fuller.

It was apparent that the going design-blindness of the lay level . . . afforded European designers an opportunity . . . to develop their preview discernment of the more appealing simplicities of the industrial structures that had inadvertently earned their architectural freedom, not by conscious aesthetical innovation, but through profit-inspired discard of economic irrelevancies. . . . This surprise discovery, as the European designer well knew, could soon be made universally appealing as a fad, for had they not themselves been so faddishly inspired. The 'International Style' brought to America by the Bauhaus innovators, demonstrated fashion-inoculation without necessity of knowledge of the scientific fundamentals of structural mechanics and chemistry.

The International Style 'simplification' then was but superficial. It peeled off yesterday's exterior embellishment and put on instead formalised novelties of quasi-simplicity, permitted by the same hidden structural elements of modern alloys that had permitted the discarded *Beaux-Arts* garmentation. It was still a European garmentation. The new International Stylist hung 'stark motif walls' of vast super-meticulous brick assemblage, which had no tensile cohesiveness within its own bonds, but was, in fact, locked within hidden steel frames supported by steel *without visible means of support*. In many such illusory ways did the 'International Style' gain dramatic sensory impingement on society as does a trick man gain the attention of children. . . .

. . . the Bauhaus and International used standard plumbing fixtures and only ventured so far as to persuade manufacturers to modify the surface of the valve handles and spigots, and the colour, size, and arrangements of the tiles. The International Bauhaus never went back of the wall-surface to look at the plumbing . . . they never enquired into the overall problem of sanitary fittings themselves. . . . In short they only looked at problems of modifications of the surface of end-products, which end-products were inherently sub-functions of a technically obsolete world.

There is much more, in an equally damaging vein, picking on other vulnerable points of the International Style besides the lack of technical training at the Bauhaus, the formalism and illusionism, the failure to grip fundamental problems of building technology, but these are his main points. Though there is clearly a strain of US patriotism running through this hostile appraisal, it is not mere wisdom after the fact, nor is it an Olympian judgement delivered from a point far above the practicalities of building.

As early as 1927, Fuller had advanced, in his Dymaxion House project, a concept of domestic design that might just have been built in the condition of materials technology at the time, and had it been built, would have rendered *Les Heures Claires*, for instance, technically obsolete before design had even begun. The Dymaxion concept was entirely radical, a hexagonal ring of dwelling-space, walled in double skins of plastic in different transparencies according to lighting needs, and hung by wires from the apex of a central duralumin mast which also housed all the mechanical services. The formal qualities of this design are not remarkable, except in combination with the structural and planning methods involved. The structure does not derive from the imposition of a Perretesque or Elementarist aesthetic on a material that has been elevated to the level of a symbol for 'the machine', but is an adaptation of light-metal methods employed in aircraft construction at the time. The planning derives from a liberated attitude to those mechanical services that had precipitated the whole Modern adventure by their invasion of homes and streets before 1914.

Even those like Le Corbusier who had given specific attention to this mechanical revolution in domestic service had been content for the most part to distribute it through the house according to the distribution of its pre-mechanical equivalent. Thus cooking facilities went into the room that would have been called 'kitchen' even without a gas oven, washing machines into a room still conceived as a 'laundry' in the old sense, gramophone into the 'music room', vacuum cleaner to the 'broom cupboard', and so forth. In the Fuller version this equipment is seen as more alike, in being mechanical, than different because of time-honoured functional differentiations, and is therefore packed together in the central core of the house, whence it distributes services—heat, light, music, cleanliness, nourishment, ventilation, to the surrounding living-space.

There is something strikingly, but coincidentally, Futurist about the Dymaxion House. It was to be light, expendable, made of those substitutes for wood, stone and brick of which Sant'Elia had spoken, just as Fuller also shared his aim of harmonising environment and man, and of exploiting every benefit of science and technology. Furthermore, in the idea of a central core distributing services through the surrounding space there is a concept that strikingly echoes Boccioni's field-theory of space, with objects distributing lines of force through their surroundings.

Many more of Fuller's ideas, derived from a first-hand knowledge of building techniques and the investigation of other technologies, reveal a similarly quasi-Futurist bent, and in doing so they indicate something that was being increasingly mislaid in mainstream Modern architecture as the Twenties drew to a close. As was said at the beginning of this book, the theory and aesthetics of the International Style were evolved between Futurism and Academicism, but their perfection was only achieved by drawing away from Futurism and drawing nearer to the Academic tradition, whether derived from Blanc or Guadet, and by justifying this tendency by Rationalist and Determinist theories of a pre-Futurist type. Perfection, such as is seen in the Barcelona Pavilion and *Les Heures Claires*, could only have been achieved in this manner since Futurism, dedicated to the 'constant renovation of our architectonic environment' precludes processes with definite terminations such as a process of perfection must be.

In cutting themselves off from the philosophical aspects of Futurism, though hoping to retain its prestige as Machine Age art, theorists and designers of the waning Twenties cut themselves off not only from their own historical beginnings, but also from their foothold in the world of technology, whose character Fuller defined, and rightly, as an

... unhaltable trend to constantly accelerating change

a trend that the Futurists had fully appreciated before him. But the mainstream of the Modern Movement had begun to lose sight of this aspect of technology very early in the Twenties, as can be seen (*a*) from their choice of symbolic forms and symbolic mental processes, and (*b*) their use of the theory of types. The apparent appositeness of the Phileban solids as symbols of mechanistic appropriateness depended in part on an historical coincidence affecting vehicle technology that was fully, though superficially, exploited by Le Corbusier in *Vers une Architecture*, and partly on a mystique of mathematics. In picking on mathematics as a source of technological prestige for their own mental operations, men like Le Corbusier and Mondriaan contrived to pick on the only important part of scientific and technological methodology that was not new, but had been equally current in the pre-machine epoch. In any case, mathematics, like other branches of logic, is only an operational technique, not a creative discipline. The devices that characterised the Machine Age were the products of intuition, experiment or pragmatic knowledge—no one could now design a self-starter without a knowledge of the mathematics of electricity, but it was Charles F. Kettering, not mathematics, that invented the first electric-starter on the basis of a sound grasp of mechanical methods.

In picking on the Phileban solids and mathematics, the creators of the International Style took a convenient short-cut to creating an *ad hoc* language of symbolic forms, but it was a language that could only communicate under the special conditions of the Twenties, when automobiles were visibly comparable to the Parthenon, when aircraft structure really did resemble Elementarist space cages, when ships' superstructures really did appear to follow *Beaux-Arts* rules of symmetry, and the additive method of design pursued in many branches of machine technology was surprisingly like Guadet's elementary composition. However, certain events of the early Thirties made it clear that the apparent symbolic relevance of these forms and methods was purely a contrivance, not an organic growth from principles common to both technology and architecture, and, as it happened, a number of vehicles designed in the USA, Germany and Britain revealed the weakness of the architects' position.

As soon as performance made it necessary to pack the components of a vehicle into a compact streamlined shell, the visual link between the International Style and technology was broken. The Burney 'Streamliners' in Britain, and the racing cars designed in Germany in 1933 for the 1934 Grand Prix Formula, the Heinkel He 70 research aircraft, and the Boeing 247D transport aircraft in the US all belong to a radically altered world to that of their equivalents a decade earlier. Though there was no particular reason why architecture should take note of these developments in another field or necessarily transform itself in step with vehicle technology, one might have expected an art that appeared so emotionally entangled with technology to show some signs of this upheaval.

What, in fact, happened is of vital importance to the International Style's claims to be a Machine Age architecture. In the same early years of the Thirties, Walter Gropius designed a series of closely related bodies for Adler cars. They were handsomely conceived structures, with much ingenuity in their furnishing, including such features as reclining seats, but they show no awareness of the revolution in vehicle form that was proceeding at the time; they are still elementary compositions, and apart from mechanical improvements in the chassis, engine and running gear, for which Gropius was not responsible, they are no advance on the bodies that had been illustrated in *Vers une Architecture*. On the other hand, we find Fuller justifying his right to speak slightingly of the International Style by designing, in 1933, a vehicle fully as advanced as the Burney cars, and revealing thereby a grasp of the mind of technology which the International Style had failed to acquire.

This failure was followed promptly, though not consequentially, by the emergence of another kind of vehicle designed to take advantage of yet another aspect of technology that the masters of the International Style seem to have failed to grasp. This was the first genuinely stylist-designed car, Harley Earle's Lasalle of 1934, whose aesthetics were conceived in terms of mass-production for a changing public market, not of an unchangeable type or norm. There is a curious point here: Le Corbusier had made great play with the idea of a fairly high rate of scrapping, but he seems not to have visualised it as part of a continuous process inherent in the technological approach, bound to continue as long as technology continues, but merely as stages in the evolution of a final type or norm, whose perfection, he, Pierre Urbain, Paul Valéry, Piet Mondriaan and many others saw as an event of the immediate future, or even the immediate past. In practice, a high rate of scrapping of our movable equipment seems to imply nothing of the sort, but rather a constant renewal of the environment, an unhaltable trend to constantly accelerating change. In opting for stabilised types or norms, architects opted for the pauses when the normal processes of technology were interrupted, those processes of change and renovation that, as far as we can see, can only be halted by abandoning technology as we know it today, and bringing both research and mass-production to a stop.

Whether or not the enforcement of norms and types by such a conscious manoeuvre would be good for the human race, is a problem that does not concern the present study. Nor was it a question that was entertained by the theorists and designers of the First Machine Age. They were for allowing technology to run its course, and believed that they understood where it was going, even without having bothered to acquaint themselves with it very closely. In the upshot, a historian must find that they produced a Machine Age architecture only in the sense that its monuments were built in a Machine Age, and expressed an attitude to machinery—in the sense that one might stand on French soil and discuss French politics, and still be speaking English. It may well be that what we have hitherto understood as architecture, and what we are beginning to understand of technology are incompatible disciplines. The architect who proposes to run with technology knows now that he will be in fast company, and that, in order

329

to keep up, he may have to emulate the Futurists and discard his whole cultural load, including the professional garments by which he is recognised as an architect. If, on the other hand, he decides not to do this, he may find that a technological culture has decided to go on without him. It is a choice that the masters of the Twenties failed to observe until they had made it by accident, but it is the kind of accident that architecture may not survive a second time—we may believe that the architects of the First Machine Age were wrong, but we in the Second Machine Age have no reason yet to be superior about them.

Index to Proper Names and Buildings

*An index to Topics, Publications, and Organisations
begins on page 335*

332

Index to Topics, Publications, and Organisations

335

337